DOCUMENTARY CINEMA IN]

DOCUMENTARY CINEMA IN ISRAEL-PALESTINE

Performance, the Body, the Home

Shirly Bahar

I.B. TAURIS

LONDON • NEW YORK • OXFORD • NEW DELHI • SYDNEY

I.B. TAURIS
Bloomsbury Publishing Plc
50 Bedford Square, London, WC1B 3DP, UK
1385 Broadway, New York, NY 10018, USA
29 Earlsfort Terrace, Dublin 2, Ireland

BLOOMSBURY, I.B. TAURIS and the I.B. Tauris logo are trademarks of
Bloomsbury Publishing Plc

First published in Great Britain 2021
This paperback edition published 2023

Series design by Adriana Brioso
Poster Image by Producer Duki Dror for Paradise Lost, Directed by Ibtisaam Mara'ana.
Courtesy of Duki Dror and Ibtisaam Mara'ana.

A catalogue record for this book is available from the British Library.

A catalog record for this book is available from the Library of Congress.

ISBN: HB: 978-1-8386-0682-4
PB: 978-0-7556-4126-0
ePDF: 978-1-8386-0680-0
eBook: 978-1-8386-0681-7

Typeset by Newgen KnowledgeWorks Pvt. Ltd., Chennai, India

To find out more about our authors and books visit www.bloomsbury.com
and sign up for our newsletters.

To my parents, Tilda and David Bahar

CONTENTS

FIGURES

ACKNOWLEDGMENTS

No one writes alone. This work could have not been compiled without the care, generosity, and patience of many teachers, family, friends, lovers, and strangers—many more than I can mention here—to whom I owe my deepest gratitude. First, I would like to thank my mentor Ella Shohat. Ella not only invited me in and walked me through the meticulous journey of research and writing during my graduate career at New York University but she also in fact made the very existence of this journey possible. From my first encounter with her groundbreaking work to her dedicated reading of my work, Ella's words and presence and her endless wisdom and resilience have been an essential ray of light keeping me going despite much hardship. She has raised and nurtured me as a writer and as a person and I am therefore indebted to her in every possible way. I would also like to thank the following mentors: Zvi Ben-Dor Benite, Bernadette Brooten, Hillel Cohen, Shayne Figueroa, Chaeran Freeze, Yali Hashash, Gil Hochberg, Dalia Kandiyoti, Orly Lubin, Shoshana Madmoni-Garber, Avital Ronell, Sami Shalom Chetrit, Eugene Shepherd, Ilana Szobel, Sarah Schulman, Helga Tawil-Souri, and Christina Vatulescu. Your thorough readership and guidance alongside your inspiring work go a long way.

My colleagues at Columbia University and at Tzedek Lab are an immense source of learning and support to me. I want to express a special thank you to Rachel Lithgow, whose faith in me made possible the emergence of my life and work as a curator and cultural organizer in New York City. My political home of the chapter of Jewish Voice for Peace-New York City has held and sustained me in immeasurable ways. I am beyond fortunate to have always had a loving family whose invaluable presence in my life informs every word of this book: my parents, to whom this book is dedicated, my brother Yair and his partner Gaya, and recently—my nibling Arian who, I hope will join this book's readership as a grown person. My friends have been a precious source of ongoing inspiration and care. Since I am immensely lucky to be part of an ever-expanding queer chosen family, I will only name a few here: Jehad Abu Salim, Neta Alexander, Mariam Bazeed, Ora Batashvilli, Ben De Witte, Faria Chaudhry, Aviv Deri, Danielle Drori, Maya Edery, Susanne Fuchs, Tal Gilboa, Allyson Gonzales, Noa Hazan, Ilker Hepkaner, Shima Houshyar, Atalia Israeli Nevo, Nadia Kader, Ella Klik, Shimrit Lee, Ayala Levin, Deb Lolai, Roni Mazal, Eman Morsi, Joao Nemi Neto, Yigal Nizri, Udi Pladott, Sary Rottenberg, Natasha Roth-Rowland, Sivan Rajuan Shtang, Tanya Rubinstein, Yasmin Safdie, Keren Soffer Sharon, Sapir Sluzker Amran, Yasmin Sasson, and Tiffany Willkins. I deeply thank the therapists who tirelessly take care of me and my family. I want to especially thank my sister and friend, Wazhmah Osman, for carrying me through it all and gifting me with the most nourishing friendship to ground my life around.

I want to extend a special note of gratitude to the filmmakers whose work I explore in this book. Beyond their celebrated contribution to our understanding of politics, representation, and pain, their films have accompanied my own journey through this swiftly changing world as a writer, an immigrant and daughter of immigrants, a queer transplant from Tel Aviv to Brooklyn dragging her thick Istanbul roots everywhere she goes.

I started writing the first chapter of the book, which was initially a dissertation, right after experiencing a painful breakup. Writing the first draft of the introduction after completing the chapters coincided with another painful breakup. The writing of this book was thus informed by the ongoing reliving, living through, and living on of personal pain, intwined with formations and reformations of local communities, new encounters, new chapters. In the midst of it all, I could have never braved the final process of fine-tuning, and letting go of the utmost charged mission of writing, if I were not blessed to meet my partner Velina Manolova in the moment when we did. Thank you, Velina, for your sharp comments, pouring wisdom, poignant jokes, and for the pleasure, magic, and joy you brought to my life. Above all, thank you—Velina and our cat, Mali—for giving me a home.

INTRODUCTION

The moment when a feeling enters the body/ is political. This touch is
political.

—Adrienne Rich[1]

Yes, and the body has memory. The physical carriage hauls more than
its weight. The body is the threshold across which each objectionable
call passes into consciousness—all the unintimidated, unblinking, and
unflappable resilience does not erase the moments lived through.

—Claudia Rankine[2]

I — who steals in and out of your thresholds as if it were my own—Sipping
from the Arab coffee, Kicking at the jug and shouting "dirty Arab!"
Smashing each and every mirror so that I will not see in them The face of
my grandfather, puzzling back at me, in Arabic.

—Sami Shalom Chetrit[3]

Documentary Cinema in Israel-Palestine: Performance, the Body, the Home
characterizes the wave of documentaries by Palestinian and Mizrahi citizens of
Israel that came out during the first decade of the 2000s and centered on Palestinian
and Mizrahi lived experiences of oppression and pain across Israel-Palestine and
beyond.[4] Palestinians and Mizrahim have undergone different and unequal yet
interrelated forms of oppression under Zionism in Israel. Fighting for their rights
to dignity and representability in Israel separately, the communities have been
reclaiming their identifications as Palestinians and Mizrahim, respectively. This
recent wave of personal and political documentaries by and about Palestinians
and Mizrahim from Israel emerged in a liminal moment of new opportunities
for representation, and backlash of extreme violence, economic distress, and
entrenching ethnonationalist segregation in Israel-Palestine. Responding to a
sense of broken hope, anticipated disappointment, and enduring quests for ways of
living on, Palestinian and Mizrahi filmmakers in Israel have paved unprecedented
access to self-representation to explore historical and structural questions
embedded in the founding of the state of Israel and the Palestinian Nakba, or
"catastrophe" since 1948, at times pondering longer histories beginning with the

Zionist colonization of Palestine in the 1880s. The documentaries foreground the ongoing repercussions of formative moments in the history of Israel-Palestine on the current lived experiences of the filmmakers, their families, and communities, under Israeli rule from within and from below, and on their cultural and political identifications across the increasingly segregated yet inseparable Israel-Palestine and Arab/Jew common binaries. *Documentary Cinema from Israel-Palestine* challenges the common tendency to study the Arab-Palestinian and Jewish-Israeli cinemas and realities separately.[5] Curating the films together not despite but precisely because of the segregation of our communities, this book underlines the threads of continuity running across experiences of state violence taking place across the armistice Green Line that demarcated Israel after the 1948 war. Examining cross-national Palestinian and Mizrahi documentaries comparatively provides a fuller picture of nation-state building and violence from the intersecting viewpoints of its marginalized citizens.[6]

The documentaries analyzed below bring forth first-person testimonies of Palestinians' and Mizrahim's experiences of pain in their own words, voices, and bodies, crafted as documentary performances.[7] Distinctively tracking how structural oppression and segregating racialization have been differentially impacting Palestinians and Mizrahim across Israel-Palestine and beyond, the documentaries share a political commitment, key cinematic and performative affinities, and the common thematization of the body and the home. Collectively, the documentaries defy the historical removal of the pain of Israel's marginalized citizens from the public realm of visibility. Thus, while pain sets them and their documentaries apart, observing documentary performances of the pain of Palestinians and Mizrahim together invites us to contest the segregation of pain and consider reconnection and relatability to others with different experiences of pain by intimating with the very relationality of pain.

This book draws on the interdisciplinary study of visual culture that, by no coincidence, solidified around the same time that this wave of documentaries— documentaries that innovate relationships between local political realities and globally newly available technologies and media—came out.[8] I join scholars who employ the lens of performance, and intimate the terms "performance" and "performativity," to challenge common boundaries between reality and representation, action and acting, phenomenon and spectacle.[9] Analyzing documentary performances illuminates how Palestinians and Mizrahim testify, demonstrate, reenact, and situate their lived experiences of pain in front of the camera, and how the documentary media transmit and shape their testimonies as cinematic and performative, personalized and politicized, relational sites. Gauging the injustices inflicted on and archived by the testifying performers, the films thus carve out the documentary performance as a complex relational site of politicized self-representation. Unpacking messy entanglements and negotiations of Palestinians and Mizrahim with Zionism and Israel, the documentaries politicize pain, portraying it as relational and multidimensional: singular and collective, constructed and real, returning from the past, formative of the present, and generative of future resilience living on within the body of the harmed resistant person in front of us. The documentary performances of Palestinians and Mizrahim convey what Zionism and Israel look like on their skins, scalps, and faces, and sound like in their voices, speeches, and silences, portraying the structures of feeling of their pain. *Documentary Cinema from Israel-Palestine* wishes to inspire conversation about vulnerability, accountability, intersectionality, solidarity, and democracy, by encouraging readers and spectators to see, hear, feel, connect, and relate to their struggles of living on in Israel-Palestine.

"They ordered him to raise his hands and shot him on the spot," a witness of a public execution explains while raising her own hands in Mohammad Bakri's *Jenin Jenin (2002)*. "My greatest wish is to go back home," a young girl in *Jenin Jenin* says and smiles for the first time; right after we have seen her walking through the rubbles that used to be her house in the Jenin refugee camp, she summarizes her vision of a return to Palestine in this way. "Wherever we held our heads high, they broke our bones," former leader of the Mizrahi Black Panthers and Moroccan immigrant Reuven Abergil says in reference to the Israeli police's violence during their protests in the 1970s, as he is sitting upright with his eyes looking right at the camera, in David Benchetrit's *Kaddim Wind (2002)*. "I have very good memories from Morocco, really good ... a nice home, good life," says leader of the Mizrahi ultraorthodox party Shas, Aryeh Deri, in *Kaddim Wind*, about the home he had to leave as a child. Such are the testimonies about pain, the body, and the home that you will read about. The chapters comprise close analyses of Palestinians' and Mizrahim's documentary performances of their formative lived experiences: they narrate and demonstrate their and their beloveds' interactions with, internalizations of, and survival and recovery from the threats of bullets, military and police figures, property owners, employers, doctors, and others— Israeli spokespersons and decision makers who reiterate structural oppression by exercising physical and verbal violence toward them. Focusing on either Palestinians or Mizrahim, the documentaries similarly explore the themes of the body and the home, correlating them to state violence in Israel-Palestine. Thus, *Documentary Cinema from Israel-Palestine* is structured in two parts, "The Body" and "Home," with each part consisting of one chapter focusing on Palestinian documentaries and one on Mizrahi documentaries.

Part I, "The Body," analyzes documentaries that address specific experiences of a physical pain due to racialization and racial profiling that translated into military and police brutality afflicted directly on the bodies of Palestinians and Mizrahim, respectively. These documentaries center on individuals reenacting violence inflicted on them, their family, or community, in the past, and the prolonged repercussions resolutely lingering in their bodies up to the present. The documentary performances politicize the experience of physical pain as emanating from state violence. Criminalizing Palestinians as "a security problem" and Mizrahim as "a social problem," the state executes violence against them and lays the blame for the violence on them, thus denying their experience of violence. Nevertheless, Palestinians and Mizrahim listen to their bodies as they retain the pain, embodying, remembering, reclaiming, and telling the stories of their becoming, thus surviving pain in and through the body. Part I includes

Figure 1 *Jenin Jenin*, "My greatest wish is to go back home," girl from the Jenin refugee camp.

two chapters. Chapter 1, "Jenin: Living with Martyrdom in Mohammad Bakri's *Jenin Jenin* and *Since You Left*, and Juliano Mer-Hamis's *Arna's Children*," situates the reader in a Jenin shelled by the Israeli Defense Forces' (IDF's) military operation Defensive Shield in 2002, causing many to experience and witness public executions and home demolitions. These films are also created against the backdrop of the attacks on Palestinian citizens of Israel in October 2000 and after, especially those who publicly exhibited support for their relatives and communities under attack in the West Bank. The films explore the performances of the residents of Jenin who testify and physically perform their embodied state of lived martyrdom. This is a state of living with the pain of constant loss of loved ones and the imminent threat of potential loss of one's own life. The documentaries illuminate the impact of both Israel's military action on Palestinians and the prior discursive labeling of Palestinians as always already terrorists. Fathoming the repercussions of these interrelated practices, the documentaries also emphasize the resistance of the Jenin residents in and by performing their pain in the documentaries. This opening chapter provides general background about the first decade of the 2000s, and explicates approaches to documenting "reality," and terms such as witnessing, testimony, and reenactment are further discussed in the following chapters. Chapter 2, "Heads Held High: Mizrahim's Coming of Age and Activism in David Belhassen's and Asher Hamies's *The Ringworm Children*, David Benchetrit's *Kaddim Wind: A Moroccan Chronicle*, and Nissim Mosek's *Have You Heard of the Black Panthers?*," analyzes documentaries about Mizrahim who grew up under the direct influence of state-mandated pathologization, medical operations, criminalization, and police brutality. The chapter centers on Mizrahim's documentary performances about their childhood and youth as they reminisce the time of their and their families' immigration to Israel in the 1950s, and speak about and against the effects of pathologization and criminalization on their bodies. Created against the backdrop of Mizrahi leaders' growing dissociation from their previous support of Palestinians after 2000, and the backlash against their previous achievements in grassroots campaigns, these films return to the emergence of the Black Panthers movement in Jerusalem in the 1970s and other key moments in Mizrahi organizing to reflect on a history of Mizrahi activism under and against the criminalization and police brutality targeting them.

Part II, "Home," analyzes documentaries tackling displacement from home and the silencing of terms, languages, and discourses that signified those homes as such for Palestinians and Mizrahim. These documentaries center on individuals who demonstrate how the loss of their or their families' homes was accompanied by a systematic, state-mandated silencing of the terms, languages, and discourses that signified their identifications with and attachments to those homes. The documentary performances politicize the experiences of silencing, shedding light on how it is understood as such and overcome in and by speech acts that reconnect Palestinians and Mizrahim to those linguistic and discursive manners of reconnecting with homes that were supposedly lost forever. Part II includes two chapters. Chapter 3, "Speaking Out about the Places of Palestine in Israel in Rachel Leah Jones's *500 Dunam on the Moon*, Michel Khleifi's and Eyal Sivan's *Route 181* , and Ibtisaam Mara'ana's *Paradise Lost*," gathers films that examine the experiences of displacement, dispossession, disorientation, and exile of Palestinians who have stayed in Israel post-1948. The chapter highlights the documentary performances of Palestinians who have been living through the remaking, remapping, and renaming of places in Palestine into Israel, thus hindered their political identifications with Palestine. The chapter focuses on scenes that portray Palestinian residents of such places who perform the ways in which ruination and fragmentation of Palestine has affected them, how they embody, show, and resist the alienation imposed on them in order to hold on to their identification with and belonging to the places they inhabit and call Palestine.

Chapter 4, "A Mother Tongue, a Daughter's Voice: Mizrahi Women's Homecoming to the Arabic Language in Effi Banai's *Longing* and Israela Shaer-Meoded's *Queen Khantarisha*," tells Mizrahi women's experiences of economic and cultural oppression, focusing on documentary performances of Mizrahi women who practice poetry and singing, reclaiming of the voices, languages, and practices related to the Arabic cultures that they came from and that came under systematic silencing in Israel. The chapter contextualizes the heightened economic distress and gentrification inflicted on Mizrahim after 2000 by reviewing the history of tracking Mizrahim to manual labor and precarious public housing, and the concomitant silencing of Mizrahi cultural practices—particularly women's. The chapter demonstrates how Mizrahi women perform their poetry and songwriting as ways to rewrite and undo the history of silencing inscribed on them, and reconnect with their Arabic mother tongue. If Part I shows that the political meanings of physical pain as caused by state violence are not lost on those who underwent it, Part II extends this point, to argue further, that the linguistic and discursive political meanings associated with their former homes—homes they dwelled in prior to the violence, displacement, and silencing—are not lost either. Thus, Part II situates the physical pain endured by Palestinian and Mizrahi racialized bodies discussed in Part I within the larger context of their dislocation from their homes.

Turn of the Century (1): Extreme Violence, Emerging Representations

There are several commonly memorable landmarks in the eruption of extreme violence in Israel-Palestine in 2000: the failure of the Camp David Summit between Palestinian Authority chairman Yasser Arafat, Israel's prime minister Ehud Barak, and US president Bill Clinton in July, marking the decline in the feasibility of the Oslo Accords to lead to a two-state solution in Israel-Palestine; Israeli parliament member Ariel Sharon's inciting visit to Al Aqsa/Temple Mount in Jerusalem in September and the Palestinian general strikes that followed; the nonviolent protests of Palestinian citizens of Israel who condemned the attacks of the IDF on Palestinian civilians in the Israeli-occupied West Bank and Gaza; and the police gunfire that killed thirteen of them in October. Living in Israel at that time, I remember how state- and military-funded panic-inducing updates on mainstream media heavily dominated the public sphere. The alarming announcements surely kept track of the violent events in the next roughly five years—events commonly known as the second intifada/Al Aqsa intifada: the frequent IDF operations in the West Bank and Gaza, and the bombings launched by Palestinians from the West Bank and Gaza. In the coming years, the Israeli (mostly male) "experts on Arab matters" painted this state of emergency as yet another round of extreme violence between two fixed entities: innocent Jewish Israeli civilians and heroic soldiers on one side, and senseless Palestinian "terrorists" and their supporters "from within" the Palestinian citizens of Israel on the other.[10] Similar to the post-9/11 US-launched "War on Terror," panic inducement served as a top operating strategy, spreading what Patricia Zimmerman called "the political economy of blindness."[11] Yet more than in previous violent crises, this time there were more viewing options other than the monotonous voices and know-all faces of the so-called experts. Globalization, privatization, commercialization, and the technological advancements that have transformed the media industries in Israel and globally since the 1990s meant that more representations of more realities in Israel-Palestine were now available. At our Turkish-Israeli home in Tel Aviv, we could watch the news in Turkish or in French on cable TV, listen to Mizrahi music on a local radio station, and, gradually more so, catch a local documentary film on TV, at the film theater nearby, and by the end of the decade, on the internet: some films delivered a different, less familiar, reality to the one we had been used to viewing.

In Israel, the commercial public Channels 2 and 10 that aired in the early 1990s and early 2000s, respectively, and Channel 8 that was available on cable since the early 1990s started sponsoring slots for local documentary productions. At that time, private funders and the state came together to establish funds primarily for documentaries.[12] In 1998, the Doc Aviv Film Festival dedicated to documentary cinema was launched in Tel Aviv's Cinematheque, and the Haifa and Jerusalem Film Festivals were slating more documentaries than before. In 2001, after years of advocacy by filmmakers and film educators, the Israeli parliament passed the Cinema Bill, which officially secured a budget for filmmaking, established the Film Council to enhance the production and display, and accelerated distribution and promotion of Israeli films around the world. Drawing attention from international funders, too, the format of the transnational coproduction became the most widely used for documentaries. Since 1999, filmmakers started utilizing the popular DV camera and, gradually, other diverse, affordable, and thus growingly available digital and cyber new media, too. As more documentary-centered festivals emerged locally and globally, and as various funders invested in documentaries transnationally, more documentaries featuring pieces of actual people's lived everyday experiences were produced and disseminated more easily and widely.[13]

One commonly correlated result of this collision of the new available digital technologies, the privatization and commercialization of the media, the new local and global resources allocated to documentaries, and the eruption of extreme violence in 2000 is the wave of Israeli documentaries critically revisiting the Israeli-Arab and/or Israeli-Palestinian conflict and winning big prizes for it around the end of the decade.[14] One of the most highly acclaimed and widely researched Israeli films was an animated documentary: Ari Folman's 2008 *Waltz with Bashir*, which received an Oscar nomination in 2009 for best foreign film. In 2012, Guy Davidi and Emad Burnat's *5 Broken Cameras* and Dror Moreh's *The Gatekeepers* were nominated for best documentary Oscars. Folman's *Waltz with Bashir* and Moreh's *The Gatekeepers* both centered on veterans of the Israeli military or security forces who opposed war and occupation.[15] Burnat and Davidi's *5 Broken Cameras* was part of a related wave of films about Israel's gradual erection of the segregation wall amid populated Palestinian areas since 2002, the everyday and organized survival and resistance against it, and the military occupation suffocating the West Bank generally.[16] The films' criticism of Israel's militarist activity and society earned them negative reactions from officials of the ultranationalist Likud government headed by Benjamin Netanyahu, which took office in 2009.[17] The controversies stirred around these films in Israel marked the government's new trend of attacks on globally disseminated liberal Zionist cinema and representation. These attacks went hand in hand with the reopening of a government office dedicated to "Hasbara" that year, where "Hasbara" refers to anything on the spectrum of public advocacy from diplomacy to propaganda, especially as it concerns non-Hebrew-speaking audiences outside Israel. The mediatized altercations between the creators and proponents of *Waltz with Bashir* and *The Gatekeepers* and the government are indicative of the general intra-Jewish, intra-Ashkenazi (mostly) ideological rift between two parties. On one end are the liberal supporters of the two-state solution who associate themselves with the Labor Party that has founded and ruled the state from 1948 until 1977; they are sometimes called "liberal Zionists," with the term "Zionist" here signifying their general support of the concept of the Jewish state of Israel. On the other side are the hardline neoliberal ultranationalists mostly associated with the Likkud party, which has replaced them in office almost continuously since 1977, except between 1992 and 1996—the years of the Oslo era—led by the Labor party. Yet the hyped clashes between the two so-called left and right camps that nevertheless have the most access to hegemonic power, media, and representation, until today, should not blind our sight from the more structural rifts and inequalities informing civil society in Israel, and the constant fight to challenge them—for our purposes, through documentary filmmaking.

Palestinian and Mizrahi Documentaries

By the time *Waltz with Bashir, The Gatekeepers,* and *5 Broken Cameras* were celebrated globally, I was already living in New York. Like Ari Folman who made *Waltz with Bashir* to face his PTSD as a result of his combat service in the IDF during the 1982 invasion of Lebanon, I turned to documentary cinema too—albeit as a spectator—to try and make some sense of the events of the first decade of the 2000s beyond my blend of memories of hyper-visualized fleshed-out violence and pain. I endeavored to fathom what happened in those years of transition, from the aftermath of the Oslo euphoria to the normalization of the current neoliberal ethnonationalist regime of apartheid, from the time documentary cinema—and cinema by and large—was starting to make significant headway globally until the Likkud administration's establishment of an official reactive and reactionary "war on the narrative." In my frequent round trips between film festivals and libraries in the United States and Israel, I found myself watching a myriad of culturally diverse and politically critical visages of contemporary Israel-Palestine made in and responding to the first decade of the 2000s, but stretched into and shaped through various personal, positional, temporal, and spatial lenses. Among this array of new representation were films by and about those who, unlike Ashkenazi Zionists, were previously historically denied access to self-representation in Israel.

Aside from documentaries by and about liberal Zionists, two other subfields of documentary work were participating in this emerging abundance of representation of Israel-Palestine while focusing on identity and fashioning self-representation in a politically committed manner. The first features documentaries by and about Palestinian citizens of Israel who were filming themselves and their families and communities, including Palestinians in the West Bank and Gaza, and Palestinians in exile around the world. The second features documentaries by and about Mizrahim, citizens of Israel of Jewish Middle Eastern descent, who were tracking their families' and communities' winding migrations to Israel, and at times filming Mizrahim around the world, too. Against the backdrop of the privatization and commercialization of the media industry and the local and global increase in investments in documentaries, Israeli filmmakers have been tackling questions of identity more extensively since the 1990s, addressing the various waves of Jewish migrations to Israel, holocaust survivors in Israel, and looking into women's and LGBTQ people's lives, gender and sexuality, the body and disabilities, while centering personal and familial pain at the forefront. While mostly made by Ashkenazi Israeli filmmakers, these documentaries began challenging the trope of "Israeliness" as a fixed ethnonational category, including more attention to Mizrahim and Palestinians, albeit typically calling them "Israelis" and "Arabs," respectively. Yet at that time, Palestinian and Mizrahi filmmakers and activists started utilizing film and media to amplify their own respective identifications and self-representation, too. The '48 Palestinian and Mizrahi filmmakers were pushing against years of limited access to representation and misrepresentation, respectively, by the dominant stakeholders in the mostly nationalized Israeli media and cultural hegemony. They began forming an unprecedented, resistant, personal, and political documentary language radically challenging the state of Israel and diversifying the representation of the histories and lives of the human fabric of Israel-Palestine and beyond.

Palestinians of 1948 or in short "'48 Palestinians," or "Palestinians fil-dahil"— Arabic for "of the interior"[18]—are Palestinian citizens who live and have lived inside the state of Israel since its foundation in 1948 after the war: Palestinians use the term "Nakba" to refer to their mass expulsion and/or flight during the war and definite prohibition of their return to their homes.[19] About 150,000 Palestinians managed to remain in or return to the country and found themselves to be a minority with limited citizenship in the newly founded Jewish state that privileged its Jewish citizens.[20] They comprise about 21 percent of Israel's citizen population today.[21] The Jewish Israeli state and society commonly refer to '48 Palestinians as "Israeli Arabs" or just "Arabs."[22] These depoliticized terms erase their Palestinian identity and affiliation to Palestine, blur their kinship to Palestinians in the West Bank, Gaza, and in exile around the world, and neutralize the history of displacement, racialization, and resolute oppression that '48 Palestinians go through inside Israel until today. Gil Hochberg has conceptualized "the principle of concealment" as "the key principle organizing the dominant Israeli (civil society) visual field,[23] a visual field restricted by a vast mechanism of erasure, denial, and obstructions of sight since 1948 and increasingly so throughout the present,"[24] contending that the term "Israeli Arabs" conceals the Palestinianness of '48 Palestinians, thereby erasing their national identity and belonging to Palestine.[25] The '48 Palestinians have been underrepresented as well as misrepresented in Israeli media, culture, and the arts, in imagery falling to reductive tropes of the "good Arab" versus the "Palestinian terrorist."[26] The official permission granted to Palestinians in the West Bank and Gaza to narrate, produce, and distribute Palestinian self-representation after the first signing of the Oslo Accords and the foundation of the Palestinian Authority in 1993, coupled with the general increasing access to and affordability of digital media, all made it possible for Palestinian filmmakers to create an abundant number of fiction and documentary films by the early 2000s and to screen them locally and globally.[27] Despite the suffocating structural restrictions due to the ongoing occupation after 1993, telecommunication, media coverage, and internet usage in and from the West Bank and Gaza facilitated unprecedented connection among Palestinians and their supporters around the world more than before.[28] As a result, '48 Palestinians were able to engage in more Palestinian-defined local, national, and cultural work, too. While sometimes showcasing their work in independent screening venues in Israel, filmmakers were also partaking in the general formative and transformative, national and transnational consolidation of the field of Palestinian cinema, which included the emergence of film festivals dedicated to Palestinian cinema in the West Bank, Jerusalem, and globally.[29] In 2003, for example, New York's Columbia University celebrated the newly growing field with the First Palestine Film Festival, with more to come in the United States. As a result of some investments of international stakeholders in the Oslo vision, more films pictured the partitioned fantasy of a Palestine demarcated around the West Bank and Gaza.[30] At the same time, Palestinian cinema was becoming one whole entity not merely located in the West Bank and Gaza—in exile—or in today's Israel; rather, as Helga Tawil-Souri has noted, the films were connecting these "dynamic geographies" into and as one entity, "one Palestinian cinema," tracking the fragmentation and threads of continuity connecting Palestinian society together into one Palestinian cinematic corpus that, like Palestine, is "multi-fold and multisituated."[31] Despite some funders' expectations, Palestinian filmmakers never refrained from addressing the need, demand, and pain of the current inability to return to pre-1948 Palestine.[32] Renowned Palestinian filmmakers such as Hany Abu-Assad, Kamal Jafari, and Elia Suleiman, who were born into the post-1948 existence of the state of Israel, challenged the in/out dichotomy of Israel and Palestine, picturing instead one whole geography.[33]

Mizrahim are Jewish citizens of Israel of Middle Eastern descent, most of them either immigrants or first generation, though some either lived in or have arrived in Palestine before 1948. The literal meaning of "Mizrahi" in Hebrew is "oriental," folding within it histories of degrading orientalization and political reclaiming. Initially, Zionist and Israeli officials and writers ascribed the label "Bene Edot Ha-mizrah," offspring of the oriental sects, or in short, "Orientals" (Mizrahi-im), to Jews from various countries in Asia, Africa, and the Middle East, lumping them all together under an orientalist term imbued with pejorative connotations. Some Mizrahim are also Sephardim, that is, the offspring of Jews expelled (alongside Muslims) from Spain, formerly Al-Andalus/Sefarad, in 1492, and migrated into the Ottoman Empire. In the 1980s, as part of their transnationally circulated grassroots activism, Mizrahi thinkers, artists, and activists in Israel and the United States started calling themselves Mizrahim as a way to reclaim their experiences of oppression proudly.[34] The term "Arab Jews" has also been used, at times by proponents of Zionism,[35] and at other times to articulate a radical criticism of it, as in Ella Shohat's "I am an Arab Jew."[36] For statistical purposes, Mizrahim are considered Israeli Jews—a practice that denies their exclusion from positions of power in the Israeli government, academia, or the media, the repercussions of generational oppression, and their relationship with the Middle Eastern, Muslim, and/or the Arab world.[37] In mainstream popular visual culture, however, Mizrahim have been prevalently represented derogatively.[38] In Ktzia Alon's words, Mizrahim are subject to "peeping, exoticization, racialization, and stereotypical labeling."[39] During the Oslo era, Mizrahi activists and artists were building on years of organizing to found the educational not-for-profit *Kedma* in 1993, which promoted equal educational opportunities for Mizrahim, and the *Mizrahi Democratic Rainbow* in 1996, which still fights for social, legal, and economic justice and fair public representation for Mizrahim.[40] In these years, popular platforms for self-representation made it to mainstream media and public theaters, too.[41] In 2001, Ella Shohat's *Israeli Cinema: East/West and the Politics of Representation* finally appeared in Hebrew. In 2002, the project *Eastern Appearance/Mother Tongue: A Present That Stirs in the Thickets of Its Arab Past* featured an art show, film festival, and an anthology, with writing from Israel and around the world.[42] For the most part, the new Palestinian and Mizrahi waves of self-representation stormed forward in parallel lines.[43] While many Mizrahi films received financial support from the state, most of the Palestine-centered films did not.[44]

Turn of the Century (2): Politicized Self-Representation, Political Backlash

The year 2002—when Israel started constructing a wall that was allegedly supposed to separate Israelis from Palestinians—marked a triumphant moment for both Palestinian and Mizrahi filmmakers in Israel. In September 2002, David Benchetrit received wide public attention and awards for his four-episode documentary, *Kaddim Wind: A Moroccan Chronicle*, which was screened on Israel's popular Channel 2 on primetime. *Kaddim Wind* followed the stories of six prominent political leaders who immigrated from Morocco to Israel, from grassroots organizers to ministers, including ex-minister of internal affairs Shlomo Ben-Ami, who had just resigned after owning responsibility for the shooting of unarmed Palestinian protesters in October 2000. One month later, in October 2002, a few months after the IDF's operation Defensive Shield in Jenin, the documentary *Jenin Jenin* by the famous theater and film actor Mohammed Bakri, a Palestinian citizen of Israel, came out in Jerusalem's and Tel Aviv's Cinematheques. Closely collaborating with the residents of the Jenin refugee camp and inspired by the new trends of Palestinian cinema, Bakri managed to bring the voices and faces of Palestinians from the West Bank and the director's voice of a '48 Palestinian citizen of Israel together and into the Israeli screen.[45] Yet soon after they first accessed unprecedented exposure, Bakri's and Benchetrit's lives were severely damaged. Against the backdrop of the Israel's new Film Council and its commitment to channeling funds to the film industry, it was easy to forget about that other, more archaic state body: The Film Review Board, established by the British mandate in Palestine in 1927, which still held the power to ban and censor film. *Jenin Jenin* was banned from public viewing almost immediately. As Bakri's *Since You Left* (2005) documented, although the Supreme Court canceled the ban in 2003, Bakri faced immense public condemnation, legal scrutiny, and loss of income for years to come, and was vilified as a helper of terrorism "from within." A sign of the heightened vulnerability of '48 Palestinians post–October 2000, the ban served as a reminder of their position throughout the history of Israel-Palestine. Correlative to the spread of hate and harm against Palestinians, identifying with Arabness in any sort of way in Israel could also lead the authorities to suspicion of terrorism.

In 2004, Benchetrit was severely beaten by security forces in Tel Aviv, upon his arrival to a scheduled meeting with the spokesperson of the ministry of security for a new film he was making about Jewish Israeli IDF officers who refused to serve in the 1967-occupied territories for conscientious reasons. Benchetrit suffered ongoing severe repercussions from this injury that restrained him from ever going back to work, until he eventually died in 2017. While the ministry of security claimed that Benchetrit looked like a suspected terrorist—that is, looked like an Arab Palestinian—his family insists that he was brutalized due to his long commitment to justice. Whether Benchetrit was attacked based on appearance or his politics, the violent incident marked the new reality that Mizrahim faced in the public sphere of visibility, as upon the permissible violence against Palestinians in Israel post-2000, Mizrahim were again forbidden from looking at Palestinians with solidarity and/or physically "look[ing] like them,"[46] as was historically the case with the conditionally included Mizrahi citizens who were always demanded to dissociate from their Arabness.

In 2002, Benchetrit's *Kaddim Wind* was screened at the Human Rights Watch Film Festival and at the Sephardic Film Festival in New York, on its third year of running. In 2007, Bakri's *Jenin Jenin* and *Since You Left* were screened at the First Boston Palestine Film Festival. That year, Bakri was involved in cofounding the *Other Israel Film Festival* at the Jewish Community Center in New York, dedicated primarily to films by and about '48 Palestinians. Making wiggle room under the global spotlight, these and the other Palestinian and Mizrahi documentaries analyzed in this book do not represent the state of Israel but rather characterize their communities themselves. The films explored questions of identity and representation through the lens of key structural features of Zionism and Israel that have impacted their lived experience and positioned them in vulnerability throughout the history of Israel-Palestine. At that (re)turning point of heightened pain around 2000, Palestinian and Mizrahi documentaries returned to events related to the formative and destructive moment of the foundation of the state of Israel and the Palestinian Nakba in 1948, while encouraging us to correlate them to a longer history of Zionism's colonization of Palestine since 1882.[47] While '48 Palestinian filmmakers questioned the separability of the Israel-Palestine geography, Mizrahi filmmakers questioned the separability of the Arab/Jewish binary. Unlike *Waltz with Bashir* or *The Gatekeepers* that star the Ashkenazi Zionist representatives of an imagined "good old Israel" seemingly legitimately tucked within the Green Line, these films do not nostalgically long for the 1990s, for prewar 1967, or for 1948. Rather, they remind us that questions about 1948, the state, and ethnonational separation have been pertinent throughout the history of Israel-Palestine. Hovering on the public discourse during the Oslo era and its delivery of cautious hopes of checkpointed coexistence between Palestinian Arabs and Israeli Jews, these questions weighed heavily on our everyday in Israel-Palestine from the translation of peace talks to bloodshed in the late 1990s. Against the backdrop of the strengthening of ethnonationalist discourses, state power, and state violence in those years, the films tailor a view of the state of Israel and of the place of Israel-Palestine from within and from below.

The heavy toll inflicted on Bakri and Benchetrit was indicative of the multifaceted knot of progressive and regressive settings informing representation and public life across Israel-Palestine and globally,[48] especially during the "War on Terror" era, upon its racialization of many who may or may not "look like" a terrorist.[49] Yet while verbal attacks by Likkud ministers against Palestinian representation reach audiences far and wide nowadays, state sanctioning of films and theater productions critical of Israeli policies is far from a right-wing novelty: it has always been around.[50] Watching *Jenin Jenin*, *Since You Left*, and *Kaddim Wind*, we reckon that the attacks on them consist of a backlash rather than a shift—that is, a throwback to common tropes of Palestinians and Mizrahim constitutive of the entire history of Israel-Palestine. Namely, the racialized depiction of Palestinians as perpetually potential terrorists and the racialized conditioning of Mizrahim's access to Jewish civil privilege pertaining to their shedding of their Arabness. The attacks are emblematic of the return of Zionism and Israel's century-long efforts to racialize Palestinians and Mizrahim as well as, importantly, entrench them into Arab-Jewish, Palestinian-Israeli ethnonational animosities. After the Israeli police shooting of '48 Palestinian protesters in October 2000, Sami Shalom Chetrit noted, the Israeli mainstream media shaped their image as the "the evils of evil" and, concomitantly, popularized the image of Mizrahim as the vulgar, primary haters of Palestinians in Israel—an "ugly" mob thirsty for blood.[51] As I elaborate below, Mizrahim today hold many low-rank duties in the Israeli police and border patrol (alongside Ethiopian Jews),[52] live in the continuously expanding '67 settlements, and vote for Shas, the ultraorthodox Mizrahi party that dropped its previous support of the two-state solution after 2000.[53] Mizrahim indeed execute much of the state violence inflicted on Palestinians. Yet in contrast to the growing trend of depoliticizing Palestinian and Mizrahi identities and rivalries as perfectly championed by some reality television shows,[54] the films mentioned above take a long, deep look at the sociopolitical conditions that position, pit, portray, and essentialize Palestinians and Mizrahim as animus criminals and cops. Bakri's *Jenin Jenin* and *Since You Left* encourage us to think critically about the making of '67 Palestinians as always already suspect terrorists, and of '48 Palestinians as always already potential terrorists or helpers of terrorism, simply by virtue of their expression of any resistance to the state of Israel that has turned them into refugees. *Kaddim Wind* traces a long history of police violence against Mizrahim, sheds light on how the state criminalized Mizrahim on one hand and recruited them as the lowest executing agents of state violence against Palestinians as a promise of upward mobility on the other hand, and how when Mizrahim do not wear Jewish religious garments and/or Israeli security uniform in public, they very well may be considered terrorists until proven Jewish.

The Documentarian Return to 1948

As *Jenin Jenin*, *Since You Left*, *Kaddim Wind*, and the other films gathered in Part I elucidate, the state's attacks on Bakri and Benchetrit were not solely a sign of the times. Emerging from the conditions of globalization, deregulation, and the civic and representational possibilities developing in the late 1990s–early 2000s, these and the other films I analyze in this book do not celebrate the Oslo era but rather destabilize the good 1990s–bad 2000s binary by asking themselves, and us, some hard, profound questions. Indeed, the years of the two-state solution, globalization, and deregulation enabled Palestinian and Mizrahi thinkers, organizers, and artists in Israel to cultivate more political organizing initiatives and, correlatively, foreground and disseminate innovative, reclaimed forms of self-representation in film and visual culture generally. Yet the films contemplate the continuous threads informing both the "peace talks" of the 1990s and the extreme violence of the 2000s: namely, the reinforcement of the ethnonational separatist binaries of Israeli Jews/Arab Palestinians, and the harsh neoliberalizing decrees of housing and employment precarity for the working class in Israel-Palestine as a whole.[55] Gathered in Part II, films about '48 Palestinians such as *500 Dunam on the Moon* (2002), *Route 181* (2003), and *Paradise Lost* (2003) and about Mizrahi women such as *Longing* and *Queen Khantarisha* reflect on how the problematic persistence of racialized and class-based ethnonational separatism of Palestine-Israel and the Arab/Jew deny and further detach Palestinians and Mizrahim from their respective homes of Palestine and the Arab world—the homes where they and/ or their families are from. Films such as *500 Dunam on the Moon*, *Route 181*, and *Paradise Lost* attend to the question of Palestinian refugees generally and displaced '48 Palestinians particularly, and their right to return and belong to historic Palestine. Beginning in the summer of 1993, the Oslo talks were trying to imagine the two-state solution as a remedy to Israel's 1967 military occupation in the West Bank and Gaza while still sustaining its prominence in the region. In that process, some crucial matters regarding Palestinian civil freedom and self-determination were neglected, remaining unresolved: most acutely, the status of the Palestinian refugees and their demanded right of return to their homes in pre-1948 Palestine in accordance with UN resolution 194.[56] The return of the suppressed issue of the Palestinian refugees' right of return, invoking the year 1948 rather than 1967, heavily hovered over the failure of the Israeli-Palestinian talks in 2000, accordingly surfacing in the Palestinian documentaries.[57] Compatibly, focusing its lens on class issues and the systematic making and maintaining of Mizrahi impoverishment in Israel, *Longing* and *Queen Khantarisha* correlate economic disparity to the racialization and discrimination of Mizrahi immigrants who originated from the Arab world. The almost instantaneous emergence and collapse of the markedly capitalist concept of "The New Middle East" such economic setbacks commonly comprise the flipside of globalization and deregulation, namely, the already most vulnerable becoming even more vulnerable, shocked and disproportionately harmed those who have been historically oppressed in and by the state of Israel. The films focus on Mizrahim but help us reflect on class disparity as a whole.

To that end, the terms of the ethnonationalist separation promoted by the two-state solution meant that Israeli Jewish and Arab Palestinian identities were supposed to be neatly divided along a soon-to-be Israel-Palestine bordered geography. Yet the majority of those expected to embody those identities—Mizrahim, '48 Palestinians, and Palestinians living in refugee camps in the West Bank and Gaza—not only suffered from the eruption of violence, but also had to face a decrease in the already meager economic resources at their disposal. Since 2002, when Israel started building the separation wall, that geography is 8-feet concretized, yet does not limit Israel's continuous colonization of the West Bank resulting in many more Palestinian residences and land to be cut to the gut.[58] This revised logic of separation did not emanate from, but rather incited, heightened ethnonational animosity. As Oren Yiftahel contended, Israel was born as an ethnocracy, as its "socio-economic and settlement policies ... have created a system of ethno-class segregation and inequality."[59] A closer look at Zionism and Israel's segregated shaping of ethnonationalism and ethno-class stratification sheds light on why '48 Palestinians and Mizrahim ended up launching split struggles and self-representations such as the documentaries analyzed in this book.

Segregating Racialization, Split Struggles

The formative thrusts of Zionism and Israel's racialization[60] of Palestinians and Mizrahim are interlinked with the Nakba and foundation of the state of Israel in 1948. Since 1950, Israel has been legalizing the appropriation of homes and land of exiled Palestinians and the prohibition of their return, criminalizing those who are attempting return.[61] This prohibition was imposed not only on the refugees outside Israel but also on the approximately twenty thousand "present absentees," Palestinians who fled their homes to find refuge in other places within the newly founded state.[62] Until 1966, '48 Palestinians lived under a military administration that mostly facilitated the confiscation of much of their land and property.[63] As detailed in Chapter 3, whether they were physically displaced from their standing village as was the case of Ayn-Hawd, lost their homes to complete destruction as in the case of Abu-Shusha, or remained in their homes as was the case of Fureidis, the dislocation and disorientation of '48 Palestinians in their homeland renamed as Israel persists in their everyday lives. Yet the collective memory and organized work of '48 Palestinians in Israel has sustained their connection to their home of Palestine.

In many cases, Mizrahim had to flee their homes in the Middle East, especially in Arab countries, due to their association with the Jewish state of Israel's expulsion of Arab-Palestinians in and after 1948, and due to the general growing Arab/Jewish national tensions.[64] The war of 1948 has placed Jewish communities under increased risk in their Arab homelands: they were associated with the emergent Jewish state in Palestine and, at times, faced Arab nationalist sentiments that negated their Arab identity. At that time, the Israeli government and security forces utilized an array of mostly dubious methods to transfer the various Jewish communities throughout the Middle East to Israel. Though the term "population exchange" was never officially utilized by the Israeli government and its proponents to describe the mass migration and flight of Palestinians and Mizrahim after 1948, it occasionally frames Mizrahim as "refugees" from Arab countries until today, mainly to relinquish any Palestinian demand for return or for compensation for their lost property.[65] Framed as "rescue missions," their mostly forced flight actuated a great loss of Jews' basic sense of stability, as most of them had to renounce their citizenship and leave their assets behind in their Arab homelands. Some Mizrahim—especially North African Jews—also went through selections.[66] Then, upon arriving in Israel, Mizrahim faced systematic discrimination and exclusion from the start—in labor, housing,[67] and education.[68] The state placed many of the Mizrahi immigrants in "immigrant settlements" or "development towns" often built along the fringes of the Green Line, as well as in areas largely populated by '48 Palestinians, criminalizing those who tried to seek work or housing, or even just walk out elsewhere.[69] The Judaization of the land and the labor force, that is, the efforts to win the demographic battle, were top priorities for the Jewish state, and Mizrahim were tracked to materialize this purpose as Israel's docile Jewish working class. As detailed in Chapter 2, Mizrahim were pathologized as inclined to ailments and to crime—pathologies prefiguring their confinement in treatment camps and in heavily policed poor neighborhoods.

Thus, while the racialization and segregation of Palestinians as the others of the Jewish state was supposed to facilitate their subordination and, importantly, curb their national demand to return to Palestine, it also isolated them from anyone in Jewish civil society who might express solidarity with them— especially, the separately intranationally racialized and inferiorized Jews from Arab countries and/or the Middle East. Accordingly, the racialization of Mizrahim in post-Nakba Israel attempted to prevent any possible cultural familiarity or political solidarity between them and the Palestinians, forcing Mizrahim to discard or closet every and any affiliation with Arabness.[70] To that end, the conceptualization of the Israel-Palestine and Jew/Arab hierarchical dichotomies and their translation into political conditions on the ground effectively segregated Mizrahim and Palestinians geographically and culturally, as well as set them apart politically.[71]

These segregated conditions of oppression and pain inflicted on Palestinians and Mizrahim, in turn, enhanced their self-organizing, albeit mostly separately— which they have been doing ever since they first encountered Zionist oppression in Palestine/Israel. The national identity of the '48 Palestinians has been strengthening ever since Israel's lifting of the military ban on Palestinians in Israel in 1966 and its occupation of Jerusalem, the West Bank, and Gaza in 1967, which enabled family and community reunifications, and the 1976 Land Day uprising against land confiscation, and the first intifada in 1987.[72] Yet the more '48 Palestinians progressed toward some sustainability in Israel,[73] and the more they partook in the shaping of Palestinian national self-determination, the more backlash threatened them. In 1998, and then more forcibly in 2000, '48 Palestinians who nonviolently protested their community's mistreatment across Israel-Palestine, were unprecedentedly attacked by the military, police, and media.[74] The protests of '48 Palestinians who, in the words of Amal Jamal, were advancing their self-determination as "a national minority and a homeland minority"[75] against years of oppression, accelerated their ongoing racialization as inherent traitors from within, helpers of their counterparts in the West Bank and Gaza,[76] in a process that Gil Eyal called "the return of the specter of the internal enemy."[77] Chapter 1 follows the ways that documentaries such as *Jenin Jenin*, *Since You Left*, and *Arna's Children*, made by '48 Palestinians, follow precisely the effort to racialize '67 Palestinians as "terrorists" and '48 Palestinians as their "helpers," the subsequent harm of this discursively prevalent racialization on Palestinian bodies and on their ability to reclaim the stories and represent themselves on their own terms, as Palestinians.

Mizrahim's long history of organizing spans from letter-writing demanding fair treatment in the Zionist settlements of Palestine,[78] to escapes from the policed camps and development towns in the 1950s,[79] to protests against police violence and poverty in Wadi Salib, Haifa in 1959,[80] to the Mizrahi Black Panthers uprisings in Jerusalem in 1971–3, and until today. Against the backdrop of the delegitimization of protesters as "anti-Zionist" and the co-optation and mobilization of their rage toward the Labor Party, many Mizrahim voted for the Likkud in the elections of 1977.[81] Yet the Black Panthers protests also inspired the small but persistent transnational cohort of leaders advocating for Mizrahi-Palestinian solidarity and the collective liberation for all, and generations of Mizrahi leaders who reclaimed the identification "Mizrahi"[82] and have been reconnecting with the Arab and Muslim Middle East from various cultural, nonnational, and anti-colonial perspectives ever since.[83] Importantly, the late 1980s saw the emergence of a direct dialogue between Palestinian cultural figures and official representatives of the Palestine Liberation Organization (PLO) and several prominent Mizrahi thinkers and artists, culminating in a series of meetings in Europe.[84] Despite Israel's attempt to illegalize them,[85] these meetings put pressure on the Israeli political mainstream to begin negotiations with the PLO too.

Alas, the deadly backlash against Palestinians across Israel-Palestine in and after 2000 brought back an intense wave of reactionary politics of fear and hate, sweeping across the Israeli Mizrahi community too.[86] To that end, while the organized struggles of '48 Palestinians and Mizrahim were already quite separate in the two-state days of the 1990s, the mobilization of Mizrahim against Palestinians further escalated in the 2000s. Ever since, the increasingly neoliberalized, albeit nationalist, mainstream media has been co-opting a depoliticized, sentimentalized representation of Mizrahim especially on reality television shows, where they often perform as docile and grateful subjects of the state and haters of Palestinians.[87] At the same time, Mizrahi organizers and artists continue to fight the harsh decrees of economic oppression targeting the working class—mainly un/underemployment and gentrification—and to create more platforms for the celebration of Mizrahi, and specifically Arabic, cultural production. As Chapter 4 elaborates, the end of the first decade of the 2000s saw Mizrahi women protest against housing and labor precarity and celebrate their Arabic mother tongue. As the struggles of Palestinians and Mizrahim continue to split, my analyses of the documentaries emphasize their common ways of representing relational pain.

From Interrelated Pain to Relational Pain: Cinematic Affinities, an Affective Community

In his 1979 *The Question of Palestine*, Edward Said has dedicated a chapter to conceptualizing "Zionism from the Standpoint of Its Victims"—the Palestinians.[88] In 1988, Ella Shohat published the article "Sephardim in Israel: Zionism from the Standpoint of its Jewish Victims,"[89] on Mizrahim. "In keeping with one of its central characters, Zionism has hidden, or caused to disappear, the literal historical ground of its growth, [and] its political cost to the native inhabitants of Palestine," Said maintained.[90] Said mentions that for Zionists, "the nonexistent Arab inhabitants [and] the complementary Western-Jewish attitude to an 'empty' territory"[91] played a key role in their imagination and/as negation of Palestine and Palestinians. In "Sephardim in Israel," Shohat concomitantly asserted that "a more complete analysis" of Zionism and Palestine "must consider the negative consequences of Zionism not only for the Palestinian people but also for the Sephardi Jews … for, Zionism does not only undertake to speak for Palestine and the Palestinians, thus 'blocking' all Palestinian self-representation, it also presumes to speak for Oriental Jews."[92] Later, Shohat emphasized the need to study Palestinian and Mizrahi oppressions relationally, since "the same historical process that dispossessed Palestinians of their property, land, and national-political rights, intimately was linked to the process that affected the dispossession of Arab Jews from their property, lands, and rootedness in Arab countries, as well as their uprootedness from that history and culture within Israel itself."[93] Similar to these historical processes, the discursive and cultural tropes that Zionism and Israel have attached to Palestine, Palestinians, Arab Jews, and the Arab world are also interlinked: "While presenting Palestine as an empty land to be transformed by Jewish labor, the Zionist 'founding fathers' presented Arab Jews as passive vessels to be shaped by the revivifying spirit of Zionism." In this view, the Palestinians, merely "the Arab masses, exploited by Arab feudalism, only could benefit from Zionist praxis."[94]

Shohat's above conversation with Said inspired various post/anti-colonial, anti-racist, and transnational scholarship on the interrelated impact of Zionism and Israel on Arabs and Jews. *Documentary Cinema from Israel-Palestine* employs the relational framework to studying Palestinian and Mizrahi cultural representation in Israel-Palestine that was braved by Shohat and developed by others.[95] Palestinians' and Mizrahim's experiences of pain should be theorized together not despite, but precisely because, Zionism presented and positioned the two groups separately, on segregated sides of the ever-devouring Israeli border, rendering the "Arab/Muslim" identification as essentially opposite and in perpetual animosity to the "Jewish" one to have us believe that a perpetual animosity has always defined the two peoples. Palestinians' and Mizrahim's circumstances of living and dying are different because they were differently interpellated under Zionism and Israel. *Documentary Cinema from Israel-Palestine* builds on the scholarly legacy that has been troubling these placed divides by foregrounding the interrelated political conditions commonly affecting Palestinians and Mizrahim—namely, that their everyday consists of enduring and resisting the same Zionist-Israeli state power and orientalist hegemonic discourses. Joining analyses of Palestinian and Mizrahi documentaries together helps shift the conventional paradigms of war and conflict commonly framing the conversation on Israel-Palestine to discussing the lived experiences of pain of Palestinians and Mizrahim under structural, differential, segregating, and complementary binary racialization.[96] Thus, understanding the interrelatedness of Mizrahi and Palestinian oppression and pain may push us to question both the recent attempt of Mizrahi leaders and cultural figures to co-opt hard-won Mizrahi battles and discourse to brownwash[97] their advance of blatant racism against Palestinians,[98] as well as the picturing of Mizrahim as the ultimate face of racism and violence against Palestinians by contrast to an alleged nice face of the reasonable and benevolent Ashkenazi Zionist liberal founders of the state.

In *In Spite of Partition*, Gil Hochberg argued: "The demographic, territorial, and economic reality in Israel-Palestine is such that the two people are forced to share an inextricably linked life ... [which] upholds alternative, latent possibilities for envisioning social emancipation achieved across national and ethnic differences."[99] I further suggest that viewing the Palestinian and Mizrahi respective relational portraits of pain side by side may inspire not only our theoretical understanding of their historical interrelatedness, but also venture the harder task of practicing our emotional relatability to one another's wholly different experiences and expressions of pain. As Sara Ahmed recommended, to examine "the politics of pain" we have to grapple with its "production of uneven effects."[100] Watching the documentaries together, we may reminisce Rebecca L. Stein's and Ted Swedenburg's perspectives on popular culture in Israel-Palestine , and ponder the ever-occurring instances of Palestinian and Mizrahi "border crossing and mutual contingency" as well as the increasingly pertinent "forms of divisions, both territorial and ideological" between Palestinians and Mizrahim, "in tandem."[101]

In the first decade of the 2000s, Palestinians and Mizrahim rarely collaborated on politically committed documentary films. From their respective viewpoints, they tackled questions of identity, self-representation, and belonging from a historical and structural perspective. Precisely because of the effectiveness of segregating pain, this book wishes to turn the lens onto these very affinities in the politically committed documentaries analyzed below. Pain sets us apart, but we may want to watch the films together to start practicing the dismantling of the principle of racialized separation commonly premised throughout the history of Israel-Palestine. When watching the films together, we can recognize some notable cinematic and performative affinities between the films. This book'sfocus on the films' shared framing of pain as personal, political, and relational inspires us to not only understand but, crucially, *to sense*, the differential, interrelated, and especially, the cross-relatable political pain informing Palestinian-Mizrahi separation and inseparability.

Rather than the exclusive focus of documentaries by and about Palestinians and Mizrahim, pain was a key motif in most, if not all, of the documentaries from Israel about Israel-Palestine in the first decade of the 2000s. Taking their pain in, the films made it easy to feel touched, and to relate to all the people in front of me and feel empathy toward them. At the same time, the ability to rewind and revisit the scenes on my personal computer allowed me to pay careful attention to the cinematic means, settings of spectatorship, and, most importantly, inspired me to better study the political context and politics of representation surrounding these scenes of pain. The different aspects of the documentaries— that is, who the filmmaker is, who the filmmaker centers at the forefront, and how they both mediate the documentary performance—speak to how differently the documentaries represent pain, and how differently the participants perform pain. The documentary genre centering on the Zionist-Israeli, mostly but not only cis male and Ashkenazi protagonists, usually veterans of the Israeli military and/or security services, is consistent with the Israeli 1980s fiction genre of the "turn to the self," which Ella Shohat had theorized in *Israeli Cinema*.[102] This genre centers on the famous Zionist Crier and Shooter psychologizing and depoliticizing image prevalent in Zionist and Israeli literature and visual culture since the arrival of Zionism in Palestine.[103] In *Waltz with Bashir*, *The Gatekeepers*, and other similar films, the psychological pain of the Israeli veteran protagonist is most often expressed as a sentiment emanating from the elaborately confessing subject's inner world— confirming his entitlement to speak his hurt heart and soul, in his own language. Constant flattering, forgiving close-ups help to cohere, authorize, and exonerate the security agent or soldier's sentimental statements as valid and evidential claims about his pained psyche. This is the case, for example, in the *Gatekeepers*, where filmmaker Dror Moreh concentrated on the torsos of the former heads of the GSS against a blank backdrop, where their facial emotional expressions stood out as the sole star of the show, crowning them as utmost reliable, legitimate, and authoritative speakers.[104] Laurent Berlant's words in "The Subject of True Feeling" are helpful here, as the Israeli veteran's expressed "national sentimentality" stems from "identification with the law" and "operates when relatively privileged citizens are exposed to the suffering of their intimate others, so that to be virtuous requires feeling the pain of flawed or denied citizenship as their own pain."[105] This sentimentality delivers the wish for redemptive relief through "identification with pain, a universal true feeling"; consequently, "populations emancipated from the pain … would reauthorize Universalist notions of citizenship in the national utopia, which involves believing in a redemptive notion of law."[106] Relatedly, in some anti-occupation films, the harshest Israeli soldier or security personal to inflict violence on Palestinians on camera—with no chance to exonerate himself—is often brown-skinned.[107] The human representation of Palestinians and Mizrahim beyond their respective stereotypical roles as victims and victimizers is otherwise often compromised.

What happens, however, when those who have been historically excluded from and subordinated to a Zionist colonial, national, and orientalist gaze and vision perform their experiences of pain to the documenting lens while within the territorial, linguistic, and discursive supremacy of Zionism and Israel? Unlike their Ashkenazi Zionist peers, documentaries by and about Palestinians and Mizrahim respond to the exclusionary and/or derogatory politics of public representation that corroborate their oppressions—politics within which they operate and against which they resist. Shifting from ontological questions about the capacity of representation to represent reality to political questions of power and access, the documentaries discussed here differ from documentaries that feature testimonial performances by executors of violence rather than that of survivors.[108] Rather than assuming authoritative power over a reality that is inevitably no more, the filmmakers exercise much self-reflexivity. They utilize the accelerated democratization of digitized documentary filmmaking to unearth previously underrepresented past events as remembered by marginalized yet persistent people whose presenting bodies have memorized their pain. They maintain a radical faith in the filmed subjects who have been deploying prolonged, brave struggles to maintain the memory and understanding of their identities, bodies, and homes alive and tell their stories to us spectators.

Most often, pain in these documentaries is excavated through interviews where the performing person or people are in dialogue with the filmmaker and/or a third person and a camera are typically placed on the latter's side. The filmmaker does not impose a dominant view as an authoritative narrator on the experiences told by the performers. Instead, some stay silent, letting the performers narrate their stories independently—as in Rachel Leah Jones's *500 Dunam on the Moon* (2002) and Israela Shaer-Meoded's *Queen Khantarisha* (2009)—while others grapple vocally and self-reflexively the information that the performers introduce and with the performer-filmmaker rapports, as in the case of *Paradise Lost* (Ibtisaam Mara'ana, 2003) or *Longing* (Effi Banai, 2009), in which cases the filmmakers star in their own documentaries. Rather than seating the performing participant against blank backdrops in a neat studio and letting us see only their face and torso, documentaries centering on Palestinians and Mizrahim find them in situ—where pain has been experienced by them or their family, which is often where they still live—situating the performers' whole bodies in front of the camera. The documentaries take intimate interest in stories told by and about family and community members, often filmed together, processing the details of painful events of political duress, personal repercussions, and larger public meaning. The lens meets and walks with them to the carob trees they lost, near the spring where they shepherd their cattle, and into their precarious homes. Making room between the human face and recording lens, the documentaries carve out a cinematic space for the performing person to weave their experiences, narrate the story of their becoming, and re-present their current way of being as a verb rather than a noun. This cinematic and performative space both simulates the political setting where the experience of violence has occurred in the past, and showcases the performing body as it constantly carries and endures the repercussions of that experience. On that note, the documentaries share many of the conspicuous characteristics listed above with the recently growing global wave of testimonies in documentaries and other media initiatives too. As Phyllis R. Klotman and Janet K. Cutler noted, African American documentaries have been pioneering "the struggle for representation," carrying "an urgent desire to … counter the relatively uninformed and often distorted representations of mass media film and television productions" of them, instead putting forth a "struggle to be seen."[109] Bhaskar Sarkar and Janet Walker have recently usefully termed the testimonial scenes from around the world as "Documentary Testimonies: Global Archives of Social Suffering."[110] Sarkar and Walker consider "the audiovisual testimonial scene as one of the most common and geopolitically significant—but as-yet-under-researched—venues for the attestation, reception, and mitigation of social suffering."[111] As they emphasize, and relevantly to Israel-Palestine, the "broadly cross-regional and transnational *continuities* in testimonial modalities"[112] elucidate the importance of assembling "ethical communities" and "affective communities" of solidarity and empathy, and even dare to surface "the popular imagination of healing."[113]

Representing Relational Pain

Scholars tackling the abovementioned Israeli documentaries from a Freudian standpoint describe pitifully the hardships that the tormenting traumatized perpetrator has to endure, especially in carrying so much guilt around his military/security services, while the sociopolitical circumstances by which he serves are lost on him, and on us as spectators.[114] Conversely, *Documentary Cinema from Israel-Palestine* shares the consistent suspicion that scholars, mainly in feminist, queer, and performance studies, have raised toward the often-depoliticizing Freudian-Lacanian psychoanalytic paradigm of trauma,[115] and their preference of the term "pain." Building on scholarship of cultural trauma[116] and on Elaine Scarry's groundbreaking *The Body in Pain*, critical theories about pain have been adamant in its commitment to politicizing and believing human injury, especially in its deliberate focus on how the systemically oppressed represent it.[117] Recently, Sara Ahmed noted that "rather than assuming that pain is unrepresentable," it is important to focus on how "the labour of pain and the language of pain work in specific and determined ways to affect differences between bodies."[118] In light of these insights, I delineate pain in the films as the relational political loci of overlapping inflictions of power and/as an oppressed situation: "the scope and magnitude of the performative as a strategy of power and tactic of resistance" that highlights "social relationality rather than identity."[119]

Above all the political, cinematic, and performative trends that the documentaries share is their determination to represent pain as relational. As interactive sites of testimony, performativity, and cinematization, the documentary performances powerfully politicize pain by shaping it as a relational event that took place between the performing person and the state and is lingering in the person's body and ways of speaking, expressing, and representing oneself. The documentary performances are the relational loci, multilayered encounters between bodies, speeches, and filmic apparatuses, in which the individuals return to the past painful experiences, performing their embodiment and endurance of the pain inflicted on them, and in which the documentary shapes these performances as relational and political. The documentaries craft these loci as relational, politicizing the ways in which the painful experiences have shaped the individual who is performing, surviving, and resisting them. The documentary performances of Palestinians and Mizrahim demonstrate and protest their relationships with manifestations of the essentializing and authoritative perception of Palestinians and Mizrahim as entities comprising racialized innate, fixed, and perforce inferior substance and destined to unfortunate futures.

The documentaries present Palestinians' and Mizrahim's various recollections of experiences of oppression that have formatively constituted their lives and identifications as such. The hit of the bullet, the demolished home, the lost carob tree, the dried fountain, the unattainable moon, the imposed mask, the interior of the home, the fence of the camp—are all cinematic and performative imagery communicating particular ways of living, hurting, being in, and becoming through political conditions of oppression. Palestinians' and Mizrahim's documentary performances refute the invisibilization of their pain as such from the public eye. By showing and narrating the injuries inscribed on their homes and bodies, the documentary performances of Palestinians and Mizrahim expose and work through the relationality embedded in personal and/as political pain. Palestinians and Mizrahim show us the direct and prolonged effects of oppression and violence on their embodied and affective states of pain. They break down for us how a hurtful event is experienced and cohered as an affect of pain, and how surviving them nurtures new becomings. They show that they have been un/made into their situation by specific political, visual, spatial, physical, and linguistic coercive policies and practices, rather than just are this way innately. Palestinians' and Mizrahim's pain is expressed by them as well as cinematically mediated; it is theirs to feel yet not stemming from any interiority of theirs. This mode of performed and mediated relational pain contests some commonly entrenched binary concepts of temporality, identification, and representation, blurring presumed divides between Arab/Jew, past/present, real/discursive, power/the oppressed, action/situation, and political versus psychological notions of pain, enabling a discussion of identifications without essentializing and/or segregating them.

The framing of pain as relational in the documentaries exposes and breaks the erasure of Palestinian and Mizrahi pain from the public field of representation by detailing the ways they have been racialized and displaced and/or dislocated from their homes and native languages and discourses, the ways in which the mechanisms of this oppression have been removed from representability, and the ways it is resisted in the everyday and by the documentary performances. To that end, the erasure of political pain is a cause of more pain. That is, the fact that the histories, humanities, and political conditions of oppression of both Palestinians and Mizrahim have been underrepresented, made invisible, exoticized, humiliated, by Zionist and Israeli channels of public memory and visibility representational mechanisms severs their very efforts to narrate and show the pain of oppression they have been harmed by. The documentaries convey that, despite the personal and generational harm, and the organized attempt to deny the harm as the direct result of state violence, making them believe that their pain is their fault, Palestinians and Mizrahim are able to return to the physical and symbolic experiences of oppression and pain, reclaim them, and recover their ways of making meaning in the world that existed prior to Zionism and Israel. There is no claim made on the part of the filmmaker or performing testifier to describe a real event of pain reliably in the ways that it happened exactly. Rather, the cinematically, performatively, and poetically crafted choice of words, silences, facial expressions, and bodily gestures of the performing testifier touch, contour, and communicate precisely the structural and historical political conditions and circumstances deeply embedded in the specific event of pain: this is what makes the documentary performance a site of politicized relational pain. In the corporeal and cinematic settings of the documentary performances I study here, comprising interactions, influence, and frictions between lenses, the filmmaker, a testifying performing person, and us spectators, we see and hear about pain taking place and shape—pain is present, represented, relived, survived, and resisted, as an ongoing formative experience of heightened vulnerability in relation to state violence. Relational pain in the documentary performances is a pain created of and as the lasting remnants of an imposed action, a harmful experience—an affect,[120] restored as a texture of life, a structure of feeling. In the films, relational pain is traveling, sticking, shaping, and shattering people, cohered as and comprising overlapping somatic and emotional, external and internal, personal and always political dimensions. A relational understanding of documentary performances trumps strict notions of temporality, politics, identity, and representation.[121]

"An Ethics That Begins with Your Pain"

When asked to pick his favorite scene from any film, renowned Kurdish Iranian Israeli actor and activist Yosef Shiloah chose the scene from *Jenin Jenin* focusing on the girl and her declaration: "My greatest wish is to go back home," stated the young girl from *Jenin Jenin*.[122] "I identify with the Palestinian people. It's simple, so simple," he explained. The girl from *Jenin Jenin* was born in the Jenin refugee camp as a refugee, and has yet to return to her ancestors' home in Palestine that turned into Israel in 1948. Although pictured as a homecoming to the promised land for Jews, the conditions informing Shiloah's immigration to and integration in Israel, to which he arrived as a child with his family in the 1950s, were far from welcoming.[123] For some of us, children and grandchildren of Middle Eastern Jewish immigrants to Israel, circumstances have changed since the 1980s and more so in the 1990s, and with some restrictions, we can now visit our families' countries of origins in Egypt or Morocco. Turkish Israelis like myself never ceased to be in touch with Turkey. So, as more Mizrahi Israeli thinkers and artists advocated their reconnections to the Middle East and its cultures, I too wanted to deepen my intimacy with Turkey. In June 2014, shortly after starting to write this book, I flew to Istanbul to spend my first summer there since I was a child. That access that I have always had to Turkey means the world to me—a window to my family's histories in Turkey. This world remains intact because I can make meaning of it, which in turn grants me with some access to the delicate layers of pain that their departure from their home in Istanbul, when immigrating to Israel, has brought upon them—that pain that we grew up in and lived by as a family. In turn, that summer, that access that I have to the Turkish language also facilitated my daily encounter with numerous visceral detailed reports from Gaza in the Turkish media that humanized Palestinian pain. Reconnecting to my home of Istanbul while sensing excessive rage, agony, and empathy when regarding the pain of others in occupied Jerusalem or in besieged Gaza may not amount to politicization single-handedly. Rather, it takes perpetual learning and training to try and relate to the pain of others in a politically informed and committed manner: this is a pivotal argument this book makes. It is driven by my outlook as a Mizrahi Turkish-Israeli scholar, and by my wish to enhance Mizrahi solidarity with the Palestinian struggle. Mizrahi thinkers, artists, and organizers like Shiloah, and like the filmmakers and subjects of the analyzed documentaries who, for years, have been nurturing an unapologetically Mizrahi opposition to Zionism and solidarity with Palestinians,[124] taught us that our pain as Mizrahi immigrants is real and, nonetheless, inextricably intertwined with the pain of Palestinians, since our homes in Israel were constituted on the expanse of their home of Palestine. But what might it feel like for a Mizrahi reader or spectator to take in and live with the hopeful eyes, fervent longings, and political demand of the girl from *Jenin Jenin* to return home? When reading about, or watching, and—if we let it—also feeling the pain of another person that has been living on through ongoing effects of an oppression that we ourselves did not, or perhaps we did but experienced or expressed it differently, what kind of emotional and ethical labor may the feeling harbor?

Documentary Cinema from Israel-Palestine emphasizes the pressing need to watch documentaries centering on Palestinians and Mizrahim side by side not in order to spread peace and love between the two victims of Zionism and Israel but, rather, to deepen our understanding of another people's pain, which is unlike

Figure 2 Renowned Mizrahi actor and activist Yosef Shiloah watching and talking about *Jenin Jenin*.

ours. Connecting the dots between the experiences of pain of Palestinians and Mizrahim, we may also hear the unequivocal demand that all of their documentary performances place on us, to viscerally engage in intersubjective accountability. "An ethics that begins with your pain," for Sara Ahmed, involves "being open to being affected by that which one cannot know or feel."[125] I encourage readers-spectators to try and believe the people who are expressing pain in a way we may have never heard before, and consider some alternative realities to the ones typically perceived and lived, even if they uncomfortably ask us to change from who we knew ourselves to be so far. This book advocates for the transformative power of relating to another fellow human's mediated vulnerability and taking on the risk of complicating, confusing, and even adding to our immediate experience of our own pain, for the sake of holding space for their humanity in ourselves. More often than not, those who care for the pain of others are found in relative vulnerability themselves—political, physical, mental—thus chancing their becoming further undone. But as Tourmaline inspires us to believe, "if we are to ever make it to the next revolution, it will be through becoming undone, an undoing that touches ourselves and touches each other and all the brokenness we are … to become undone is the greatest gift to ourselves."[126] *Documentary Cinema from Israel-Palestine* hopes to be of interest for anyone who wishes to understand their own feelings of powerlessness as not one with them privately and naturally but, rather, as public, political, relatable, and changeable.

Part I

THE BODY

Chapter 1

JENIN: LIVING WITH MARTYRDOM IN MOHAMMAD BAKRI'S *JENIN JENIN* AND *SINCE YOU LEFT*, AND JULIANO MER-KHAMIS'S *ARNA'S CHILDREN*

"This is a film about people in the Jenin camp, whose experience was very very hard": this is how Mohammad Bakri described his film *Jenin Jenin*.[1] Screened in Israel in October 2002 for the first time, then banned, and enduring several trials and much public bullying, *Jenin Jenin* has been widely covered by Israeli mainstream media for more than a decade to come: indeed, its display of the Jenin refugee camp struck an unnerving chord in the Israeli psyche.[2] Filmed in five days in Jenin in April 2002, *Jenin Jenin* travels around the camp ruins right after the IDF destroyed large parts of it to the core, in what Israel called "Operation Defensive Shield," and Palestinians, "The Battle of Jenin." Bakri collected heartbreaking testimonies from the residents of the camp about their experience of the assault, as many of them had just lost their beloveds and homes. The screening of *Jenin Jenin* in Israel pushed against the normalized absence of their faces and voices from Israeli media.

In turn, *Jenin Jenin* ignited a wave of responses, engendering more documentary filmmaking about Jenin.[3] Gil Mezuman's *Jenin: Reserves Diary* (2003) and Pierre Rechov's *The Road to Jenin* (2003) dismiss Bakri's film, propagating the legitimacy of the IDF's operation in Jenin. *Invasion* (2003) by Nizar Hassan, a Palestinian citizen of Israel like Bakri, explored the battle of Jenin from the viewpoint of an IDF Bulldozer driver and of the residents of the Jenin refugee camp who fought against the IDF's invasion. In 2004, Juliano Mer-Khamis's *Arna's Children* joined the conversation, with a personal film about his mother, Arna Mer, and the children that both of them mentored in theater in the Jenin refugee camp in the 1990s. Alongside the footage from the theater classroom and stage, *Arna's Children* features Mer-Khamis's visit to the camp in 2002, after most of the children are no longer alive.[4] In 2005, Bakri released *Since You Left*, which, among other endeavors, elaborated on the making of *Jenin Jenin* and confronted the fervent criticism that it drew. Like *Jenin Jenin*, *Since You Left* and *Arna's Children* focused on the people experiencing the harsh consequences of the military violence against Jenin—yet in the latter two, the filmmakers included themselves in their films.

This chapter reads key scenes from the closely linked *Jenin Jenin*, *Since You Left*, and *Arna's Children*. To start off the discussion, I attend to a couple of scenes from Bakri's *Since You Left*, tracing living circumstances of '48 Palestinians during and immediately after October 2000—circumstances that influenced Bakri's decision to make *Jenin Jenin*. *Since You Left* illuminates that even when focusing only on their communities in the West Bank, documentaries by '48 Palestinians are also very much about them. Rather than merely communicating the stories of Jenin of the 1990s and the 2000s, *Since You Left*, *Arna's Children*, and *Jenin Jenin* unpack the complexities of living on in the refugee camp in Jenin since its foundation in 1953 to settle the survivors of the Nakba of 1948, and throughout years of Israeli military occupation since the 1967 war.[5] Carefully attending to the documentary performances of witnesses of violence and death, the chapter works through the terms testimony, reenactment, and witnessing used afterward, while grappling with documentary approaches to representing "reality": the chapter complicates theorizations of witnessing and testimony formative to trauma studies by indulging the power embedded in the documentary performance. The chapter unpacks the concept of "martyrdom" as it relates not to armed but to audiovisual, mediated, and mediatized Palestinian resistance. "Martyrdom" is a term fraught with meaning: in inciteful Islamophobic discourses in Israel and the United States, it has often been used interchangeably with "terrorism." Yet an important meaning refers to the Arabic translation of "martyrdom," or "shuhada," as "witnessing." The witnesses of violence and death in the Jenin refugee camp may thus be viewed as "living martyrs":[6] survivors of witnessed destruction who embody and carry the painful experience in and as their very own physical and affective state.

When performing their testimonies of what they have seen as reenactments, the witnesses filmed for *Jenin Jenin* do not guarantee to posit "what had exactly happened" with any measure of empirical accuracy. Rather, *Jenin Jenin*'s documentarian approach underlines whose pain gets to be filmed and shared depending on the circumstances of power informing the distribution of representation. As has been established, the trauma of witnessing destruction directly harms the usage of language about it. Yet on top of running the risk of unifying and depoliticizing the diversely positioned human experience, the Freudian genealogy of trauma carries harmful legacies of disbelief to survivors.[7] In this chapter, I harness a politicized view of both the testimony of trauma and of documentary distribution in Israel-Palestine to show that the precise ways in which their testimonies have been performed and cinematized, including the testifiers' bodily gestures, chosen words, silences, and the filmic general edited sequences, provide us spectators with poignant clarity regarding how pain had hit their bodies when the bullet hit the witnessed executed person. Additionally and no less importantly, the testimonies communicate how the conditions of the military occupation on the ground that pulled the trigger also made it difficult to communicate the pain of that experience outside the camp, by depriving them of audiovisual means of communication, and painting all the camp residents as unreliable speakers perforce who were responsible for their own suffering. When testifying in the film, the witnesses' reenactments of the pain of witnessing destruction politicize their pain, framing it collectively and relationally—as impacting their bodies, as well as recovering by their very telling of their own stories of their embodied pain. In and by these reenactments of their absorption of the pain of the killed one, they transform from racialized and potentially targeted innate "terrorists" whose pain is their own fault to living martyrs—survivors who reclaim agency over their own becomings, personally and collectively. *Arna's Children* extends this message by delving into the structure of feeling of living with potential death—of a beloved one, or one's own—throughout life. The film traces how, even as children, the theater students lived with the encompassing threat of death under military occupation much before many of them died. The formative experience of knowing death intimately in life is not only a collective one but also one that challenges the temporal understanding of pain: rather than a past event, the pain of living with death is present and constant and projects onto the future, all at the same time.

"I Decided to Enter Jenin with a Film Camera": Mohammad Bakri's Journey to Jenin

Where is Mohammad Bakri coming from, when traveling to Jenin to film? What is the context begetting Bakri's journey to Jenin in the first place? Such are the questions that *Since You Left* excavates. Addressing the heavy personal toll that Bakri had to endure after making *Jenin Jenin*, Bakri recounts the events that led to his portrayal as "a terrorist" in Israel, where he lives as a citizen and has been celebrated as an actor for decades. *Since You Left* demonstrates the escalation in inciteful discourse against '48 Palestinian after 2000, when they were vehemently stigmatized as fifth-column and clandestine traitors.[8] Yet this escalation marks the return of established racialized terms incriminating '48 Palestinians as always already suspected traitors since the foundation of Israel. By reviewing the events that sent him to Jenin, *Since You Left* sheds light on the political conditions to which he and '48 Palestinians at large are subjected to when depicted as the enemy from within, asserting that the making of the film did not simply invite an attack on Bakri but, rather, it was actually the position of '48 Palestinians in Israel that enabled the attack on Bakri.

A valuable resource for assessing the rebuke inflicted on Bakri himself, *Since You Left* focuses on Jewish Israeli society's demonization of Bakri after *Jenin Jenin* came out: it traces the changing esteem of the Palestinian public figure in Israel from a celebrated actor to a demeaned enemy. In *Since You Left*, actor Bakri's will to become a documentary filmmaker and visibilize the witnesses of violence in Jenin disrupted the conditions of non-representability inflicted on Palestinians everywhere, and hence brought about the punishment: lumping Bakri in the category of "terrorists" typically ascribed to the Palestinians living in the West Bank and Gaza. This connection across historical Palestine, in and outside the Green Line, is important to Bakri, though in a different way. *Since You Left* resists the common naming of '48 Palestinians as "Arab-Israelis," which omits their affiliation to historical Palestine and dissociates them from the Palestinian struggle for self-determination. In the film, we see that any attempt of Palestinians to reclaim their identification as such in Israel endangers them. Tracing the occurrences of the early 2000s while paying particular attention to the circumstances informing the making and the reception of *Jenin Jenin* in Israel, Bakri employed a personal perspective to share his own experiences of these turbulent times in *Since You Left*. Bakri's mode of the first-person singular develops as both a monologue as well as a dialogue: rather than informing the audience about the occurrences, Bakri communicates them to his late long-time mentor, the well-acclaimed Palestinian writer Emile Habibi. At the cemetery by Habibi's grave, Bakri delves in an imaginary conversation with Habibi, recounting the latest events and recalling the times they spent together, as archival footage from both the near and far past inundate the screen. As the next few pages argue, Bakri attempted to follow the footsteps of Habibi and convey his message in creative manners to Jewish Israeli society. His role model and a citizen of Israel like him, Habibi wrote and directed the text for the play *The Pessoptimist*, in which Bakri starred.[9] *Since You Left* focuses on the personal journey of the one who, through his winding ways from Israel to Palestine, from 1948 to 1967, leaves the profession of acting, dons the position of the writer and director, but is consequently and reluctantly deemed to dwell under the label of "a terrorist."

Bakri's narration of the visit to Jenin in *Since You Left* begins in Israel, where "on the 29th of March 2002, at the night of the Seder, a young Palestinian from the West Bank entered the Park hotel in Netanya, and blew himself up. This was one of the most severe attacks," Bakri explains. Consequently, "the attack gave the green light to Sharon's government to declare war and re-occupy the West Bank." Bakri's decision to go film in Jenin thus follows on the heels of the IDF going to war. One central scene from *Since You Left* especially focuses on Bakri's embarking on the road to Jenin—a road that begins in Nazareth. There, he and his colleagues at the El-Meidan theater participated in Federico Garcia Lorca's play *The House of Bernarda Alba*. There, on stage playing Bernarda, Bakri acts "the part of a mean woman that beats her daughters"; together with Bakri, an actress named Valentina plays Adela, the youngest and most rebellious daughter of Bernarda. In this scene, immediately after showing Bernarda fervently pulling Adela's hair and dragging her sideways on the stage, the film suddenly shifts to foreground an IDF tank driving through Jenin. In this way, images of a theater act merge and interchange with images from a war zone, while the figure of oppressive and violent Bernarda converses with that of an IDF soldier. Juxtaposing Bernarda's staged figure played by Bakri with that of the IDF soldier, the figure of Adela played by Valentina accommodates an important role in this narration as well, especially in her suffering. As the tank completes its patrol, the frame returns to Bernarda, who first stands on top of her supinely dropped corpse, and then slowly bends toward her; Bakri's voice simultaneously communicates that "we went, me and Valentina, my 'daughter' whose hair I tear, to a demonstration that took place north to Jenin, at the Jalame checkpoint." Then, as footage from that demonstration inundates the screen, Bakri describes how "an Israeli soldier passed by us and began shooting at us. Valentina was hurt. She was standing beside me. And I went nuts." Finally, while crying Bernarda slowly caresses her dead daughter Adela on stage, Bakri's voiceover explains Valentina's hurt to be the reason why he "decided to enter Jenin with the film camera." Thus, whereas Bernarda the theatrical figure thrashes Adela, tacitly precipitates her suicide, and finally embraces her corpse, Bakri the filmmaker follows the wounds of actress Valentina as guiding footsteps leading his way to Jenin.

Directed and staged in various renditions, *The House of Bernarda Alba* traveled worldwide since the 1930s: accordingly, it is here possible to consider not only El-Meidan's show but also Bakri's directed scene discussed above, as one of these adaptations, though a unique one. When the repressive and oppressive power, embodied in the figure of the IDF soldier, again aggressively appears, Bakri decides to enter Jenin with his camera. Thus, Bakri utilizes and revises the play's notions cinematically, expanding and literalizing Lorca's attention to the means and mechanisms of artistic production and/as political predominance. Thus, while the IDF imposes its hurtful presence on the screen and on the body of the actress, Bakri aims to render the predominance of its power visible, both in this scene and also through his expressed plan to film in Jenin. In designing this scene through interpolations of soldiers' images, and intending to direct *Jenin Jenin*, Bakri exposes, explicates, embodies, and mediates the implicit yet intrinsic connection between the ruler and the matriarch, structuring Lorca's play. As soon as he gets off the stage, Bakri is interested in pulling the mask of acting off of his face and switching to stand behind the camera, so that he can see, hear, and audiovisualize the power apparatus that is actually running the whole show.

Figure 3 *Since You Left*, Mohammad Bakri playing Bernarda Alba in "The House of Bernarda Alba."

What are, in turn, the consequences of the decision to take off the mask of theater and wear the lens of documentary for Bakri? Although much concerned with the turbulent events surrounding the public reception of *Jenin Jenin*, *Since You Left* minimizes any account of its processes of production: "I spent five days and five nights in Jenin Camp," Bakri merely mentions. The subsequences and repercussions that *Since You Left* weaves around the mostly muted experience of making *Jenin Jenin*, however, speak to its potent effects. Coming back first from Jenin, where he filmed, and then from Italy, where he edited the film, Bakri encounters an entirely new reality, when the Israeli newspapers claim that the Bakri family from El-Baeina in Israel is involved in executing the suicide bomb attack in Meiron, thus demonizing them as the "assistants of death." About a month after the first screening of *Jenin Jenin* in the two independent theaters of Tel Aviv and Jerusalem, Bakri received an official notification that his documentary was banned from public screening in Israel.[10] The official banning of the film by the Film Review Board led to an abundant series of legal prosecutions and public condemnations. Correlating the attack with the content of the film, hateful speakers zealously defaming and demeaning Bakri inundate the screen; at one crucial moment, against the backdrop of one vile voice calling the film "Palestinazi propaganda," defeated Bakri declares: "They made me out to be at least Bin Laden." Once Bakri steps down from stage and attempts to take his mask off, uproar erupts. According to the narrative of *Since You Left*, that single moment when Bakri decided to employ the means of audiovisual documentation in order to expose the works of the oppressive powers sentenced him to years of accusations associated with the term "terrorism." Thus, when pointing to and generating criticism against that power as the aggressor behind the scene, Bakri was immediately accused of being the aggressor himself.

In this state of affairs, is it still possible to say that Bakri indeed did succeed in taking the Bernarda Alba mask off of his face? I think not. Rather, it seems that the mask is insistently stuck on his face, so tightly that it became one with it. It is an already established preconception of his face as that of an aggressor that facilitates its casting in the image of the aggressive mask. To that end, this perceptual act of prejudice in fact connotes the general inclination of the Israeli entertainment field to let Palestinian actors play and portray only Arab and/or Muslim figures. "When Bakri decided to become an actor, there weren't many roles for Arabs on the Israeli stage or in films. The few roles that existed were stereotypes,"[11] contended Ginger Assadi based on his interview with Bakri. Refusing to collaborate with this trend, Bakri declined some job offers, as, in his words, "most of the characters were Palestinians or Arab terrorists."[12] Alas, although insisting on his ideological values within the professional game, stereotypization haunted Bakri nevertheless, rendering him from an actor to "a terrorist."

In closely juxtaposing Bakri's performance in the theater with his relegation to a terrorist, the scene sheds important light on an ubiquitous yet particular cultural and political phenomenon of anticipated exclusion occurring under the auspices of the terminology of terrorism. Here, another key scene, read through the lens of the local Palestinian context as well as global theories of terrorism, may assist in further clarifying Bakri's degradation. Taking part in the historical, political, and discursive manifestations elaborated below, the film may be said to comment and commentate on the overall local and temporal changes in the status and position of Palestinians within the recognized state of Israel in the early 2000s. Communicating the events of the early 2000s, one particular scene paves the path to an understanding of the discursive, cultural, and political conditions facilitating the immediate relegation of Bakri from actor to terrorist. Early in the documentary, Bakri tells Habibi all about the Israeli police's killing of thirteen innocent Palestinian citizens of Israel who, following the break of the second intifada, participated in a series of protests in October 2000. Summarizing the bloody events known as the October ignition as the backdrop of atrocious footage, Bakri communicates how "they took away 13 youngsters, like stems of basil, of ours. From within. Yes." In this scene, Bakri identifies with the victims in a shaken voice, mainly by ascribing the collective location of and affiliation with the Palestinian interiority of the state of Israel not only on them, but also on himself, and on Habibi. The claims to and negations of Palestinian indigenousness harness several competing namings and groupings: here, Bakri refers to their identity as "Palestinians min-al-dakhil"—"of the interior" in Arabic. Elucidating the term "the interior," Edward Said explained that it initially mainly referred to Palestinians living within the founded state of Israel, that is, along the 1949 armistice demarcation of the Green Line.[13] The term then was forced to evolve after Israel occupied further territories in 1967, to include all Palestinians living under Israeli rule. Bakri's employment of this term thus subverts the common usage of the ascription of the Palestinians in Israel as "Arab Israelis."[14]

The production of "Arab-Israeliness" and erasure of Palestinianness, as the year 2000 finally proved and as the films echo, did not succeed. Within this context, the documentary's framing of the October 2000 events by centering it on the protesters—Bakri being one of them—reverberates with the reestablishment of an indigenous and national Palestinian identification within Israel. In shooting the protesters, moreover, the Israeli police exercised the punishment of immediate death typically operated against those marked as dangerous to state security. Rendered as traitors and/or terrorists, the resisters to ethnic-based state violence are right thereafter exposed to even further fervent violence. This is thus a circular situation well-known in advance: '48 Palestinians protesting against the intentional and institutional years of systematic discrimination, land confiscation, and more, always corroborate the already established view of them as inherently potential traitors and/or terrorists. Writing about such instances of racialization, Said also examined the "noisy consensus"[15] created around "pseudo-scholarship and expert jargon about terrorism"[16] in *The Essential Terrorist*. As his case study, he critiques *Terrorism: How the West Can Win* edited and commentated by Benjamin Netanyahu—then the Israeli ambassador to the United Nations, today Israel's prime minister—who wrote his Zionist and orientalist convictions into the book. It is thus far from surprising that Netanyahu's definitions of terrorism "depend on a single axiom: 'we' are never terrorists; it's the Moslems, Arabs and Communists who are."[17] This determinist demonization, Said explained, relies on and stems from the systematic erasure of certain historical events, as well as the consistent exclusion of the demonized Arab and/or Muslim from the pages of the history books. In the case of Palestine, the denial of the ongoing Palestinian Nakba conditions and enables the ontological portrayal of Palestinian resistance as unexplainable and disproportional violence.[18] Thus, "if you can show that Libyans, Moslems, Palestinians, and Arabs, generally speaking, have no reality except that which tautologically confirms their terrorist essence as Libyans, Moslems, Palestinians and Arabs, you can go on to attack them and their 'terrorist' states generally."[19]

Now, it is possible to revisit the theme of the mask in the documentary once again, and better comprehend the imposition of the terrorist's mask on Bakri's face particularly. In the chapter "Our Terrorists, Ourselves," Arjun Appadurai analyzes the typical structures of contemporary global struggles between state and anti-state politics, identifying the latter as the flagship of what is otherwise known as "terrorism."[20] According to Appadurai, the state attempts to eliminate the "social uncertainty" that ethnic diversity, multiplicity, and ambiguity pose through imposing "vicious certainties" at and about them: these certainties comprise not only mass body violence but also corroborative racialization of perceived ethnic minorities.[21] A readily validated and deadly suspicion against these minorities thus simultaneously and consequently produces them as inherent traitors: the state imagines that "the ordinary faces of everyday life ... are in fact masks of everydayness behind which lurk the real identities not of ethnic other but of traitors to the nation conceived as an ethnos."[22] Rather than conceived as minority groups corresponding to "large-scale bodily violence" that "becomes a forensic means for establishing sharp lines between normally mixed identities,"[23] anti-state counterviolence confirms the already established distrust against its executers. As a result, instead of veiling her/his face, "the masked face of the armed terrorist actually reflects and confirms the suspicion of many dominant ethnic groups" among which s/he used to live. "When terrorists wear masks, and even when they do not wear masks, their ordinary demeanors are seen as organic masks for their real identities, their violent intentions, their treasonous loyalties, their secret betrayals ... what they reveal beneath the mask is another mask, that of an ordinary Muslim, or Palestinian, or Afghan, or Chechen, a traitor by definition."[24] Trying to transform uncertainty to certainty ultimately backfires, however; for, once the minoritarian individual dares to fight back, his actions immediately enhance further uncertainty, as "terrorists blur the line between military and civilian space and create uncertainty about the very boundaries within which we take civil society to be sovereign."[25]

Reluctant to accept the edict and determined to utilize his right as a citizen of Israel, Bakri sued the state and won the case, thus managing to lift the ban on screening the film in 2003. The canceled ban and subsequent trials stimulated prolonged and abundant heated debates on the dubious freedoms of speech and the politics, prospects of, and expectations from, documentary filmmaking in Israel. And yet, what this extensive discussion still lacks is a dedicated close theoretical analysis of the cinematic performances appearing in the documentary itself, alongside the key claims and discursive premises as well as actual repercussions surrounding it.[26]

Bakri's journey from his place of birth and residence in Israel to the camp and city in the occupied West Bank led him to his unobvious decision to screen *Jenin Jenin* in Israel. Bakri aspired to address an audience fluent in the linguistic and discursive circles of Jewish Israeli culture. Yet Bakri's decision meant that his film would have to be subjected to the inspection of the Israeli Film Review Board, like all artwork designated for display in Israel. Placed under the surveillance of the guards of Israeli cinematic audio-visibility, the film thus failed to meet the unwritten requirements and regulations of representation contoured along the confines of national and colonial Zionist discourse. At the same time, this supposed "failure" may point precisely to the documentary's success to both expose as well as irritate these confines. But what if Bakri actually endeavored to foreground the effort to exclude Palestinian testimonial activity from the regulated realm of credible representation to the anxious outskirts of nonrepresentability? What if the film directly targeted the Israeli desire and/as militarized strategies to shape Palestinian witnessing as a deadly and deadening experience of extreme unintelligibility? What are the tactics that the film employed to both deliver its message as well as demonstrate the effective restrictions that conditioned its garbled character? The following section endows *Jenin Jenin* with a much-deserved and long-overdue close reading, carefully analyzing the performative, cinematic, and discursive acts it accommodates. While Bakri attempted to challenge the invisibility and silence of Palestinian war witnesses, the testimonies of the residents of Jenin unearthed the broad and crude context of the war that, among many other atrocities, also deprived them of the capacity to access the witnessed event sensibly and coherently. Below, I place the wish to push Palestinians into unrepresentability by banning the film and/or delegitimizing the testimonies as a force that *Jenin Jenin* portrays, reenacts, and rejects. I trace the ways in which the filmmaker and his interviewees embody and display the state of emergency that the military carnage imposed on them. I fathom how the survivors' alarming testimonies effectively emphasized the unrepresentability of the witnessed reality of destruction. Military operations, *Jenin Jenin* communicates, not only murder and physically offend many[27] but they also, crucially, try to shatter its witnesses/testifiers/survivors and their verbal and audiovisual means of communication. In other words, these operations of state violence attempt to exclude its witnesses/testifiers/survivors from representability. Yet as I show, the inseparability of the surviving Jenin residents from that death that they have seen and sensed in their bodies as witnesses, and their inability to testify on it in accordance with conventional codes of credibility, births and coheres as a unique cinematized reenactment of the political setting that brought about the suffering in the first place.

The war on the Jenin residents' representability neither began nor ended with the 2002 Jenin operation/battle. This explains why, while the witnesses centered their injurious experiences of witnessing at the heart of their testimonies, Jewish Israeli critics, rendered them as unreliable speakers right thereafter, immediately dismissing the speakers and filmmaker, denouncing them as either liars and/or as terrorists, interchangeably. The dehumanizing relegation of those involved in representing Jenin and their compatible exclusion from representability contributes to their embodied state of martyrdom—a state and term that I explore elaborately throughout the next section. Indeed, the Jewish Israelis' gestures of disbelief toward the testifiers in *Jenin Jenin* adequately reflect the unbelievability of what they have witnessed, embodied, and survived.

From Terrorists to Witnesses to Testifiers: Witnessing and/as Martyrdom in Jenin Jenin

Listed as the first factor in the Film Review Board report, the members claimed that *Jenin Jenin* "is a distorted presentation of events distended as a documentary truth, which might mislead the public."[28] In the statement of claim, Bakri's attorney Avigdor Feldman utilized documentary theory to tackle this accusation: using legal definitions as well as quoting from Claude Lantzman's statement on his documentary *Shoah* (1986) to corroborate his claim, Feldman desisted that "a documentary is not required to be balanced, objective … it is not obligated to presenting the absolute truth and does not aspire to do so. It falls under the definition of a cinematographic work."[29] Feldman emphasized that freedom of speech protects not only truthful claims but "expressions that are not truth": "even if the film was describing facts that did not exist in reality, it would still be included under these freedoms."[30] Feldman concluded that "the protection of the freedom of speech becomes relevant and significant *especially* for expressions that the Film Review Board sees as expressions that are not truth" (my emphasis).[31] Thus, the determination of what is true or false is shaped by the politics of power at play that stir processes of production of and exclusion from what is constructed as "the domain of legitimate discourse."[32]

The language employed in this appeal addresses some of the most core issues embedded in documentary filmmaking and theory, while also illuminating Bakri's artistic and political approach to documentary film, particularly in making *Jenin Jenin* in occupied Palestine and insisting on its showing in central movie theaters in Israel. By bringing previously underrepresented scenes of Palestinians' human pain to wide public attention in Israel, *Jenin Jenin* challenged spectators and news consumers to ask themselves which reality is commonly represented, in what way is it represented, how much does the filmmaker attest to their presence in any representation and, most crucially, what are the political and power conditions informing any quest after representing a reality? *Jenin Jenin* encourages us to avoid old paradigms in documentary studies, especially the trap of treacherous discussions on verisimilitude that recourse to prescriptive ideas as to what documentaries should, should not, can and cannot, do or be. Instead of again reaffirming documentary media's incapacity to touch reality directly, we are invited to watch and appreciate the transformative power of documentary scenes—especially performances of pain of Palestinians that are mostly unavailable through Israeli mainstream channels.[33] In that regard, *Jenin Jenin* aligned itself with the myriad of documentaries emerging from the US-occupied Iraq around the same years: As Ryan Watson asserted after Patricia Zimmerman, representations of everyday "real lives and real affects" in documentaries became radical political acts in the face of the blinding power of the US mainstream media's meta-representation of the "war on terror" imbued with terms such as "democracy" and "freedom."[34] In the words of Jane Gaines, who refuted the reactionary employments of discussions of documentary and verisimilitude while advocating for the politicized usage of documentations of lives under war and occupation in the context of Iraq: "Yes, mimetic technologies do have the power to explosively reproduce, to reproduce the world before us as well as to reproduce its intensities onscreen and to reproduce them most strategically in the bodies and hearts of viewers."[35]

Yet the *Jenin Jenin* epic sagas do not end, but rather only begin, with the acceptance of Feldman's claims as valid for juridical purposes. Prior to the trial, as well as many times after its conclusion in favor of the documentary, the loud speaker against *Jenin Jenin* and later an enthusiastic proponent of the *Jenin Jenin* law David Tzanegen stated a similar accusation against the documentary: a doctor and officer who participated in the "Defensive Shield" operation, Tzangen proclaimed that "Bakri weaves together lies and half-truths," and listed seven presumable lies that the documentary presented.[36] In particular, Tzanegen referred to one specific interview that Bakri conducted with Dr. Abu-Rhalli, the manager of the Jenin hospital at the time of the operation. Tzanegen attempted to disconfirm the doctor's claim that the IDF destroyed the western section of the hospital while intentionally damaging its water and electricity supply. Tzanegen seemed especially worried that "this Abu-Rhalli serves as one of the 'authoritative' sources to substantiate the 'massacre' claim."[37] Throughout his meticulous list, however, Tzanegen refrained from addressing the claim directly. In what follows, I look at this particular scene that foregrounds Dr. Abu-Rhalli's statements that upset Tzanegen so much by tackling the aspects that he dubiously overlooked. Reconstructing the execution of Abu-Jandal, the head of the resistance movement in the camp, Abu-Rhalli's performance treasures several, utmost crucial, messages between its lines. Rather than debating on whether or not the IDF deliberately bombed the western section of the hospital, and whether or not the IDF has executed a formerly planned massacre of Palestinian civilians, I focus on a careful analysis of the scene to ask a different, if related, set of questions. How can we stretch Feldman's stakes further to not merely acknowledge the ideological biases that truth claims always display, but also consider the conditions that affect, validate, and/or obstruct the production of codified credible truth and audiovisual knowledge? How is Abu-Rhalli's—as the other documentary participants'—documentary performance informed by, and how do they converse with, claims of the kind that Tzangen made, thus underpinning our understanding of the reception of *Jenin Jenin*?

"I examined the corpse and found out it was Abu-Jandal, the commander of the battle of Jenin," Dr. Abu-Rhalli confidently states. He thus volunteers to provide his diagnosis and identifies the corpse as that of the deceased Abu-Jandal. *Jenin Jenin* thus presents Abu-Rhalli's medical forensic assessments to determine the identity of the dead. Yet additionally, Abu-Rhalli also testifies on other occurrences related to the public execution that convey other, deeper significances of his and others' experience of witnessing it. A close analysis of the entire scene reveals how, like an explosion in the happening, Abu-Rhalli's stated official and knowledgeable identification of the body that kicked off the scene disperses in multiple alternative directions, to delineate the ongoing and collective contours of the pain of witnessing a public execution. Abu-Rhalli not only medically identified the person but also ideologically names him as a freedom fighter. This naming is in conversation with the common Israeli premise that labels all fighters of the occupation as always already and merely terrorists, holding Abu-Jandal accountable as "one of the main coordinators of terrorists."[38] Yet on top of this identification, *Jenin Jenin* finds additional, more radical ways of expanding and subverting the terminology of "terrorism." To shed light on the trajectories in which *Jenin Jenin* and its protagonists lead the filmmaker and his plans, let me now explore Abu-Rhalli's testimony across its several framing layers.

It is important to understand here not only the post-death identification but also, more profoundly, the wobbly conditions of witnessing death in the happening as highlighted in the scene. For this task, I alternately rewind and forward the documentary by few seconds, to track down the several statements Abu-Rhalli madeon—just before and right after—identifying the corpse of Abu-Jandal. I encircle Abu-Rhalli's medical diagnosis with two interpretive layers that shed light on the performative and discursive components that enable his statement of knowledge: the first indicates the representational characteristics comprising Abu-Rhalli's performance, and the second unpacks the systematic power relations within which it is given. Right before plunging into Abu-Rhalli's medical diagnosis, the camera directs its lens elsewhere, preceding the diagnosis with something else: a testimony of an anonymous woman. "What upset me the most is that when they arrested Abu-Jandal," says the woman, then pauses momentarily, looks right at the camera, at her interviewer's eyes, and at us, and recounts how the IDF soldiers "tied him before they shot him down, here and here." Then, right after Abu-Rhalli delivers his forensic assessment, he repeats and re-performs the woman's movements, and corroborates: "They had him sit down on the rubble and shot him twice in the face." Separated by few crucial moments, both the woman and the doctor, respectively, and complementarily testify on an execution and also physically point to their very own chins and foreheads to indicate how the IDF shot Abu-Jandal. As their verbal description somewhat differs, so is the order of their physical movements distinct: for, while the woman places her finger on her forehead first, the doctor initially touches his chin. Rather than a document of evidential knowledge, it is thus two performed testimonies of a witnessed execution that surround and substantiate Abu-Rhalli's medical claim.

What kind of witnesses do the woman and the doctor perform? Giorgio Agamben differentiated between two kinds of witnesses: the superstes and that of the terstis.[39] A person who lived an experience in his own life and is thus able to report the experience as the one who bears witness, the superstes, "has lived through something, who has experienced an event from beginning to end and can therefore bear witness to it."[40] However, to produce credible testimony for legal

Figure 4 *Jenin Jenin*, the woman witness, "tied him before they shot him down."

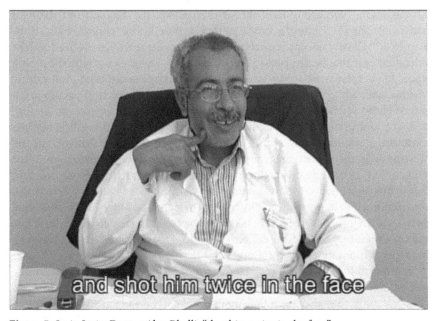

Figure 5 *Jenin Jenin*, Doctor Abu-Rhalli, "shot him twice in the face."

usage, the superstes is insufficient: in that case, the witness needs to perform a terstis, someone who may testify on something that happened to other people as an objective third party; only a terstis may be considered as the producer of factual legal evidence in trial.[41] Besides these two prototypes, Agamben also followed Primo Levy in mentioning a third witness who, rather than the still relatively privileged survivor of the catastrophe, is the absolute victim, the dead, whose absent voice echoes in the survivor's testimony as "a lacuna."[42] While the two kinds of witnesses preoccupy the positions of the "almost witnesses," only the victim, or, in Levy's phrasing, the Muslim, is the "true" and "complete witness" who, ironically, may not account for her/his experience as it has happened. The absent presence of the third witness elucidates that, actually, "the value of testimony lies essentially in what it lacks: at its center it contains something that cannot be borne witness to and that discharges the survivors of authority." Finally, for this reason, "the survivor speak in their stead ... they bear witness to a missing testimony."[43] Agamben finally concludes that indeed "there is something like an impossibility of bearing witness."[44]

Seen through Agamben's lens, the woman and the doctor in the scene oscillate between an attempt to serve as supersteses as well as account for the dead, true witness or missing Muslim, while altogether unable to obtain the requirements of the tertis. To further analyze the tasks, positions, and gestures that the woman and doctor take on as witnesses, as testifiers along Agamben's theorization, it is useful to explore Faisal Devji's concept of the witness as a martyr. In Devji's interpretation, "witnessing itself means martyrdom, the Arabic word shahadat translating one term into the other, so that to have borne witness is also to be martyred."[45] Devji's concept of martyrdom thus connects between the dead and the living that bear that death's consequences, so that it "involves not only the person whose life is voluntarily sacrificed ... but also everyone annihilated in this cause whether willingly or not."[46] If examined through these theoretical paradigms, it is possible to see how the concrete and metaphoric threads of context, destiny, mimicry, and performativity connect the already dead and the still living, the witnessing enactors and the murdered martyr, in the scene. In that split second of witnessing, the woman and the doctor both observe the victimization of the dying as well as become the victims of disdaining sights themselves: accordingly, they demonstrate not only how instantly and alarmingly the killing of Abu-Jandal occurred, but also how intensely it inscribed its wounds on other—in this instance, their—witnessing skins, rendering them as subjected to an experienced death too, and the experience as political, collective—indeed, public—loaded with meaning and repercussions for everyone around.

In order to transmit the atrocious occurrence in front of Bakri's camera, the woman and the doctor thus play and portray the dying of Abu-Jandal himself. Concomitantly, they also instantiate how they absorbed and embodied his killing and death at the moment of the execution. In this fashion, the woman and the doctor may be said to stage victimization and survival as interrelated, performing them as not only temporally simultaneous but also metonymically similar. One of the tasks of testifying therefore becomes to underscore the very relationality of their experience of pain, and the resilience in their competence to still conceive themselves as separate entities intelligibly witnessing pain, despite the debilitating effect of watching death in the making. "All representational practice, and indeed all communicative behavior, is composed in reiteration, is engaged in citation, is already a practice of reenactment,"[47] contends Rebecca Schneider in her study of contemporary performances. In reenactment, Schneider continues, "Affect can circulate ... in material remains or gestic/ritual remains ... shifting in and through bodies in encounter."[48] On the threshold between the binarized archival concepts of history and memory that is "layered with anxiety about verity, authenticity, falsity, theatricality, truth, and claim," Schneider reminds us, reenacted "physical acts are a means for knowing."[49] Schneider's generous definition helps frame the woman's and the doctor's testimonies as reenactments of their witnessing experiences of and as martyrdom. In turn, thinking of their performances as reenactments of martyrdom enables the equally expansive employment of Devji's conception of Shahadat alongside and against Israel's confining definition of the Shahid. First of all, by contrast to the narrow conception of the suicide bombers, Bakri's martyrs—the dead and/as the witnesses—do not sacrifice themselves voluntarily but, rather, reluctantly experience the execution that the IDF conducts. Yet moreover and most importantly, the woman and the doctor here reenact, embody, and become the martyr at his disappearance, showing how it immediately and destructively impacted and permeated their beings. The woman and the doctor reiterate the acts of the execution itself on their own bodies, thus reenacting the execution as well as embodying the executed. Thus, they trace and stage the way in which his death haunts, captivates, and ultimately, engulfs, their lives.

As a result, the audience's knowledge about the loss of life does not come from an authoritative source but is rather presented as an audiovisual affect that the testifiers deliver through their reenactments. In turn, the interchangeability between the martyr and the witness seems to reverberate with the representational traits that the documented performances obtain. How can the woman and the doctor testify on the witnessing of/as martyrdom? What, finally, ties together the acts of observing, reenacting, and becoming martyrs, and brings two witnesses to perform audiovisual moving, as well as martyred, images? Correlating the sufferings of the already dead and the still living as he does, Devji contends that the conception of the martyr as witness instantiates the "close link between seeing and dying in the etymology of martyrdom."[50] Ample with connotations of media and mediation, Devji explains that this link also appears "in the televised image of the landscape that as news is simultaneously seen and destroyed."[51] To probe the connection between martyrdom, media, and mediation more thoroughly, Devji discusses the practice of Jihad martyrs who, before conducting suicide attacks, videotape their testaments. As Devji demonstrates, they draw their inspiration to conduct mediated and actual acts of martyrdom from various mediatized imagery, such as videotapes of suicide bombers and television broadcasts of war.[52] For them, Devji explains, "the mediated witnessing of terror in Beirut" and "the equally mediated witnessing of terror in New York, together make up a media narrative in which one scene is exchanged for another, together creating a community of exchanges."[53]

On one level, it is possible to view the woman's and doctor's testimonies and reenactments of witnessing as corresponsive to the global mediated imagery of martyrdom and thus proactive in the participatory community of exchanges that Devji delineates. Similar to the flickering image of the martyr in popular global media, moreover, the woman and the doctor take upon themselves to mediate and mediatize, carry and pass along, what their eyes have formerly and horrifyingly observed. As a result, the reenacted execution, upon the inevitable discrepancies they display, speak to the elusive and precarious representational status of the transition between mediated witnessing and martyring, and mediatized showing, appearing, and performing. Yet moreover, the woman's and the doctor's congruent yet not identical performances highlight the grave circumstances that shaped them as witnesses and testifiers: they foreground contested testimonies of death as well as witnessing of/as martyrdom. Capturing how witnessing became martyrdom, the woman's and the doctor's testimonies thus illuminate the obstacles informing the efforts to transform this specific event into representable audio-visibility. Here, it is not only the traumatizing effect of witnessing destruction[54] but, rather and most importantly, the particular restrictive political-representational conditions that wounded the witnesses in the first place, that designed them as unreliable observers and reporters right from the moment of witnessing. Indeed, the woman's and doctor's acts of mediation operate within the discursive territory of Israeli occupation, and restrictions on representation and visibility. Thus, the woman and the doctor do not ritualize an already mediatized image but, rather, are forced to memorize and commemorate an intentional and equally ritualistic live execution. To examine the specific political-representational restrictions within which the mediation of martyrdom comes to being, I now analyze the second statement Abu-Rhalli made, right after identifying the corpse.

Politicizing Witnessing, Testimony, and the Embodied Experience of Pain

"When I saw the second corpse, I was obviously in the process of filming when the soldiers confiscated my video camera," states Abu-Rhalli at the outset of the scene. Thus, prior to testifying alongside the woman and providing his forensic diagnosis, Abu-Rhalli details both the aspiration for, and, the inability to live up to the required standards of the corroboration of death under military, discursive, and representational occupation. Here, Bakri endorsed the importance of the audiovisual documentation of the corpse as the most efficient means of proving that an event has really occurred. Yet he also let Abu-Rhalli describe the deliberate deprival of this important task from them at the same time. Abu-Rhalli's statement thus not only retroactively explains why he may not provide audiovisual evidence to that which is about to be told, but also tracks down the acts by which he was deprived of any capacity to produce this audiovisual evidence. Thus, the testimony foregrounds the standards from which Abu-Rhalli's testimony emerges as well as those in which it is given: not only that Abu-Rhalli had to retell what he observed from memory that could not audiovisualize its own processes of registration, but also he is relegated to a status where any other possible way of communicating the testimony would be considered insufficient and unreliable. In the absence of any capacity to produce audiovisual evidence, he thus draws the spectator's attention to his own voice and movements.

Here, it is possible to view the IDF's confiscation of the camera in one line with the conditions of witnessing imposed on the woman and the doctor: the lack of the camera metaphorizes and materializes the inherent inability of martyrized witnesses and testifiers to see and speak properly about live death. Witnessing and wanting to testify that which cannot simply and smoothly register as representability resembles the impeded and thus failed will to hold a camera in front of an execution: both activities have to, and also may not, be done right. On the one hand, the accentuation of the conditions of witnessing shed significant light on how Abu-Rhalli arrived at a situation where he testifies in front of an audience that does not believe him. This audience of non-believers, in turn, is inexorably affiliated with the soldiers who committed the execution and deprived him of the opportunity to corroborate his testimony audiovisually. This is how, on the other hand, these testimonies become so useful in exposing and emphasizing the state of martyrized witnessing that precedes, informs, and impedes the task of testifying. To that end, whereas the scene began with a confident identification that corresponds to the common accusation of Abu-Jandal as a terrorist, it closes with some turbulent and excessive performances poignantly speaking to an inability to identify the dead. These final frames visibilize the presence of corpses: Dr. Abu-Rhalli aims to seek, find, and examine corpses, in order to determine the identity of those killed. Here, however, it is not merely one but, rather, a plethora of corpses that are at stake. The IDF hinders Abu-Rhalli from pursuing the task of identifying the corpses, claiming that "the area hasn't been cleaned up yet"; despite this prohibition, he decides to check the area with his own eyes. "Cleaned up for them means: cleaning up the area from bodies," Abu-Rhalli deduces after violating the IDF soldiers' permission and checking the area for himself. "I can smell the decomposed corpses from where I am standing," Abu-Rhalli reassures, and finally indeed reports that "while searching we found a corpse, mutilated and scattered." The doctor then concludes his testimony by addressing the IDF with the confident assertion: "Here is the evidence of your execution."

Abu-Rhalli solely saw and smelled, rather than identified, corpses, bodies, and/or past lives: the malodorous sight does not assist Abu-Rhalli in identifying the corpses as he identified Abu-Jandal. No name associated with terrorism is mentioned: in fact, no name is mentioned at all. Bakri thus does not trace and name the identities of most of the victims of the "Defensive Shield" operation. Instead, fragmenting, unifying, ubiquitous, and contagious acts of execution are repeatedly scrutinized. Yet where no identification is possible, there dwells the evidence for a horrendous offense, Abu-Rhalli emphasizes. Indeed, if examined as a whole, the scene asserts the need, attempt, and frequent failures to identify and name as many dead as possible, as well as highlights the important inevitability of identifying with and as the dead through witnessing (as) martyrdom. As a personal and collective resistant act, identifying with and as the martyr becomes a way of exposing the occupation's strive to push witnesses into unintelligibility, as well as a way of retaining intelligibility against all odds: death, it seems, is the one intelligible experience that witnesses and/as martyrs can testify on. On the one hand, verbally testifying on both the will as well as the incompetence to document the execution, Abu-Rhalli calls forth Israel's responsibility for both the demand for, as well as the exclusion from, evidential visibility. Similar to the martyrs described by Devji, Bakri, the doctor, and the woman all "take democracy … seriously." In this scene, "the assignation of responsibility … is itself an inclusive and even democratic act because … it presupposes the existence of a global community of equals."[55] And yet, on the other hand and precisely because of these conditions, the woman's and the doctor's scarce resources and capacities do not qualify as proper means for producing evidential documentation. Devji asks: "how can such responsibility either be claimed or assigned in a world of media distortion and political coercion"?[56] To adjust the question to the case of the discussed scene, we can ask: How exactly are Bakri, the doctor, and the woman to demand the Jewish Israeli audience to recognize their responsibility for the hurtful discourses and occurrences if their medial and political state coerces and constitutes them as perforce distorted? In other words, what are the tactics necessary for compellingly proving and protesting one's undocumented death?

Not only Agamben, but Avital Ronell too, addresses the problem and possibility of the testimony on traumatizing events to perform reliability and receive respective recognition: her conceptualization of the witness and testifier assists in attending to the above questions. Referring to witnesses and victims interchangeably, Ronell shows that "the demand to establish the reality of a phrase according to normative procedures can wrong a witness"; this often occurs when "the victim asked to account for the reality to which she points, sometimes mutely, is under pressure to produce reference."[57] For, "you yourself, as lacerated victim, cannot believe this has happened."[58] Ronell offers to consider that "the disturbing complicity between fiction and testimony cannot be erased or simply overcome"; thus, and in utter relevance to the case study of the scene, Ronell concludes that "testimony comes forward to pose a knowing without cognition, a memory without prosthetic or technical support, an exemplarity that must be repeated and replaced by more testimony without ever resolving itself into a proof."[59]

Along this thought, it is possible to consider that while the lack of evidence might possibly and presumably prevent the testifiers from properly and directly accusing the IDF of the execution, this lack may actually also be regarded as the exact required evidence: a look at one more segment of the scene may clarify this point. "I told the soldiers I knew why they would not let me film; because it was an execution," Abu-Rhalli infers when concluding his testimony. Referring back to its point of departure and explaining it more elaborately, Abu-Rhalli's words—juxtaposed with an image of a soldier armed with a rifle and a camera passing by on a jeep—manage to turn the deprival of documentation on its head: for, the missing footage not only testifies on a deliberately disabled reliability but, rather, itself indicates that an atrocious execution and/as elimination has occurred. In this fashion, the actual deprival of the camera thus becomes the very evidence for the occurrence of the execution; there where the entrance of the documenting eye is denied, the corpse probably lies, Abu-Rhalli's testimony thus communicates. Indeed, it is the lack of the camera that forced the woman and the doctor to perform a reenactment to begin with. At the same time, it is in fact only this kind of reenactment that can best capture, highlight, and instantiate the inherent performative and ritualistic element embedded in the execution. Here, the woman, and then Abu Rhalli, both point to the preparatory acts of tying and seating that the IDF carried out on Abu-Jandal preceding his actual execution: "They ordered him to raise his hands and they executed him on the spot," the doctor corroborates the woman's testimony. As they don the execution upon themselves through reenactment, they actually hold the IDF accountable for initially and intentionally planning and staging it. Thus, it is the theme of the ritual inherent to the deeds of the IDF that comprises the crux, and delivers the message, of the testimony. Rather than creating the ritual themselves, the woman and doctor only reiterate and absorb its grave repercussions: the woman and the doctor are the ones burdened with its corporeal consequences.

No documentary endeavor seeking knowledge could ever capture the ritualistic element and effect of the execution, which both echoes its repetitiveness as well as the impact it has on others observing it. To that end, the woman's and the doctor's forced position as mediated imagery carries within it an inflammatory potential: as the woman and the doctor track down the paths and take on the labors involved in the rendering of an act into an image, they also highlight the salient and immanent shortcomings of any desire to obtain knowledge through documentation. The woman and doctor do not solely emulate and embody images: their documentary performances commentate on the very taboos and limitations inherently generating the image crafted after the act. If to employ Devji's claim one last time, the ritualized embodiment of the woman and the doctor "demonstrates its truth by pointing to the same media images that are otherwise denounced as distorted and deceptive, thus suggesting that knowledge in some objective sense is not an issue at all."[60] Blurring all boundaries between witnessing, appearing, enacting, and experiencing, Devji concludes that "media images of martyrdom have no epistemological status … their truth never becomes a subject … knowledge as an epistemological category does not exist in the jihad."[61] Finally, Bakri, the woman, and the doctor find a way to overturn and resist the imposed deprival of and exclusion from both Jewish Israeli and global media's knowable audio-visibility by reclaiming, rather than dissociating from, martyrdom as means of mediation. Here, it is not so much the soldiers that looted the camera and conducted the execution who are held accountable in particular but, rather, Israeli discourse as a whole. Addressing the Jewish Israeli audience as it does, the documentary importantly underscores the imperative of audiovisual documentation for the production of normatively accepted knowledge as well as the deprival of Palestinians from any ability to live up to that standard. It does so by illuminating, as well as resisting, the attempted exclusion of Abu-Jandal, the woman, and the doctor, from the right and competence to participate in the global distribution of documented knowledge.

In the midst of Bakri's legal efforts to lift the ban, some have charged the film and its participants as already culpable of crimes far exceeding cinematic inadequacy. Here, the accusations made by the public participants in the polemic around *Jenin Jenin* further reinforced the Zionist ritual, and performed the cinematic theme, of Palestinian exclusion from representabiliy that the Film Review Board dictated. By discrediting the testifiers as illegible speakers, the opponents of the film disallowed their entrance into the realm of credible representation once again. At the same time, these loud antagonists acted out, and thus further highlighted, the impeded conditions of audio-visibility that informed the Jenin residents' attempts to witness and testify on Israel's ubiquitous atrocities. In this way, the announcement of the board's formal decision and the enunciations of the documentary's opponents may be seen as public reenactments of the themes that the *Jenin Jenin* intentionally implicated. To that end, the film enables the filmmaker and testifiers to narrate and articulate stories and performances that counter and construct, correspond to and stem from, precisely this exclusion, in creative alternative ways.

Flickering on the screen before the official introduction, *Jenin Jenin* opens with a dedication to its executive producer Iyad Samoudi, who was murdered by the IDF just as the filming was coming to a close. Right thereafter, the sun comes up on Jenin, throwing solely several hesitant rays of light to the sky and the screen. Finally, as the screen slightly brightens, it shows a man running in an alley, stopping between two corners, and reenacting a rifle shooting using bodily gestures, sign language, and some vocal sounds. Pointing and then striking at his forehead with his finger as if it were a shooting gun, the man then spreads his arms horizontally and leans back as if ready to fall: it is this last posture that the documentary slow-motions, and thus ponders on, in particular. A somewhat extended variation of this scene appears right after the woman finishes her testimony as well: there, too, the same man reenacts shootings, ending his act with the same posture. In this way, even before its title surfaces, and right after the key testimony finishes, the documentary already presents two of its very central themes: first, the act of killing, its ritualistic reenactment, and the embodiment of instant murder by the living on whose bodies death was inscribed; second, the communication disconnect with the audience that hardly acknowledges that its inability to believe the testifiers directly stems from the Israeli occupation's martyrization of witnesses. To that end, Bakri opened his lens and began filming despite systematic silencing—as a result, the voices he recorded speak to the audience from beyond a deafening layer; yet through reenactments of witnessed martyrization, the testimonies of both the already dead and still-living martyrs nevertheless penetrate this deafness.

In the Midst of Life We Are in Death: Arna's Children and the Theater of the Occupation

"My greatest wish is to go back home," says the young girl from *Jenin Jenin*, as mentioned in the introduction of this book. Her reference to the ruined house we have seen her walk through before is as plausible as it is to pre-Nakba Palestine.

But the girl has a vision. "Yes, they destroyed everything but we will rebuild it despite their presence. We will rebuild everything on the basis of resistance," she continues in full confidence, her performance piercing the screen. "The camp is like a tall, eminent tree. The tree has leaves, and each leaf of the tree bears the name of a martyr … even if they break a few branches, others shall grow in their place, they were not able to reach the top of the tree." In the young girl's narration, it is neither the trunk nor the lower branches of the tree that sustain and signify its strength; rather, it is the leaves, especially those hanging from the treetop, which guarantee its long-lasting stability. Inscribed with the names of the martyrs, these leaves are under constant danger of disappearance. It is unclear whether the breaking of branches targets the living witnesses or the witnessed dead; yet this ambiguity precisely renders their interchangeability unfortunate but also useful. For, while martyrs do fall, the memory of their falling holds the tree high. As this section shows, it is this liminal state of ambiguity between life and death that the residents of the Jenin refugee camp experience daily, and not only when faced with a killing as it is happening. Retaining, remembering, and memorializing the names of the lost ones is the important task that survival and resistance prescribes, *Jenin Jenin* affirmed. witnessing (as) martyrdom makes the witnesses realize the unintelligible sense of death that they were carrying within themselves all along, prior to or regardless of witnessing dying in its happening, and thus renders the unintelligibility of death intelligible. This is one of the deeply painful problems that *Arna's Children* explored.

Told from the perspective of the actor and drama instructor Juliano Mer-Khamis (directed with Danniel Danniel), *Arna's Children* foregrounds his farewell from Ashraf and Youssef, his former theater students, and from his mother, Arna Mer.[62] The day when Mer-Khamis was notified that he received funding to make a documentary about Arna, the founder of the Stone Theater program for the children of Jenin, he was also informed that she has only one more year left to live.[63] On her part, Arna refused to be the sole protagonist of the film, insisting that it should focus on the theater project and its participants as a whole—and, mostly, on the children. And that is what Mer-Khamis did. The first part of *Arna's Children* features footage from the early years of the theater in the 1990s, and the children who participated in the theater program—particularly Youssef and Ashraf, in the shadow of ongoing attacks on Jenin. Years after his mother's death, and after many further attacks, Mer-Khamis returns to Jenin that has lost Ashraf and Youssef as well—they died in attacks and/or acts of resistance against Israel and Israelis: this later visit comprises the second part of the film. Two years of time separate *Jenin Jenin* and *Arna's Children*. While the participants in *Jenin Jenin* and *Arna's Children* wish to name lost martyrs and put them to rest, the latter provides an account of "living martyrs"—of people's lives in front and under the shadow of constant possible destruction. Besides their shared interest in witnessing (as) martyrdom as a collective experience of pain, the films foreground different momentums, tempos, and temporalities: while *Jenin Jenin* was shot in five days and released within several months, *Arna's Children* includes archival footage collected for over a decade. Moreover, as *Jenin Jenin* illuminates the production of Palestinian witnessing as martyrdom during the battle of Jenin, Bakri left it to Mer-Khamis to ask questions about mundane life in Jenin prior to the deadly 2002. Finally, the juxtaposition of the documentaries enables a glimpse into the disturbing circularity of martyrdom: when witnessing and experiencing death, potential destruction was already installed around the residents of Jenin in advance, questioning the differentiation between the past, present, and future of martyrdom. How does Mer-Khamis's account of an everyday life constantly hovered by a possible destruction in *Arna's Children* contribute to our understanding of the experience of witnessing (as) martyrdom? This question motivated the following analyses.

One register in this study runs along and against the grain of Ariella Azoullay and Adi Ophir's differentiation between two types of violence that the Israeli occupation manifests: withheld and bursting violence,[64] offering to consider the implications of beheld violence too. Both *Jenin Jenin* and *Arna's Children* foreground the aftermath of bursts of violence, one that "penetrates, dismantles, damages, hurts or digests" and altogether demonstrates "forms of destruction," thus demonstrating "an explicit aspect of visibility."[65] Yet by focusing on the experiences of witnesses of destruction, they also inquire the production of a "withheld violence" that, rather than conducting "a direct contact with the exposed body," exacerbates an already installed "presence of the threatening power"[66] within the witness. In a relational situation of beheld violence, seeing someone or something else destroyed under the Israeli occupation's burst of violence immediately inflicts power on the witness, as *Jenin Jenin* shows; furthermore, as both films demonstrate, this situation reflects the presence of a power that formatively, continuously, and relationally impacts Palestinians' lived experiences and identifications. *Arna's Children* expands on the Palestinian subject formation around destruction by deploying not only the instantaneously productive, but also the incessantly permeating, effects of power. Since it has burst before, violence is anticipated, until it again explicitly appears afterward: between these simultaneous temporalities, the power of withheld violence maneuvers and manufactures identifications with and as ubiquitous potential destruction. In many ways, Arna's children, who rehearsed and performed their lives under the gazing threat of withheld violence in the 1990s in theater as well as in the film, are similar to the testifiers in *Jenin Jenin*, who witnessed and absorbed death and/as martyrdom under Israel's bursts of violence in the deadly 2000s, which exposed the Jenin residents to many devastating occasions of dying in the happening. Yet as *Arna's Children* communicated, the dying martyrs only reminded the witnessing martyrs that, beholding violence, they have seen the face and felt the threat of destruction long before the Israeli forces reinvaded Jenin in 2002. In both *Jenin Jenin* and *Arna's Children*, making sense of the political conditions constitutive of bursts of violence helps to understand the relationalities informing the everyday experience of one's body, and to reclaim one's sense of ownership over the story of the becoming of the body. Below, I follow the documentary performances of Ashraf and Youssef on and offstage as children maturing into death. The film's oscillating focus between the two media apparatuses of the theater and the audiovisualized performance speaks to these children's temporal experiences of continuously beholding and being in violence. The scene capturing the demolition of Ashraf's house during the days of his participation in the theater project depicts his pain in ways that collapse binaries of destruction and construction, past and present, public and private, national and personal. Finally, Youssef's video performance before his deadly attack in Israel delivered his identification with and as this heightened alertness of constant destruction under the conditions of the occupation.

Violence Withheld: Arna and Ashraf

At the outset of *Arna's Children*, we are situated in a theater hall: rather than merely focusing on the scenes on stage, however, the camera intrudes the noisy space, framing and exposing the ample and subtle occurrences both on as well as off the stage. As the play comes to a close, a young actress dressed in a princess outfit shuts her eyes, letting the projector hit her spot. Joining hands and voices to applaud the show, the engaged audience ignites the event, playing their part in both the theater show as well as in its documentation. Mapping the ado from above, below, and within, the opening scene of *Arna's Children* accentuates the dynamic movement of the camera lens as it negotiates with the accelerated energies of all those engaged in the event. Acknowledging the means and mediations of theater and cinematic production, we also reckon our own accentuated presence as the play's and film's audience. Here, *Arna's Children* deciphers the multidimensional aspects of theater as facilitated by play directors and actors, cinematic means and spatial settings, and spectators. Theater depends on the surrounding conditions that enable its standing, and that can just as much cause its colossal collapse.

Amid the artistic excitements of theater and filmmaking, Arna walks around hastily, switching platforms alternately: first found within the crowd, she occasionally looks up, then embarks on the stage to sing along with the participants in the performances, and finally provides her concluding words: "The intifada, for us and for our children, is a struggle for freedom. We call our program 'Learning and Freedom.' These are not just words. These are not just words. They are the basis of our struggle." It is indeed one figure, the one the film is named after and who endowed the filmmaker with his name, who sabotages Juliano's aesthetic research, punctuates it with the pains of politics, and blurs the boundaries between aesthetics and politics: wishing to liberate "words" from their limited role in the title of the theater program, Arna resurrects the context and conditions of the event, rendering it a part of a larger "struggle." Rampaging Mer-Khamis's lens, Arna's disruptive presence reminds us of the ongoing oppression, and potential destruction, that decisively impact the performances in the film.

Soon thereafter, we are introduced to the reminiscent yet distinct filmmaking style in which Juliano films, collects, and edits cinematic portraits of the children who participated in the theater program, too. Crafting several shooting sessions that depict different eras in the children's lives, Juliano stands behind the camera, asks the children guiding questions, and, at times, also clearly instructs them to provide certain answers. "I want to be the Palestinian Romeo!" says Ashraf when filmed for an Israeli television crew that visits the camp to learn about the theater program. Ashraf's performances inhabit a central locus in the film. Nevertheless, standing behind the lens, Mer-Khamis tells Ashraf what to say, thus shaping his stated future dreams. This particular scene highly interests Emine Fisek in her essay on *Arna's Children*: analyzing this and other scenes, Fisek correlates between the film's focus on theater practices and its exploration of filmic representation of performers.[67] "The theatrical experiment serves as a reference point for understanding the development of life histories, as the individuals in question are tethered to this experiment and their participation in the theater serves as a temporal mark through which their life trajectories are examined," Fisek contends.[68] At the same time, the scene with Ashraf delivers "the manner in which theatrical practice is in fact depicted, and the formal interventions of filmic technique … make 'theater' out to be an unsteady, precarious enterprise."[69]

How are Arna's performances of life in times of death converse with the children's recorded and cinematic performances of ephemeral lives in the film? How do they negotiate the film's conceptualizations of various modes of representation? Fisek elaborates further on the scene discussed above, comparing two theatrical tenets within Ashraf's articulated approach to theater. On the one hand, when Ashraf states that "when I am in theater I feel *like* I am throwing stones," he in Fisek's words "highlights theatrical action's status as symbolic representation." Yet when explaining how theater is an opportunity for him to "say what I feel," he develops

Figure 6 *Arna's Children*, Ashraf, "I want to be the Palestinian Romeo."
Source: Images from *Arna's Children* are courtesy of Trabelsi Productions.

"what we might label an embodied approach" to theater, thus conveying that "the link between 'art' and 'violence' is not simply one of symbolic protest, nor is the theater a space for *safe* action."[70] Correspondingly, Arna recounts a conversation she has had with one of her students who similarly grappled with resemblance, symbolism, and the "like." Early and rarely in the documentary, Arna looks straight at the camera and replies to the interpellations posed at her, while speaking specifically, if connotatively, about her upcoming death. In the first instance, a woman asks Arna, "How long will you go on this way?" Arna replies, "Yesterday, one of the children said to me, 'You *look like* you are an old lady,' so I said to him, 'No, I *am* old! So he said, no, you're young, you only *look* old. The question is the physical strength available." Rather than taking it at face value, it is possible to discern an approach and advice about theater and representation between the lines of Arna's performance: collapsing the difference between appearance and substance, between what "looks" and what "is," Arna affirms the decisive existence of the image that not only represents, but also is ingrained in, matter. In this way, Arna both implements embodied theater as well as emphasizes its ultimate finitude: one's image may not remain immune, and ends up carrying and marking the forthcoming ceasing of the corporeal, insinuates the theater organizer.

Arna's performances, however, not only enrich our thinking on theater on stage but also pave the path to thinking of the theater of colonization, appropriation, and occupation, which the state of Israel concurrently runs on Palestine, and which the

Figure 7 *Arna's Children*, Ashraf, "When I'm on stage, I feel like I'm throwing stones."

children and budding actors of Jenin are living, dying, and performing under. "Her head is covered with a kaffiah because she lost her hair as a result of chemotherapy treatment" is the second sentence Mer-Khamis says about his mother, right after presenting her name. Mer-Khamis asks Arna about the kaffiah only halfway through the film, though. Sitting in a car on the way to bid the residents of Jenin her last farewell, Arna makes her final, and most significant, monologue in the documentary. With his brother driving, Mer-Khamis sits behind the camera and in front of his mother, in an attempt to obtain some final words about her lifelong journey. "You know something, I don't even remember how it started," states Arna in reference to her habit of wearing the kaffiah, and begins to obfuscate our sense of ideological and identity categorization. For, while Arna's kaffiah demonstrates her commitment to the Palestinian national fight for freedom, it also performs the Zionist appropriation of a Palestinian cultural object that was prevalent in the Jewish Brigade of the Palmach.[71] "Those were the most beautiful years," Arna replies exuberantly when asked if she enjoyed her Palmach service.

Toward the end of her monologue, however, her most crucial message emerges: this occurs when Arna talks about how, as part of her service in the Palmach, while on duty as the driver of an officer, she conducted deportations of Bedouins in the Nakba of 1948. "Do you regret stuff you did while there?" Juliano's brother asks his mother in reference to her past service in the Jewish infamous militia. "Not even one thing ... oh, maybe one thing ... that I deported Bedouins ... that is the only thing, that I can say, is real ... otherwise, nothing." Here, the scene's correlation of the kaffiah to the actual activity of deportation and land appropriation realizes and materializes its symbolic significance and firmly anchors it in reality. If again to consider Arna's statements as comments on representational activity, they may be said to demonstrate how the Zionist symbolic appropriation of Palestinian objects formulated, fostered, and facilitated a *real* dispossession. Finally, this real talk coming out in Arna's final act in the film places her on the directing and deporting end of the theater of Zionist appropriation. Arna's acknowledgment of her deeds, moreover, serves as a reminder of the related and ongoing harsh state of occupation that Jenin is very notably still under: her deportation of Bedouins is mirrored in the continuous Nakba that conditions the lives and deaths of her theater disciples, as well as informs the making of the film.

Arna Mer

"In Ashraf's narrative," Fisek writes, "stage activity is a continuation of life lived offstage."[72] Ashraf's statement, "we won't let the occupation keep us in the gutter"[73] demonstrates how "aggression transfers fluidly between the world and the stage."[74] Questioning the competence of theater symbolism to "diffuse a grievance [and] render it 'art,'" Fisek endorses what she sees as Ashraf's desire to enact "affirmation of liveness in the midst of loss."[75] Most importantly, Fisek insisted, these affirmative enactments reckon and resist the present and persistent aggressive context stirring around the theatric acts. While Fisek emphasizes the blurred boundaries of art and

Figure 8 *Arna's Children*, Arna, "pride, beauty, power."

life in theater, she says very little about the theater of life, that which accommodates symbolic and/as real actions such as colonization, appropriation, occupation, and deportation. Consequently, the productive and frequently destructive impact that symbolic concepts and texts inflict on the performing children in the theatric of the everyday, and the ways in which the performers in the documentary reckon this infliction, in the theater of life and death, remain outside the scope of her theoretical framework. Yet Arna's performances in the film demand that we further ask: What about the symbolic acts of the occupation endorsing and reenacting the 1948 legacies of appropriation and deportation in new means and ways? How are these acts represented in the children's theater, cinematic, live, and lived, performances?

"I met Ashraf for the first time when he was 9 years old, in the ruins of his house. His house was destroyed when the house next door was blown up by the Israeli army," Mer-Khamis's voiceover informs us. In this primal encounter, we get to know a child in the midst of his ruins: as Ashraf cleans and arranges the few interior items of his home, the filmic frame accommodates the fragmented liminality of a house, showcasing both what it used to be and how it is becoming. "What about the collateral damage, the neighbors' houses that were not slated for demolition but whose windows and doors were torn out when another house was demolished?"[76] Azoulay asks, as if directly referencing Ashraf's unfortunate situation. Mer-Khamis's first encounter with Ashraf provides a useful point of departure to attending the theater of occupation that the children of Jenin live in and by.

Like the testifiers from *Jenin Jenin* who walk between the rubbles of their houses, Ashraf too is affected by a destruction directed at someone else. Foregrounding Ashraf in the aftermath of destruction and an emerging construction, however, this scene asks that we also contemplate not only its immediate impact on the individual, but also on the historical and collective aspects of systematic house demolitions. Here, someone else's house demolition not only brings forth the consequent demolition of Ashraf's house, but also epitomizes its recurrences elsewhere and in other times: it thus explores the historical collective identification that the no-longer demarcated space provides across times. Where ruination marks a past loss and present and future processes of production for more than one person experiencing it not merely once but at least twice, the spatially and temporally unstable home instantiates the un/makings of simultaneous and collective de/construction.

Since the 1948 foundation of the state of Israel and alongside Arna's deportation of some Bedouins, "the demolition of houses has been, and continues to be, the most extensive and consistent disaster carried out by the regime that came into power,"[77] Ariella Azoulay writes. House demolitions, Azoulay theorizes, manifest the precarious status of Palestinians who, since 1967, are "not considered or counted in a regime's discourse" around "the separation between the private and the public domain."[78] Yet while indicating Palestinians' exclusion from decision making, house demolitions can also be seen as manufacturing the private as perpetually and punitively public: they render the Palestinian refugees as relentlessly exposed to the menace outside when within their own refuge. This is finally how "this regime has turned the home into the arena where the boundaries of the body politic are demarcated,"[79] where it "designates as refugees, stateless, or displaced persons"[80] the bodies who wish to build their residence and personhood in it.

When, as part of the 1993 Oslo Accords, Jenin was designated as Zone A, thus placed under the auspices of a newly founded Palestinian Authority, but since Palestine was yet to become a state, Jenin remained subjected to Israeli invasions, assaults, and house demolitions. Thus, for Palestinians, building a home implies rendering it highly susceptible to the fragile conditions of a possible destruction; an undoing inherently informs every making, and destruction becomes the principal material for any construction for them. There in the home, where the private and sovereign subject is supposed to independently emerge and consolidate, and, since the 1990s, also identify as a Palestinian, the potential destruction publicly performed around her supervises and thus shapes her personal and/as national constitution. As in Ashraf's house, so in Arna's Stone Theater, too: established on a private person's rooftop, the theater embodies exactly the vulnerable overlap between the private and the public.[81] Indeed, Ashraf believes he can fully and freely resemble and embody that sovereign figure he portrays and, as he says, "say what I feel." And yet, when performing on stage, some destructive gaze installed in site silently scans his performances from every corner of the theater hall. Absorbed within the very settings of the theatric space, the gazing danger of destruction also perforce dictates the stage directions for the performers' plays: in other words, the theatric script carries, construes, and is constituted by an acute awareness of the fact that the ceiling might crash on the performers at any given moment. Thus, the more Ashraf wants to say what he feels, the more the scripted stage directions, already underwriting his speech act, end up forming, framing, casting, and castrating his performance. The personal performance of identification with Palestinian nationalism—the topic of the following pages—will desire to expose this script precisely.

From its very first sentence—"this is my mother Arna"—and until the visit to the deceased's room, *Arna's Children* seeks the trope of the inspiring figure, political leader, and mother of all of her children in Arna. Alongside footage of Arna as a vibrant and driven woman who is organizing, and is also placed within, the setting of the theater, some of her filmic portraits already deliver information on her forthcoming death. Arna repudiates any attempt to corner her against a camera and frame her in the fixed and frozen death pose. Piercing the screen in her fluctuating performances, Arna's figure roams from one place to another, reels between one action and another, waves her hands sideways as she speaks, and allows no memorialization. "This kaffiah is an age kaffiah ... age, age, age ... whoever lost, lost," she concludes right before stepping out of the car and out of the screen forever. Incoherent as it sounds, this key sentence highlights that the performances of Arna the Palmachnic and Arna who is dying both warn that her "children" were threatened by a possible, if not probable, destruction throughout their short lives, way before their untimely death. As Mer-Khamis's filmmaking prepares him for the farewell from his mother Arna, *Arna's Children* depicts a very beloved and vibrantly lively person, whose death is nearing. This theme of a life already implicated by death, I argue, serves to illuminate the state of the performing children in the film too.

Violence Videoed: Youssef

Throughout *Arna's Children*, Juliano's voiceover instructs and navigates the cinematic depiction of children's joy, anger, and acting, imposing and exposing his role as the narrator—a role compatible with his job as the drama instructor of the children. In particular, Mer-Khamis's voiceover obtains horrifying tones when, overshadowing the children's amused performances in the rehearsing room, he announces some of their henceforth deaths. In one of the film's first scenes, Mer-Khamis takes us back in time, introducing us to the children of Jenin who participated in the theater group under his guidance between 1989 and 1994. Playing animals as part of the rehearsal training, the children all stand in a circle, each in his turn crawling at one another while barking and mewing. "This is Nidal, he's the youngest of the group," Mer-Khamis's voiceover lets us know. From being the youngest, Nidal then quickly turns into the first one whose future death becomes a known fact: "In six years' time, during the Al-Aqsa intifada, Nidal will join the Islamic Jihad, and will be killed during the fighting against the Israeli army," the voiceover adds. Not only Nidal, but the other children appearing in this scene, will die in a matter of few years, we later find out: these children thus perform a spectral state between life and death. Here, while we encounter and acquire empathy for the smiling Nidal, we are also burdened with the knowledge of his later death right from the start.

Confronting a "catastrophe that has already occurred,"[82] in Laura Mulvey's words, Mer-Khamis's informative voice marks the scene with a cease: it is as if the announcement on Nidal's henceforth death interpolates a troubling congealment into the continuous narrative of the film.[83] Punctuating the performers' rehearsals with information on death, Mer-Khamis also exposes filmmaking's inherent occupation with temporality, hence disallowing the smooth dissemblance of a linear cinematic narrative.[84] It is thus the announcement on death, signified and executed by Mer-Khamis's voice, which shakes the structure of the time of the documentary: this is the know-all narrator's way of calling attention to the documentary's temporal and constructive dimensions. An exchangeable reciprocity between death and the means of cinematic construction is thus established through Mer-Khamis's voiceover announcements on deaths: it is upon its various vocalizations of death that the documentary repeats, dismantles, and stitches together its multiple fragments, scenes, and temporalities. To that end, the rehearsal in which death is announced already prefigures what is about to come later: not only live shows, but also, sadly, events of death. Along these lines, as Mer-Khamis oscillates between what "will" and what "already has" happen/ed as two overlapping marks of time, he crafts the documentary as a product oscillating between the "meantime" of life and the "after" of death.

Here, the announcements on deaths known in advance not only break open, but also carve, a space within cinematic time, to both postpone a forthcoming death and also mourn the already dead, and dwell in the liminality of the meantime until the anticipated after arrives. As if trying to keep them safe from death for the time being, Mer-Khamis seems to orchestrate and concoct his very own chemotherapeutic and cinematic meantime by vocally narrating audiovisual archival moments and performances of lives that are allegedly not yet in death. And yet, at the same time, once Juliano announces the previous death of the protagonists of his documentary, meantime itself perforce becomes the time of the after, the afterward, the afterlife, of the dead: it thus alas fails to protect the children from what is about to, but already has, come. To further delve into the nuances of these temporal and temporary dynamics within the documentary, it is useful to examine the ways in which *Arna's Children* presents and inculcates Youssef, Nidal's brother, via his various performances, throughout it. When introduced for the first time, he too crawls in the theatrical circle mentioned above, but Mer-Khamis merely names him "the joker in the group." Only later in the film, against the backdrop of a recording of their final testament, Mer-Khamis declares that "in five years' time, in October 2001, Youssef and his friend Nidal will commit a suicide attack in Israel." At this point, Mer-Khamis narrates the video footage of a performance of Youssef of a different time, kind, and mediation constellation than children's theater. In this video, Youssef wears military uniform, carries a rifle on his shoulder, and behind him is the formal scenery of a black curtain, posters, and slogans. Looking straight into the camera at first, Youssef then looks down and starts reading out loud from a piece of paper. "To my brothers, my family, my dear mother, my loved ones," Youssef confidently calls, "I greet you and say goodbye." As he continues and asks them: "Please pray for me and all Muslims," his voice starts cracking, repeating stutteringly and specifically the pledge to pray twice. "God help us defeat the oppressors. Heaven is precious and jihad is the way," Youssef concludes his performance, not before he cites prescribed hopes phrased and said by others, and directed at other others: the oppressors.

A scene inscribed by an announcement of death—just like the rehearsal scenes, the videoed farewell further investigates the concepts of live and recorded theater performance that the film implicates. Key to understanding the film's oscillation between the meantime before, and the after of, death, and its overall occupation with the constant hovering of death in the midst of life, Youssef's video navigates matters of time by negotiating them with the adjacent theme of the live performance, which it both addresses and accommodates. Arguing that live performance always takes place "in the meantime," Schneider notes that dictionaries provide "meantime" with two possible interpretations: "both between times and simultaneous."[85] In accordance with Schneider's observation, Mer-Khamis both edits the testament in between other times in Youssef's life, as well as

Figure 9 *Arna's Children*, Youssef and Nidal in the testament video.

probes and produces representational simultaneity through it. Within the twofold framework of the meantime, simultaneity haunts the heels of betweenness. Piecing together fragments of the short life of young and dying Youssef, the video mediates between the scenes of the rehearsals and those of the live performances at the theater. Yet importantly, the video serves to illuminate some of the subtle occurrences at play in the rehearsing room, and demonstrate the theme of simultaneity echoing in the live performance's "meantime." In the video, the scripted text that commonly precedes and facilitates the hitherto live performance explicitly appears simultaneously to it, as Youssef in fact reads out loud from it. To that end, while the text that Youssef is reading from dictates his performance, the video foregrounds a simultaneity that exceeds the trouble of temporality. "Many have claimed temporality itself as theater's primary medium," writes Schneider, only to immediately add that, "however, this fundamental temporality is volatile, easily swerved."[86] This is because, Schneider contends, the category of the live may not be neatly polarized from that of the recurring recorded.[87] Thus, she states, "the problem of the record in relation to the live here slips away from tidy distinction … in theater … the live act succeeds, surrogates, or comes after a precedent textual script."[88] This is relevant for "any inscribed set of performatives written to require repetition where repetition is *both* reiteration of precedent *and* the performance of something occurring 'again for the first time'"(emphasis in the original),[89] Schneider concludes. Driven to liberate the theatrical category of liveness from its presumed ontological status as an ephemerality anchored in experience, Schneider thus reinstates its inherent reliance on reproductive reiterations and scriptural mediations.[90] Thus, in the film and in general, the testament video teaches us of the interrelatedness of the written text to any live performance, and thus of the text's persistent presence and potency, even or especially if invisible, in it.

Youssef's video appears between a rehearsal and the live show of the same theatric play, thus both separating as well as mediating two mirroring re/enactments of Youssef's performance. "OK, lights out," Mer-Khamis orders at the outset of the scene. Standing in his supervising position in front of the mock stage back in the rehearsing room, he then watches Youssef climb up a ladder and proclaim: "I'll bring the sun!" Right thereafter, Youssef continues reasoning this wish: "If the princess brings in the sun, she'll be the Queen. If I bring in the sun … I will be King!" Furthermore, the same act is later repeated, only slightly differently and more elaborately: Youssef is now on stage, under the projectors, wearing the proper costume, participating in the live show at the actual theater. Significant here are the very first voices heard from stage right after the testament closes and right before Youssef begins his live performance. Unanimously, the children call "the King is dead!" at that point. Juliano's announcement of death follows the rehearsal, prefigures the live performance, and is almost simultaneous to the announcement of the king's death. Thus, the path from rehearsing to performing live goes through two declarations of death. Furthermore, the figure of the king is both in death in the children's calls, and is verbalized as a wish by Youssef thereafter. To that end, death here comes before, marks, runs through, enables, and enlivens the aspirations voiced in the live performance that follows—a performance that, in

Figure 10 *Arna's Children*, Youssef as a child, "If I bring in the sun."

filmic time, occurs after death. Indeed, this is a live scene from after death. As I discuss elaborately in the next pages, this scene appears repeatedly to illuminate the experiences of those living on after the deaths of their beloved ones, hanging on to the dead's live, haunting, and deadening memory and recorded representation. As I further deliberate, the previously recorded and already dead Youssef and his friends were already under the constant hovering danger of death as children and young actors performing life in their community theater in Jenin.

A Burst of Violence

Mer-Khamis's general efforts to capture, and in some ways talk to, the dead, culminate in the scene appearing right before the video: an analysis of this poignant scene follows. In 2002, right after the battle of Jenin, and about a year and a half after Youssef had videotaped his farewell and executed his attack, Mer-Khamis visits Youssef's and Ashraf's friends Majdi and Mahmud, two former participants in the children's theater activities. Upon Mer-Khamis's return to Jenin, Majdi and Mahmud begin to explore their own experiences of losing their friends, and describe the ways in which Ashraf's and Youssef's lives were severely inscribed by loss. In this way, Majdi recounts how Youssef was affected by someone else's path to death: "He was deeply shaken by this: a little girl dying in his arms. From then onwards he never stopped talking about her," Majdi and Mahmud explain, telling Mer-Khamis about a girl shot by the IDF whom Youssef tried and failed to save from dying. It is then that the film shifts to repeat the scene of the video for the second time: this time, however, our attention is particularly drawn to the photo hanging behind Youssef and Nidal, which shows that same girl after her death. Here, the image of the dead girl as the backdrop of Youssef's monologue emphasizes the attempt of the living to follow the traces of the dead.

"He felt like he is about to explode ... he felt dead ... he said: 'I'm dead anyway,'" Mahmud recalls what Youssef used to say to him. According to Mahmud's words, and aside from its unbearably dreadful implications, it seems that Youssef's final performance also delivered the sense of deadness that he had experienced already throughout his life. Thus, Youssef formed relations with the dead while alive, found himself living with a conscious connection to death, and then, eventually and unfortunately, dead just like the girl. Along these lines, Youssef may be understood as a "living martyr"[91] who lingered on the threshold of death long before he physically died. As Mer-Khamis, Majdi, and Mahmud stand by Ashraf's grave, Majdi shares his experience of Ashraf's death, recounting that "I didn't believe it until I saw his body. I didn't recognize him but people told me it was Ashraf, because they were with him when it happened. I wanted to bury him, but I couldn't, because the army was still in the camp." It was thus important for Majdi to acknowledge the death of Ashraf by seeing him, recognizing him, and burying him; his attempts to fulfill these needs, alas, failed. All Majdi can do now is visit Ashraf's grave and his photo placed right on it. Similarly, Ashraf too desired to see his beloved dead friend, Mahmud remembers: "The day Youssef was killed, Ashraf was still alive," he reconstructs. "We watched a video tape. Ashraf said, 'It was a good life.' It was the video of the play we did together ... that day. Ashraf said, 'Where is Youssef?'"

As Mahmud speaks, moving images from the live performance of Ashraf and Youssef as children, dressed in their costumes and trying to bring the sun and become kings, inundate the screen as well—a filmed, re-produced performance punctuated by, and preceding, their death. If Ashraf was "*still* alive" the day Youssef died, by the time he watched the tape, Ashraf already employed the past tense, stating that "it *was* a good life," thus desisting that the now is neither good, nor perhaps a life at all anymore. Majdi and Mahmud describe Youssef's experience of witnessing death right as it takes away a young innocent girl, and Ashraf's desire to comprehend where his beloved dead friend went. Their accounts insinuate the horror of witnessing death and the danger embedded in the quest for the lost paths of the witness who became a martyr: this quest casts death in the midst of the seeker's life. Here, watching the recordings of formerly living performers who are already dead is metonymically and metaphorically akin to witnessing someone else passing from life to death; in other words, the dying is equated to the recovered, reproductive, recorded life. A second glimpse at the dictionary clarifies this: looking up "live" this time, Schneider reports that "we are given two antonyms of note: 'dead' or 'recorded.'"[92] I accordingly argue that it is this equation that *Arna's Children* teases out, as it probes the possible interchangeability of the "recorded" with the "dead." Indeed, the recordings of the rehearsals, as well as the live performances appearing after death in the film, all highlight that "theater can never be 'live.' Or, never only *live*" (emphasis in the original).[93]

Recognizing the correspondence between recordings of childhood and futures of death in *Arna's Children* enables the emergence of curious perspectives on the experience of Palestinian martyrdom in the past twenty years. Talal Asad elaborates on Palestinian martyrdom upon its Islamic and secular political significances in the 2000s and explains: "Palestinians, when employing a religious vocabulary, call all their civilians who die in the conflict with Israel *shuhada*—including innocents killed in Israeli operations" (emphasis in the original).[94] This is because "the violent death of all Palestinians in confrontation with Israelis, so one might suggest, is regarded as a sign that they have died as witnesses (shuhada)."[95] Asad thus reminds us of Devji's theorization of martyrdom as witnessing which, as recalled, facilitated the argument that witnesses of martyrdom become themselves martyrs in their witnessing. And yet, what about those civilians who experience the presence of withheld violence and thus sense that its offspring—the destructive burst—might be making its way toward them? Taking these civilians—in this case, children—into account, we might want to correlate two interchangeabilities: that between martyrdom and witnessing in *Jenin Jenin*, and that between witnessing the dying and watching an image of the already dead when s/he was still alive in *Arna's Children*. Here, Mer-Khamis may be said to expand the theorization of martyrdom, conveying that the children were subjected to martyrdom in their lives too, and not only in their death: having experienced withheld violence throughout their short lives, they anticipated the upcoming witnessing of burst destruction in front of their eyes and in their arms; the experience of watching the images of them living and performing thus compatibly enfolds their short lived experience of waiting for the witnessing of/as martyrdom.

Here, *Arna's Children* assists in further contesting the exclusive usage of the term martyrdom for physically dead Palestinian victims of the occupation solely, rather than for victims—witnesses—of the occupation as a whole. Furthermore and consequently, the documentary shifts the discussion on Palestinian suicide fighting from the presumable psychological and religious motives of those who attack innocent Israeli civilians, and recognizes that, even if not always and entirely, their "death here is an effect not a motive."[96] *Arna's Children* thus corroborates Asad's criticism of those theorizers of so-called terrorism who claim that "it is the free intention of the perpetrator that leads to the criminal act and not (as is often alleged) brutal subjection to Israeli occupation."[97] Thus, delineating destruction expansively rather than exclusively as death, the film compels us to regard all "Palestinian civilians who are destroyed under the Occupation ... as shuhada."[98]

As *Jenin Jenin* elucidates, the Israeli invasion and consequent battle of Jenin in April 2002 left the camp and city gut-ruined. Arna's Stone Theater and the children's program were demolished as well.[99] And yet, *Arna's Children* presents that the call for destruction, potentially and practically informing the reality of the occupation, always conditioned the lives and live performances of the children: that is, death overshadowed their existence much before it materialized. While Arna "expresses her anger at the occupation ... she is raising the next intifada's martyrs," Adam Shatz wrote: "Their decision to fight, as shown in the film, is as inevitable as it is tragic: they are patriots defending their homes, not Islamic zealots; their cause, it suggests, is no different from Arna's."[100] Rather than evaluating the grown children's decisions to fight the occupation, the film traces the potential destructions that were always dwelling between the walls of their derelict rehearsing rooms and performing stage. *Arna's Children* discerns and depicts the context of witnessed destruction that shaped the performing children as always already shuhada, ascertaining that about fifteen years before the IDF physically destroyed it the withheld violence of the occupation already harbingered the threat of destruction on the Stone Theater.

In Conclusion: Keep in Touch

One question densely threading *Since You Left*, *Jenin Jenin*, and *Arna's Children*, and leading my concluding remarks is: How does one keep in touch with another who has died? Let us take a final look at Arna's approach to performance, pedagogy, touch, and to living with the constant weight of death. Early in *Arna's Children*, we encounter Ala as he is sitting in the midst of the ruins of his home, and then we see him again in Arna's classroom. Arna leads a group discussion with the children of the theater: the topic of the discussion—the children's experiences of the IDF's practice of house demolition. "Can you go back to your home?" asks Arna, to which Ala replies: "No. Our house has been demolished." When Arna pressures him to provide further details, he replies: "We were told to leave the house. Then they blew it up." Arna then turns to Ashraf and asks him too to explain: "Why are you angry?" Ashraf replies: "First they blew up Ala's house, and then that damaged our house." Finally, Arna wishes to know what Ashraf would want to do to the IDF, and subsequently suggests that he enacts his reply on her, for, as she states, "I am the army." Ashraf then gets up and begins to push Arna against a table; both verbally encouraging him to go on and physically trying to remain standing, Arna ends the role-play by declaring "very good!" Finally, as a series of similar exercises ends, Arna explicates the lesson to be learned: "When we are angry, we have to express it."

This scene is of particular interest for Fisek: "This statement on the relationship between anger and self-expression is positioned as a tentative, albeit universal, truth ... the experience of anger necessitates both its recognition as such and the presence of an expressive outlet."[101] Yet beyond that, the expression of anger may also be regarded as a way to form corporeal relationships and memories that do not disappear with death. In one line with the reenactment exercise, Schneider challenges many performance theorists by contending that "performance does remain, does leave 'residue,'" on the very flesh of the performers, simply by virtue of the vulnerable bodily touch that they have mutually bestowed to each other. Schneider explains that it is important to challenge the axiom associated with archiving methods, according to which "flesh is given to be that which slips away";

Figure 11 *Arna's Children*, Ala sitting amid his house's ruins.

Figure 12 *Arna's Children*, Arna and Ashraf in a classroom theater exercise.

instead, she offers to think of the ways in which "the place of residue is arguably flesh in a network of body-to-body transmission of affect and enactment—evidence, across generations, of impact."[102] In this way, "death appears to result in both disappearance and remains," for, "disappearance, that citational practice, that after-the-factness, clings to remains—absent flesh does ghost bones."[103]

To that end, Schneider illuminates the general role of physical reenactments in and as testimonies. When she writes about affective transmission, or "the way affect jumps between bodies—crosses borders of bodies, getting into and out of bodies as if there were no material border of consequence,"[104] the testifiers who witnessed executions in *Jenin Jenin* come to mind. In the aftermath of the battle of Jenin, the woman and the doctor reenacted the ways in which an execution, as well as the executed, remained with them, communicating how their witnessing and testifying capacities have been martyrized. Further, Bakri's conversation with his late mentor, Emile Habibi, in *Since You Left*, demonstrates how Bakri holds on to the traces of shared experiences with Habibi as he lives through the backlash targeting him. Yet as *Arna's Children* indicates, the ubiquitous experience of anticipating destruction before it bursts renders the residents of Jenin living martyrs of the everyday, and not just of times of war. For the Palestinians performing in these documentaries, witnessing death in the happening, in life, concretizes and renders verifiable the ambiguous ubiquity of the experience of withheld violence, thus making intelligible the otherwise vaguely felt formative connection to death, and assisting in making sense of the relational experience of violence and pain and in reclaiming ownership over the story of one's body. Against all odds, and as Mer-Khamis did until he was shot too, all the participants in the Jenin documentaries follow the advice of the young girl from *Jenin Jenin* and mark the names of the martyrs—at times, their names—on the leaves of the treetop at the heart of the camp.

Chapter 2

HEADS HELD HIGH: MIZRAHIM'S COMING OF AGE AND ACTIVISM IN DAVID BELHASSEN'S AND ASHER HAMIES'S *THE RINGWORM CHILDREN*, DAVID BENCHETRIT'S *KADDIM WIND: A MOROCCAN CHRONICLE*, AND NISSIM MOSEK'S *HAVE YOU HEARD OF THE BLACK PANTHERS?*

Had he been alive, David Benchetrit would probably continue to transform the field of documentary cinema in Israel and globally. But in April 2004, Benchetrit was harshly battered by Israeli security forces, and as a result, he struggled with ongoing physical and mental traumas.[1] In October 2017, shortly after losing the prolonged trial against his batterers, Benchetrit died. Senyora Bar David eulogized Benchetrit, her longtime partner, on social media, describing that morning when he headed to a scheduled appointment in the offices of the Ministry of Security in Tel-Aviv, and was battered by the guards. "When Benchetrit, a filmmaker of documentary films, arrives uphill next to the meeting spot ... several security guards approach him and begin an identification procedure that turns to a severe physical assault, in the light of day, in front of the passersby ... the security guards batter him in all of his body parts ... when the assault ceases they announce in their walkie-talkies that 'the target has been neutralized'... an ambulance is called and he is sent to the hospital ... that day, there were alerts about a suicide bomber."[2] The authorities' statement reads: "This morning at 10:30 am the security guard of the ministry of security ... identified a man that looked suspicious. The security guard turned to the suspect asking him to identify himself, and when not granted collaboration, suspicion grew—this is why the security guard was compelled to use force in order to disconfirm the concern." During the trial, the Ministry of Security refused to release the surveillance tape that recorded the battering. "The security guards have conducted a *Targeted Elimination*; the court has supplemented by *Verifying the Killing*" (emphasis in the original): this was how Bar David titled her heartbreaking, raging eulogy. Reclaiming the jargon typically used to describe killing operations against Palestinians marked as "terrorists," Bar David argued that the security forces deliberately targeted Benchetrit for his filmmaking and political activism that have always been highly critical of Israeli policies. While the motivation of the battering security guards is hard to speculate about, their instinctively executed master narrative underlies their abrupt acting-out on suspicion. That is, whether the immediate suspect here was someone who is an Arab Palestinian, and/or an Israeli Jew advocating for Palestinian rights, their battering is somehow justified simply based on suspicion.

Within the confining Arab/Jewish binary division informing this narrative of "suspicion of terrorism," Benchetrit was indeed not easily identifiable. A Jewish immigrant from Morocco, Benchetrit may be simplistically said to look and sound somewhat like an Arab Palestinian because he was an Arab Jew. As a filmmaker and organizer, he dedicated his life's work to raising awareness and seeking justice for Palestinians and Mizrahim, often intersectionally, and honoring their Jewish-Israeli allies in the struggles. Benchetrit thus lived and contemplated on being Mizrahi in the most political sense of the term—as both an embodied position as well as a position of solidarity with others—a resistant, multilayered, and vulnerable stance. Prior to the violence that brought an end to his creative life almost entirely, Benchetrit directed eight films and shot many others. His first feature documentary, *Through the Veil of Exile* (1992), about three Palestinian women refugees living under occupation in the West Bank and Gaza, won him international recognition and respect.[3] Benchetrit was one of the cofounders of The Mizrahi Democratic Rainbow (1996) and of The Forum for Documentary Cinema (1998). In 2005, Benchetrit managed to complete *Dear Father, Quiet, We're Shooting*—the film about Israelis who refused to serve in the IDF's operation in the 1967-occupied, which brought him to the Ministry of Security in the first place, to interview the then-IDF spokesperson, Nurit Yaron, from which he barely came out alive.

Yet in September 2002, about a month before Mohammad Bakri released *Jenin Jenin*, Benchetrit's *Kaddim Wind: A Moroccan Chronicle* was broadcast on Israeli television's commercial Channel 2, reaching more local audience than ever before. The fruits of many years of persistent fights with the overwhelmingly Ashkenazi film and media industry, Benchetrit attributed his long-overdue access to primetime broadcasting to the privatization and denationalization of television in Israel in those years.[4] In this four-part documentary series, Benchetrit excavated the history of his own community—the Moroccan community in Israel. *Kaddim Wind* traces the migration of Moroccan Jews to Israel since the 1950s, amid the harsh political conditions that have constituted their lived experiences, and the struggles for resistance that they generated. Compassionately capturing them in their homes and towns, in the fields that they were coerced to plow or on the streets where they protested their evictions, Benchetrit interviewed prominent political leaders and thinkers who emerged from the Moroccan community, such as the Mizrahi ultraorthodox party Shas leader Aryeh Deri, former minister Shlomo Ben-Ami, and Reuven Abergil, who was one of the cofounders of the Mizrahi Black Panther movement in Jerusalem in 1971. Benchetrit thus traced the history of the state of Israel from the viewpoint of Moroccan immigrants who arrived in Israel as children in the 1950s, suffered through the racializing, exclusionary, and discriminatory mechanisms of state violence upon its foundation, and became organizers against the oppression of Mizrahim, thus helping to retell the collective histories of Mizrahim in Israel.

This chapter explores *Kaddim Wind, Have You Heard of the Black Panthers?*, and *The Ringworm Children* from 2002 to 2003, all following well-known Mizrahi political leaders, as they narrate their and other Mizrahi immigrants' survival through pathologization, criminalization, and police violence throughout their childhood and youth since their arrival in Israel in the 1950s, and their organized struggles against that oppression. In 2002, Nissim Mosek released *Have You Heard of the Black Panthers?*, which focused entirely on the Black Panthers movement, revisiting old footage that he took in the early days of the Black Panthers, and reassessing where the leaders of the movement are thirty years after its foundation. Both *Kaddim Wind* and *Have You Heard of the Black Panthers?* feature archival materials taken at the demonstrations organized by the Black Panthers in 1971–2, among them many depictions of the police's violent treatment of the protesters. Two other films from around that time return to the events surrounding the uprising of the Black Panthers in the 1970s too. In 1998, on the state of Israel's fiftieth anniversary, Israel's state-mandated Channel 1 also dedicated part of the documentary series *Resurrection* to the Black Panthers and their experiences of police violence, yet from a more normative perspective. While referencing *Resurrection* briefly, this chapter primarily carefully analyzes the scenes about police brutality in *Have You Heard* and *Kaddim Wind* alongside testimonies about the pathologizing of Mizrahi youth as prospective criminals, which is also discussed in the films—a criminalization that took place before they took to the streets as activists. First, this chapter examines the operation of radiations applied on the same Mizrahi youth when they were children, upon their arrival in Israel in the 1950s, following the pathologizing diagnoses of many of them as suffering from the sociomedical aesthetic problem of ringworm, which resulted in death, brain tumors, and other terminal and chronic illnesses for many of them as adults. In 2003, David Belhassen and Asher Hamies directed *The Ringworm Children*, which unpacks the operation of radiations through interviews with the survivors of the treatments, some of whom led the important campaigns to hold the state accountable for the operation in the 1990s, and with medical professionals. The operation of radiations is mentioned in *Kaddim Wind* too, linking it as one of the motivations for the organized uprisings of the 1970s. Delineating the devastating long-term repercussions of pathologization, criminalization, and physical violence on the bodies of the testifying Mizrahi leaders who immigrated to Israel as children, the films trace how they managed, against all odds, to remember and politicize, embody, reenact, retell, and show their ongoing experiences of pain in their own voice, on their own bodies, and base their organizing initiatives on that politicized experience of bodily pain.

"More than half of all immigrants who came to Israel after the establishment of the state came from culturally backward areas," asserted education scholar Carl Frankenstein in his famous study.[5] Yet "the immigrant can overcome his feelings of dependence, helplessness, and resentment by identifying himself with those who constitute the absorptive society," he then quickly corrected.[6] "Why did the Jews of North Africa, more than others, obtain most of the hereditary characteristics that cause the Mediterranean fever?"[7] asked physician Chaim

Sheba with regard to the same Mizrahi immigrants that Frankenstein assessed; corroborating Frankenstein's observations, he determined that "amongst Yemenite and Babylonian Jews, we found most of the cases of heredity flaws that cause brain retardation";[8] similar to Frankenstein, he also believed in the power to cure the immigrant: "Through heredity, we can not only solve the mystery of his disease, but also take preventive steps in the midst of his family, that carries the same mutation."[9] As Shohat demonstrated, Zionist leaders, thinkers, and doctors have portrayed Jewish immigrants from the Middle East as an insoluble inadequacy, while at the same time promptly purporting to repair them.[10] Identifying the problem, offering the resolution, and insinuating its probable failure in this same typical way, Frankenstein's and Sheba's teleological articulations resonate with the Zionist establishment's approach to these immigrants as a whole. The cyclic predictability that Nissim Rejwan has termed "the Workings of the Self-Fulfilling Prophecy"[11] invoked ramified and multilayered discursive acts of investigation, fictionalization, narration, and corroboration of Mizrahim and the Mizrahi body. The first section sets the scenes by situating the Ashkenazi professional perspective in front and against the examined Mizrahi body. While scholars of Mizrahi history referred to Frankenstein's and Sheba's work ubiquitously yet mostly briefly,[12] this section engages several key texts comprising the systematic pathologizing production and relegation of Mizrahim as "Orientals"—Jews of an inferior and fixed Oriental ethnicity. In particular, I probe the textual transitions between descriptive deciphering and active attempts to produce bodily difference.

Upon purporting to see, scan, and diagnose their objects of research, Frankenstein and Sheba promoted the state's projects of both administration of populations on the one hand, and their presentation as free individuals responsible for their unfortunate failures on the other hand. The second section plunges into an analysis of David Bellhassen's and Asher Hamies's *The Ringworm Children* (2003), following the film's exposure of the political mechanisms of the state- and military-coordinated operation of radiations led by Sheba that targeted children, mainly from North Africa. A particular case study of the impact of the pathologizing perspective of Ashkenazi Zionist medical and social scientists on Mizrahi bodies, *The Ringworm Children* centers on its survivors who re-weave back the stories of their bodies' pain, of becoming, and of organizing to demand reparations. The third section in this chapter contextualizes Frankenstein's pathologization of "the Levantine Man" in the 1980s in light of the changing image of Mizrahi youth and masculinity that was taking place in Israel since the 1970s. *Kaddim Wind* and *Have You Heard of the Black Panthers?* illuminate that multifaceted turning point in the representation of Mizrahim against the backdrop of the state's continuous racialization of them, which was partly built on Frankenstein's legacy. The primary photography and video images circulating in mainstream media in the 1970s depicted Mizrahi protesters as they were suffering the police's crackdown on them at the demonstrations organized by the Black Panthers. Mizrahim's critical appearance in the media at that time is thus also a moment when police brutality against civilians was audiovisually distributed more widely. The section about youth explores several crucial scenes from the films that reclaim the hegemonic representation of Mizrahi youth and masculinity by revisiting that key moment in which state-operated nationalized media covered the demonstrations. Featuring portraits of Mizrahim as they were severely brutalized by the Israeli police, these scenes decolonize the memory of the Mizrahi body's experience from the national media's ill representation, returning it to the organizers to own again.

The Ringworm Children, Kaddim Wind, and *Have You Heard of the Black Panthers?* are part of a larger wave of documentaries about Mizrahi organizers who launched various grassroots campaigns to fight for equal and fair access to housing, education, work, and to representation in politics and cultural production. Indeed, the advent of the Black Panthers in the 1970s created a transformative momentum that inspired Mizrahi younger leadership to continue struggling in various means and capacities for years to come. Eli Hamo's and Sami Shalom Chetrit's *Black Panthers (in Israel) Speak,* from 2003, told the story of the emergence of the Black Panthers from Musrara in Jerusalem after the 1967 war, the influence of the US-based Black Panther Party on them, and their ideological vision as articulated by its leadership. Yet other films traced less glamorous but no less crucial battles of Mizrahim, especially with regard to labor. The late 1990s and early 2000s brought about increased neoliberal deregulation measures. The factories that closed left many working-class Mizrahim unemployed and/or ununionized, to add to years of labor exploitation as part of their overall discrimination. Such films include Ayelet Bargur's *Nearby but Far Away* (2003), about the damage done by the American Intel Corporations to the Kiryat Gat residents, Tali Shemesh's *White Gold, Black Labor* (2004), about contract labor in the Dead Sea factory, and Asaf Sudary and Amir Tauziner's *Strike* (2005), about the employees' unionization and strike in Haifa Chemicals South, convey the oppressive labor conditions prevalent in the increasingly privatized job market in Israel and its disproportionate harsh impact on Mizrahim. On a related note, Nissim Mosek also followed the lives of Mizrahi human rights activists who fought against state policies, militarism, and violence. Mosek's films include *Who Are You Mordechai Vanunu,* which was about the Moroccan nuclear whistleblower who was released after serving eighteen years in prison in 2004—the year that the film came out, and *Citizen Nawi* (2007), which was about the Iraqi Israeli activist Ezra Nawi who fights for Palestinians' rights, especially in South Hebron.

As Chapter 1 reviewed, *Jenin Jenin* and other Palestinian films illuminate how the label of "potential terrorist" hovers over '48 Palestinians who are construed as the "fifth column" living within the territory of the state of Israel while maintaining an alleged incriminating kinship to Palestinians living in the West Bank and Gaza. Unlike '48 Palestinians, Mizrahim's access to Jewish privilege generally spares them of the constant threat of death due to security determinations, which is placed on Arab Palestinians—an access presumably disrupted only in case of racial mistakings. To earn this privilege and enter the Jewish fold, however, Mizrahim needed to successfully go through a process of assimilation that involved shedding any connection to Arabness and becoming as purely Jewish as possible. The state's suspicion that Mizrahim, that is, Jews who "look/sound/talk like/are" Arabs—Jews unable to remove the stain of bodily or ideological Arabness from them—may become an enemy of the Jewish state was just one in many justifications for the Zionist Ashkenazi establishment's attempt to racialize all Jews from various localities in the Middle East as "Oriental Jews" and place them on the Jewish side of the Arab/Jewish binary construct of ethnonational animosity exclusively, apart from non-Jews and against Arabs, and especially, Arab Palestinians, all the while foreseeing and sanctioning their failure to get in line with the program.[13] Thus, Palestinians and Mizrahim were historically differentially positioned in relation to Jewish supremacy, society, and Israel's system of state security—positions that are further instigated at times of heightened violence, as the films' show. *Jenin Jenin* and *Since You Left* explore the direct violent manifestations of the exclusionary "suspicion of terrorism" of the security and military apparatuses on Palestinians in the West Bank and on '48 Palestinians. Both foregrounding the heavy police brutality directed at Mizrahim, *Kaddim Wind* and *Have You Heard of the Black Panthers?* also reflect on the ramified conditional treatment of Mizrahim who were welcomed to serve the Israeli police as well as threatened to face immense, at times deadly, brutality if they protested against it. The intentional recruitment of Mizrahi immigrants into the Israeli police since the 1950s purported to start "a process of legitimizing a system of inequality"[14] and to pit them as "communal civilizers"[15] against fellow Mizrahi immigrants and, if serving in the Border Patrol that is also under the auspices of the police, against Palestinian returnees—whom Israel called "infiltrators"— trying to access their homes. The films also portray the ambivalence of Mizrahi leaders toward Palestinians, and some leaders' active dissociation from them in times of violence. The opening scene of *Kaddim Wind* captures the dramatic moment in September 2000 when hundreds of thousands of supporters of Aryeh Deri, the leader of Shas and one of Benchetrit's interviewees, gather to mourn and protest his incarceration—after which, Shas started to gradually employ a racist agenda against Palestinians. Shlomo Ben-Ami, who Benchetrit also interviewed, served as the minister of internal affairs—the ministry in charge of the police, typically given to a Mizrahi minister—during the time of the shooting of the unarmed '48 Palestinian protesters, and resigned after the shooting. In other most striking scenes, *Kaddim Wind* follows organizer Oved Abutbul, who, as part of his grassroots campaign against the eviction of the Mizrahi residents from Mevaseret Tzion in 1997, is joined by a community of activists who rent a bus and ride to Jericho, in the territory of the Palestinian Authority, to seek asylum. The activists additionally send a letter to the king of Morocco asking to return there, and receive his blessing. These scenes speak to the intensified waves of gentrification that took place and hurt mostly Mizrahim in the early 2000s (more on this in Chapter 4) and the subsequent charged confrontations between evictees and policemen who shut down their protests—all being Mizrahi. Thus, while *Jenin Jenin* attends to Palestinians' persistently urgent matter of living and dying as a "security problem," *Kaddim Wind* and *Have You Heard of the Black Panthers?* contextualize the historical, conditional inclusion of Mizrahim as a "social problem" that may be eligible for redemption by participating in executing state violence against Palestinians and other working-class Mizrahim. This filmic contextualization questions Mizrahim's complicity in state violence while holding the state itself accountable for mobilizing Mizrahim to hate.

Like *Jenin Jenin*, *Kaddim Wind* made unprecedented waves in Israel. Yet while *Jenin Jenin* was removed from the theaters and displaced to the courthouse, *Kaddim Wind*'s slot on primetime television's programs remained unchallenged and, furthermore, the film won the prestigious Wolgin Prize for Israeli Film at the Jerusalem Film Festival in 2002. Yet the violence against Mizrahim that Benchetrit depicted in *Kaddim Wind* caught up with him eventually. The public condemnation of Bakri in Israel post–*Jenin Jenin* continues until this day. But they left us with precious documentations of how Palestinians and Mizrahim have been resisting violence throughout history.

White Fantasies: Carl Frankenstein's Search for Ethnic Interiority

In a government-sponsored, highly circulated, newspaper photo from June 1951, a white man wearing a white robe stands behind a giant device; from beyond his glasses and mechanic lens, he observes a person wearing a white gown who poses for him, fists on his waists and elbows spread, on a pedestal: "Avraham Salah, seventy years old, who was a real-estate agent in Iraq, going through medical examinations," the attached caption informs.[16]

Similarly, Carl Frankenstein sharpened his pens, employed the proper methods and parameters of scientific investigation, and composed his report. "It is relatively easy to discover and describe the negative manifestations of primitive mentality in

Figure 13 "Avraham Salah, 70 years old who was a realtor in Iraq, goes through medical examination, June 1951": photograph from Israel's National Photography Collection, caption in the original.

our culture-clash situation," Frankenstein confidently asserted at the outset of an essay that, like many of his essays, centered research on children.[17] He appears to express "an extreme weakness of the power of intellectual and social abstraction, and, consequently, an inability to understand the meaning of inner rules which require understanding, conscious consent, comparison, identification, and introjection; and an inability to control affects and impulses, as the result of the ego-weakness; these are some of the most significant characteristics of primitive mentality."[18] In these words, Frankenstein sums up and specifies the absolutely problematic traits of the immigrant arriving from Asia or Africa. Thus, out of the written impressions of an expert, a primitive immigrant emerges.

What sounds like the conclusion of a prolonged probe, however, merely marks Frankenstein's point of departure for a scientific study of the deeper nature of primitive mentality. Meticulously delineating his winding paths of thought, Frankenstein dons the mantle of a third-person professional and explains: "We are inclined to judge cultural realities and patterns by the degree of the opportunities they offer to the individual for realizing his potentialities, expanding his consciousness, achieving integration *autonomously*" (emphasis in the original).[19] Frankenstein presented his seemingly objective, unbiased criteria for tracing solid academic findings; with these premises at his disposal he embarks on a journey beyond the easily accessible and into the dimensions of the deep, in a search for empirical inferences based on observation rather than preconceptions.

"More than half of all immigrants who came to Israel after the establishment of the state came from culturally backward areas in Asia or Africa, Yemen, Persia, Iraq, Kurdistan, North Africa"; Frankenstein declared right in the beginning. Indeed, Frankenstein adopted a common orientalist dogma by which, in the words of Edward Said, "it is assumed that a highly generalized and systematic vocabulary for describing the Middle East from a Western standpoint is inevitable and even scientifically 'objective.'"[20] Later, however, Frankenstein seemingly assuaged his initial harsh assertions to communicate "an attitude and a conviction, the conviction that positive forces *are* hidden in the structure and mentality of men who belong to one of the so-called primitive groups" (emphasis in the original).[21] Apparently ready to admit to these cultures' possession of a limited yet existent and relevant number of positive traits and values, Frankenstein accordingly initiates a re-search for the pleasant qualities of the now only so-called "backward cultures," and asks: "How can we recognize these assets and how can we actuate them?"[22] Equipped with an eye that may invade the veil of the externally perceived negative mental expressions, Frankenstein desires excavation—to capture the cloaked positive traits out in the light. The immigrants' trend of conducting blood feuds, he gives an example, clandestinely cloaks what may otherwise be seen as capability of appreciating close intimacy, strongly identifying with their family members; also, their laziness that imbricates their ways of blamelessly enjoying free leisure time, for example, functions, for Frankenstein, as evidences of pure intentions and earnest motivations.[23] This approach of acknowledgment should be followed by an honest account of the negative traits and tendencies of the Western man who extensively identifies with his profession and rejects the casual possible delights of daydreaming. Indeed, Frankenstein encourages a relativist approach by which "we have to recognize the relativity of assets and liabilities in the mentality of so-called primitive or culturally backward immigrants *as well as in ours!*" (emphasis in the original).[24]

Frankenstein went back and forth between derogatory judgments, merciful mitigations, and bridging apologetic articulations. Today, his essay may come across as a clumsy attempt to arbitrate contradictory assessments and narrate them into a coherent and legitimate analysis. It is indeed as difficult to overlook the zigzagged alterations between negative and positive, negations and positions, as it is to tell the difference between supposedly scholarly objective observations and stereotypical generalizations. Yet, a more careful reading of Frankenstein's utterances reveals a sophisticated structure of argumentation. Frankenstein promises that the recognition of positivity "is not a mere tactical means"[25]with which the educators should methodically approach the primitive immigrants in order to win their hearts; and yet, it is possible to read Frankenstein's profound probing of hidden positive forces otherwise presumably secretively lying behind the obvious negative mentality of "the primitives" as a useful textual and theoretical strategy.

Frankenstein's reiterated employment of "recognition" aspires to attest an omnipotent capacity to see, capture, and deliver real cultural behaviors and traits reliably. Concomitantly and complementarily, Frankenstein's use of the adjective "positive" amplifies an attempt at positing cultural components as inherently, veritably, and inevitably found in the individual's mind. In this way, exploring the primitive mentality while also mentioning the good intentions and qualities of backward cultures work collaboratively to foreground and fix "cultural patterns" as visible and inexorable dwellers of the "individual's structure."[26] Here, Frankenstein's will to "actuate" the hidden positive forces is put to work in its full significance: assisting to access, capture, and thus construct the immigrant's innate inner mentality, the recognized positive qualities purport to corroborate and confirm, rather than contradict, the existence of evidential cultural traits in the individual. Thus, besides and beyond evaluating cultural behavior along the good and evil axis, Frankenstein's examination particularly strives to locate ethnicity as a personalized embodied animated essence. He "sets out to understand a given behavior within a specific group represented by the family";[27] for he believes that "the education of the child towards the desired social aim must proceed within the family."[28] As Frankenstein extensively employs the rhetoric of a researcher aspiring to encounter cultural essences, the individual in general, and—concretely and perhaps also metaphorically—the child in his family environment in particular, becomes his site not only of explorations but also of experimentations; through this linguistic mechanism and psychological discourse, he hopes, an ethnic self may be found, verified, and stably grounded.

As safely and smoothly as possible, Frankenstein thus attempts to essentialize and legitimize his ethnocentric judgments as professional diagnoses, structuring them as the linguistic and discursive instruments and components of ethnopsychology. Frankenstein's edifice of ethnopsychology, as Nissim Mizrahi phrases it, may in turn function as "a set of psychological approaches that provide the theoretical foundation and the logic of practice by which cultural attitudes are regarded as cognitive, emotional, behavioral, and structural characteristics of the individual."[29] Yet, does Frankenstein follow through with this desire for essentialization? Is he able to find and fix cultural traits in and as the individual? Doubtful. Soon thereafter, and right as Frankenstein announced the final resolution, he also quickens to express some caution and lists several somewhat surprising reservations. "Recognition of cultural patterns in the individual's structure is one step towards the normalization of interpersonal relationship; understanding of the genesis of these patterns is a second step."[30] And yet the third and final step of "discovering the 'assets underneath the liabilities,' to which he had just allocated so much textual space, is something that sometimes "we will not be able to reach."[31] In such a probable case, the agents of socialization "will have to build our educational approach and activities on the basis of our achievements on the two first levels."[32] Frankenstein provides no explanation to this impasse that brings him back to the precise perceptual point from which he initially departed.

It is possible to fill this gap in his reasoning by returning to the image of the white-robed doctor and place Frankenstein once again in his shoes. As a closer look at Figure 13 reveals, apart from the immense medical device allegedly enabling the doctor's gaze at the pedestaled Iraqi Jew, another adjunct layer separating the two is the latter's white gown. While it may seem that, by contrast to the doctor's device, the gown donned by Salah stands in the way of the expert's eye, hindering its full access to the examined body, it is also possible to conceptualize the gown as fostering, and even facilitating, the operation of visualization. To that end, that which Salah is conceived to carry over from Iraq to Israel, the gown mediates Salah to the doctor, becoming the exposing and explicating, rather than veiling, object through which the doctor not only analyzes and assesses Salah, but, ultimately, sees him.[33] No wonder, then, that it is just as white as the doctor's professional robe. Shedding light on the means and conditions cushioning the doctor's gaze, the Figure provides an illuminating insight into Frankenstein's discursive tools, settings, conditions, and action. Culturally encoded by and as the white gown, the negative embodied yet external appearance of ego-weakness both blocks Frankenstein's sight as well as becomes the one visual site fully accessible to him. Similar to the doctor, Frankenstein seeks to literally look at his primitive immigrant through the cultural patterns and observe him in accordance with, rather than above and beyond, them.

"I came into this world anxious to uncover the meaning of things, my soul desirous to be at the origin of the world, and here I am an object among other objects," Frantz Fanon famously wrote about the experience of racialization in *Black Skin White Masks*.[34] From his place "locked in this suffocating reification," the racialized subject realizes: "The Other fixes me with his gaze, his gestures and attitudes, the same way you fix a preparation with a dye."[35] In an imaginary conversation with Frankenstein, his contemporary, Fanon would have surely reminded him that it was precisely "certain laboratories" with their "test tubes" and "scales" that have assisted "the other, the white man, who had woven me out of a thousand details, anecdotes, stories."³⁶ Fanon's concept of "denegrification,"³⁷ the development of a "historical-racial schema"³⁸ for the body of color, is hard to materialize: "In the white world, the man of color encounters difficulties in elaborating his body schema";³⁹ this is because "the body schema, attacked in several places, collapsed, giving way to an epidermal racial schema."⁴⁰ Stuart Hall's perspective on looking and visualization in Fanon's work further unearths the assault of racialization, or "epidermalization as an inscription of race on the skin and bodily schema under scrutiny and surveillance by the medical gaze of the white Other."⁴¹ Like the white-robed men in Fanon's work, Frankenstein's research mechanisms seem to lead him in several alterative and not necessarily coherent turns. As Hall's reading of Fanon elucidates, and as Frankenstein's research findings and failures demonstrate, elements of racial and racist perception, metonymically named as negative cognitive and mental capabilities, remain to serve as the sole proof of "the power of a science to fix and stabilize racial difference."⁴²

Can Frankenstein's racialized "primitive immigrant" speak? In the films that I henceforth analyze, they absolutely do—reconstructing the making of their historical-racial scheme that have been informing their lives since. For some, as *The Ringworm Children* foregrounds, this historical process of racialization started at childhood, upon their arrival in Israel: by bringing their performed stories, *The Ringworm Children* undermines that power of science to stabilize racial difference precisely.

Childhood: Politicizing the "Social Problem" of *Ringworm* in The Ringworm Children

"During the 1950s, masses of Jewish immigrants emigrated from North Africa. About 100,000 of their children were subjected to X-rays' radiation, as a treatment against ringworm. Thousands of them died, and those who survived suffered cancerous aftereffects." With these subtitles, *The Ringworm Children* begins, stating its mission: "To identify the people who were responsible for this calamity." Against this statement, some informational background, and archival materials from the Zionist Archives that documented the operation of radiation, medical experts explain the lethal repercussions of the X-ray radiation operation on the immigrant children, contending that ringworm, which causes a mild damage in the hair and scalp that naturally passes away in adolescence, never required such intense treatment as the radiations. Considering this, they try to assess the behavior of the medical institution that ordered and executed the operation in the 1950s. After we have learned about ringworm, we meet the then-immigrant children, now adult Mizrahi testifiers, in the film. They recount the suffering that they underwent since their scalps were radiated upon their arrival in Israel, and reenact the forced medical procedures they went through as part of the operation, showing us the physical remnants that they live with, and telling us about the overall pain they endure as adults. The testifiers thus delineate the ongoing harm that they have been going through ever since. As the film reviews, elaborate research and investigations into the scandalous operation started in the 1970s, when the first victims of the radiations started getting sick with cancer, dying, and suffering other serious harm, rendering evident the correlation between the radiations they underwent as children and their concurrent situation. Since 1996, the state has partially compensated the survivors of the operations and their families; yet the severance packages were hardly sufficient and difficult to obtain. The survivors' struggle for recognition and reparations thus continues.

In line with its stated mission, *The Ringworm Children* places the direct responsibility for the colossal long-lasting offense on human life on Chaim Sheba, who supervised the radiations when serving as the deputy director of the Ministry of Health and a veteran of the IDF's medicine unit. The prominent figure advocating for the opening of The Institute for Ringworm and conceptualizing its agenda, Sheba ordered the gathering of children with ringworm from immigrants' reception and transit camps in Israel. The institute's operations were initially planned against the backdrop of the debate around selective immigration that mainly referenced the Jews of North Africa. After prolonged discussions around the question of whether or not to regulate immigration from North Africa, the Jewish Agency's Absorption Department and the Ministry of Health headed by Sheba had reached an agreement in December 1951: "In exchange for having its people put in charge of overseeing Aliyah [Hebrew for immigration] preparations in North Africa, the Ministry allowed a small number of ringworm patients (150 per month) to immigrate and be treated in Israel."[43] In this way, "instead of banning the entry of children with ringworm," as Sheba originally advocated, they would be sent for concentrated treatment in Israel.[44] Although appearing to hold conflicting opinions with regard to selective immigration initially, the agreement ultimately reflects the common underlying ideological ground from which both parties' views on the prospective immigrants from North Africa stemmed: for, the participants in the discussion finally univocally believed that many of the immigrants carry contagious sicknesses.[45] The agreement, furthermore, deposited much power in Sheba's hands, as it enabled him to partake in the selection procedures as a member of the committee that articulated the regulations for immigration before treating these selected immigrants in an orderlymanner.[46] As elaborated later, Sheba's orchestration of the radiations was closely linked with his research interest in heredity in non-Ashkenazi Jewish communities.

As the recent television report by Amnon Levy about the ringworm affair[47] shows, the debates about whether Sheba and his collaborators deliberately radiated the Mizrahi children as part of a US-funded experiment or whether he and his peers naively utilized the then-available and partially legitimate means to fight ringworm are still at their height. Interviewing for Levy's article, filmmaker Bellhassen took back his critical filmic message from 2003.[48] Far from arbitrating who is to blame for the immense suffering, I follow several scenes from *The Ringworm Children* featuring testimonies and reenactments of the survivors' past experiences as Mizrahi immigrant children treated for ringworm and their animated bodily performances of their subsequently injurious physical and mental states. As the film communicates, the bodily experiences of *The Ringworm Children* were formed as such by the state's definition of ringworm as "a social problem" and the resolute decision to apply extremely high levels of radiations on the children's scalps in forced isolated camps right as they arrived in Israel. Rather than defined by the sociomedical issue of ringworm itself, it is the radiations that shaped their lived experience as children and later as adult Mizrahi immigrants, injecting lasting illness into their then-tender scalps. The immigrant survivors perform the relational position of embodying sickness as a repercussion of the radiations while resisting the reasoning of "ringworm" behind it as a sickness—a reasoning that, as the state's official narrative claimed, hindered their access to their own politicized understanding of their pain in their bodies for too long. *The Ringworm Children* thus illustrates how a collective was created, and started organizing as such, under the dire conditions of the forced infliction of radiations rather than existing as an a priori fixed biological identity beforehand. The "ringworm children" were made sick because they immigrated from North Africa as children, rather than being sick prior to immigration: the film discloses the mechanism of diseasing that followed the phantasmatic, questionably scientific, construction of ringworm as "a social problem."

At the outset of the film, we meet David Deri. "I am going to go back 46 years in time, to go back to such a place where, I know, I left my childhood, I left my youth. This is where life was destroyed, actually," Deri's statement opens the film. A victim/survivor of the ringworm operation and an activist seeking fair reparations for all survivors, Deri drives his car to the place where the treatment facility for ringworm, part of the Sha'ar Ha'aliya reception facility and transit camp, used to stand, and where, according to him, he may revisit the traces of the events that painted his coming of age and adulthood with destruction. Yet the farther we drive with Deri, the more the destination seems like a non-place: in a wide court of concrete, Deri parks the car, walks out, and halts in one spot, from which he begins animating the industrial void around him, and reliving his relation to it. "There!" Deri calls when recognizing the familiarity of the space, and as he reconstructs his memory of mountains behind him and the sea in front, his verbal description of that memory responds to the view that is still there, albeit the warehouses currently hide the sea that he used to see directly as a child. "I remember how we would hang ourselves on the fence and watch the train, and also, some trucks that brought transports of children, of victims … they brought them here, and here they did all the atrocities," Deri recalls, reenacting the child that used to climb the gridded bars of the fence to look at the other children who were being delivered to and placed in that prison where he dwelled. Smiling as the childhood memories return to him, Deri's hands hang on to a fence that is not there anymore and the sea is no longer in sight.

The final scene of *The Ringworm Children* takes us back to the same Sha'ar Ha'aliya, only this time Deri stands right across from the visible sea, where an actual fence stands today. Deri's hands hang onto it in the same way that they did in the first scene. Starting with a slow shot of a breathtaking sunset captured from within the fence that today separates the remnants of the camp from the rails of the train and the sea, the ending scene first shows a hand and fingers clutching the bars, and as the camera pulls back we see Deri's entire body holding onto the fence, watching the sea and the train go by. This time, Deri is shown only from the back, his eyes gazing toward the sea are unseen, with the camera focusing on his head and his fingers tightly squeezed around the bars.

Recollecting his memories of traumatic events from a very long time ago, Deri starts with the simple, retained movements of the body of the then child. Displaying Deri's movements, the camera also captured his angle of vision, with the bars both conditioning and confining his performance and position. The scene thus speaks to Deri's situation as relational: he is an intrinsic part of the space and scenery of horror that he himself beholds and depicts, instantiating the captivated realm from, despite, through, and on which Deri reflects his ongoing lived experience of pain. To that end, the opening and closing scenes speak to how formative Deri's stay in the Sha'ar Ha'aliya camp has been to him as a child, an immigrant, and as the adult person he grew up to become, for the rest of his life. Indeed, Deri's painful experiences in The Ringworm Institute at Sha'ar Ha'aliya have made him a perpetual inmate in a body marked by the ongoing pain resulting from radiations: he, as do the other treated children, still looks at the world through the bars of the imprisonment of his own body. The circular citations within which Deri is caught throughout *The Ringworm Children* illuminate, as Meirav Aloush-Lavron notes referencing this scene, his "epistemic sensation and victimized consciousness,"[49] accentuating his overlapping placements as a testifying survivor who is also still living the recurring victimization of the treatments. Further, the framing of the film between Deri's reenactments of his childhood memories of climbing the fence from a time past and through memory gaps of imaginary and real bars portray the film as an investigation of the intertwined processes and circumstances of building the fence: those involved in the state's diagnoses of immigrant children as sick with the "social problem" of ringworm—diagnoses that constituted the gate and constructed the fence behind which Deri was then placed, and that lead to the actual, physical, destructive repercussions within which his body is still imprisoned. Watching through the 43-minute film stretching between a remembered yet invisible fence and a solidly existent one, we watch the gradual transition from imaginary to real bars embodied in the film's development. This metaphor of transition indicates how state imaginary misconceptions of authorities such as Dr. Sheba about presumable social ailments consolidated to becoming a horrifying bodily reality of different ailments for people. This metaphor goes hand in hand with the film's construction of an alternative narrative for the experience that the immigrant children went through, focusing on radiations as a mechanism that served as the formative experience rather than as the solution and cure for their ringworm.

Sha'ar Ha'aliya—Hebrew for "the gate of immigration"—was a reception facility established after the foundation of the state and operative in the years 1949–62, for the claimed purpose of preliminarily administering the waves of immigration that inundated the shores of the Haifa port. A camp "near Haifa, where newcomers were first taken,"[50] Sha'ar Ha'aliya "was intended to serve as a central, contained environment through which the immigrants of this period would undergo bureaucratic processing before being allowed into the larger community."[51] The Ringworm and Trachoma Institute began to operate as part of Sha'ar Ha'aliya in 1952. As a result of this addition, "Sha'ar Ha'aliya became a central institution for the treatment of ringworm in immigrant children,"[52] where they were held in isolated forced concentration camps for up to three months and received radiation treatment. Although ringworm patients were treated in other medical facilities too, "the significance of Sha'ar Ha'aliya lies in its focus on ringworm in new immigrants … either immigrants whose families had passed through Sha'ar Ha'aliya or immigrant children from the transit camps"[53]—that is, immigrants mostly from North Africa.

The film loads the Sha'ar Ha'aliya camp with meaning, both deconstructing the scientific validity of "ringworm" and reconstructing how it functioned as a political and discursive racial armature around which the operation of radiation was constituted. First, the film follows the state's medical and other institutions' conceptual construction of the correlation between the ringworm disease and the migrant children of North Africa that set them apart as having the "social problem" of ringworm, and then served as the reasoning for their forced confinement in the camp. "A disease which [appears in] children [and] passes spontaneously in adolescence. We treated a disease that would pass on its own. The whole intention was … the thing … the social problem … the inconvenience … etc. etc.": this is how medical doctor, Peretz Yekutiel, who worked closely with Sheba in the Ministry of Health in the 1950s, describes the ringworm and the rationale behind the operation of eliminating it. The social dimension of the operation, which Yekutiel initially only stutteringly mentions, seems more significant later, when he further notes that he was deprived of the responsibility to treat children with ringworm due to its ascription as a social matter. "It was very odd that this treatment, including the radiation part, was under the responsibility of a different division in the ministry of health, which was called 'the division of social medicine,'" Yekutial explicates. Scholar Haim Malka, who is then interviewed, quotes from some of the most racist opinions that Zionist and Israeli authority officials held toward Mizrahim—opinions that translated into policy and common discourse.

According to Malka, Sheba "believed in the supremacy of Ashkenazi Jews." Ruth Bondy's biography of Sheba corroborates this, describing how Sheba promoted and planned the process of selective immigration from Morocco since 1954 by contending that the immigrants may transmit and spread contamination. "Sheba's main argument was that the health services are not capable of serving such a large community, of whom many were contaminated with diseases, among them contagious diseases," Ruth Bondy argues. While acknowledging "the lack of cleanness, lack of water, lack of services" in the transit camps, Sheba did not try to better these dehumanizing living conditions or prevent the placing of so many immigrants there for extended periods of time. Rather, Sheba favored the idea of circumscribing a group of people and identifying them as ethnically coherent while scrutinizing their biological commonalities as fixed rather than resulting from their shared living circumstances. Even before his interest in ringworm, Bondy contends, Sheba seemed to "cling to heredity reasons,"[54] theorizing the immigrants' presumable problematic biological predispositions to substantiate his political demand for selective immigration. The statements from Sheba that Bondy quotes confirm that the issue of heredity was one of Sheba's most passionate fascinations for years. "I was mainly interested in one area: why are the red blood cells of Askenazim more durable than those of non-Askenazim," Sheba thus explained the main purpose of his IDF-funded research trip to the United States in 1950.[55] Upon his appointment as the director of the state-supervised Tel-Hashomer hospital in 1953, Sheba finally found the time to properly deepen his research: "I returned to my old affair, the red blood cells ... indeed my first work ... I wrote back in 1942."[56] Eager to harness the resources of the hospital for furthering the special research project, Sheba remembered: "I said: we are transferring to the country [Israel] Jews from different diasporas, that lived among different nations ... we see people who have different physical traits."[57] The project was made possible since "Israel had a live lab, like no other nation had. Thanks to the strict preservation of tradition, prayer phrasings, and folklore, it was possible to follow the members of different sects and easily determine to which sect the patient belongs. Through heredity the mystery of his disease was resoluble."[58] To substantiate premises and presumably precipitate reparative resolutions, Sheba and his colleagues took and tested blood samples from immigrants upon their arrival.[59]

In Sheba's writings, he expresses a special fascination with the social aspects of immigration. "Sheba approached the genetics of the Jews first and foremost from a social, Zionist, historical interest ... medical research and Jewish intuition were brought together here," Bondy confirms when describing Sheba's research on heredity. Underlying the lines of Sheba's theorizations, the delimiting cultural differentiation between Ashkenazim and non-Ashkenazim is presumed rather than inferred, in turn giving way to the conclusive delimitation of them as two biologically distinct groups. Sheba's eager constructions of theories of medical anthropology and epidemiology that focused extensively on non-Ashkenazi communities in Israel and their genetic mapping attest to his desire to track down their consistent and segregated origins and lineages.[60] The direct correlation and loose exchangeability between cultural folkloric habits, seeming sects, and physical traits, were Sheba's basic materials with which to assemble an edifice of essentialist medical and racial observations that lay the foundation for Sheba's programs of selective immigration and the ringworm operation. *The Ringworm Children* turns Sheba's "science" on its head by narrating his correlation of the "social problem" of ringworm and non-Ashkenazi immigrants as a social correlative construction, naming it the main political factor behind the ringworm operation rather than some physical phenomenon of ringworm per se. The fences surrounding Sha'ar Ha'aliya were there before Deri and the other children were forcibly brought into it: Sheba's theorizations preceded and precipitated the formation of the fences, consolidating the social, political, and racial structure into which Deri and the others were implanted. In other words, *The Ringworm Children* breaks down for us the discursive materials from which the fenced camp is made: the conceptual racial construction of a light disease as a social problem and the subsequent translation of that "problem" into a physical ongoing painful problem and state of being—an actual making of the migrating body into a new body in the new country they have just arrived in.

After covering the scientific opinion regarding ringworm and elucidating the political circumstances in which the children were placed in the camps for treatments, the film turns to focus on how these circumstances produced their ongoing physically and mentally painful states of being concurrently. "Not all ringworm children passed away prematurely. Those who survived suffer from tumors, epilepsy, sterility, and more," informs the narrator of *The Ringworm Children* as the film leads the way to investigate the outcome of the radiations by featuring testimonies from the survivors who live with various terminal and/or chronic sicknesses. To contrast the archival footage that sterilizes the ringworm operation as a necessary procedure of medical aid, the film follows the survivors as they reenact the forced infliction of treatment that the medical staff applied on the children's bodies. Although the film establishes that it was the extremely high level of radiation that caused the later sicknesses, it also emphasizes the ongoing pain that resulted from the routine systematic activity surrounding the radiations, including the medical staff's use of physical force to pull the children's entire hair off of them, often for good. "They held me forcibly," Deri communicates, and then "she pulled my hair by force, actually scalped me," Deri shows the pulling of his hair from his scalp. Ilana Fahima demonstrates on a plastic object how the nurse violently treated her: "She grabbed my head between her knees and started plucking (my hair) with tweezers, as if she's cleaning a chicken ... and don't you dare move, because if you moved, you got some" (colloquial for "you were battered"). Thus, in line with the transporting of the children depicted in the first scene, the film exposes the mechanic, ritualistic workings of an entire system surrounding the radiations as a treadmill of destructive production of altered, sickened, traumatized bodies.

Within this context of the productivity of the system of the ringworm operation, the film introduces us to the long-term effects of the radiation treatments etched in the bodies of the then children forever.[61] Destined to undergo recurring surgeries, Deri lives with cancerous brain tumors as a result of the ringworm treatments: the scars on his head attest to the ways in which the first treatment anticipated a lifelong series of subsequent treatments that would engrave their signs on Deri's scalp. "My head is burning, my head is burning" Fahima repeats five times, crying out, reenacting the way she has been screaming for many years since the ringworm treatment. "It's always itchy, it's covered with inflamed sores" shares a third survivor of the treatment who, like the others, exposes her partially bald and damaged scalp. Echoing the first and last scene with Deri and the fence, these difficult scenes frame the survivors' pain as an affect that they are imprisoned within. Thus, the film accentuates not only the entrance to and through, but also the long-term, formative, embodied experience of the pain of remaining locked behind the gruesome "gate of immigration" for the rest of your life.

The grave repercussions of the ringworm operation were a direct result of the exaggerated radiations—way over the quota permitted in several publications of that time, inviting much more dangerous and often deadly diseases into the children's lives. Revising the state official ringworm narrative by shifting the focus to the evident results of the radiations that the survivors unearth instead, the film reconsiders the operation as an operation of radiation rather than against ringworm, demanding us audience to consider radiations as an active and productive process rather than as a reactive cure. Here, one of the working logics historically embedded in the practice of the X-ray devices since its emergence in the late nineteenth century may shed further light on the perhaps unconscious yet nevertheless inevitable causality between Sheba's desirous diagnoses and the active treatment that he deliberated and delivered. "Although it developed primarily within medical and scientific institutions (Rontgen was a professor of physics at the University of Wurzburg in Bavaria), the x-ray image has always hovered at the intersection of science and art, technology and fantasy," Akira Mizuta Lippit wrote.[62] X-ray, psychoanalysis, and cinema—all recognized as inventions in the same year, 1895, and all exploring notions of the interior—"seek to expose respectively, the depth of the psyche, body, and movements of life … which changed the terms by which interiority was conceived, imagined, and viewed."[63] Notably, X-ray technology received much popular attention due to its reliance on the medium of photography. It is against this cultural backdrop that, as Allen Grove shows, "X-ray pictures immediately captured the imagination of a people who for sixty years had associated photography with ghosts," and/or had aimed "to discover 'real' ghosts." Igniting phantasmagorical whims, Wilhelm Conrad Rontgen's accidental discovery of X-ray technology drove some to link "the etherealizing scientific gaze to supernatural terror."[64] Yet this is perhaps no wonder, given that this technology was "so named because the nature of the rays was unknown at the time of their discovery." The specters of the X-ray technology that haunted scientist-fantasizers like Sheba were believed to engender "penetrating rays … discovering realities not available to the naked eye" that can "look through the flesh, and gaze upon the inner workings of the body." The X-ray image visually displayed that "the body, which was then and continues to be the primary object of the X-ray gaze, was irreversibly transformed under the scrutiny of radiation";[65] in this way, "the x-rayed body exposed the subject to an aspect of itself it actively suppresses—namely, death."[66] As more and more symptoms revealed "the destructive capacities of the x-ray," Lippit writes, "the body moved from a referent to a sign, from a figure to the primary site of inscription. X-rays turned the body into a photographic surface."

Drawing attention to the productive and destructive quality of the X-rays, *The Ringworm Children* foregrounds the horrific outcome of Sheba's transition from scholarly research on heredity to the practical treatment of immigrant children. What began as a quest for interior biological characteristics horrifically ended as an external programmed infliction of epidemics on the children—indeed, what Fanon would call "an epidemization." Materializing the wish to see and investigate in the form of a framing "treatment," Sheba in fact artificially imposed a harmful illness on innocent so-called patients, and in this way created them as a distinct group burdened by specific medical concerns. Handling all the children who immigrated from the same place—in this case, North Africa—in a unified and unifying manner, the treatments finally managed to create some correspondence between their geographic origins and an ailed explicit physical condition.

Yet rather than defining them as a different race, this physical condition pushes them to become the storytellers of their own bodily oppressive histories and political advocates of their own cause. As we hear more and more testimonies of survivors and medical opinions, the second half of *The Ringworm Children* also provides us with a closer look at the organizing work that has been taking place around the radiations operation since the 1990s. The survivors who we have been seeing recounting and reenacting their pain as monologues, the camera centered only on them, we now see together, interacting with each other, and traveling together to the parliament to stake their claims. In 1996, the parliament constituted the "law of the ringworm victims" that guarantees meager monitory reparations for the survivors and their families. Yet this law denies any imposition of negligence or harm by state medical officials who were well aware of the harsh implications of the radiations, arguing that this was the common treatment for ringworm in the 1950s worldwide; and the reparations for each survivor was based on the condition that they do not file any lawsuits against the state in the future. Additionally, the survivors wishing to claim the reparations have to go through meticulous, exhausting medical committees first to prove that they were harmed by the radiations. "I don't know if there's anyone who attends their own execution with witnesses, photographer, telling them to take photographs," Fahima says, ragingly and rightfully condemning the ridiculous request of the committee to provide evidence of the treatments.

Fahima's and the others' valid complaints reaffirm that the struggle for recognition and fair reparations for the survivors of the ringworm operation must go on—and in fact it does until this day. Moreover, Fahima illuminates an important aspect of the ringworm operation, which the film as a whole stresses from beginning to end: the way that the state's narrative of correlating ringworm and children from North Africa affected the immigrants' perception of their own stories and selves, until they learned to rely on their own memories and organize around and against that narrative. Being held forcibly behind bars, the immigrant children were also importantly away from the public eye, and as the archival footage incorporated throughout the film shows, the witnesses, photographers, and filmmakers around were all recruited for the mission of propagating that state narrative of ringworm. *The Ringworm Children* demonstrates how this has been impacting the lives of the survivors and forming their identifications, as well as how the survivors sobered up from the harmful narrative to take back their agency over their bodies and the stories of how they came to be, and to fight back for recognition and reparations.

This note on embodied effects and continuous organized resistance concludes *The Ringworm Children*. "I feel that there is a duty of the heart, a duty of the hour, a conscientious duty, and certainly this is also my testament," Deri's statement ends the film, as the camera zooms out from his fingers on the fence to his head, his back, and entire body from behind. Deri, the narrator, and ending subtitles of the film all make references to the "shoah of the ringworm children," complementing the imagery of the train going by and the clutched fence heavily associated with the Holocaust. I take this striking ending statement as a criticism of the lack of attention to and visibility of the pain of the survivors of the radiations conversely to the Holocaust which is well commemorated in Israel—a lack that *The Ringworm Children* importantly repairs.

The film tracks down how the infliction of tremendous ongoing pain by the operators of the radiations and the forced rituals around it are all forever embodied by the survivors. Yet it also offers an alternative to the harmful state narrative of ringworm as the survivors' "social problem" and the programmed system that it generated precisely by centering on embodied and performed countermemory and reclaimed agency. Instead of being defined by ringworm, *The Ringworm Children* are organized activists taking their bodies, stories, and destinies in their own hands despite constant pushback from the state, despite the erasure of any respectful commemoration of the oppressive operation of radiations. The survivors listen to their bodies and to their peers to recall, remember, and get-together around their shared lived experience of systematic oppression. Together with Deri, we audience face the bars of the fence, and as the relationality embedded in the fence encourages our relatability, we are asked to not only feel empathy but also a sense of responsibility for Deri and the others still struggling to heal from the atrocities that happened behind the fence.

Youth: *The Levantine Man, the Black Panthers, and Representations of Police Brutality*

The Ringworm Children emphasizes the harm resulting from putting a scientific racializing examination and racist perception of people—in this case, immigrant children—to practice as a medical treatment. In a similar spirit to Sheba's desire to take his medical theorizations of human bodies a step further, Frankenstein too insisted on formulating a more active strategy that would not only assess, but also fundamentally repair, the immigrant. "The immigrant can overcome his feelings of dependence, helplessness, and resentment by identifying himself with those who constitute the absorptive society,"[67] Frankenstein promises doctors, educators, social workers, and judges. "We can free him from the fetters of his primitive ego-centricity and reactive impulsiveness, and make him aware of the individuality of the other person."[68] This is as long as the agents of socialization are not too overwhelmed by the appearances of "egoism, lack of control, or even overt asociality"[69] in their "encounter with Evil."[70] As it were, several institutional procedures attempted to "free" the immigrant child and adolescent from their alleged primitivism. Frankenstein's prescriptive studies crucially enabled institutions' direct actions of oppression, exclusion, and discrimination in the name of absorption and socialization. As Henriette Dahan-Kalev argued, Frankenstein's research comprised a significant factor in a whole systematic effort to count, depict, analyze, and administer Mizrahi immigrants as objects for design and re-indoctrination.[71] Shalom Chetrit as well as Yossi Yonah and Yitzhak Sporta demonstrated how Frankenstein's research served to facilitate and legitimize the new educational methods formulated specifically for Mizrahi students.[72] Designating them to vocational training presumably more suited to them, the education system construed and constructed them as creatures of lower capabilities.[73] Furthermore, Rakefet Zelshik noted that Frankenstein's employment of discourse of "primitivity" encouraged psychiatric research and the mistreatment of Mizrahim according to his pathologization of them as proved "primitives."[74]

If Frankenstein's writings from 1953 offered that the institution of the modern state can redeem the "primitive immigrant," especially children and adolescents, how did he assess the progress of the immigrant in the new society in his later work? In *Externalization—Its Social Aspects* from 1983, Frankenstein characterized a type of an adult male defined by his inability to fully develop a real masculine self by adapting to and internalizing the new modern society's values: he therefore becomes merely a fake exteriority. Frankenstein called this type *The Levantine Man*. Frankenstein explains that the primitive possesses no self in their original habitat—before they immigrate to the Western modern world. It is solely the transition from their former reality to modernity that triggers a perceptual and existential crisis in the immigrant and inculcates their first sense of a shallow surface of a weak ego.[75] Alas, in this new world, "the society absorbing the people who move into it cannot absorb them out of consideration of their cultural past," Frankenstein stated in explaining the "pathology of transition."[76] For this reason, Frankenstein inferred, the immigrants are "compelled to segregate themselves in their own neighborhoods" that then, in turn, serve as environments exacerbating the emergence of The Levantine Type.[77] Frankenstein dedicates a separate section to theorizing *The Levantine Type*, who suffers the "pathology of the self." Of special interest for this chapter is Frankenstein's description of the masculinity of *The Levantine Type*, which he coins as "deformed masculinity." The traits that "this mentality" possesses include "fancying and role play, lack of honesty and lack of identity ... externalization of feelings and opinions ... exaggerated vulnerability."[78] Frankenstein contended that "this person tries to prove to himself and to others his heroism and masculinity" in various ways, such as sexism and misogyny, arrogance and imprudence. The Levantine Man brags about his success, wears fancy colorful clothes, is sentimental, and inclined to homosexual relationships. Lacking "honest feelings and true involvement," The Levantine Man is merely imitative and not real. Basically, "his exhibited masculinity is nothing but an outward appearance."[79]

Nissim Mizrahi contended that in this text, Frankenstein "offers a typology that characterizes the different forms of pathological transitions from primitive to Western culture."[80] For Frankenstein, "the line between 'primitive' and 'modern' is absolute and is congruent with the essential and qualitative difference between the primitive and the modern mind."[81] I suggest that Frankenstein's *Levantine Man* should also be viewed within the larger framework of the increasing and shifting representation of Mizrahim, especially Mizrahi masculinity, in the Israeli public sphere in the years following the uprising of the Black Panthers movement during 1971–2. Founded by young Mizrahim such as Saadia Martziano, Reuven Abergil, Kochavi Shemesh, and Charlie Bitton to name the famous ones, The Black Panthers started mobilizing in the neighborhood of Musrara in Jerusalem after the 1967 war, organizing massive and memorable demonstrations against concurrent and ongoing conditions of impoverishment, oppression, and racism defining their and their families' lives since their arrival in Israel. Highly documented in photography and video, the uprisings contributed considerably to Mizrahim's growing visibility and changing image in the public sphere and in the media.[82] Raz Yosef wrote: "The Black Panthers movement … inculcated a sociopolitical Mizrahi consciousness, which involved the invention of the image of the macho, erect, and proud Mizrahi. This image challenged the dependence and inferiority that the Ashkenazi hegemony had imposed on Mizrahi men."[83] State-controlled mass media, however, quickly responded with backlash. Noa Hazan shows how the dominant newspapers of the time were representing the demonstrations of the Black Panthers "as violent confrontations between cops and outlaw protesters."[84] Highlighting masculinity played an essential role in "the attempt to construct it as a real national threat to the Western and Modern State of Israel."[85]

On the face of it, Frankenstein's construction of *The Levantine Man* can be read along the lines of the general historically derogatory hegemonic representation of Middle Easterners in general, and the overall backlash against the increasing visibility and self-representation of Mizrahim in the public realm in Israel, particularly. Yet his insistence on not just dismissing and mocking *The Levantine Man*, but also characterizing him specifically as an inauthentic extrovert, a mere appearance, is interesting to examine in light of the documentaries about the Black Panthers that came out in the early 2000s. These documentaries revisit the archival materials such as photographs and videos taken at the demonstrations organized by the Black Panthers to critically discuss the appearance, disappearance, and representation of Mizrahim both out on the streets and in the media at the time. Benchetrit's *Kaddim Wind* and, more elaborately, Mosek's *Have You Heard of the Black Panthers?* reframe the mainstream photography and video representation of the demonstrations that was circulating before the films came out—especially depictions of the violence that the police inflicted on protesters. The films also feature more rare materials from private archives of people who supportively participated in the demonstrations. Denouncing the reaction of the police to the appearance and presence of the Black Panthers leaders and Mizrahim generally at the demonstrations, the films also question the interrelated treatment of the state-owned mainstream media in representing them. Just like Frankenstein's pathologization of *The Levantine Man*, the representation of police battering is a formative moment in the larger state efforts to criminalize and racialize Mizrahim. Yet as the films show, those moments can be reclaimed to serve as just one perspective in the ongoing negotiations on the image of Mizrahim and Mizrahi masculinity and youth in Israel. Frankenstein deprived Mizrahim of authenticity, credibility, authority, and ownership over their stories of becoming adults, on their gendering, and their appearance, performance, and presence in public. Opposing years of state racialization, the films tell intimate powerful stories about what happened to their very bodies in the processes of racialization, pathologization, criminalization, physical battering and pain, in their own voice, sitting face-to-face with the filmmaker and us spectators to represent and pose their resilient and persistent ways of protesting against oppression.

All the films about the Black Panthers incorporate both state-mandated and independent archival photographs and video footage of the demonstrations to communicate a different message. Instead of photographs that are allegedly illustrating the threatening and tamed Mizrahi body, we see moving images that provide context and clarity about the making and becoming of this body. The scenes that portray the demonstrations in *Have You Heard of the Black Panthers?* and *Kaddim Wind* focus mainly on the leaders and followers of the Black Panthers, placing their formerly erased bodies, faces, and voices at the forefront. We see Abergil and Martziano delivering their speeches to a mass, cheering crowd. We see them taking the streets with signs calling for racial and social justice. Additionally, we constantly see the police crash into them with overwhelmingly militarized full force, as the films inundate brief snippets of the clashes between the cops and the protesters back to the screen, incorporating them alongside the other images of the demonstrations. Abergil and Martziano contribute their voiceover to the videos, explicitly naming the videos of the clashes as documentations of police brutality against them, and highlighting its impact on their very bodies. In *Have You Heard of the Black Panthers?*, Martziano testifies: "I didn't feel the beatings anymore, at all. Really, I didn't feel them anymore. They cracked open my eye, broke my head. Broke my hand, my leg. I ... when they threw me in the hallway and more detainees would arrive ... they didn't recognize me. They didn't know who that was." In *Kaddim Wind*, Abergil details: "Suddenly, an attack, of cops, with horses, with water sprinklers, and they ruined us, broke our bones ... the police lost control in its brutality, and crashed people with their horses ... they took the first row of the demonstrations—and, I have photographs of the guys looking blue from head to toe—and, with sticks, they took them to the corner, about 50 people would take 5 guys, and every ten cops caught the leadership, and broke their bones, one by one." Martziano's and Abergil's testimonies about their experiences of the battering reflect a feeling of being reduced to a mere body, an objectified, fragmented, and dehumanized material of the flesh.

On top of adding new voices, faces, and narration, the reframing of police brutality in the films also includes tackling directly the larger political conditions informing the very presence of the Black Panthers leaders in, and the attempt to disappear them from, the demonstrations, particularly, and the public space as a whole, by arresting them beforehand or beating them up right when the demonstrations start. Hazan notes that the erasure of the Black Panthers' leaders and followers from the newspapers went hand in hand with the actual, physical removal of most of the leaders and organizers of the demonstrations from the venue altogether: before the first demonstration on March 3, 1971, the police conducted "preventive arrests" to hinder the participation of the leaders of the Black Panthers in the demonstration.[86] In *Resurrection*, Yigal Naor's authoritative narrating voiceover explains that the March 3 protest was not approved by the

פתחו לי את העין.
שברו לי את הראש.

Figure 14 *Have You Heard of the Black Panthers?* Footage of police violence.

police, and went ahead anyway without most of the Black Panther leaders: "The Black Panthers, most of them having criminal records, saw themselves as a legitimate protesting movement. When they decided to demonstrate, they went by the book, and asked for permission. The police was determined to not let people with criminal records demonstrate. There was a concern that the demonstration will fall into violence. The heads of the Panthers were detained for interrogation."

While *Resurrection* subscribes to the state's master narrative and presents the Black Panthers leaders' "criminal records" as a fact and valid reason to hinder them from protesting, the other documentaries respond more critically to that claim. In *Have You Heard of the Black Panthers?*, Martziano explains that during the time of the demonstrations, "they suppressed us and perpetrated us ... trials ... you still haven't done nothing, you're already arrested, you still haven't done the protests, you're already arrested ... they cracked down on us." In *Kaddim Wind*, Abergil elucidates the broader state mechanisms of criminalization, by which one is not born but rather becomes a criminal, not just by demonstrating but way earlier in life. Abergil explains how the lack of proper education opportunities left the Mizrahi children residing in Musrara but to dwell in the streets. "The police, that was patrolling here every day, would catch children, beat them up, gather them. ... I experienced that on my own flesh, as did my brothers. ... I used to wake up and ask ...'where's this person? He's been taken to juvenile prison ... where's that person? He's been taken to juvenile prison' every single day ... you didn't need to do anything for the cop to come and assault you."

Thus, the first Black Panthers demonstration is far from the first time that Mizrahim have had to deal with police brutality. Rather, all throughout their upbringing, many of them would get beaten up and/or sent to juvenile prison upon merely entering the public sphere. For young Mizrahim, appearing in the streets was prohibited regularly regardless of any crime they have conducted. Rather than sanctioning a crime, beating marks the criminalization of Mizrahim's appearance in the highly policed public sphere, thus enforcing and enabling their exclusion from it. Construing the protester as a perpetual criminal justifies the prohibition to demonstrate placed on them, as well as the beating that follows their disavowal of that prohibition and the demand to materialize the civil right and show up in protests. Here, the testimonies of the police's continuous criminalization and repeated battering of bodies for their mere appearance in the public sphere paint a larger picture of the state's racialization that Mizrahi bodies have been enduring ever since they have arrived in Israel. As part of this racialization, the state's teleological narrative about the always already Mizrahi criminal upon-appearance translates as not only a physical but a psychological abuse, where the sense of temporality of the battered protester is distorted: that is, the present moment of the battering is presumably evidence of a criminal mirrored past and predetermined future.

Have You Heard of the Black Panthers? and *Kaddim Wind* teach us of the orchestrated media and police efforts to delegitimize the Black Panthers movement taking place as part of the broader operating state mechanisms of criminalization and racialization against Mizrahim. Indeed, right after the scenes of police brutality, *Have You Heard of the Black Panthers?* reminds us of the famous speech by Golda Meir, then prime minister of Israel, as she openly instigated against them on television. Additionally and importantly, however, right before the scenes about police brutality, the film also featured a short video segment that captured a Black Panthers leader appearing and speaking his mind. In that video, we watch young Martziano stating concisely: "What way is there left? That, I can't say, what way is there left. But you think about it, yourselves, what way is there. If the good way doesn't work, what's left?" This video was previously featured in *Resurrection*, where it was tailored to corroborate the police's "preventive arrests" of the Black Panthers leaders prior to the March 3 demonstration. Taking Marztiano's statement literally, *Resurrection* utilized this video to validate that while they had "good" reasons to protest, the Black Panthers leaders were inciteful in alluding that the demonstration might escalate to "bad" violence. Yet Martziano never said the word "bad" because, as he reckoned, he could not "say that"; that is, he knew there were limits to what he is allowed to say on the record when he had so many criminal records on his name already. *Have You Heard of the Black Panthers?* emphasizes precisely that sense of Martziano's limited choice and persistence of agency against all odds. Here, the black-and-white video is transmitted to us through two monitors: one looks small and old, placed on a cardboard box, and another is set up for the filming of the scene, like a video within a video, both replayed and on display. The double framing of the two monitors recalls the state's double framing of the Mizrahi body as criminalistic: once as a youth and then as a protester—protesting among many other things, his criminalization precisely. Perpetually at work, the double framing keeps repeatedly affecting the present and haunting the future, just as the screens are framed by our own screen as we watch the video. Yet the film's reframing of Martziano's statement, especially in comparison to *Resurrection*, elucidates that imagery depends on the mediation to enable, contextualize, and politicize it. Martziano thus "can't say that" and says it anyway: by legally curbing their civil right to protest, the police left them with no choice but to go ahead and break the law: the way that is "left" for them is to claim this right anyway.

While explicating the reiterative process of framing that continues till the time of the filmmaking, the video also renders Martziano's message as a powerful, personal and collective address releasing itself out from the framings as if to physically touch the audience directly. Indeed, passing through the layered and multichanneled videoed, televised, and cinematized mediations and mediatizations, Martziano's statement comes across crystal clear: for he looks straight into the camera, his eyes thriving beyond it in what feels like he is looking us spectators straight in the eye, and sends his hand out as if to point to us and almost touch us when pleading: "What's left?" I suggest that the human contact initiated by Martziano should encourage us to think for ourselves: What is left of this and other videos previously utilized to incriminate and hurt its recorded subjects? What is left for the protesters, for their supporters, for us, present and future spectators of police brutality, to do to reinstate our hope in humanity?

To explore the full significance and potential of this video and of videos of police brutality featured in the films, it is useful to recall another memorable, videoed, and well-watched case of police brutality: the LAPD's battering of Rodney King on March 3, 1991 (exactly two decades after the first demonstration of the Black Panthers in Jerusalem). The battering was filmed by George Holliday who lived nearby, and those 81 seconds were supposed to serve as solid evidence of criminal police brutality in the *California v. Powell et al.* trial of the four cops responsible for the battering. However, the jury preferred to focus on the first few extremely blurry seconds of the otherwise credible video, coercing a misreading and projection of their racist ideas onto it, and acquitted the cops. The jury interpreted King's attempts to save himself from harm as physical gestures of violence of an ex-yet-perpetual criminal deserving of brutalization. Paula Rabinowitz reminds us of this case in her article about Michael Brown, who was killed in 2014 in Ferguson, Missouri, by Darren Wilson, a cop who was later acquitted. Rabinowitz noted that like Brown, King was similarly rendered a criminal in hindsight of the deadly harm placed on his body. Rabinowitz recalled how the "defense attorneys surgically dissected the tape, frame by frame, reinscribing each instant with a narrative judging Mr. King as the perpetrator of violence—his 'leg is cocked' and his 'arm is triggered'—while the officers fearing for their lives, benignly administer 'strokes' to his 'bear-like' body."[87] Time and again, "a young man, African American, deemed criminal (Rodney King was an ex-con; Michael Brown allegedly a thief) after the fact, ends up face down on a street—put there by the violence of police, in full view of those who happen to live nearby."[88] The insensible acquittal of Wilson and the cops who beat King, alongside the horrifying, repeated "placement of the brutalized black male body in public view, streetside, is an unbearable trace of racism's dehumanization and its visual record,"[89] Rabinowitz raged.

Twenty-one years prior to the killing of Michael Brown, Rabinowitz dedicated a chapter to Rodney King in her book about documentary cinema, where she elaborately criticized the defendants of the battering cops for their racist portrayal of King in the trial as "'a duster,' 'an animal,' 'bear-like,' 'buffed out,' thus 'an ex-con,' 'a monster with one-track mind,' 'super-strong,' and so forth."[90] "Of course, his [King's] body was nowhere in the courtroom; instead, his presence was graphed through the tape onto the monitor, a visual image open to interpretation. Furthermore, by emphasizing the taped visuals, Rodney King can only be seen as body: he lacks a voice."[91] Rabinowitz's revisiting of the King case speaks to the high volume of police brutality endlessly practiced in the service of racialization in the United States at large. Yet we may also correlate her analysis of the video with her later noting on the historical protests that followed suit. This correlation shows the compatibility between the image traces graphing the objectification, fragmentation, and dehumanization of King's absent body in the trial and the "images of the confrontations that occurred regularly between demonstrators and police beginning on the day of Mr. Brown's death."[92] That is, the protests may be viewed as the locus where everyday, mostly unrepresented, police brutality in the service of criminalization and racialization comes out in the open, is seen and experienced in public, and circulated in the media. Thus, the inability of videos of police brutality to serve as hard evidence leading to just charges against battering cops stands in stark contrast to their power to bolster rightful rage and public protests, visibility, and criticism—and later on, sometimes, lead to justice in court.

Despite every attempt to induce fear around the Black Panthers leaders and demonstrations, many people actually took to the streets and joined as protesters after watching the pictures of police brutality in the media. If to build on Rabinowitz's analysis, and to go back to Martziano's question, "What's left?" we can see videos of police brutality as that which is left—an important trace and piece of evidence that may assist in the possible politicizing code-switching that we can perform when watching incriminated protesters and exonerated police brutality in the media. A document of a past remaining relevant, the video itself—of the battering of King, and/or of the Black Panthers leaders, and/or of other people of color in the United States and Israel/Palestine—is "what's left" to distribute and accumulate meanings after the fact and mobilize people to protest.

The scene doubly framing Martziano's videoed statement with television monitors in *Have You Heard of the Black Panthers?* directly explicates the general critique of mainstream media weaved through the films as a whole. Present at the demonstration, the person filming the videos of police brutality was witnessing, communicating, and experiencing, the chaotic manner of violence. Even if we watch them repetitively, the videos evade our ordering scrutiny: yet the very unintelligible nature of the videos illuminates the inability to comprehend the trauma caused by witnessing and/as experiencing violence. Further, that illuminating lack of clarity is partly what enabled the audience watching television at home at the time to view the battering through and against the dismissive framing of protesters by mainstream media generally. In *Trauma TV: 12 Steps beyond the Pleasure Principle*, Avital Ronell analyzed the critical role of the recording of the battering of King in the aftermath of the trial. Ronell focused on the function of the video when tailored into redemptive, reactionary narratives on television portraying the perpetrating cops as victims. Video "produces an ETHICAL SCREAM which television has massively interrupted," in calling television "to itself."[93] Thus, "when testimonial video breaks out of concealment and into the television programming that it occasionally supersedes, it is acting as the call of conscience of television," for, video "requires a reading; it calls for a discourse … and instead of voyeurism, an exegesis." Ronell highlighted the power of the several few blurry seconds of the video in communicating the inability to refer to a traumatic event through credible means—an inability systematically denied by television. Broadcasting the video's blurry seconds, "television showed a television without image, a site of trauma in which the experience of immediate proximity involved absolute distance … through video … rhetoricity of televisual blindness emerged … something was apprehended."[94] That "something" was a politicized glimpse into the ongoing trauma that structural racialization and racism imposes on people of color everywhere: by foregrounding blurriness, the video brought back the "phantom body of the police" represented by "this ghostly relationship that the image produces between phenomenal and referential effects of language."[95] Ultimately, what "made it possible for the taped brutalization of King to blow out of teleproportion and into the streets" is the spectators' encountering of "the fact of fundamental disruption in traditional modes of consciousness and understanding, a disruption that occurs traumatically in the very experience of our history."[96]

In line with Ronell's analysis, I suggest that viewing the disruption in audio/visual clarity as a trace of structural racism speaks precisely to our agency as spectators to read between the lines and against the grain of hegemonic messages. Indeed, we can see the human behind the misreading and wrongdoing of the televised blurry images, we can see the residues of humanity, of human memory, and human connection that cannot be destroyed by police brutality. When Martziano asks us "What's left?" we can thus interpret his appeal as pondering: What can remain human after the perpetual criminal has been beaten up and is recriminalized? What can remain human after the consistent racialization of the body? And simultaneously, physically, and performatively, answering: we remain. The lasting and growing power of the video where a person reaches out through his eyes and hand to touch and impact the audience directly may serve as precisely the trace of his humanity and the failure of the police's attempt to dehumanize him with militarized force. In turn, every protester joining the demonstrations carries within and as themselves the racialized, criminalized, beaten yet always human, body of color, represents their rage and disgrace, and claims their right to return to the public sphere.

Figure 15 *Have You Heard of the Black Panthers?* Young Saadia Martizano.

In Conclusion: Heads Held High

"Wherever we went to hold our heads high—they broke our bones": Abergil declares when testifying about his experience of police brutality in *Kaddim Wind*, as we spectators visit his home, seated by a table, speaking calmly to the camera, to filmmaker Benchetrit, and to us. Seeing Abergil reflect on his experiences in *Kaddim Wind*, as Martziano did in *Have You Heard of the Black Panthers?*, we see them living on, despite and in resilience to the constant repeated battering and criminalization. How does one keep their head high when one's bones are being repeatedly and systematically broken? Or when one's very head is burning in pain after absorbing deadly amounts of radiations in childhood, as we saw in *The Ringworm Children*? Abergil's testimony about his experience of police brutality in *Kaddim Wind* may assist us to wrap up our thoughts about survival and resilience critically informing the films analyzed in this chapter. In the opening moments of the scene, and in other moments throughout the film, the camera walks with Abergil through the streets of Jerusalem, around Musrara and the nearby Mahne Yehuda market, following the lead of his erect, proud step, and instantly capturing his eyes gazing forward. "I, as a Black Panther, I rebelled against the conventions imposed on me by society ... but I, when I rose up as a panther, I did not know where I'm going and where I'm striving ... and then I realized, I am rebelling here—my first protest was a protest against myself, not against the institution. Because I was shackled inside my conventions, inside the obsequiousness which was my life, inside the big null that I grew up in. That's where I came from." Abergil walks and talks, seemingly explicating a process of rebelling that sounds like an actual shedding of a skin—a skin condensed on him like the heavy winter coat he is wearing—a thick skin of a myriad of conventions that were imposed on him, the nothingness of his life that was cuffing and confining and crafting him. By "imposed conventions" we can assume that Abergil is referring to the mechanisms of criminalization that he described earlier, as well as the ringworm treatment that he underwent as a child, which he talked about in his first testimony in this film.

On the one hand Abergil describes the mechanisms of state racialization of Mizrahim as both donned on and suffocating him so much that they became his own self, and on the other, as events that he could, in a long and perhaps perpetual process, reflect on, and somewhat liberate himself from. If to revisit the destructive racializing and pathologizing theories about Mizrahim reviewed at the beginning of the chapter, perhaps what Carl Frankenstein saw as the "personality pathology" of *The Levantine Man* may be reclaimed as a useful defense mechanism for Mizrahim who, against all odds, try to keep the racialization inflicted on their bodies at

Figure 16 *Kaddim Wind,* Reuven Abergil, "Wherever we held our heads high." Photo courtesy: *Kaddim Wind's* editor and co-producer Senyora Bar David.

bay. "This is the form of exterior and exteriority characteristic of the transition of the 'primitive' person to the modern culture,"[97] Frankenstein contended when rendering the "Levantine Man" as a type of "exhibited masculinity" who externalizes his gender, opinions, and feelings because he lacks significant values and human ties, like a retarded child.[98] While explicitly offensive, a reading against the grain of this text can sabotage Frankenstein's scientific framing of extroverts as observed empirical phenomena. Pressed under Frankenstein's casting hands, Mizrahim may only survive practiced pathologizations by refusing to internalize them as fixed facts of ethnicity. Frankenstein's theorization of exteriority may thus be reclaimed as Mizrahim's way of grasping and managing racialization as a set of operations conducted by the state—that is, as inflicted *from the outside*, with its harsh implication to be kept *as an exteriority* to the body as much as possible. For this purpose, let me advise the perspective of another astute reader of Fanon.

Theresa De Lauertis addressed exteriority in her reading of Fanon's work alongside Freud's, Homi Bhabha's, and Hall's. Dialoguing with Hall, De Lauretis articulated her worries that "in so emphasizing the discursive character of racism as a social category, something of the value of Fanon's text, perhaps the thing that makes it most radical today, may slip out of sight and out of mind."[99] De Lauretis then revisits Hall's definition of epidermilization and highlighted its concrete dimension as "the introjection of racist stereotypes in the individual psyche." For De Lauretis, racist discourse and its acts of racialization directly target and simultaneously strike both the body and the ego, or, as she phrases it while referencing Freud, take "their consequent hold on the body-ego."[100] To explicate and complicate her response, she quotes from Bhabha's reading of Freud to render this action as "a pressure, and a presence, that acts constantly, if unevenly."[101] All the more, however, we must not forget that it is "*beneath* the body schema" that Fanon has "created a historical-racial schema" (my emphasis);[102] as Hall highlighted, the elements of racial discourse inscribed on the surface of the skin also evoke what seems as "real effects."[103] Importantly, for De Lauretis, the body-ego is a "sense organ ... it must lie *on the borderline* between outside and inside; it must be turned towards the external world and must envelop the other psychical systems" (my emphasis).[104] De Lauretis rewrote Freud's body-ego as "a permeable boundary—an open border, so to speak—and a site of incessant material negotiations between the external world, on one side ... and, on the other side, the internal world."[105] Finally, "the epidermal schema, culturally constructed by racist discourses, is superimposed onto the corporeal, phenomenal schema that is the source of bodily sensations and comes to displace it altogether," De Lauretis concluded.[106] As the epidermal schema thus dwells instead of and struggles in negotiation with the body-ego, a dynamic reality of exteriority emerges and evolves. In this state of affairs, that which has been attacked from the outside also inevitably becomes an inseparable component of the body under arrested assault, making it impossible to differentiate the outside from the inside. Frankenstein's theorization of externalization as both stemming from the systematic "outside" as well as eventually belonging to the individual's "inside" captures precisely this situation of the embodied epidermal schema. Frankenstein's textual endorsement of exteriority may thus tacitly and reluctantly pave the path for reclaiming the visible individuality of the immigrant as "a primitive" as both imposed from the outside as well as simultaneously embodied as his reality in this precise process.

To that end, coming back to the photo of the white doctor standing in front of the immigrant from Iraq, Salah, that I started with, it is possible to think of the gown not only as the image mediating the latter to the former but also as the casting pattern pushed against Salah's very body, forming and shaping it from without. Rather than attempting to unravel the alleged layers within, and as the act of unraveling reveals its inherent underlying creative and constructive capacities, Frankenstein is now sculpting him with his very own hands. Compatibly, fortunately for Abergil, and unlike many others as we saw in *The Ringworm Children*, he survived the ringworm treatment. While it might have taken a miracle for his scalp to be spared from the results of months of radiations, Abergil explains that the first step in the complex, winding, and uncertain way to shedding the extra skin of racialization was to hold his head high and speak his mind on behalf of himself, his family, and his community at the demonstrations. The demonstrations were thus the very first point of departure in a path one needs to embark to start personally resisting and physically snapping out of everything that Frankenstein prescribed for Mizrahim, such as Abergil.

In Conclusion of Part I: "The Body"

Encouraging us to consider filmed, performing bodies as always "bodies too much," Ivone Margulies asked: "How is one to grant a corporeal weight to faces, places, and events through a medium that can imply but lacks depth? Where the body appears as theater, as third dimensional, how does it highlight cinema's constitutive hybridity?"[107] The films analyzed in Part I, "The Body," correlatively ask: How may a film represent and care for the filmed performing person who is carrying the repercussions of physical pain in them, and how to encourage spectators to believe them as testifiers? How may the encounters of the filmic media with the medium of the body, the voice, the face, the head, the pointing fingers, the reaching hands, conjoin as multidimensional sites of documentary performances to illuminate some of the deeper, lasting implications of structural oppression? Centering on the documentary performance of a person in prolonged physical pain adds crucial dimensions to the study of the documentary media's relationships to the past event of physical harm recounted and reenacted in film. The documentary performances analyzed in Part I convey that the represented physical experiences of past events have been lasting and vastly recurring in their communities due to structural oppression. The documentary performances shift the focus from an interrogation of whether what happened to the person may be transmitted in exactly the way it happened to the persistent and survived effects of the experienced past event on the person, on their body, in the performed present. In the documentary performances analyzed above, the filmic media and the human body interact with and impact one another: they comprise the very means and core ingredients of the documentary performance. The films touch upon the relationality inexorably informing both the surviving and becoming of the body in conditions of structural oppression, and the site and event of the documentary performance.[108]

Watching Palestinians' and Mizrahim's different experiences of physical pain side by side, we begin to learn about the interrelated strategies of state violence deployed when differently racialized bodies are harmed, and about the shared methods that differently racialized hurt bodies utilize to reclaim agency over the story of the body and obtain the resilience to live on. As we learn from the documentary performances analyzed above, the bodily pain resulting from the operation of radiations on the scalp that David Deri testifies about in *The Ringworm Children* significantly differs from the pain resulting from witnessing your neighbors and friends die in the hands of the IDF's military operation and knowing you may be next, as we see in *Since You Left*, *Jenin Jenin*, and *Arna's Children*. In many ways, differential experiences of pain set people apart, commanding that they organize themselves differently to oppose it. The infliction of differential pain by the same state is part of the ongoing attempt to position Palestinians and Mizrahi apart and encourage Mizrahim to congregate around Zionist-Israeli national identity. Yet the analyzed films by and about '48 Palestinians and Mizrahim engage with bodily experience and memory of pain in several shared ways. Like the protagonists of *Jenin Jenin* and *Arna's Children*, the Mizrahim who suffer prolonged physical injuries and sometimes premature death due to radiation treatments and police brutality track the political circumstances and conditions affecting their ongoing pain. Their performed testimonies show that the pain inflicted on them was not the result of them being "a social problem" as the Zionist Ashkenazi doctors claim, and is not their fault. Similarly, the Palestinians in Jenin reject their treatment as "a security problem." Rather, they refuse to buy the master narratives imposed on them a priori by so-called empirical studies, knowing that the ways in which they were labeled—terrorists, sick people, criminals in essence—in the textbooks and media almost deprived them of accessing the memory and representability of their own bodily pain as a political, rather than a scientific, matter. They understand bodily pain as relational: they know the infliction of pain has actual embodied implications, but are not the hostages of those implications, affirming that hurting them cannot be justified. The films find ways to access, recall, retell, and politicize bodily pain by centering on the documentary performances of the survivors who point out the evident effects of the actualization of racializing discourses in the form of physical violence on their bodies. The films' cinematizing means such as reframed archival footage, editing, camera perspective, and the testimonial reenactments of the participants all emphasize the ways in which they resist the reasons that the state assigns for their pain, reclaiming the story of how their bodies came to be that way, and owning their body and legacies of politicization and protest. Just as *Jenin Jenin* and *Arna's Children* help us understand the discursive and physical mechanisms affecting the lives of Palestinians collectively living under the vivid threat of death throughout their lives, this chapter tracks how the physical assaults on Mizrahi bodies such as the ringworm treatment and police brutality were put forth to un/make Mizrahim in the shape of the racializing discourse formed around and against them in the first place.

Part II

HOME

Chapter 3

SPEAKING OUT ABOUT THE PLACES OF PALESTINE
IN ISRAEL IN RACHEL LEAH JONES'S *500 DUNAM
ON THE MOON*, MICHEL KHLEIFI'S AND EYAL
SIVAN'S *ROUTE 181*, AND IBTISAAM MARA'ANA'S
PARADISE LOST

"After that, we never returned," Sa'ad Abu al-Hayja, a Palestinian refugee residing in Jenin since 1948, concluded his testimony in Rachel Leah Jones's *500 Dunam on the Moon*. Prior to this conclusion, Sa'ad relayed a visit that he paid to his place of birth known as Ayn-Houd until 1948, and since 1953 is called Ein-Hod, an Israeli artist colony by Mount Carmel. Although managing to reach Ein-Hod and even getting a taste of its native carobs, Sa'ad did not revisit ever since: upon arrival, he was told that the carob tree is not his and never will be. Silenced, Sa'ad took off and never returned. "Where are we?" inquires filmmaker Michel Khleifi in *Route 181*, as he and his co-filmmaker Eyal Sivan encounter a Bedouin shepherd with his cattle in today's "Kibbutz Gezer." "Ayn-Yarka," the shepherd replies repeatedly, exacerbating Khleifi's suspicion and doubt. "Ayn-Yarka? Is this the Arabic name? Where is the 'ayn' [Arabic and Hebrew for "well"] then? Do you use it?" Khleifi further stresses when unable to locate the well on the map; but the shepherd says nothing further than the same name, and merely points in a general direction—at the end of the trail and outside the frame—and admits that he does not use it. "I don't know what really happened in that war. But ever since, my father is silent," filmmaker Ibtisaam Mara'ana shares at the outset of *Paradise Lost*. Filming in her hometown of Fureidis, one of only two remaining Palestinian villages along Israel's coastal line, Mara'ana explores the attempts to intimidate the residents of Fureidis into silence, especially regarding the destruction inflicted on the neighboring village of Tantura. Mara'ana's conversations with Fureidis-born and -raised scholar and activist Suaad Genem also convey the risk of vocally identifying with the struggle to liberate Palestine, which led to her persecution as "a terrorist." Yet the documentary performances of Sa'ad, the shepherd, Mara'ana, Suaad, and others analyzed below show how they survived and spoke out about, through, and beyond the imposed silence all at the same time, to identify with their birthplaces and histories of Palestine as such in order to hold on to their homes and sense of belonging and of imagining a future of return.

How do documentaries about 1948 Palestine represent Palestinian places that have been removed from the discursive contours of today's map of Israel? This chapter probes the impact of Israel's unmaking, remapping, and renaming of the places in Palestine on '48 Palestinians as shown in *500 Dunam on the Moon*, *Route 181*, and *Paradise Lost*. The chapter focuses on documentary performances that trace and resist the attempts to silence '48 Palestinians' identification with and belonging to Palestine vis-à-vis their displacement, precarious relocations, and continuous state of alienation—all comprising the Nakba. That silencing occupies Israel's common discourse, current maps, and everyday spoken language, operating by the new spatial narratives, terms, and names, applied to places in Palestine as a whole. That silencing translates to an effective denial of the pain of loss that '48 Palestinians are living through by the day in Israel. Yet in the documentary performances analyzed below, Palestinians speak out and about places in Palestine, recounting and reenacting the mechanisms of silencing as these were imposed on them, accessing and articulating their own stories of the places where they are from and/or where they are at, thus reorienting themselves toward a past of Palestine to rehearse its possible futures. I focus on scenes portraying the speakers in situ, in the places where they found themselves after the physical loss or the redefinition of their homes in Palestine. There, they speak about and despite the silencing of their belonging to their places and reclaim their attachments to their villages, their olive and carob trees, their well, their sea.

Focusing on the residents of Ayn-Hawd, *500 Dunam on the Moon* reconstructs the displacement of '48 Palestinians that the state of Israel has defined as "present absentees": forced to leave and prohibited to return to their homes in 1948, the approximately twenty thousand "present absentees" found refuge in other places within the newly demarcated territory of Israel. The first section of this chapter addresses Israel's remaking of the land, nature, and architecture of Palestine as represented by '48 Palestinians and several Jewish Israelis in *500 Dunam on the Moon*. The film consists of testimonies of the displaced Palestinian residents of Ayn-Hawd who have lost and then rebuilt their village on a nearby hill, as well as statements by the Israeli current residents of Ein-Hod, which was built on the ruins of Ayn-Hawd, and, finally, reenacted dialogues between them. The scenes I analyze tell us about the appropriation of Palestinian land and the displacement of its people, uniquely showing how Israel attempted to depoliticize the things that make up a home such as trees and stone structure, crafting them as untouched objects of the orient, denying the ways they were altered, and thus silencing the Palestinian histories and people removed from and still affiliated with them. Against these attempts, the documentary performances of Palestinians speak out about the land's histories of cultivation, demolitions, and re-demarcations, and reenact the ways in which silencing takes place in everyday conversation between Palestinians and Israelis. The interlinked demolitions, re-demarcations, and silencing, the testimonies convey, attempt to fragment '48 Palestinians' attachments to and affiliations with the land of Palestine, its trees, structures built before 1948, and other objects related to the very place they inhabit. The testifiers resist these mechanisms by reclaiming their ongoing attachments to their olive and carob trees and to their stone structure in Ayn-Hawd, thus relating Palestine as a home.

The second section explores how Palestinians and Jewish Israelis living around the ruins of the village Abu Shusha destroyed in 1948—where "Kibbutz Gezer" is today, close to Ramle and Lydda—relate to the place they inhabit as shown in *Route 181*. In *Route 181*, filmmakers Michel Khleifi and Eyal Sivan, a '48 Palestinian and an Israeli Jew both based in Europe, return to Israel-Palestine to embarked on "a cinematographic journey in their country," conversing with "all those who cross their path."[1] They utilized the map outlining the United Nations' 181 partition resolution from 1947, which sought to constitute two bordered, Arab Palestinian and Jewish Zionist states. The filmmakers follow the map of their trajectory, and, along the way, approach Palestinians and Jewish Israelis to inquire about their thoughts on the Palestinian villages destroyed in 1948. In one scene, a Jewish Israeli resident of Kibbutz Gezer talks to Sivan about Abu Shusha, which used to be around there. In another key scene, a Palestinian Bedouin shepherd answers Khleifi's questions in Ayn-Yarka, which Israel designates as a land of the Jewish National Fund (JNF), and which appears on no official Israeli map, a result of the constant displacement of and refusal to recognize Bedouins' existence in that area (and in other areas in Israel). The scenes assist me in describing the continuous silencing of both the destruction of Abu Shusha as well as of the factuality of Ayn-Yarka, both linking the past and present of Palestine and Palestinians' ongoing attachments to it. Particularly, I spend time delineating the shepherd's performance of embodied silence besides and in between his brief utterances of the place's name, Ayn-Yarka, and the film's emphasis of the structural silencing of his relationship to the space.

The final section analyzes Mara'ana's *Paradise Lost*, which centers on the residents of the village Fureidis—including the filmmaker herself and her family. Particularly, I focus on several scenes where the filmmaker dialogues with her protagonist and childhood hero, Suaad Genem. Fureidis was occupied in 1948 but was one in only two villages along the coastal line that was not destroyed in the war (the other village being Jisr al-Zarka), because of pressure from residents of the nearby Jewish towns, who were their employers, to spare them.[2] Mara'ana captures herself, her family, and other residents of Fureidis on camera, as they endure the continuous reality of living as Palestinians under the state of Israel. Positioning herself behind and in front of the camera alternately, Mara'ana conducts conversations with her father, friends, students, and neighbors. Centrally, Mara'ana talks to Suaad—a former resident of Fureidis who had left the town in the 1990s to Exeter in the United Kingdom. Suaad was perpetrated by the Israeli authorities for many years, imprisoned and tortured occasionally due to her activism in Palestinian national campaigns. Mara'ana captured Suaad as she verbally describes and reenacts her embodied experiences of the attempt to suppress her activism and identification with Palestine in the Israeli jail.

The Ayn-Hawd centered in *500 Dunam on the Moon* was not recognized by the state until 2004 and hence did not appear on the map at the time the film came out. Ayn-Yarka and the once adjacent village of Abu Shusha brought up in *Route 181* appear on no contemporary map of the state of Israel. To represent the Palestinian places ruined in 1948 and after, filmmakers Jones and Khleifi and Sivan focus on how those exist in the spoken discourses of the everyday of both Palestinians and Israelis living nearby, and especially in the conversations among them. Conversely, Mara'ana films at her and her family's hometown, which remained physically intact in 1948 and appears on the map. While not depopulated, Fureidis has been significantly impaired as a result of the Nakba as a whole, and especially as the coastal village of Tantura that was located nearby was destroyed, and its residents killed or exiled, with some of them initially escaping to Fureidis but eventually mostly expelled.[3] In *Paradise Lost*, pain is associated not with the erasing or silencing of the very physicality or name "Fureidis," but with the harsh suppression of both the catastrophes that it witnessed and of the liberated futures it may imagine for Palestine as a whole. The scenes I focus on foreground an embodied emptiness carved within the women starring in them—filmmaker Mara'ana and her admired interlocutor, Suaad Genem—as personal inner spaces that remember the histories of Palestine, which they keep within themselves wherever they go and even after leaving Fureidis, and as an inner room from which to dream, speak up, and resist and break the silence about a possible free Palestine of the future. Complementary to its former accounts that the Abu Al-Hayjas and the shepherd provide, the concluding analysis of *Paradise Lost* depicts another way of speaking of and surviving through silencing, adding the important perspective of the two feminist freedom fighters—each fighting for her own and collective freedom in her own way.

The films, *500 Dunam on the Moon*, *Route 181*, and *Paradise Lost* deeply contemplate upon the lives of '48 Palestinians post the years of the decline of Oslo, and especially post–October 2000, when the community lost thirteen unarmed protesters to police fire, and was becoming increasingly vulnerable in the public sphere at large. The films' centering of the question of Palestine and of 1948 resonates with the return of the suppressed crucial issue of the Palestinian refugees' Right of Return according to the UN resolution 194, which resurfaced and stirred the general discourse on Israel-Palestine around 2000, and then was vetoed by Israel, comprising a major cause for the failure of the Oslo talks. Moreover, beyond the politicized aspect of these films, they also join other films depicting the civil everyday facets of lives of '48 Palestinians in Israel and against the backdrop of globalization and global politics at large, with a focus on cultural production and activity that questions Palestinians' ability to partake in Israel's cultural life as equals. Duki Dror's *Raging Dove* (2001) was centered on boxing world champion Johar Abu-Lashin, following his rise to fame after winning two world championships as part of two World Title Fight games in the United States in 1992 and 1997. Yet once Abu-Lashin, a citizen of Israel from Nazareth, publicly exclaimed that he is Palestinian his career came under serious jeopardy. Similarly focused on sports, Ram Levy's *Sachnin, My Life* (2005) accompanies the members of the Bnei-Sachnin soccer team representing the city of Sachnin in the north of Israel, as they ponder on winning the highest cup of Israel's national championship in 2004. In her *Dancing in Jaffa* (2013), Hila Medalia captured the ballroom dancing performance and contest held between Jewish Israeli and Arab Palestinian mixed and segregated elementary schools in Jaffa. Led by Palestinian American instructor Pierre Dulaine, the children had to learn to dance with one another. These are examples of films about '48 Palestinians' cultural lives made by Jewish Israeli filmmakers who trace success stories that are not without conflict, oppression, and pain. In the case of *Dancing in Jaffa*, the success story runs the risk of presenting a depoliticized neoliberal narrative along the infamous slogan, "Anyone can succeed if they only worked hard." This is why it is so important to celebrate such achievements as *500 Dunam on the Moon*, *Route 181*, and *Paradise Lost*. Although *500 Dunam on the Moon* was not made by a Palestinian filmmaker—it is the only film analyzed here that was made by an Ashkenazi Israeli woman, Rachel Leah Jones—I chose to include it here because of the high and impactful involvement of the residents of Ayn-Hawd in the making of this film and the way that Jones refrains from providing any kind of authoritative voice(over) to the story. Finally, it is important to add a note about the extensively prolific film work of Ibtisaam Mara'ana who, aside from *Paradise Lost*, created many other films, all centering on Palestinian women. Along the lines of the abovementioned films, her *Lady Kul el-Arab (2008)* focuses on culture and competition too, as it stars Angelina Fares who launches a battle to try and participate in Israel's national beauty pageant. Mara'ana's additional films, *Al-Jisr* (2004), *Badal* (2006), *Three Times Divorced* (2007), *77 Steps* (2010), and *Write Down, I Am an Arab* (2014), lifted women's voices while not sparing her sharp criticism of patriarchy throughout.

Centering on the physical destruction and pain caused to human bodies, the backdrop of rubbles framing the films about Jenin discussed in Chapter 1 begs an account of the longer histories and deeper workings of ruination, and of reconstruction and remembrance, in and of Palestine. In *Jenin Jenin*, soon after situating us audience in the ruined camp, the film immediately, almost simultaneously, also takes us to Saffurriya of 1948. Bakri walks into the ruins of the Jenin refugee camp and, there, a man in the background calls "I am Saffuri, my friend … Saffuri," orienting the film toward historic Palestine. Amid the rubbles of a tragedy of a near past, more and more scattered narrations of the Nakba and traces of Palestine rise to the surface to join the identification with Saffuri as the film moves along. "In 1948 we went through the same suffering, but it's worse this time," says another old man who was shot in his hand and foot. Palestine persistently dwells not only in the hearts and mouths of those old enough to remember 1948 but, as *Arna's Children* stressed, the children and youth of Jenin carry Palestine with them and forward just as much. These ruins of and in *Jenin Jenin*, Nurit Gertz and George Khleifi suggest, always reverberate with the "language, structure of description, and terms taken from another trauma, that of 1948."[4] *Since You Left* too highlights the theme of return that *Jenin Jenin* harbingers, as Bakri's journeys take him from Nazareth, through the Jalame checkpoint, Jenin, then all the way to Rome, and back to his hometown of El-Baeina, within the Green Line. The filmmakers who examined embodied experiences of pain in Jenin were prompted by the attacks on Jenin in 2002 as well as the killing of the unarmed protesters in October 2000, identifying with the national and overall struggle to end the occupation of Palestine. The films analyzed below, complementarily, go back to '48 Palestine—Israel—to consider the structural conditions informing the prolonged collective distress of Palestinians, on their present everyday lives, and spoken languages, all across Palestine. Writing about contemporary Palestinian fiction cinema, Helga Tawil-Souri encourages us to discern how Palestinian films "collectively communicate that Palestine is the disappeared past/places, and the shrinking contemporary reality of the Territories, and the pan-territorialized experience of exile, and an uncertain future, and more. Neither Ramallah nor Beirut alone does Palestine make; so too, neither 1948 Galilee nor 1998 Shatilla nor 2009 Jaffa, and neither the 'non-place' of outer space. Rather it is the negotiation of these spaces and the im/mobilities they engender that are part and parcel of Palestinian spatiality. In other words, the real and the cinematic Palestine is multi-fold and multisituated."[5] Mostly taking place in '48 Palestine, imagery of the outer space of the moon, the refugee camp in Jenin where Saad lives, and the exile in the United Kingdom where Suaad resides, are all part of the documentary performance that I analyze. Tawil-Souri helps us see the Palestine of the disappeared past as constantly reappearing within the real and representational flow linking the different places of an inside-out, complete Palestine together.

Ayn-Hawd: The Moon

Seated on a plastic chair in the midst of the everyday happenings of the outdoors, Muhammad Abd al-Raouf Abu al-Hayja introduces himself and his family, and recounts a central occurrence in their history in *500 Dunam on the Moon*. "I was born in this village, which we call Ayn-Hawd, after our old village. Until 1948 my family lived in Ayn-Hawd, which today is an artists' colony." This piece of information is followed by a pause that amplifies anticipation for further details on what has occurred until, and during, 1948. Yet when Abu al-Hayja's words reappear, they skip right to providing the outcomes of the occurrences, elaborating neither on that which had been ceased by it, nor about the course of it: "after the war, the residents of Ayn-Hawd, who numbered 900 people, were dispersed." Abu al-Hayja stresses that "we were expelled but became refugees on our land, 1.5 kilometers from the village in which we lived for some 900 years." Around his chair and through his words the new Ayn-Hawd receives a name and some visibility, thus acquiring our recognition. And yet, as the back of the DVD cover of the film previews, "this new Ayn-Hawd cannot be found on official maps, as Israeli law doesn't recognize it."[6] In this opening, *500 Dunam on the Moon* paves the path to challenge the situation of nonrecognition at hand, by asking us spectators to see and hear Muhammad, and better understand where he is at. Some of the residents of the old Ayn-Hawd are among the '48 Palestinians defined as "present absentees," many of whom are of the Abu al-Hayja family.[7] Establishing its new legal framework, the state of Israel has formed laws that legalize the appropriation of lands of exiled Palestinians. According to the Law of Property of the Absentees

I was born in this village,

Figure 17 *500 Dunam on the Moon*, Muhammad Abu al-Hayja, "I was born in this village."
Cinematography for *500 Dunam on the Moon*: Philippe Bellaïche.

from 1950, Palestinians were prohibited from returning to their homes, as the state attempted to congregate as many of them as possible in limited and segregated areas. Until 1960, some hundred thousands of dunams were confiscated by the government, the local municipalities, and/or the JNF.[8] Yet the Abu al-Hayjas defied the attempts to relocate them, and resettled on a slope to the east of their lost home—a land officially recognized as owned by the Israel Land Administration and maintained by the JNF.[9] Although the new Ayn-Hawd was preliminarily recognized by the government in 1994, the master plans necessary for the minimal development of the village had to wait another decade for ratification..

The intertwined now and then of Ayn-Hawd continues to appear in Abu al-Hayja's testimony, when he unpacks the events of the year 1965 to further illuminate the outcomes of the 1948 war. "In 1965," Abu al-Hayja proceeds from his spot on the plastic chair, "the Israeli government ordered the Ministry of Interior to draft a map demarcating the cities and villages. A zoning map of Israel." Abandoning the official rhetoric at this point, Abu al-Hayja describes how, in drafting the map, the Israeli authorities decided to omit some "Arab presence in Palestine." "Naturally," Abu al-Hayja ironizes, "a village like ours wasn't included on the map of Israel." As Abu al-Hayja speaks, the old map appears, providing a guided tour through the names of the towns and villages that once were, and no longer are, part of the cartographic image and living texture of Palestine: to visually illustrate the verbally made point, the screen also draws our eyes closer to the word "Ayn-Hawd." As the speech articulations and moving images draw an analogy between the graphic and the verbalized Ayn-Hawds, it becomes clear that, in order to observe the old Ayn-Hawd on the map, one would need to look for the pre-1948 version that still showed the old one or, otherwise, physically go visit the new version of it on the ground. In other words, it is possible to think of the new Ayn-Hawd not only as a residential replacement but also as a commemorative, three-dimensional monument, standing for the vanished two-dimensional mark on the map. Abu al-Hayja communicates how "using this map, they [the Israeli government] drafted plans as if these villages didn't exist. So on top of our village they planned the Carmel National Park." As a result of the decision, the village residents were forced to endure new suffocating boundaries. The military forces "gathered the people, put barbed wire around the village and said all the land outside the wire is theirs, and the land inside the wire is ours. Inside the wire … the few houses we live in. Outside the wire was the land that we farmed and lived from." On top of that, the trees planted outside the wire further fostered the new imprisonment, as "they came and planted cypress trees among the olives." Abu al-Hayja's statement refers to the making of his family's place of residence into a national reserve and a fire zone overnight, following the passing of the Planning and Construction Law in 1965. All the spontaneous relations that the residents maintained with their environment until then were thus severed: the cultivation of their terraces that were full of fruit trees, for example, had to cease, and the untended terraces eventually withered.[10] Here, Abu al-Hayja also verbalizes a common case where the state of Israel, if to use Irus Braverman's words, makes "mundane uses of law and landscape in the national war between Israelis and Palestinians."[11] Braverman described Zionist afforestation as means of naturalization of the land that is used as "a convenient cover for state power"[12] by rendering the planting of trees not a political but, rather, a "neutral, inevitable, and immutable"[13] activity. For the Israelis, the materialization of the National Park described by Abu al-Hayja was a symbolic national and nativist project of breathing life into and endowing presumable "higher truths" to the land. Braverman detailed at length the ritualistic meaning of the "enthusiastic act of planting trees for the Zionist project,"[14] adding that the ideational and ideological planting practices presume and promote a binary polarization delimitating olive and pine trees, "wild trees and human forests," according to which "the forest is considered human made" and "wild trees are regarded as natural."[15] Under this discursive dichotomic equation that dates back to the British mandate in Palestine and generally references colonial and orientalist practices, Zionists, and later Israelis, embraced the planting of pine forest trees, such as cypresses. For, as Abu al-Hayja phrased, "nature, for these authorities, is a sterile entity … in a gradual process of limitations, marginalization, and discipline of movement and employment, the life tissue of an Arab rural community has deteriorated."[16] Thus, the wire that Abu al-Hayja discusses is another way in which the state implements its division between the natural and the human: segregating where the Ayn-Hawd residents "live in" from that which they "live from" in effect denies the instrumental, material, and cultural meaning of the olive trees for the humans who depend on them, as if rendering the olives nature's excessive error.

The planting of forests as national park projects and the polarization between the pine and the olive tree,[17] the sovereign Zionists and the disturbing Palestinians,[18] are structurally embedded in Zionist and Israeli legal and cultural discourse. However, it is important here to attune to the minute details of Abu al-Hayja's testimony, as it emphasizes his lived experiences under the oppression of the map and of those discourses, verifying just how much power a graphic or legal construct can acquire. Braverman shows that while afforestation laws and ordinances proclaim to protect both the pine as well as the olive (and carob too, on which I will say more momentarily) trees, they are posed as perpetual rivals on the ground, with the latter much more inclined to be relentlessly uprooted than the former.[19] Abu al-Hayja, however, indicates the constant encounters and inevitable fusion of the allegedly distinct genuses, telling us that the state planted the pine trees "*among the olives*" (my emphasis), thus merging the legally and commonly discursively separate species of vegetation into one geographic field. Naama Meishar indeed briefly states that "the JNF planted the orchards *over with* cypress trees" (my emphasis).[20] Here, it is possible to posit this refrain from uprooting the olive trees and understand it as an active doing: rather than standing in the way of the Zionist project of planting the cypresses, the olives assist them in their cultivation and corroboration of the Hebrew identity of the land and the Hebrew self as allegedly naturally belonging to it. Most importantly here, on the very everyday level of experience that Abu al-Hayja speaks about, this is also a process that is supposed to dissociate the olives from any human connotation as interconnection to the very real human lives of the Ayn-Hawd Palestinian residents. The Zionist afforestation mission of planting of cypresses among the olives thus acts like a depoliticizing conceptual sculpture: it is as if the cypresses strove to suckle the Palestinianness out of the olives, empty them from their various political contextual significances, and disconnect the human from their land and trees, in this way fragmenting their sense of identification with that land—that is, with their home.

Similar to the conquest, remapping, and renaming of places in Palestine, the physical appropriation of the olive trees and other trees in Palestine and their discursive resignification in Modern Hebrew go hand in hand, underlying the constitution of the Israeli Hebrew-speaking subject and culture.[21] These trends are also markedly orientalist. As is the case with many new names for Israeli places, the choice of the name Ein-Hod for the new Israeli colony built on the ruins of Ayn-Hawd follows the Zionist orientalist perception of Arabic names as authentic,[22] and rendering them as merely sounds that a new word and name bases itself on. Yet the Hebraization of space through naming would not be sufficient for the Zionists: for, they also need to substantiate their naming as unconditionally right, and show that the names they grant are the only possible way to reliably refer to these places. The orientalist categorization of olives as wild nature serves as a complementary orientalist practice, enhancing the Zionist project of renaming and remapping. Precisely because they are delimited from the intentionally planted and humanly designed forest, the discursively naturalized and presumably wild olives compensate for the alleged artificialness of afforestation, thus substantiating the Zionist ideational claim for real rootedness in the place. The presence of olive trees that are constructed as natural organisms "assists" as they endow, perhaps literally feed, the planted cypresses with the legitimate character as natural. After Daniel Monk, it is possible to call Zionist planners and planters "instrumental orientalists," for whom "orientalism as a discipline establishes dominance over an imaginary domain and rehearses there, within the space of representation, the West's historical cathexis with the actual Orient of material history."[23]

How does the system of non/recognition operate to excavate a fantasized realness and disregard an actual existence? This is what the young girl who appears with Abu al-Hayja in several scenes throughout *500 Dunam on the Moon* wants to know. "Isn't this the moon? Why is there writing on it? Why isn't it like the real moon that we see up in the sky?" the girl asks him while sitting by his side and pointing to some framed image which itself turns its back and sharpens its edges against us spectators. Abu al-Hayja responds to her, "They've divided it into sections. This area belongs to someone. This belongs to someone else. It's been partitioned," he explains, passing his fingers as if drawing parallel lines on the image. Thus, while the girl wishes that there would be a compatibility between the real and the image, Abu al-Hayja has to disappoint her and didactically explain how this system of representation in front of her works. "Ahhh, now I get it … now I get it," the girl understands. In this scene, the desired real is taken over by the imaged and dividing lines marked by someone else, now understood as that which can be represented by a set of segregated sections that carry written letters. Just as the invisible image of the moon that the girl addresses desired, decoded, deformed, and perhaps even destroyed, the real of the moon, the map of Israel has ordered the devouring of the olives through imposing its methods of re-signification on them. At the same time, this imposition conceals itself by purporting a referential connection to the wild and natural, real olives of Eretz-Israel. To put this more firmly: this zoning of Palestine through an employment of a Hebrew index, paralleling to renaming it as Eretz-Israel, exhibits what may be called a Zionist desire to naturalize and depoliticize the land as "the real." As my following analysis of the next scene indicates, not only vegetation, but architecture too, is utilized to enhance the interrelated and subsequent Zionist projects of re-signifying the (Palestinian) land and (Hebrew) body.

Ein-Hod: The Appropriated Stone

As the case of the olive trees teaches us, remnants of Palestinian culture are to be sought right in the midst of the erecting Israeli endeavors. In order to find the old Ayn-Hawd *500 Dunam on the Moon* takes us on a visit to Ein-Hod. To locate and look at the lost village, one needs to rewind the film by few minutes to the former scene that departs from the new Ayn-Hawd and travels back to the spirits of the old Ayn-Hawd residing in Ein-Hod. This journey back thus unavoidably tracks down a leap forward as well: Ein-Hod was built in the stead and future of the old Ayn-Hawd, and precipitated the foundation of the new Ayn-Hawd. "The view: Marcel Janco's Ein-Hod. The place: the Ein-Hod artists' colony. Once it was an abandoned

Arab village on the foothills of the Carmel, filled with ruins, without a living soul; today it is an artists' colony," the authoritative voiceover of the Zionist archival footage about the colony's formation informs us. Alternating between black-and-white and color images of stone houses and arches, figurative and abstract artwork, the voiceover explicates that Jewish Israeli artists "discovered" the village," and "began to fix it up"; nowadays, "the talents of the Ein-Hod residents can be seen in every corner," he summarizes. "The place was an 'abandoned Arab village,' replete with 'scenes of biblical desolation,'" Susan Slyomovics critically cites the common descriptions of the Ein-Hod artists of the new colony.[24] Slyomovics sees these descriptions as "full circularity, a kind of intertextuality of reinforced beliefs," containing repeated "key words and phrases"; it is on this intertextuality that the scene comments. In particular, Slyomovics elaborated on the recurrent employment of the word "ruins"—"hurvot" in Hebrew—which, ascribed to the different stone structures ubiquitously found in Ein-Hod, "features prominently in every discussion."[25] In this context, the term "ruins" indicates the utilization of Palestinian stone structures as aesthetic objects and/or architectural elements for the construction of private and public residences. "Ruins are to be understood as anonymous creations from the ancient past,"[26] which was "redefined to encompass the many centuries in which Arabs inhabited Ayn-Hawd."[27] Then as today, "the Israelis of Ein-Hod live in an Arab Palestinian past, an architectural past."[28]

"This is an olive press house. Here they used to make olive oil. I don't want to make olive oil, no, I'm an artist, an artiste! So what do I do? I take this example, yes, this olive press house, and make it into a gallery!" the Ein-Hod tour guide declares in the scene that follows the archival presentation of Ein-Hod. Slyomovics elaborates on the artistic vision of Ein-Hod as conceptualized by Romanian-born Dada artist and architect Marcel Janco. A former participant in the avant-garde activities of Dada, Janco was appointed by the state of Israel to establish the artists' colony of Ein-Hod in 1953, on—and importantly, with—the remnants of the Ayn-Hawd that was depopulated in 1948. Demonstrating "the ways in which Zionism and Dada, two seemingly unrelated movements, have intersected and sustained each other,"[29] Slyomovics mentions the overlapping ideology and strategies of the Zionist settlers and/as Dadaist artists. Janco and his followers "privileged especially the primitive and naïve craftsworker, and the local, traditional, vernacular material culture," which resulted in "preserving yet adapting the surviving Arab architecture."[30] The Dada Zionists wanted to touch original objects, natural colors, and primordial sensations, and romantically fantasized the stone structures as abstract remnants of the archaic orient. The Hebrewness of the stone structures cannot be textually corroborated by biblical references; but it suffices that they are imagined as backward innocent realness fixed in the far ahistorical past. The Zionist discursive operation of naming structures as "ruins" in Ein-Hod works in line with the remapping of the olive trees in the new Ayn-Hawd. Stripped of their context of the Palestinian human, practical, cultural, and historical settings they emerged in, the trees and structures newly marked in Israel are appropriated as well as depoliticized—with depoliticization assisting in denying that the appropriation ever took place.

To that end, the two scenes examine the deliberate disappearing of Ayn-Hawd within Zionist discourse. The scenes demonstrate how, rather than simply coming to existence after the elimination of another village, Ein-Hod is grounded in Zionist discourse and built on the erasure of the old Ayn-Hawd. Yet the scenes nevertheless emphasize the significance of the "ruins" as retrieved monuments. "Ruins are not just found. They are *made*" (emphasis in the original),[31] Ann Laura Stoler affirmed in conceptualizing "ruination." More than merely demolition, ruination may mark a productive constitution of "compounded layers of imperial debris" that "do" rather than solely are.[32] "A virulent verb," ruination expands on the perception of ruins as "sites of reflection—of pensive rumination" that, like the Ein-Hod stone structures, "condense[s] alterative senses of history."[33] Similarly, Monk determined that the work of "instrumental orientalists" eventually "cannot but be condemned to the status of a 'second nature' (or a 'fallen nature'), in all its brutality, precisely because it enters into a chain of eternal sameness that works through the very idea of 'natural history.'" Like the "naturally wild" olive trees, the stone structures depoliticized as "ruins" still stand as solid reminders of the exploitative act.

After Abu al-Hayjas's testimonies and the hegemonic introduction of Ein-Hod, the film travels to the interior spaces of Jewish Israeli homes in Ein-Hod. An unnamed family greets the filmmaker and her crew in Hebrew at the threshold of their new house in Ein-Hod. Rather than composing a temporally based narrative like Abu al-Hayja, the anonymous Jewish Israeli Hebrew-speaking man welcomes the filmmaker to an instructed tour inside the whims of an interior space currently under construction. "We simply went from arch to arch in the village, took their exact measurements, and reproduced them. Our conception was that the people who used to live here brought their materials from nearby … so that's what we did. We brought materials from nearby," the man initially clarifies. In line with this praxis of replication, the man concludes: "In fact, what needed to happen was to take the Arab construction, which is actually a style that developed here over the years, and use it as a starting point for developing an Israeli style … so, if this developed here over time, why not take it as a model and emulate it?" Functioning as an attempt for resolution, the specific details that the man provides in between the two statements illuminate: "They used to bring wood from Lebanon, known in Arabic as 'Qutran,' but it's difficult to obtain—only from demolished houses. So we wanted to get wood like that, but couldn't." To overcome this "problem," at hand, the man suggests that "what we could do is get it for the windows, because it could be polished—the windows are made from old wood collected from demolished houses." Within this flux of desire, admiration, inability, and recovery, the man would have wanted the Arab construction to remain intact so that he could imitate its aesthetic principles but, alas, would have to solely recycle the very raw substance from which the lost and longed-for structures were made of.

The attempt to reason the lack of wood soon becomes a quarrel, when a woman's voice disrupts the scene. On the face of it, the woman is just clarifying what the man was saying earlier: "Actually, this entire house was built from houses demolished in Haifa. The stones outside aren't new. They're from demolished houses," she adds.

Figure 18 *500 Dunam on the Moon*, Jewish-Israeli man, "took their exact measurements and reproduced them."

The woman frames the making of their home precisely as a ruination: the practice of construction underpinned by demolition. The timing and fashion of her clarification render the subject of demolition as highly significant too. Sitting next to the abovementioned man—her partner—the woman blatantly intrudes the man precisely as he was trying to verbalize why the "the Arab construction"—provider of architectural models and Lebanese wood—suddenly vanished. "There was a war," the man was saying before this interruption, "in fact, I often ponder over it. There was a living culture here … we're living in a place that … we don't even know the … all of a sudden there was a kind of culture ceasing … and … " the rest is cut-off. As the three dots—appearing in the original subtitles—indicate, neither the man nor we spectators know what he was going to say next. This mention of a war that certainly was and passed, but also apparently lingers in the mouths of speakers and writers about Ein-Hod, is ubiquitous in Hebrew spoken language.[34] Trying to gather fragments of the ceasing of the Arab culture in the area, the Israeli man is cut-off by the woman, thereby resolutely unable to enclose his statement—as the woman's silencing interference affirms that recognizing the existence of Palestine and Palestinian culture prior to 1948 is too threatening. Instead, she impedes the acknowledgment, renders it dialogic, and seemingly changes the subject: she thus explicitly causes and reassures the negation of that which could have been otherwise recognized. "What conditions the core endeavor of the consolidation of our house and of ourselves is the utilization of demolished stones in an alleged available space," the woman says. Moreover, her spoken utterance performs and perpetuates the silencing prohibition on talking about the Arab Palestinians' former presence in, and possession of, their land, and their temporal, spatial, and cultural routines.

Thus, when the woman is saying, "The demolition of random houses for the recycling of elementary resources is inevitable to structuring our home," we are actually able to attend and interpret it as follows: "The very anonymous fragments composing the household we are constructing were initially and formatively earned through a demolition and a denial." In other words, by abruptly recalling demolition as necessary for Israeli homemaking, she exposes the verbal denials that condition this construction. Here, the woman's underscored usage of the word "demolition" assists in reminding us that a denial inherently conditions every Zionist construction—material and/or discursive—in the colony of Ein-Hod. As I now show, this denial translates into an active silencing of anyone trying to tell the history of Israel-Palestine, especially Palestinians, as a verbally reiterated dispossession of their trees and other things that mean home, and the fragmentation of Palestinians' sense of belonging to everything Palestine.

Jenin Refugee Camp: The Lost Carob

While one of the film's trajectories directs us to a possibility of identifying the persistent trees, structures, and objects of the old Ayn-Hawd, another, albeit more winding way, points to the impossibility of embarking on the trajectory of return for Palestinians—for now. As Muhammad Abu al-Hayja closes his monologue, *500 Dunam on the Moon* takes us to Jenin where some others of the Abu Al-Hayja family members have been living in a refugee camp since 1948. Sitting in a shadowed passageway, between several walls and staircases, under the sound of the muezzin, the Abu al-Hayjas in Jenin say their names and state their affiliation to the old Ayn-Hawd. Of special interest is the story of Sa'ad Abu al-Hayja who, right after recounting the Zionist violent conquest of Ayn-Hawd, recalls a subsequent verbal violent silencing that he experienced years after. Sa'ad tells us about the carob trees that, similar to the olive trees, still stand in front of his house yard in the eastern bloc of the old Ayn-Hawd—which is now the new Ein-Hod. "I went there, saw the carobs, and I wanted one," he explains, lifting one finger, as well as his eyes, upward, to reenact his place under the carob tree. "I threw a pebble on a carob, and got it," Sa'ad affirms. While able to get the carob, Sa'ad concludes his testimony saying, "After that, we never returned." Sa'ad reasons this henceforth inability to return by describing the encounter he had with a Jewish Israeli resident of Ein-Hod, who assaulted Sa'ad verbally and silenced him. "Why are you throwing stones at the carob?" the Israeli man blamed him. After Sa'ad assertively said, "This carob is mine, and I wanted one," the Israeli man informed him that the carob is not his but, rather, "used to be" his. "I didn't tell you to leave it," he added. After recreating that hurtful interaction, Sa'ad stares at the camera, silent, reenacting that state of shock he was in after being brutally silenced, and asks the filmmaker, and us: "See?"

Figure 19 *500 Dunam on the Moon*, Sa'ad, "and I wanted one [carob]."

While able to approach the abandoned physical remnants on the ground once, Sa'ad is hindered from again returning to that which he had lost—his house, his trees, and his carobs. Beyond their arches, houses, and trees—which are, already, so much—that have been stolen from Sa'ad and the other Palestinians, something else has also been, and is, constantly afflicted upon them, as they live through an ongoing physical and affective experience of a refused return. Similar to the olive tree, the carob tree too received legislative protection by both the British mandate and the state of Israel.[35] Yet the carob tree lacks biblical reference, and is posited as an immigrating plant and Talmudic textual trope within the national and natural intertwined canons.[36] While the carob tree did not earn the special Zionist treatment that its fellow olive tree did, this ideological neglect provides us with an opportunity to unpack Sa'ad's performance while thinking through the carobs differently. In Sa'ad's testimony, I not only find the lost carobs but also track down the abandoned stones. The speech practice of the Israeli man that Sa'ad encountered in Ein-Hod deprived Sa'ad of his right to name the carob as his own, and later return for another one: he cannot have it since it is part of the carob tree that has been appropriated from him. If rephrased, the Israeli man's speech act implies that "if the house and the tree are not yours anymore, then none of their components can be yours either." Let us note Sa'ad's emphasis on his ongoing attachment to his singular carob, rather than the carobs and/or carob tree. By particularly referring to the fruit of the carob rather than the entire tree that he grabbed but cannot reclaim or return to, Sa'ad reenacts and relives not only the Zionist acts of appropriation but also those of ruination—a ruination of a life and its essential attachments. The carob here is one of many residual fragments of a life, community, culture, people, and bodies once in vibrant touch with and now removed and disjointed from not only its lands, houses, and trees but also its "smaller things," such as fruit and stones. Unlike the stone structures and olive trees, some specific "things" cannot be claimed as such, for they were fragmented, deconstructed, and thus altogether dissociated, and violently, physically detached and disjointed, from the wholesome entity and signifier that coheres, names, and defines them—such as the stone structure or tree. While inherent to all acts of appropriation and re-signification discussed above, it is harder to discern a deprival when that which has been confiscated is but a singular carob of an entire demolished entity. Indeed, instrumentally, the utilization of a stone from an unknown structure demolished elsewhere and embedded in an ambiguous context resonates with the confiscation of carobs from Sa'ad. Yet the carob in Sa'ad's dialogic reenactment also foregrounds an act of disjoining that is connotative of the demolition of the stone structure into their stone components: if the carob no longer is Sa'ad's, then Sa'ad is no longer solidly and wholly who he was when he lived close to the carob tree, in his house, in his yard, as a Palestinian in Palestine. The challenging endeavor of communicating such a subtle yet significant silencing, lingering fragmentation of Palestinianness is precisely what the scene accomplishes.

This scene culminates the film's accounts on the depoliticization of the appropriated and/or demolished Palestinian things that make up a home/land such as trees and stone structures, exploring their interrelated manifestation as a silencing occurring in conversation. Hindering Sa'ad's continuous relation to elementary and unmarked "things" such as carobs is an attempt to break the cohesion of Sa'ad's identification with Ayn-Hawd, so that he cannot taste an immediate connection to his home. Yet while Sa'ad determines to "never return" after the incident of silencing, he also, importantly, had already returned one time, and is telling us audience about it. He is telling us how silencing works to keep Palestinians away from their belongings. The power of the scene lies where the pebble meets the carob to endeavor the devouring of that which is Sa'ad's own. The documentary performance of Sa'ad thus reiterates, demonstrates, and resists silencing, to become a scene and a rehearsal of a return, inspiring us to think about it as a future possibility. By pointing his finger up to the carob as that thing which he obtained, Sa'ad emphasizes those singular components surviving the destruction—such as stones, and such as himself. Sa'ad consumes the carob, thus relating to it and becoming one with it, and together they belong to a larger entity of being.

Route 181: *The Map*

Whereas the map appears only here and there in *500 Dunam on the Moon*, it is a central trope upon which *Route 181* builds its formation. Outlining Khleifi and Sivan's plan for the film, the voiceover that opens *Route 181* informs: "For

this journey in their homeland, they drew a route on a roadmap and called it
'Route 181'… their journey across route 181 goes through the partition border, a
border that has never come to existence." A thick marking line then makes its way
from the bottom of the screen upward and inscribes the partition lines against
the backdrop of a contemporary map of Israel, thus intruding the product and
procedure of the current predominant systems of mapping. Subsequently, a 1947
map of the area enters the frame as well; deploying the partition plan, this map
contains designations of Palestinian existence before their destruction in 1948.
Conceptualizing the trip ahead on a map that was never actualized, the filmmakers
wish to bring back a time before the drawing of the map of Israel to subvert the
prevalent perception of the place formerly known as Palestine.

In *The Right to Look*, Nicholas Mirzeoff coined the term *visuality* to describe "the
making of the processes of 'history' perceptible to authority"; to "present authority
as self-evident," Mirzeoff explains, "visuality classifies by naming, categorizing,
and defining … visuality separates … it makes this separated classification seem
right and hence aesthetic";[37] in this way, "visuality sutures authority to power and
renders this association 'natural.' "[38] Yet as Mirzeoff proceeded to show, far from
vigilantly competent and victoriously omnipresent, visuality may be and has been
constantly contested by actions of *countervisuality*, carrying with them "the claim
for the right to look," and to "decolonize the real" and to "imagine new realities."[39]
Reinscribing the forgotten map of unrealized partition on the contemporary map
of Israel, the act of drawing the line lining in the opening scene is such an act of
countervisuality, as it reclaims the national authoritative graphic signification of
space—such as the 1965 map that redesigned the lives of the Abu al-Hayjas in
500 Dunam on the Moon. In Mirzeoff's words, the renewed map "predicated a
different possible means of imagining the real," as it "offer[s] a different possibility
of real existence."[40] Mirzeoff then further asks, "How can a right to look, framed
in the language of Western colonial jurisprudence, be sustained as the place of the
[de]colonized inside history?"[41] If countervisuality draws from and dwells within
discourses of visuality, then how can the former display its dissent to the latter?
Accordingly, the question persists: Can the pre-1948 model of mapping, here
inspiring the old/new map, be completely vacant of any colonizing Eurocentric
singularist viewpoint such that the maps that design national parks manifest? As
Nabil I. Matar demonstrated, the cartographic prototype of Palestine as a biblical
desolation lacking any population dates back to as early as 1570.[42] May any map
of Palestine alter its historical and foundational "viscously unique status of a
'meta-land'?"[43] One possible thread that may lead us in that general direction is
insinuated in one of Matar's first points in the essay, when he paraphrased Foucault
and asked: "What are the rules that 'allow the construction of a map'?"[44]

As the opening scene of the film progresses, stills and moving images shuffle
while multilingual subtitles translate verbal content into visual format and vice
versa. Also, literal messages collide with, and transform into, formal layouts,
while lines and stains simultaneously condense into comprehensible captions.
In this way, the solidity and coherence of the map are deconstructed; the scene
thus tasks not to replace visuality's printed product of colonial signification as

spatialization but to point to its instability as an objective artifact of realism, and to the possibility of alternativity. Seconds before the journey begins, a black stick cuts through the frame, tearing down the old/new partition map. Translating physical space into a two-dimensional paper product the map here thus also occupies space, becoming an actual physical and multidimensional object. It may thus be challenged by an alternative graphic proposition as well as corrupted by an aggressive act of scratching and slandering, as its material existence impacts as well as limits its functional capability as a navigating tool. With this allegory, the film now shifts to the cinematic journey itself. The difficult negotiations between visuality and territory remain the setting of the film throughout, while the presence, performance, and responsibility of the people that the filmmakers meet comes to the forefront.

Kibbutz Gezer and Abu Shusha

Inspired by Deleuze and Guattari, Gil Hochberg addressed the possible conjunctions of territories and language, stressing the "metaphorical imagination of language as a territory: a well-defined terrain to which 'one belongs,' to which 'one returns' and into which one does, or does not, allow others to enter."[45] Discussing Hebrew literature primarily, Hochberg centered language "imagined as a cultural territory" to critique the possessive claim that Zionists imposed over Hebrew through modernizing biblical Hebrew, Jewish religion, and ethnicity.[46] Similar to Hochberg and some of the novelists she read, Khleifi and Sivan go out to travel within the spatial realized realms of hegemonic Hebrew, both metaphorizing and referring to the territorial terrain of Israel that is resulting from visuality. Down from the smooth speedway and up on an unpaved road, the car and camera slowly drive straight toward a pedestrian passing by who soon clears the way for them; as the car gradually slows down, the passerby turns to the driving filmmakers and opens an instructive conversation. "Gezer?" the passerby asks, referring to a Jewish Israeli residence that earned its name from an ancestral biblical venue; without waiting for an answer, he diligently begins to provide directions, thus prematurely assuming the destination of the filmmakers. Setting the tone for the rest of the scene, the passerby confidently subscribes to a realist and referential discursive status quo of visuality between modernized Hebrew and the ground under his interlocutors' feet. The usage of the Hebrew name to signify the space both sets the terms for the verbal exchanges to follow and serves as an imperative for further orientating the filmmakers' journey.

Quickly, however, the conversation goes astray; noncoincidently, this occurs right with the incorporation of Arabic. "So this is what was Abu Shusha … no, El-Qbab?" Sivan suddenly, seemingly innocently and somewhat confusedly, asks, immediately arousing the passerby's stammer as a result: "Eh … hmm … opposite of here, on the hill, where … where the … pines are," the passerby replies, uncomfortably vacillating in and out of the frame, "that was Abu Shusha." With one short yet poignant question, Sivan manages to introduce an unwelcomed intruder—the Arabic—to the seemingly stable status quo. Sivan's act of renaming in Arabic abruptly attends a conversation anticipated to be conducted in Hebrew solely, disrupting the anticipated discursive conditions of this small talk by dropping the Arabic bomb right into the hegemonic Hebrew. Resurrecting the Arabic name of the place from the depths of the repressed, Sivan's act also disconnects the Hebrew name Gezer from the space to which it is commonly ascribed—denaturalizing the highly accepted and rarely contested status quo of the occupying Hebrew language and the land beneath it—and contributes to their conceptual divorce. Sivan simply takes Hebrew for a short walk in the destabilizing districts of Arabic naming, encouraging us audience to question the entire apparatus by which language and territory engage in an uncritical, referential tango of presumable mirrors. Sivan thus elevates the constructive mechanism of mapping to the conscious cinematic surface.

Introducing constructivism here prefigures the deconstruction of Jewish Israeli identity. Central to the modernization and revival of Hebrew, Hochberg highlighted, is the Zionist figure of the New Jew, who performs a Westernized nationalism and masculinity in his alleged authentic homeland in the East.[47] The precursor of Modern Hebrew, the New Jew employs and embodies the renewed language "which was itself considered not only 'authentically Jewish' but also 'masculine.'"[48] Seemingly exemplary of the New Jew, the passerby is somewhat perplexed when Sivan deflects the direction of his Hebrew narration as hegemonic navigation and asks: "Where are you from originally?" "In this country? Yahud," the passerby quickly and symbolically utters, reluctantly already facilitating Sivan's next question: "And before that?" Here, the passerby halts, calculates, and answers: "I was brought here. No one asked me. My parents brought me. If they'd ask me I would say no." "Where from though?" Sivan pushes for the last time "My parents are from Russia," the passerby finally falls to the trapping thralls of full disclosure. After much concentrated effort, Sivan thus manages to send the passerby back and away, to one of the many places where Jewish existence evades and exceeds the identiterian confines of the New Jew: the homeland of old Jew and/as Ost-Jude.[49] Directing the passerby there is also Sivan's way to highlight his literal and metaphorical stance as a passerby.

In a sense, Sivan's diasporization of the passerby similarly equates the latter's position and situation to that of the deported Palestinian; here, however, as one of the passerby's passing, yet not least important, comment demonstrates, the passerby is not like the Palestinian but he does rely on them. Just before he is cast aside, the passerby attempts to tighten his grip on the grounds for a little longer. Still pointing to the pines that replaced the wrecks of Palestinian villages, the passerby smilingly utters: "Come, I also have a beautiful landscape view ... come film!" This polite and seemingly innocent invite ends up outing the passerby's bewilderment in the face of Sivan's question. While "also" here might mean "like the view from Gezer" it also just might mean "like the view from, or of, or on, the old destroyed Abu Shusha." Tacitly and reluctantly, as his "also" reintroduces and re-presents the absence of the village into the hegemonic Hebrew, the passerby renders the specter of the village an object compatible and crucial for convoluted comparisons.

Metaphorically and more profoundly, he also marks loss and disappearance as the necessary activity preceding colonial establishment and existence. Today nothing but a commemorative name, Abu Shusha, is thus revealed to function as the very discursive platform upon which the Jewish Israeli Hebrew speaker constitutes his red-roofed home as well as his authoritative gaze. Here, it is the wreckage of the Palestinian village that conditions the Jewish Israeli colonial cultural project in Palestine. Sivan wants the passerby to look down in acknowledgment that his secure home by the beautiful landscape view is built on destruction, if only for few minutes, perhaps hoping to make him feel some shame. Neither he nor we, however, hear anything too substantial about Abu Shusha itself. The car now drives by to speak to one of the people most affected by the new precarities embedded in the silencing of his and his ancestors' home.

Ayn-Yarka: The Well

Providing but a glimpse of the airy slopes spreading under the road, and submitting to the shadows of the trees lurking from the left, the lens shatters the horizon, allowing the paper road map to support the frame and lead the way. Through these layers of visual forms and forces, and in front of the eyes sitting behind the wheel and the windshield, the protagonist of this next scene emerges. As the car enters the narrow and muddy margins of the road, a young person shepherding his sheep begins to respond to the questions he is asked by the filmmakers who are driving towards him: here, two interlocutors—one with a voice and one with a face—now initiate an interactivity of naming, navigation, and negotiation.

"Where are we?" inquires Khleifi, approaching the shepherd in Arabic; with the map and the passerby's directions, he still seeks to orient himself.. "Ayn-Yarka," the shepherd replies, exacerbating Khleifi's suspicion. "Ayn-Yarka? Is this the Arabic name? Where is the 'ayn' [Arabic and Hebrew for "well" or "fountain"; ayn is sometimes spelled as "ein," as in the film's subtitles] then? Do you use it?" Khleifi thus further stresses. Giggling as his look alternates between the camera and the ground, the shepherd points in the direction of the well—at the end of the trail and outside the frame—and admits that he does not use it. Here, Khleifi's pressing questions insinuate and instantiate a crisis in orientation: traveling through the trail of hegemonic Hebrew as designated by the passerby's instructive speech act, Khleifi's interrogatory performance bears and voices, and also ponders and probes, the specific preceding, presumptive, and oppressive perception of space from and with which he enters the scene. Khleifi's staged reality test is not only unveiled but also dashed, as he is confronted by the unexpected: far from a familiar name that he may relate to either based on the map, the passerby's directions, or his former knowledge, Ayn-Yarka marks no specific symbolic signification. Similar to Abu Shusha, Ayn-Yarka evades the referential status quo of Israeli colonial visuality of the current map. Additionally, however, the latter is also omitted from the pre-Israel map, and probably appears on no map at all; it thus attaches solely to the immediacy of absence and literality. Khleifi is here deprived of that soothing satisfaction of a straight coherent answer.

- Where's this?
- Ein Yarka.

Figure 20 *Route 181*, the shepherd in Ein Yarka.
Cinematography: Philippe Bellaïche.

Leaning on his rod, an antenna popping out of his shirt pocket, the shepherd looks at the camera and then to the ground and replies to Khleifi's tenacious questions: "Kakal allows us to shepherd here, then we leave and go home." Khleifi then further asks the shepherd whether he plans to join the army. "Next year, god willing," the shepherd states, "maybe … 'Mishmar Hagvul.'" In his answers, the shepherd uses terms in Hebrew: Kakal to mean the JNF, and Mishmar Hagvul for the Israeli Border Patrol. "So are you going to beat Arabs? Aren't they of your people, of your religion, the Arabs?" Khleifi asks, bewildered. "The Arabs are dogs!" the shepherd laughs and explains: "Today Arabs and Jews are cousins. You cannot say 'dirty Arab' or 'dirty Jew'; for me, they are all the same. All are completely crazy." Visiting an area consisting of multiple illegalized and unrecognized Bedouin villages around Ramle, Lydda, and the ruins of Abu Shusha, Khleifi assumes the shepherd is Bedouin, and hence asks him about his prospects of joining the IDF—which imposes a mandatory draft on most Bedouins. Yet the shepherd never explicitly identifies as Bedouin. This unconfirmed assumption of Bedouinness is significant: for it speaks to the conditions of precarity embedded in the lives of Bedouin communities striving to survive against the backdrop of Israel's systematic refusal to recognize their right to their lands since 1948. Bedouins have inhabited the Arabian Gulf and the Middle East for centuries, living in the Naqab area specifically since around the seventh century. Today, Bedouins' unrecognized existence is perpetrated by constant home demolition and displacement of their villages and living fabric in the Naqab and north of it.[50] Israel bases this practice of erasure on arbitrarily chosen and written Ottoman laws of land appropriation while ignoring the common custom of respecting Bedouin sovereignty over their lands, practiced by both the Ottomans and the British. Concomitantly, Israeli discourse exoticizes, essentializes, and depoliticizes Bedouinness to refer to abstract nomadic tribal Arab life that, rather than being oppressed, brought backwardness upon itself. Contrary to this hegemonic approach, I suggest that the shepherd's film performance in *Route 181* is in line with Palestinian cultural production from the interior that is responding to Israel's spatial and discursive colonization of Palestine and Palestinians. Let me juxtapose this scene with a landmark novel in the archive of Palestine of the interior: Emile Habiby's *The Secret Life of Saeed, the Ill-Fated Pessoptimist*.

Thirty years before *Route 181*, another man found himself stuck in a place designated on no map, with an antenna and a rod-like object a stake. A young Palestinian refugee who manages to return to his former home of Palestine that has recently turned into Israel, Saeed is the narrator and protagonist of Emile Habiby's *The Secret Life of Saeed*. A high-ranked security agent Adon Safsarsheck, who Saeed says is "a man who was very close to my heart,"[51] allows Saeed to remain in Israel due to his father's connections: "Your father served us. Take this and eat!"[52] Safsarsheck commands giving Saeed food and the dubious right to be his informer. Later in the novel, Saeed finds himself sitting on a "flat surface, cold and round, not more than one yard across ... sitting on the top of a blunt stake."[53] Saeed testifies: "My legs seemed to be dangling over the side of a fathomless pit ... that surrounded me of all sides"[54] Trying to rescue himself by either gripping to, or climbing down from, the stake, Saeed worries: "Is there, then, no place under the sun for me but this stake?"[55]

As noted at the outset in the novel, Saeed writes about, yet not from, the stake, but rather from outer space, where he arrived after an extraterrestrial friend had carried him away from the stake. Cloaking this location with enigmatic ambiguity, the novel contextualizes the site of outer space with neither recognizable connotation nor accessible association to specific spatial signification; however, Saeed's trip to the outside of space informs and forms his very initial entry into the possibility of personal historical narration. "As I write to you on my fantastic mystery," Saeed informs us, "I'm soaring with them high above you."[56] Although narrated subsequently, Saeed's arrival at the allegorical state of the stake may be seen as parallel and symmetrical to his departure to the magical yet metonymical place of outer space: here, stepping out to outer space emphasizes that the outsider's stake is already inherently within the terms of colonization. Thus, rather than reading his trip to outer space and his enforced experiences on the stake linearly and sequentially, it is possible to conceptualize Saeed's entrance into, and/ as departure from, colonized Palestine, as spatially simultaneous, metaphorically symbolizing Israel's occupation of his very existence. These two congruent movements—out and in—instantiate Saeed's return to a homeland formerly familiar and currently estranged, a home appropriated and thus alien to him. Reading the return to the inside and/as retreating to the outside, this multifaceted event blurs the boundaries between inside and outside, insiders and outsiders, and effectively captures the experiences of the returnee back in his home in the interior. Parallel and commensurable places where one is in Palestine while in Israel, outer spaces provide a significant advantage, however. As we learn from Saeed's story, the one in the interior is unable to speak from and about his stake in his own terms—unless, he departs en route to outer space. Only upon his trip to outer space, Saeed may begin to narrate from the stake "His Life in Israel" and his entire family history prior to 1948.

Caught within similarly suffocating confines, the shepherd and Saeed both need to serve the state that has been depriving them of their world. As both Saeed and the shepherd reside in venues that are imprisoned within colonial Israel yet escape the gaze of its official map, their ayns and stakes respectively shed light on their situation of silenced stuckness. And yet, whereas the shepherd persistently, if reluctantly, stays in Israel and, cinematically speaking, within the terms of documentary filmmaking, Saeed yearns for a way out of the reality and realism of Israeli silencing. Here, Habiby's methods of narrating Saeed—the one who returns—and his trips in and/as out of the space occupied by silencing illuminate the shepherd's situated film performance in *Route 181* as the one who remains and endures silencing. The shepherd is trapped within the territory authorized by the hegemonic territory of Modern Hebrew, and the referentiality embedded in the framework of the documentary interview. He testifies his daily entrance and exit to and from the colonized space and, importantly, demonstrates the silencing that is taking place there. Equipped with a canteen and a hat, the shepherd is prepared for a long and durable stay. The shepherd and Saeed practice various tactics of personality presentation and expression of pain to survive and resist humiliation. In *The Secret Life of Saeed*, Saeed dons the antiheroic figure of a fool.[57] Saeed's staged "foolishness" serves to cover up for his words and actions of resistance which otherwise would place him in danger: perceived as an obedient idiot, he is not taken seriously and in this way escapes sanctions. Stupidity thus becomes a useful crack through which he may breathe in his own skin and be forgiven for that. In *Route 181*, the shepherd inhabits a similarly situational submissive stupidity when citing the authority of "Kakal" and repeating the otherwise unknown name "Ayn-Yarka" to his interlocuter. Here, the shepherd's speech recalls the work of another Said, Edward Said, and the chapter he dedicated to '48 Palestinians—Palestinians "min-al-dakhil"—in *After the Last Sky: Palestinian Lives*.[58] There, Said listed creative ways that "help those fil-dakhil to keep their precarious foothold."[59] On one hand, Said observed that "to be on the inside is not to be yourself on the outside world, which means you have to use 'their' codes, but to mean something quite different ... the problem of the inside is that it *is* inside, private, and can never be made plain or evident."[60] Yet at the same time, Said contended, those in the interior develop "special languages—sometimes evasive, always idiosyncratic—that only you and others like you can understand." Practicing repetition as discursive resistance, "those on the inside" are "repeating familiar patterns to the point where repetition itself becomes more important than what is being repeated."[61] I suggest that the shepherd's speech performance may be heard and viewed as the localized verbal and physical vernacular of the one who remains in the Palestine within Israel.

Ayn-Yarka exists, yet evades the referential authority of state violence. Struck by space control, silencing, and stupefication, Ayn-Yarka bewilders and enrages the filmmakers, who rightly and importantly endeavor to break the silence and thread the stories and identities of the currently colonized. Yet the temporary unavailability of the shepherd's personal and collective histories then ends up becoming the point of this scene. Toward the end of the scene, the shepherd takes advantage of the silence informing the conversation and, taking on the role of the interviewer himself, asks Khleifi, "Who are you?" Khleifi, for his part, does not answer. As the shepherd's question remains unattended its reverberations float in the air, calling attention to the filmmakers' position as guests to Ayn-Yarka and to their participation in producing his assumed, ambiguous, performed Bedouin identity. As the scene closes, Khleifi's and Sivan's overturned expectations to derive an informative monologue from the shepherd culminate in a trip to the ayn. There, alas, they find but a small empty well surrounded by a swamp. Yet this failure may be viewed as a success too. For, wells and their documentation are evidence of a past, continuous, and potential future life on the ground that, though currently erased from most maps if not physically shut, may be proven and reclaimed. As Said sharply encapsulated, "Every direct route to the interior, and consequently the interior itself, is either blocked or preempted … the most we can hope for is to find margins—normally neglected surfaces and relatively isolated, irregularly placed spots—on which to put ourselves."[62] While transmitting the limits of documentary filmmaking, the scene eventually arrives precisely at the actual well. The well is the place of inassimilable loss that is also a well-known personal and political historical trauma: it evades colonial and state representability but we can see it clearly. Recognizing their predetermined, unrequited desire for documentary coherence, Khleifi and Sivan deliver the oppressive conditions embedded in this very scene and their whole project. At the same time, they close with a hopeful picture: for, while that well today might be covered up by Kakal crimes of forestation, we have verbal and visual documentation of Ayn-Yarka still living on.

Paradise Lost: *Fureidis*

Centering on her hometown of Fureidis and her relationship to it, filmmaker Ibtisaam Mara'ana outlines the general details regarding the unique history of the village early in the film: "After the war, the refugees who were expelled from their villages arrived at Fureidis, which was not depopulated." Yet she wants to know more: "I always wondered why the village remained, but the people here won't talk about it." Letting her viewers know about the reasons for her own unknowing, Mara'ana further explains: "What frustrates me about Fureidis is their lack of cooperation; they don't share anything with us, the young generation, about the history … that's why we always have a sense of emptiness. I always feel that inside, I'm an empty person … because I don't know anything." Expressing a core inner feeling, Mara'ana verbalizes the quest that informs *Paradise Lost*: the wish to fill the hole, and know more about the history of her family and community related to "that war." Mara'ana attempts to excavate a history beyond the fortified silence suffocating the beloved place and its residents. As this is a personal family matter to her, she begins with her father. "My father was born in Fureidis. I heard that he was sent to help dig mass graves in Tantura, the neighboring village that was ruined after 1948. I don't know what really happened in that war. But ever since, my dad is silent," Mara'ana's voiceover states what she does know and understand, as the camera looks at a tree from above, and then slowly coming down to list the details of its ripening figs, and her father holding tightly to it, his hand almost amalgamating with one of the branches. Mara'ana here indicates her understanding that the silence has to do with the 1948 war to whose victims her father provided one final honor, at only twelve years of age. Yet her father insists that he knows nothing about the massacre in Tantura; that he, just like her, had just heard, but cannot say anything, about it.

In Fureidis, we learn, the shattering events of war brought about a prolonged structural silencing just like the one that the refugees of Ayn-Hawd, Ayn-Yarka, and the rest are experiencing. Yet unlike the previous ones, this concluding section looks at a film about a Palestinian village that remained intact after 1948. "Along with Jisr al-Zarqa" Ilan Pappe noted, Fureidis was one in "only two out of sixty-four villages on the road between Haifa and Tel Aviv that were not wiped out by the Jewish forces."[63] Focusing on the destruction and massacre in the coastal village of Tantura in the 1948 war, and Israel's attempts to silence it continuously and more thoroughly so after 2000, Pappe reviews the ways in which the nearby Fureidis was affected by the events. Mainly, the massacre meant that Palestinians from Tantura escaped into Fureidis at first, before the authorities kicked most of them out to the West Bank. Additionally, residents of Fureidis participated in the burying of many of the victims of the massacre. They thus witnessed firsthand the consequences of the massacre, interacting with their dead neighbors for one more physically intimate last moment and most likely, just as the residents of Jenin who witnessed killings and death of neighbors and relatives in 2002, the people of Fureidis understood well that they could be next. The reluctant, unbearable role imposed on the living was thus to lay the horrific past to rest and still, somehow, survive.

Exeter, the United Kingdom: Freedom

With the conversation between Mara'ana and her father recurring throughout the film's progression, she poses a set of questions that inform her investigation: "Where were you in the 1948 war?" "What did they make you do to survive?" And importantly: "Do you know what Suaad did?" For Mara'ana, Suaad is a childhood hero, a lead figure in the mystery she is trying to unravel, and the protagonist of her film. That is because "Suaad was not afraid of politics": politics as in that general name to everything that her father warns her to stay out of, including "history … the present … the future," and even "dreaming." Yet Mara'ana was warned to "not become like Suaad" while growing up. Suaad Genem is known in the village as a rebellious woman who was involved in what the Fureidis residents call "security matters" and, for that reason, they refuse to provide but small disconnected details about her, and deny any relationship to her. Born in 1957 in Fureidis, Suaad founded the village's theatre circle in 1975 and, in 1979, joined the Black Panther squad affiliated with the Palestine Liberation Organization (PLO). Mara'ana's voiceover tells us how, in her bravery, Suaad "dared to wave the flag of Palestine" and for that "she served time." Mara'ana thus follows the footsteps of her lifelong, admired hero Suaad. Upon finding out that today, Suaad goes by the name Suaad Genem George and works as a university professor of international law in the United Kingdom, Mara'ana travels to meet her and hear her story firsthand.

Mara'ana's declaration of Suaad as her biggest hero, conversely to her infamous reputation as a "security problem," perhaps even a "terrorist," in the eyes of the state of Israel, and her dedicated gathering of details about Suaad through rumors and gossip despite the silencing, are heroic in and of themselves. Yet the film does more than that and, for the second half, leaves Fureidis and travels outside the confines of silencing to narrate the story of Suaad and of the Palestinian struggle for liberation from her point of view. For the most part, the second half of *Paradise Lost* focuses on Mara'ana's conversations with Suaad while in the United Kingdom and, later back in Fureidis, where Suaad visits during the summer. In and by her house in the United Kingdom, Suaad begins to shed more light on her story. Some clarifications become available as Suaad mentions having been arrested several times for waving the Palestinian flag. "The state of Israel did not recognize the PLO. That's it," states Suaad, reminding us that, prior to the 1993 Oslo Accords and agreements with the PLO, Israeli authorities criminalized Palestinians' expressions of any form of Palestinian nationalism. When they are back in Fureidis, Suaad explains how her research in the British libraries has yielded clarity about Mara'ana's other question regarding how come Fureidis remained standing and populated in 1948 unlike most of the Palestinian towns and villages. Suaad conveys how Fureidis remained standing after the 1948 war just so that the Jewish settlers in the neighboring city Zichron-Yaakov could go on exploiting its residents for cheap labor. The economic distress of the Fureidis residents due to their dependence on their Jewish employers for income thus translated into political silencing. The scapegoating of Suaad as a "security problem" was thus another means of scaring the village, and added to the already prevalent fear widespread across the village.

If history was to be shared with her properly then the frustrating emptiness dwelling within her would be fulfilled, Mara'ana fantasizes. Hearing about her throughout her life, and in person upon their meeting, Suaad inspired Mara'ana to keep searching for the facts of the history of Fureidis and the Palestinian struggle for liberation. Yet with many answers provided, it still seems that *Paradise Lost* is after something additional, just as substantial, if less definable, to extract from the intergenerational encounter between the young filmmaker and her veteran hero. This is already apparent in Mara'ana's visit in the United Kingdom, as their intimate exchange is loaded with heated tones, brief sentences, and many tears. Mara'ana asks: "What did Suaad do?" employing the third person to echo the rebuking tones of the suspicious, scared village residents who tried to talk her out of the trip. "That's precisely the question that has no answer, 'what did Suaad do … what did Suaad do … I am free. That's what I did. I am a free woman!" replies Suaad, repeating the third person several more times, and raising her voice with pride, grief, and

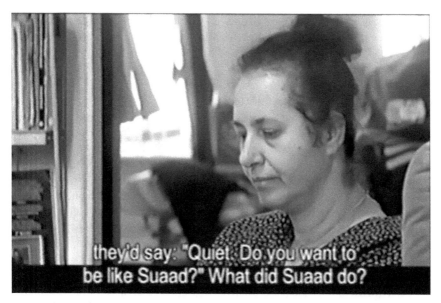

Figure 21 *Paradise Lost*, Suaad, "What did Suaad do?"

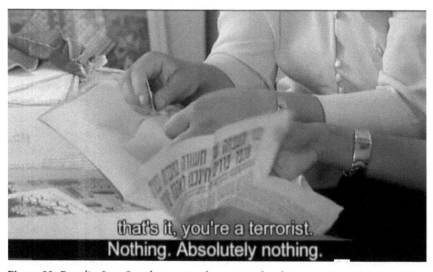

Figure 22 *Paradise Lost*, Suaad reopening her personal archive.

outrage. The emotional weight of the past is further unpacked toward the end of the film, when they meet in Fureidis. As they explore freedom and its tolls more thoroughly, the last two scenes of *Paradise Lost* also specifically tackle the sense of emptiness that, as she conveys from the start, is heavily burdening Mara'ana's inner world. As my following analysis shows, emptiness here is reshaped and reclaimed as a "nothing" that is also a "something." In the closing scenes of the film, Suaad grants Ibtisaam with a profound understanding of emptiness. While she herself is found in and operated by the emptiness of the unanswerable, Suaad's longtime life work and experience have taught her how to posit and politicize that emptiness, hold on to it, and offer it for the younger generation as a source of power: a lesson from the past that may pave a future of possibilities.

During her annual summer visit to Fureidis, Suaad climbs up to the family storage space and pulls out an old bag: oblivious of what it contains, she opens it only to stumble upon a personal archive of documents related to her imprisonment in the Ramle prison in the 1980s. Sitting next to Suaad, curious, Mara'ana quotes out loud from the old Israeli newspaper articles that reported the case in Hebrew, and asks her to confirm or deny the report. Suaad replies ragingly, shifting to read excerpts of the letters that she wrote home while imprisoned. Wrestling with different kinds of documentation, they find themselves in a verbal quarrel: Mara'ana insistently asks Suaad, "What did you do that first landed you in jail?" while Suaad fervently repeats the word "nothing!" and then states that "just by thinking and saying the word 'liberation,' that's it, you're a terrorist." Whereas Mara'ana turns to the adequate archival document and flagship of dominant discourse, the state-sponsored newspaper, Suaad focuses on personal thoughts and feelings. Whereas Mara'ana wants to understand how Suaad was imprisoned, Suaad interrupts her investigation to offer her something else instead. Rendering her written letters taken out of the bag into speech, Suaad stages a spatial element in the form of imprisonment, attempting to reconstruct the harsh memory of prison not only as a story but, most importantly, as a persistent affective structure perpetually housed inside of her. Here, Suaad tries to point to the bars forcibly installed in and around her that inhibit the smooth, consistent flow of language. In this heartbreaking moment, Suaad discloses the torments she went through while in the Israeli prison, "The tears have dried … my cry is lacking conscience, my eyes, body, and voice are weary … we cried, but they wanted more, they were thirsty for tears." Suaad then attributes the thirst for tears to the institution's will to attempt an emptying of the Palestinian inmate from her being: "I call it an attempt to empty us," she concludes. "They emptied us."

The outrage in Suaad's announcements that she did "nothing!" indicates that nothingness here is a thing: indeed, liberation is the basic right of every person to seek, and "nothing" beyond the very basic, yet it is this "nothing" that landed Suaad in jail. "Nothing" thus is a thing in the eyes of the occupier who henceforth builds a prison around that nothingness in order to null the work for liberation—indeed, render liberation into a nothing. As harmful and scarring as the experience of prison was and continues to be for Suaad, this important scene instantiates her ways of embodying and politicizing the act of emptying so that she can convey and commemorate this crime of state violence to others, the younger generation of the village, such as Mara'ana. "'We continue to be strong behind these walls,'" Suaad reads her own writing, and also explains: "I carved it on the walls with my fingernails." With the same fingers that previously wrote, and now hold, the letter, Suaad had etched her message on the walls of the prison and, thus at the same time, affixed the touch of the walls and imprinted their memory onto her. Through reading fragments from the letter in the presence of Mara'ana, it is the structure of that memory as a feeling as it is etched and entrenched within her that Suaad is trying to echo and contour. This architecture of pain that Suaad endows to Ibtisaam is her legacy: the emptiness we feel is the prison that was imposed on us; Suaad imparts the message that, relationally, emptiness is the result of emptying. Providing Ibtisaam's emptiness with a shape, and rendering it as a verb instead of attempting its eradication, Suaad uses the same fingers that absorbed the prison to point to the authority of the Israelis as its architects and constructors. This empty space within her is now the space where the history of the Palestinian struggle emanates from. It is an inner space to remember Fureidis, remember prison, remember the silencing and/as the emptying that was imposed on all of its residents, and the place from which to continue to fight for personal and collective freedom.

In *Living a Feminist Life*, Sara Ahmed reread Audre Lorde's landmark and often-quoted essay *Your Silence Will Not Protect You* (1984). "Over time … I have come to understand, to know and to feel, the costs of speaking out. I have thus come to understand, to know and to feel, why many do not speak out. There is a lot to lose, a lot, a life even. So much injustice is reproduced by silence not because people do not recognize injustice, but because they do recognize it. They also recognize the consequences of identifying injustice … we are not all in the same position; we cannot all afford to speak out … we have to find other ways for the violence to become manifest … there are so many ways to cause a feminist disturbance."[64] Ahmed concludes that "even if speaking out is not possible, it is necessary." I propose that what Suaad is gifting Mara'ana, and by extension the younger generation of '48 Palestinians, and us spectators, is an interrelated understanding of why some could not, and still cannot, speak out, precisely as a way to explain why it is important to nevertheless do so. The Israeli security forces used Suaad's arrests to further scare the village into silence, portraying her as "a terrorist" to induce terror on the residents who are already struggling economically. Their silence emanates from the state's intimidation of them, especially as they fear losing the little income that they rely on for an already impoverished living. Yet silencing and speaking out here are intertwined: the more people recognize the history of injustices against Palestine and Palestinians, the more the state strategy of silencing seems necessary; and the more silencing occurs and forms its occupation on people's voices, the more it is clear that a significant body of knowledge and basis for resistance lies underneath it.

From the start, Mara'ana trusted that meeting Suaad would allow her to break the silencing imposed on the village. Yet it is this scene that unlocks major details around Suaad's imprisonment that endows the film with its crucial closure. Mara'ana's cinematic searches reach their culmination when the film renders emptiness as an entity and a possibility, rather than doing away with it. Mara'ana's dialogue with Suaad in front of the camera brings to light and life that inner space of emptiness so that the inside and outside constantly converse and mingle, switch and interchange, and imbue one another with meaning. We may want to call the exchange between Mara'ana and Suaad a complex feminist "communication system," in Ahmed's words, where a multilayered analysis shows how silencing works and how to thus both rely on the analysis and break away from the silence. Suaad gives emptiness caused by silencing a meaning because she has struggled to break it for many years. The story of the making of this emptiness and the ability to speak from and about it is precisely the precious gift of the labor of activism and learning that Suaad is able to give Mara'ana after all these years.

In Conclusion: Tantura—Holes of Hope

Walking down the streets of the village where everyone stares at her suspiciously, or searching for traces of the past in the old vacant house of her deceased parents, Suaad is an unwelcome guest in the place she could have been at home the most. In this unhomelyness, the prison, the old house, and the village where she was born and raised become commensurable in their dismissal and denial of her stance and voice, paralleling their reluctant submission to the silencing of any "political" talk about Palestinian history, present, and future. "The problem is I loved the village very much. I love our village too much. And that's the problem," concludes Suaad, trying to hold back her tears, as if in order to prevent the full completion of the mission of emptying, at the end of the pivotal scene in her parents' old house. The emptiness she carries within marks the loss, longing, remembrance, and love for where she came from, all safely restored within her wherever she goes. Yet that emptiness is a home that spreads hope too.

In the film's closing scene, we see that Suaad's tears have not dried, nor are they handed over to the prison guards anymore, as the film shifts from Suaad's almost-teary eyes to the almost-endless spaciousness of the Mediterranean sea, connecting the large reservoir of salty water to Suaad's own eyes. Mara'ana and Suaad sail to Tantura, "the village that is no more." Silence, Mara'ana says, began with the massacre in Tantura, and that was the silence that "motivated me to speak." On a little isle between the waves, with Fureidis and Tantura behind them, Mara'ana urges Suaad to look to the horizon and to think about her dreams; Suaad refuses the invitation: "Whose dreams? There are no dreams. ... What are the dreams of the refugee camp in Jenin?" but at the same time encourages Mara'ana's wish to dream: "Go ahead, dream! You're free," she tells her younger friend. "See those holes? Those are our dreams, those holes," Suaad says, pointing to the holes within the rocks on the seashore. Upon Mara'ana's further pleas, Suaad adds that the state of Israel "is tearing our dreams to shreds." Here, where the emptiness within tries to contain, and ends up spilling over some tears, and those merge with the enormous container of waves, the holes remain intact, punctuating but also structuring the rocks. Suaad refrains from redressing neither her nor Mara'ana's painful holes: those remain the memorial monuments to the deliberate atrocities inflicted on them. Yet those are also the vessels from which the dreams and freedom emanate, and from which Mara'ana draws inspiration to weave her own dreams, films, and futures. As in *Jenin Jenin* and *Arna's Children*, *Paradise Lost* shows not only how much pain and fear emanates from witnessing your neighbor's devastation, how it distills the surrounding community with grief and fear, but also how it can move them and, importantly the later generations, to action. The struggle to free Palestinians continually stands on the shoulders of giants— activists, artists, thinkers, community—who keep it alive, as they understand, cope with, and break the silencing, by practicing unique ways of speaking through it.

Chapter 4

A MOTHER TONGUE, A DAUGHTER'S VOICE: MIZRAHI WOMEN'S HOMECOMING TO THE ARABIC LANGUAGE IN EFFI BANAI'S *LONGING* AND ISRAELA SHAER-MEODED'S *QUEEN KHANTARISHA*

"He sent me to a spy," says Margalit Engel to filmmaker Effi Banai in one of the key scenes of *Longing* (2009). A Palestinian Jew born and raised in Salame, a neighborhood in Jaffa that was occupied and annexed to Tel Aviv in 1948, Margalit was recruited to the Zionist far right militia Irgun when she was only fourteen to eavesdrop on her Palestinian neighbors and report back to the head of the "Irgun," Menahem Begin. Margalit's words take us back to the formative time when Arabic-speaking Jews like her were asked to start utilizing the capacity to hear and understand Arabic for war purposes.[1] Around that time and in the coming years, Arabic-speaking Jews had to minimize speaking Arabic in the public sphere too,[2] and the traditions of Jewish immigrants from Arab countries, previously practiced in Arabic, were undermined.[3] Born in Yemen and immigrating to Israel with her family at ten, feminist and anti-racist poet Bracha Seri learned how to elegize from her mother. Yet as she tells Israela Shaer-Meoded in *Queen Khantarisha* (2009), her elegizing does not consist of spontaneously singing in Arabic and then crying climactically, as the Yemenite Jewish tradition goes: instead, Seri wrote the elegies on paper, as poetry. While writing mostly in Hebrew Seri brought back Arabic in and through her poetic work, weaving Arabic words and sounds to expose and explode the silencing force of Hebrew. Margalit Engel, Bracha Seri, and Naomi Amrani, another poet and songwriter also appearing in *Queen Khantarisha*, are three Mizrahi women who speak about and perform their ongoing relationships with the Arabic language despite Israel's silencing of the Arabic language in the public sphere. This chapter takes a close look at how the documentary performances of the Mizrahi women deliver their multifaceted, contested connections with their home. For Margalit Engel, Bracha Seri, and Naomi Amrani, home is the physical location where exploitative labor takes place and where the Arabic language is supposed to serve a very limited utility. Yet home is also where their connection to Arabic lives on. *Longing* and *Queen Khantarisha* foreground speech performances of the women in or by their homes, where the national and patriarchal measures of silencing were placed on their voices and their Arabic mother tongues, and where their access to Arabic nevertheless remained intact.

In *Longing*, filmmaker Banai centered the Mizrahi residents of Kfar-Shalem, including himself and his family who arrived from Iran. The neighborhood Kfar-Shalem was once part of Salame in Jaffa. After it was conquered by the newly founded state of Israel in 1948 and renamed Kfar-Shalem, the neighborhood was populated by Jewish immigrants from the Middle East, who like the others arriving in Israel, were designated to manual labor, vocational schools, and impoverished public housing that they were prohibited from purchasing—unlike the Ashkenazi residents around them—and later were asked to leave, often with no compensation.[4] Banai retrieved the family and community stories of the residents—immigrants or first generation in Israel—documented the protests of their planned evictions, and emphasized the ongoing cultural relationships of these residents with the countries they came from and with their mother tongues, mainly Farsi and Arabic. I especially focus on the scenes centering on Margalit Engel, Banai's veteran neighbor who was born in Salame and lives in Kfar-Shalem. Margalit's recruitment as a spy ended her relationship with her deported neighbors in Salame and rendered her identification as a Palestinian Jew impossible. In 2007, at the time of the filming, Margalit was fighting her own deportation from her home—her and her Mizrahi neighbors'—in Kfar-Shalem,[5] in one of the most brutal waves of gentrification launched by real estate developers and the Tel Aviv municipality against Mizrahi-populated neighborhoods in the city's south.[6] Margalit testified on her broken-yet-existent connection to Arabic and to Arab Palestinian neighbors, and shares her disillusionment of believing that her service as a Jewish spy for the emerging Jewish state of Israel as a young girl would not grant her the basic human rights of decent housing in her old age. Hurt, remorseful, and nostalgic, she affirmed her longing for how relationships between neighbors of different religions in Palestine used to be before 1948; toward the end of the film, she is reunited with an old Palestinian neighbor from Jaffa to reimagine how the place once used to be in the past, and could be in the future, in Arabic.

A major focus of this chapter are the stories, poetry, and songwriting of Bracha Seri and Naomi Amrani in *Queen Khantarisha*. Centering on Seri, while featuring additional Yemenite women artists such as poet and songwriter Naomi Amrani and other women who practice elegizing, *Queen Khantarisha* follows the speech performances of these women in their homes. Seri and Amrani simulate and contemplate on the unique production and distribution of their poetry and song as continuous to and inspired by the old Yemenite Jewish tradition of elegizing in Arabic and on the material, vocal, corporeal, live, and performative dimensions embedded in writing poetry and song—which Seri has named "Written Speech."[7] Seri's and Amrani's performances of and as poetization take place in the interior space of the home, where their voices and the spaces they inhabit amalgamate to become cinematic tropes of poetry making. Quests for the cry in the home, signing "on an empty stomach," walking and trespassing in and out of the home, and utilizing Yemenite Arabic accents amid and against Hebrew, are all habits of poetization that Seri and Amrani practice. As Mizrahi women poets in Israel, Seri and Amrani had to endure the national and patriarchal oppression binding them to homemaking, reproduction, and endless labor and silencing of their voices, in order to keep poetizing, writing, and singing in Arabic like their mothers and foremothers used to. Intricate expressions of elegizing and/as poetizing, survival and/as resistance, Shaer-Meoded's feminist lens[8] centers on Seri's and Amrani's performances in *Queen Khantarisha* as ramified, complex processes of narrating, retelling, and rewriting patriarchal discourses that have silenced their mothers and their Arabic mother tongues. With etymological roots in Persian and Turkish and associated with Mizrahi subculture in its iteration in Israeli Modern Hebrew, the word "Khantarisha" is used today to mean silly, flippant, unreliable; yet here it also reclaims an insult commonly directed at Mizrahi women.[9] The film's title, *Queen Khantarisha*, taken from one of Seri's poems, thus alludes to the film's emphasis on the subversive, poignant, and playful power of language and speech, poetry and its public performance, to extract and unravel all the possible sub-meanings embedded in an enunciation.[10]

Engel, Seri, and Amrani were burdened by the oppressive imperatives that Zionism and Israel assigned to them: as Mizrahim in Israel, they were supposed to contribute their physical presence and manual labor for the Judaization of Palestine, as they were placed in state-owned former Palestinian residences in order to prevent the Palestinians' return to their homes,[11] and designated to low-paying jobs such as construction and working the fields in these areas.[12] As Mizrahi women, they were supposed to bear the added tasks of homemaking, as well as carry out the demographic mission of reproduction of Jewish children.

Figure 23 *Queen Khantarisha*, Bracha Seri, reading her poem "Queen Khantarisha."

Nationalism and patriarchy in their respective configurations as state and domestic violence are interrelatedly responsible for the oppression of Mizrahi women in Israel. Henriette Dahan-Kalev and Pnina Mutzafi-Heller explained that the oppression of Mizrahi women under patriarchy is desired by Zionism and Israel who have tried to produce and, then point to Mizrahim, prove them as an innately inferior "Oriental" collective.[13] Manar Hasan has framed the sustainment of this vicious circle as an "'Orientalist' approach": referring to views of domestic violence against '48 Palestinian women in Israel, Hasan contended that this approach "attributes various social practices of the Arab Middle East, among them the practice of murder of women for the sake of family honor, to inherent and axiomatic cultural factors, while ignoring almost entirely the political factors that influence the stabilization and even the shaping of these practices."[14] Hasan's work is useful in analyzing Mizrahi women's situation under the orientalizing male Zionist gaze too.[15]

Yet as this chapter contends, Mizrahi women like Engel, Seri, and Amrani understand, verbalize, and politicize the pain caused to them in the process of their gendered orientalization, depicting the labels and roles imposed on them as a force that has been silencing their own stories, voices, and connection to their Arabic mother tongues. They break the silencing to find new ways of returning to Arabic—a return that the documentaries picture as a homecoming. While Engel's testimony in *Longing* addresses Zionism and Israel directly as the institution that shaped her as a spy but refrains from spelling out the gender dynamics embedded in her exchange with her commander, Seri and Amrani do not tackle Zionism and Israel directly but, rather, focus on patriarchy as the power responsible for their oppression. Engel discusses the silencing of Arabic as a spoken language and her audial usage of Arabic instead to facilitate the ethnic cleansing of the newly Hebraized territory of the state of Israel; she also uses her Arabic to recover the history of Arab Jewish neighboring in Palestine before 1948. Seri and Amrani do not historicize their relationships with the Arabic language per se but only indirectly, when they reenact their mothers' usage of Arabic to criticize patriarchy. *Queen Khantarisha* thus shapes Seri's and Amrani's usage of Arabic in their creative work as a quest to reconnect with their mothers and mother tongues through and beyond the impact of and resistance to patriarchy. "I know I am a medium of writing," Seri once said in an interview, defining the poet's relation to and embodiment of poetizing;[16] "I am like an editor of some other [male] author that wrote it [the poetry]," she then added, framing poetizing as an intervention in, and a revision of, some other, certainly male, author/ity's writing.[17] Mediation, however, has additional connotations with regard to the lived experience of Mizrahim in Israel, and of Mizrahi women specifically. Becoming a spy for the "Irgun" as Engel did is also a way of mediating the Arab Palestinians and their language with the Zionist Hebrew-speaking occupier Hebrew speaker—that is, a way of providing the labor of linguistic and cultural mediation for purposes of military occupation. We can discern the process of mediation in Amrani's story too, as she details the conditions that commanded her reluctant mating and reproduction of babies at a very young age, objectifying her body as a tool in the hands of the husband to whom she was married in Yemen and the medical institution in Israel since she was a young girl. Amrani, like Seri, and like the Yemenite elegizing women that inspired them, reclaims mediation as a poetic process that saturates her spiritually and births her creative work. The women's testimonies thus complement one another. My analysis of Engel's performance in *Longing* in the first section leads right to my review of the oppression of Mizrahim in and by the state of Israel, which *Queen Khantarisha* does not explicate, in the second section. The third and fourth sections detail Seri's and Amrani's ways of speaking about and performing their practices of poetizing and songwriting about, through, and beyond the silencing imposed on them by patriarchy and—if one can listen carefully and hear between their lines—by patriarchal violent procedures of the state too. I close this chapter by analyzing Seri's and Amrani's vocalizations of Arabic through and within Hebrew in their speech. Expressing loss, oppression, and resilience, Seri and Amrani let their Arabic mother tongue and mothers' tongues infiltrate and punctuate their Hebrew enunciations, inundating their and our ears with accents and puns in the tabooed Arabic and destabilizing the forceful imperative of Hebrew.

I chose to examine *Longing* and *Queen Khantarisha* because they contemplate on and explicitly politicize pain at the intersection of several other themes that are recurring in Mizrahi documentary cinema from the first decade of the 2000s. As in other films, some of them mentioned in Chapter 2, *Longing* and *Queen Khantarisha* both foreground the hardships of precarious housing, debilitating labor, and the erasure of Arabic culture in Israel, due to the marginalization of Mizrahim. These films do so while highlighting specifically the implications on and resilience of Mizrahi women, and portraying them in situ—where they live, while contemplating the question of where is home. Along the same lines, Julie Shlez's and Doron Tsabari's *To the South* (2002) was centered on women's successful protest against the closing of the Sewing Factory in Mitzpe Ramon. Simha Lev's *Living in Boxes* (2004), which was about evictions in the Ha'argazim neighborhood in the south of Tel Aviv, tells the story of Mizrahi residents who, like Margalit Engel, struggle to remain in their homes. Finally, while not centering on women yet addressing the issue of gender in stories centering on marriage and family, I should mention Nizar Hassan's and Danae Elon's film *Cut* (2000), which focuses on Agur, a formerly Palestinian village and, after 1948, an Israeli colony largely populated with Mizrahi Kurdish, Iraqi, and Turkish Jews. Importantly, this film dwells on what Ella Shohat has called "the Mizrahi/Palestinian nexus,"[18] in that Hassan, a '48 Palestinian filmmaker, deeply reflects on the convoluted, ambivalent attitudes of the Mizrahi residents toward the Palestinian returnees—Palestinians who attempt to return to their homes of Palestine after 1948. I say more about this film in my concluding notes.

Additionally, *Longing* and *Queen Khantarisha* are also part of a larger wave of Mizrahi documentaries centering on Mizrahi women's lives more generally. Films about Mizrahi women include Michal Aviad's *Ramleh* (2001), about Mizrahi women living in the mixed Arab Jewish city of Ramle; Yochi Daddon's *Gifted* (2001), about Mizrahi women who were sent as girls to a predominantly

Ashkenazi boarding school because they were "gifted"; Sarit Haymian's *Gole Sangam* (2006), which follows two Iranian women who were set up in arranged marriages when they were young, examining their lives and thoughts about relationships; Sami Shalom Chetrit's *Az'i Ayima* ("Come Mother" in Arabic, 2009), about his mother and her community of women friends who all immigrated from Morocco; and Yitzhak Haluzi's *Breaking the Walls* (2012), about the life and work of renowned Mizrahi feminist thinker, organizer, and poet Vicki Shiran who cofounded the *Mizrahi Democratic Rainbow*.[19] On another note, *Longing*'s and *Queen Khantarisha*'s deep contemplation on the Arabic language and in the case of *Queen Khantarisha*, Yemenite culture, related to the wave of films that revived the historically marginalized images and sounds of Arab Jewish cultures and their persistence in celebrating Mizrahi cultures in the first decade of the 2000s in Israel, including Rami Kimchi's *Cinema Egypt* (2001), about the filmmaker's mother's emigration from Egypt and the place of Egyptian cinema in the life of the Jewish Egyptian community; Duki Dror's *Taqasim* (1999) and *My Fantasia* (2001), about memories and cultural practices of the filmmaker's family who emigrated from Iraq; and Eyal Halfon's *Chalery Baghdad* (2002), about the Iraqi musicians who, upon their emigration to Israel, helped found the Arab Orchestra of the state-mandated Israel Broadcasting Authority.

Importantly, in 2009, the same year that *Longing* and *Queen Khantarisha* came out, a group of Mizrahi organizers and artists gathered, as Heart at East: The Coalition for Equal Distribution of Cultural Funds in Israel, to produce a report about the systematic neglect of Mizrahi representation in Israel.[20] Many of the writers of the report were part of the Mizrahi Democratic Rainbow, and many were also women involved in the foundation of the Mizrahi Feminist Movement, *Achoti* (Hebrew for "My Sister") in 2000, after organizing as feminist Mizrahi activists since the 1990s.[21] Among many other struggles, Achoti members also supported the march of Mizrahi single mothers to the Jerusalem parliament in 2003 led by Vicky Knaffo, a Mizrahi woman from Mitzpe Ramon. While the focus on Mizrahi women and cultures in the abovementioned documentaries is directly linked to these organizing initiatives, this decade also produced quite a few apolitical films that center on Mizrahi women yet address neither Mizrahi nor feminist politics altogether. Rina Papish's *Ladino: 500-Years-Old Young* (2005) followed worldwide popular musician and music performer Yasmin Levy, when she was at the early stages of her career, developing and renewing a musical repertoire in the Ladino language in Israel. Eyal Goldberg's *Rita Jahan-Farouz* (2012) followed the famous Iranian Israeli musician Rita while she was recording her first album in Farsi, after a long successful career of singing in Hebrew. Perhaps Margalit Engel's story in *Longing* may serve as a cautionary tale for those Mizrahi activists in Israel who uncritically praise the increasingly popular, always depoliticized, and often offensive representation of Mizrahim on Israeli TV, and question the Mizrahi image of "the loyal server of neoliberal media," as coined by Shoshana Gabai while referring to the Mizrahi image of the commercialized and still state-dominated Israeli mainstream culture.[22]

"He Sent Me to Spy": Margalit

Today a neighborhood in the south of Tel-Aviv, Kfar-Shalem was called Salame before 1948: Margalit Engel, one of the main participants in Banai's *Longing*, had lived through this change. Comprising the occupation of Palestine and the foundation of the state of Israel, the remaking and renaming of her hometown, this multifaceted change had a direct impact on the status, position, and performance of Margalit—a Palestinian Jew and native speaker of Arabic and Hebrew, who was born, grew up, and has been living in Salame/Kfar-Shalem most of her life, and who, after the 1948 war and under the auspices of the state, became an Oriental Jew. As noted above, upon immigrating to Israel, Middle Eastern Jews like Margalit and Banai and his family all became Oriental Jews. Recounting and reenacting the process of that becoming in front of the camera, Margalit speaks her history in her own voice, tracing the Zionist attempt to make her into an Oriental Jew and the repercussions of this attempt—which she lives with till this day. "Kfar-Shalem was the village where the new ascendants from Arab countries arrived. They were housed in the Arab houses of the village Salame, which was abandoned in the war of liberation," Banai narrates at the outset of *Longing*. Employing the Zionist terminology of "ascendants" and "the war of liberation" to describe the arrival of immigrants from Arab and Islamic countries to Israel after the 1948 war, Banai states that he learned about the history of the neighborhood from Margalit, his veteran neighbor. Margalit, however, uses not only a different terminology but also, one might say, a whole different dialect of Hebrew, to describe what happened to the Palestinian village Salame, and how it became Kfar-Shalem, a Jewish neighborhood whose existence and population were to fortify the new borders of the new state post 1948; for, she had experienced the making of Kfar-Shalem on her body. "My girl, you speak Arabic, correct?" Margalit says, lowering her voice and looking right at the camera: at the scene's outset, she begins to reconstruct her experience of becoming, by imitating her maker, Menahem Begin. While commander of the Zionist paramilitary group "Irgun," Begin approached the then fourteen-year-old Margalit with a question, and a mission: "I have a mission for you," Margalit continues to imitate. Upon the request of her commander, Margalit became a spy for the "Irgun" or, in her own words, this is how "he"— Begin—"sent me to spy."

Perceiving Salame as a strategic location for Zionist conquest, Begin's plan was to "cleanse" Salame of its "Arab" residents, Margalit explains. Accordingly, Margalit's mission was to eavesdrop on her non-Jewish Arab Palestinian neighbors, to find out if they were preparing for any Jewish attacks. "Nothing," Margalit says. Far from militants, "the Arabs" were simply and solely "farmers." Indeed, Margalit remembers how the Irgun's attacks on her non-Jewish neighbors took them completely by surprise, just as she predicted, and how they ran away screaming, some of them even "leaving their food on the stove." Listening carefully to Margalit's monologue, we hear about the Zionist deportation of the Arab Palestinians from Salame, and the consequent separation of Jewish and

Figure 24 *Longing*, Margalit, "Child, you speak Arabic, right?"
Cinematography/photo credit: Netanel Peretz.

Arab Palestinian neighbors. Yet furthermore and very importantly, we witness the categorization and partition, of the Jew and the Arab, across separate linguistic and discursive realms—a making occurring prior and alongside the consequent spatial partition. The ethnic cleansing of the non-Jews of Salame followed on the heels of another unfortunate process: the remaking of the Palestinian Jew from a neighbor into a spy. In this process, the neighbor-turned-spy established new relationships with her two simultaneously spoken tongues: Arabic and Hebrew.

When Modern Hebrew culture was emerging in Ottoman Palestine in the 1900s, only few Arabic-speaking Jews advocated the importance of learning Arabic, which at the time was the official language of the Ottoman authorities;[23] most ceased to teach, learn, and write publicly in Arabic.[24] Yet as Liora Halperin notes, some parties in the Zionist establishment, including the labor movement and the Hebrew University of Jerusalem, did develop spaces within which people could study Arabic around the 1920s and 1930s, stressing its importance for several purposes: introducing them to the Arabic grammar would connect Jews to their imagined Semitic past in the Orient, strengthen their knowledge of Hebrew, and, finally, assist in utilizing Arabic "as a strategic tool—a means to build up a systematic body of information about the Arabs, conduct military intelligence activities, and create an apparatus to identify and predict trends in Arab activity."[25] Born into the times when Arabic was repurposed in this way in Palestine, Margalit was recruited to execute the third mission.

"Father, I know what Arabs are like. I grew up with them," Margalit reassured her suspicious commander; "I know, I know," Begin replied to "his girl." Yet Jewish-Arab Palestinian coexistent upbringing that he presumably knew about was dwindling as a direct result of Begin's ordered actions. An Ashkenazi Zionist who does not speak Arabic, Begin's Modern Hebrew dictates the redesigning of a girl who, here, becomes both a New Jew who dons the Hebrew orders upon her as well as a New Arab, whose usage of Arabic has to change. Begin does not simply recruit Margalit to the mission but, rather, tests her knowledge of Arabic first, by bringing along a Palestinian Arab to converse with her. This "Arab," as Margalit now calls him, asks her, "How are you?" Margalit, in turn, replies, "Better than you are. Good morning my neighbor, you mind your business, and I mind mine." Here, upon introducing them to one another, Begin verifies the two Arabic speakers' vicinity while paving the path to their future animosity. To properly execute the spying mission, Margalit needs to be fluent in Arabic; as she testifies, "Arabic is my language." Yet in becoming the loyal, first and foremost Jewish, spy, Margalit's Arabic also has to break from the Arabic of the one who here becomes an "Arab" who speaks "in an ancient Arabic accent." Unlike him, Margalit is now the New Arab Jew—the one that both understands the "ancient" Arabic as well as takes it in a new direction. Yet, I want to argue further that Margalit also becomes the New Oriental Jew here. As a newly designed spy, Margalit goes out to "check, feel out, smell, if there is any alertness for something" among the non-Jewish Arab Palestinians. Margalit thus becomes a sensorial seeker of possible Arabic-spoken dangers, while ceasing to speak Arabic herself. That is, Margalit's Arabic language migrates from the mouth to the ears, and also, as her monologue shows, to the throat: for, subjected to the spoken Hebrew's command, Margalit's Arabic becomes but an accent—a residue haunting the Semitic sibling that took over the public space of Palestine. This linguistic and corporeal reshaping is what I would like to call the making of the Oriental Jew, the Jew whose former ties to the Arab and Muslim world are now entrenched in her body, as physical traits obeying the Hebrew order—an order craving to reconstitute Eretz-Israel and, for this purpose, cleansing Palestine of its ancient accents, forms of communication, and human ties. Begin's Hebrew orders imply both the making of Margalit—a name connoting the word spy, "meragelet," in Hebrew—as well as the eradication of the myriad possibilities of linguistic, discursive, symbolic, and political communications between Arabic-speaking Jewish and non-Jewish neighbors in Palestine. Margalit describes how different the role of the Oriental Jewish spy was from the Jewish Palestinian neighbor she had been before. In particular, Margalit mentions how Arabs used to honor their Jewish neighbors' holidays, providing them with the food that they are prohibited from making according to Jewish law. When describing the long-gone past days, Margalit runs around, in and out of the frame, seeking that food tray that used to symbolize respect and good will, and physically connect the neighbors together. The symbolism of the tray is magnified in her spoken Hebrew, as the word for "tray" in Hebrew, "magash," is associated with "gisha," which means access. Alas, Margalit cannot find the tray or, perhaps, cannot find any access to previous times and neighborly practices of coexistence in this scene. While demonstrating how she used to hold it, the frame remains punctuated with its absence.

In 2007, at the time of the film's shooting, Margalit was living under the danger of deportation from her home, as yet another in a long series of decrees of eviction was hovering over people's homes in Kfar-Shalem. More than sixty years after the

deportation of her Palestinian neighbors, Margalit too is far from safe from the
harms of the ongoing Israeli spatial conquests. Given her unconditional loyalty
to the Irgun as a young girl, and the fact that her son died in a plane crash while
on duty for the Israeli Air Force, Margalit is deeply offended and declares she will
not come out of Kfar-Shalem alive if anyone tries to evict her. Despite serving as a
Jewish spy in 1948 and being a patriotic citizen of and a sacrificing mother for the
state of Israel since its establishment, Margalit's presence in Palestine-turned-Israel
is conditional: no longer needed as an intelligence agent and human shield in the
mission of turning Salame into Kfar-Shalem, she is regarded as an opponent of real
estate and the municipality, and especially of the state that made her a temporary
tenant in her own home. It is her raging pain that drives her to disillusionment
and nostalgia as expressed in her monologue: "You want to kick me out?? Me??
I prefer life back then to life now. Here, there are differences between the Jews.
Someone is at the top, and someone else is their slave, shining their shoes." In this
proclamation, Margalit's resentment is evidence of her deep understanding of the
process of demobilization of Mizrahim who were designated to cheap labor after the
foundation of Israel. To correlate this statement with her previous depiction of her
becoming a spy, we can picture the thread that binds the racialization of the Oriental
Jew as a provider of labor and the muteness imposed on their previously spoken
Arabic language. I say more about this thread in my analysis of *Queen Khantarisha*.
For now, let me mention that like Bracha Seri and Naomi Amrani, the protagonists
of *Queen Khantarisha*, Margalit too writes poetry: as we can see toward the end of
Longing, her poem is engraved on a stone as a monument for her fallen son. And
yet, by contrast to Seri's and Amrani's work, this poem expressses the nationalist

Figure 25 *Longing*, Margalit and her neighbor.
Cinematography/photo credit: Oded Kirma.

and tragic sentiment that Margalit repeats throughout the film: that she sacrificied so much, even her son's life, for the homeland, because she "wanted a Jewish state."

It is in the final 15 minutes of the film, right after visiting the poemed monument, that Margalit's rage translates into nostalgia and perhaps even remorse. Adjacent to the youth community center of Kfar-Shalem, which used to be a mosque in Salame, Margalit meets with an old neighbor, an Arab Palestinian refugee from Jaffa. Only then, Margalit slowly retrieves her Arabic mother tongue and, instead of speaking about her lack of access to long-gone times and relationships, she speaks in Arabic with her neighbor. Conversing and reconnecting, the two trace the lines of transportation that used to be available between towns and villages before 1948: in this way, they reinstate their live shared memory of Palestine's map in and by their shared Arabic. I suggest that, in speculating about what could have been their present if matters turned differently, the conversation in this closing scene of *Longing* also imagined what still could be the future of Israel-Palestine.

Queen Khantarisha: *The Woman Collector of Dry Branches, the Elegizing Women*

In the opening scene of *Queen Khantarisha*, we encounter two anonymous women as they cover their eyes with a handkerchief to compose and conduct elegies in their homes. Captured amid the act of elegizing, the first woman raises her voice to chant, and then weeps—her crying culminating and concluding the elegy. After elegizing and weeping, filmmaker Shaer-Meoded asks the woman if she writes the elegies herself. The woman replies that she "does not know how to read, and does not know how to write, unfortunately." Instead, "the words arrive straight to my heart," she shares. The second woman waits until her husband leaves the house and

Figure 26 *Queen Khantarisha*, a woman collecting twigs.

then covers her eyes to elegize. She explains that women often elegize together, "each bringing a voice, bringing a few words." In the following scene, we watch a woman in the woods, her body and head covered, as she silently tears and collects dry branches from the trees around her in what seems like difficult, meticulous labor. Developing sporadically throughout *Queen Khantarisha*, the scene later shows the woman carrying the branches on her back, as appearing on the cover of the DVD. Before we meet Bracha Seri and Naomi Amrani, the elegizing women's accounts of their creative work and the woman collector of branches set the scenes to *Queen Khantarisha's* exploration of women's elegizing, labor, and their labor of poetry and songwriting. "The film did not create a political position in front of the spectator, but requested the spectator to create that position ... we are demanded to think politically only after we understood the cultural and gendered exclusion, without [the film] truly signifying the excluding institution itself," Matti Shmueloff asserted when commenting about *Queen Khantarisha*.[26] To start off my discussion of *Queen Khantarisha* where the film itself starts, let me then think politically, allegorically, and correlatively about the two scenes of the elegizing and working women.

The Jewish Yemeni tradition of elegizing, Vered Madar contended, used to be passed from generation to generation in Yemen, mainly through teachings that the mother imparted to her daughter: these were transmitted orally, mostly in the home.[27] Commonly segregated and at times imprisoned, the room where women used to elegize in Yemen was an exclusively women's environment.[28] This is because women's practice of elegizing was prohibited from the public realm of the funeral's official rituals that men used to run. Whereas the men elegized in Hebrew solely, the women elegized in colloquial Yemenite Arabic, as we see in the film. "The expression 'Yemenite Jewish Home' carries various meanings, including the original location of the female voice," wrote Tova Gamliel.[29] As Yemenite Jews started arriving in Palestine and later in Israel since the late nineteenth century, the changing circumstances of immigration placed elegizing in a state of possible extinction—thus compelling the writing, recording, and other methods of restoration of the elegies. Madar affirms that "the immigration to Israel, to an environment where the network of social and familial connections is sparser, has created an intergenerational rift,"[30] which "is not a result of forgetfulness, but it is rather because a special cultural context and social situation are necessary in order to continue to preserve the creation" of elegies.[31]

A reading through of Shoshana Madmoni-Gerber's groundbreaking work on Yemenite Jews in Israel sheds important light on the pain embedded in this intergenerational rift caused by the oppressive conditions in which Yemenite Jews have found themselves after immigrating to Palestine/Israel. Since the 1980s, scholars have shown that Ashkenazi Zionist activists consistently essentialized and racialized Yemenite Jews in their writing.[32] Yaakov Tahun, for example, described the Yemenite Jews in a strictly physical manner as "an element" with the "natural" capacity to work the fields.[33] Proponents of this perspective such as Shmuel Yavnieli had organized the emigration of Jews from their mostly safe home in Yemen to the increasingly Zionizing land of Palestine since the 1880s: the main practical reason behind this was the European Jews' desire to hire Yemenite Jews as cheap labor in the newly evolving Hebrew exclusionary workforce. Placed at the margins of Jewish settlements and/or—as in the renowned case of the Kibbutz of Kinneret—collectively removed from them, the Yemenite workers of agriculture were treated with contempt and brutality. Especially oppressed were the Yemeni Jewish women, who were assigned to grim physical work in domestic labor. Later, the newly founded state of Israel exacerbated and institutionalized the systematic migration, exclusion, and oppression of Yemeni Jews: since 1948, state clerks organized collective transportations—framed as "rescue missions"—in which they dispossessed the Yemeni Jews' cultural assets before they embarked on the planes to Israel. Upon their arrival, Yemeni Jews, as the other Jewish immigrants from Arab and Muslim countries, were placed in detrimental transit camps that often became their permanent residences, and were assigned degrading work. Finally, as Madmoni-Gerber demonstrated throughout her book, the Jewish Agency separated parents from their babies who, often times, they never saw again; waves of kidnapping of Yemenite and other Mizrahi babies henceforth followed.[34] As it were, the Zionist systematic mistreatment incarnated into an official policy of the state apparatus. Of the many horrific occasions of oppression against them, one particular event strikingly illustrates the Zionist approach to Yemenite Jews and, specifically, to Yemenite Jewish women. Around 1907, the time of their first arrival at the Zionist settlement—today an Israeli city—of Rehovot, three Yemenite Jewish women were publicly abused by Yonatan Makov, one of the settlement's young Ashkenazi residents, and the son of one of the settlement's founders. In this event, Makov had found these women collecting dry twigs in his field, with the intention of using the trifling twigs for their firewood, and began to beat them up; consequently bounding their hands, tying their wrists to the tail of a donkey, and dragging them in the rocky roads back to the settlement.[35] As the Yemenite Jews protested, Makov was tried and found guilty; yet his punishment amounted to merely a small fine.

To that end, Makov's violence toward the Yemenite women in the settlement of Rehovot enacted the violent imperatives of the Modern Hebrew of Zionist thinkers in Palestine of his time on Yemeni (and) women's bodies—in particular, Zionist writers' subjugation of Yemeni (and) women as innately designated to mute manual labor. In her article about object making and objectification in the early years of the Betzalel School of arts and crafts, Sarah Hinsky focuses on the gendered and racial meanings attached to crafts such as rug weaving and lace sewing.[36] Founded in Jerusalem in 1906 by Zionist entrepreneur Boris Shatz, the Betzalel School structured disciplinary differentiations and gendered segregations between the modern high arts designated for the Zionist Ashkenazi male newcomers and the low-esteemed yet highly useful crafts framed as folkloric assigned to girls and women from the native Jewish community of Ottoman Palestine and from the Yemenite immigrant community.[37] Shatz and his fellow Betzalel administrators posited that "the female worker is a natural resource ubiquitously found in any street corner ... a natural resource whose producing skill lies in the female body ... the skill of the female workers is native, just as the skill of the Yemenites in Betzalel is constructed as native."[38] Native producers of folkloric crafts, objectified yet natural workers, are placed in the Betzalel system according to how they are imagined by Shatz, Martin Buber, Yosef Klaussner, and other Zionist thinkers: "Here, a complete congruence between entities and their nature is argued … vis-à-vis the description of the character of folk art, there is also an implicit premise regarding the essence of the producers of folk art: those have no personal character … to keep the authenticity of their representations, of their objects, it is vital to prove that they do not stem from any subjective will, but are rather the collective product of the spirit of the people."[39] Buber's romanticization of folk art as " 'the mute development at the heart of the people' " in turn "demands the producers of folk art, to maintain their silence, and perhaps even to produce their silence as a characterizing component of folk creation."[40] This endeavor required the "active utilization of absence, of silence, of gendered traits of women, to render these women as necessary objects for the realization of the projects of the invention of folk Hebrew art."[41] In this context, Hinsky also notes that Shatz and his fellow Zionist modern artists' study of Modern Hebrew as the language of cultural revival stood in compatible opposition to their derogatory construction of the crafters' spoken languages—Yiddish, Ladino, and, importantly, Arabic[42]— as "the languages of slackness and muteness."[43]

Hereby, the "natural," mute labor of Yemenite Jews was expected to mediate the making of Palestine into Eretz-Israel and later the state of Israel. According to this paradigm, the Yemenite Jewish women's enslaved bodies were placed under danger both in the public sphere and in the home. The home is also the marginalized space where Yemenite women elegize, sing, cry, or speak in Arabic: they are confined to that public sphere because nationalism and patriarchy have muted their public expression in Arabic, crowning Hebrew as the language that dominates the outside. Turning it into a language for gathering military intelligence against Palestinians, the Arabic of Jews was naturalized and depoliticized as a cultural and corporeal trait, like sweat or a scream, that resulted from hard physical labor; in other words, Arabic was to become an emptied yet essential mechanical tool assisting in the reproduction of Israel in Palestine. In this process, the Yemenite Jews' Arabic language was thought to become a physical and internal trait of a fixed and traditional corporeal culture rather than a politically charged apparatus employed in and as a public discourse: this is how Yemenite Jewish culture in particular, Arab Jewish cultures in general, and the Arabic languages of Jews, were pushed into the realm of the personal and the private.[44] The Yemenite woman and her spoken Arabic are thus simultaneously silenced outside and pushed into the home. Juxtaposing the voices of women elegizing in Arabic with the silence of the woods in which a woman struggles to collect some dry branches, *Queen Khantarisha* alludes to the harsh work that Yemenite women have had to endure in order to keep the tradition of elegizing of their mothers and foremothers alive. As I now show, *Queen Khantarisha* affirms that the home is both where mute domestic labor is supposed to take place and also the realm of the creative work of elegizing women in and with Arabic and, later, of women poets and songwriters like Seri and Amrani.

The Home Is a Grave: Bracha Seri's Poetizing

I came to you beaten, and wretched,
And mute.
And you spread your clenched fists on me,
To embrace me with fire and suffocation.
I came to you with null will,
As if led to the slaughter for exoneration.
And you licked my wounds with poison,
And you leaned on me like an inundation.
So we clung together for trouble, for awesome abhorrence,
And I hated you sturdily, and heat welled up in me,
The lust of the mortified flesh imprisoned in the pit of destruction.

We meet Bracha Seri for the first time a few minutes into *Queen Khantarisha*, right after we met the elegizing women and the woman collector of dry branches, in the square crowded with tents where Seri invites passersby to sit in front of her for a reading, and then reads these words from her poem to them. An unsettling first-person woman's feminist reflection on domestic violence, the poem "I Came to You Beaten, and Wretched, and Mute" first appeared in *Seventy Poems of Wanderings*, a collection of poems that came out in 1983.[45] Matti Shmueloff explains that the poems collected in this book were initially gathered under the title *The Scrolls of Ga'asha Meri-Dor*—a Hebrew pseudonym that means "a Storm" (first name) and "the Generation's Rebel" (last name).[46] In their initial version, the poems were formed as handmade scrolls reminiscent of tampons. Seri inscribed the poems on rolls of calculation paper, designed fabric containers for them, and then sold or gave them away personally to people at public events.[47] *Queen Khantarisha* introduces us to Seri by reconstructing the context in which this and other scrolled poems were first created and distributed: the 1980–1 activism of *The Tent Movement* in Jerusalem—a movement born out of the work of the Black Panthers and other grassroots Mizrahi initiatives.[48] With Seri's voice reading the last two lines of the poem still in the background, the scene quickly shifts—taking us to Seri's home. First capturing the outside of the house, the camera then follows Seri as she walks into the house; we hear her voice not as a reader, but as the narrator of the film, for the first time. As the lens follows Seri's footsteps, lingering in rooms that are crowdedly furnished yet vacant of people, we see the intimate interior space of her furniture, writing desk, and personalized mess—with these serving as the voiceover's spatial backdrop and repository. "My mother used to elegize, so I also elegized. That's my crying. I write it in elegies," Seri's voiceover says, as she appears walking between the rooms while humming some tunes; in one line with her evocation of the elegy, Seri's voiceover adds: "My mother called her house 'gabr' [Arabic for "a grave"]."

These two intertwined scenes set forth *Queen Khantarisha*'s journey through the winding paths and points of conjuncture between the public and private spheres embedded in Seri's work. From the start, *Queen Khantarisha* foregrounds Seri's poetry writing as intrinsically intertwined with her public life. Seri's political involvement in various struggles in Israel and worldwide since the 1970s, from the Black Panthers through *The Tent Movement*, from her projects of public education for Mizrahi girls through her participation in feminist circles, inform her highly political poetry, in which she criticizes the Yemenite community in Israel, Israel's wars and nationalism, and, perhaps most consistently, patriarchy in many of its ethnonational configurations.[49] Rather than spelling out her political activism, however, *Queen Khantarisha* asks us to think of the political conditions, circumstances, and limitations of poetry writing that Seri lived through and created within as a Mizrahi woman immigrant poet in Israel and, especially, her insistence of reinstating the Arabic language and culture that Israel wishes to eradicate from the public sphere. To be politicized, the voice of poetry first needs to be heard in the place where it emerges. *Queen Khantarisha* stimulates us spectators to see the setting of the film—the indoors, the outdoors, the transitions between them—as the sociopolitical conditions and circumstances from which their voices are heard. Poetry readings taking place at home and outside are poignant themes that this film uses to enliven written words by leaving the page, ceasing to be a text solely, and presenting itself as a lived embodied reality.

"For both Amrani and Seri, their articulation of womanhood is inseparable from their experiences as Mizrahi," Yaron Shemer wrote about *Queen Khantarisha*.[50] Born out of her mother's and other Jewish Yemenite women's tradition of elegizing in colloquial Arabic, Seri's poetry exists in and politicizes a continuous, intricate, multilingual, and transnational mother-daughter, woman-to-woman creative dialogue. Threading the lineage between Yemenite elegizing women and Seri right at the outset, *Queen Khantarisha* historicizes Seri's poetry as directly emerging from the women's elegizing in Arabic while spatially situating her own elegizing and/as poetry writing as emanating from the home, where the poet lives, works, and writes, and where the residues of her mother's voice still dwell. The home that her mother experienced as a grave, where women's elegizing takes place, and the confines of the house where nationalism and patriarchy decided that women will stay to elegize, inform Seri's practice of poetry writing—these aspects are the main concern of the film. It is in this context that we are to hear Seri's framing of crying as an aim materialized by writing. Like the elegizing women we met before her, Seri's practice of elegizing paves her path for some wailing; yet she does not simply cry while elegizing, but rather, her crying occurs as Seri "writes it"—writes the crying, that is—"in elegies." Therefore, for Seri, crying is only obtainable through the practice of writing poetry: writing poetry, in other words, is for her the ultimate application of elegizing that the women previously shown are leading—that is, the practice that leads them to cry.

Seri's renewed version of elegizing as writing and as crying drew my attention to the various uses of the very sound of her voice in the film. I suggest that Seri's quest for the cry through writing is an acutely focal theme in *Queen Khantarisha*. Ronit Hacham wrote that Seri's poems "do not refer to the specific places of wandering, but, rather, to the movement itself—a movement arriving nowhere."[51]

In the non-place of poetic language, Seri explores the districts of the speech, of the scream, of the very sound, in all their unintelligible potential.[52] Wandering thus consists of "a withheld yell"[53] that both remains within as well as breaks from the limitations of language. Audiovisualizing the poet in the last years of her life, recording her autobiographical narrations of her lived experiences, her thoughts about her poetry, and her readings of some of her poems in her own voice, *Queen Khantarisha* foregrounds Seri's various voices to explore the quest for the withheld yell that Hacham theorized. Similar to the abovementioned scrolling and wrapping acts that illuminated the poems' materiality, the withheld yell—that is, the scream within the poem—points to some concrete crux treasured within poetry. Against the backdrop of the Yemenite Jewish women's traditional reliance on the voice in elegizing, and the consequent transformation of the elegy into a sheer text, the voice in this film is both restorative and transformative. *Queen Khantarisha* contemplates on Seri's writing through centering the movements of her voice as metaphorical writing—movements both heard on the film's surface and reflecting on inner processes inherent to writing. Rather than merely read it in her books, we spectators may hear Seri's elegizing voice as it seeks for the cry that it lost. Voiceover narrations and visualized speech performances amalgamate to constitute the narrator and protagonist of *Queen Khantarisha*. If elegizing promises some access to touching, and ultimately attempts to embody, the runny howling that informs vocalization, I ask: What can we learn about Seri's ways of poetizing from her articulations and activations of elegizing as a quest for the cry and the voice's journey to its utmost birthing element?

To embark on this journey toward the core of the voice, we should first listen to, and trace the movement of, Seri's voiceover in the film. Narrating it as her mother's locus of lived burials, Seri's voiceover describes the home as nested with the absorbed sediments of her mother's absent presence. Performing homemaking as her mother used to, the daughter thus dwells in the site of repetitive and potentially deadly activities that contains the traces of her mother. In that venue of death, Seri's voiceover reiterates the mother's experience of her position and labor in the home, thus rendering the home as informed by the residues of the dead mother as well as recovers the mother's voice that named the home a grave. Narrating the home as the grave of the mother while also locating her instructive echoes there, Seri constitutes it as the source and telos of her elegizing—contemplating on the material and maternal origination of her own voice. The home and the practice of homemaking are here the fertile ground from which Seri's elegizing voice essentially emerges. "The image of the infant contained within the sonorous envelope of the mother's voice is a fantasy of origins," Kaja Silverman explained in her work on women in cinema, images of motherhood, and the voice.[54] Silverman also warns that this fantasy that "identifies the mother with sound" sometimes conceives the sonorous mother as a "suffocating confinement" within which the daughter "resembles a prisoner or prey."[55] Indeed, the cinematic site housing Seri's voiceover, which thus becomes the primal scene of vocal emergences, may be said to recall and reverberate with some established and charged, cinematic and fantasmatic fables built around the voice as an indicator of authenticity.

A concomitant analysis of the commonly perceived nature of the sound and, more importantly, the voice, in cinema, upon their possible attached associations, is thus in place here. "It is not so much sound in general as the voice which would seem to command faith in cinema's veracity," Silverman asserted in her seminal work on the voice in classic Hollywood cinema.[56] Founded on "Western" philosophical traditions, "the notion that cinema is able to deliver 'real' sounds is an extension of that powerful Western episteme, extending from Plato to Helen Cixous"; to her, this episteme "identifies the voice with proximity and the here and now—a metaphysical tradition which defines speech as the very essence of presence." If endorsed, not only the idealized meanings, but also the excessive powers, that this framework ascribes to the voice, may provide vital corroborative substantiation to the quest for, and design of, the place where Seri's voice sprouts. Taken from this perspective, the visual scenery of the maternalized home not only begets Seri's voice but also becomes the archaic, anatomic, and authentic arena of interior depths due to the commonly credited role that the voice receives in cinema: it is thus both generative of, and also painted by, the vocal, in this context. To that end, Seri's narrating and/as elegizing voice seems to be emerging from the visual scenery of the home solely by virtue of the traits that the voice in general allegedly comes with, and grants to the scene. To weave the cradle from which Seri's elegies presumably primarily emerge the scene thus weds the visual travels through the interior cozy rooms of the home with Seri's voiceover narration of their layers, legacies, and significances: it is this creation of alleged audiovisual synchronization between the seen and heard homes that in turn renders the home as the symbolic source of Seri's very capacity to voice her elegies.

What happens, however, when the camera consequently faces Seri to absorb her seated speech act and record her voice? Still in the home, the camera takes its spot in front of Seri to center her vocalized appearance, precipitate her speech act, and consolidate her cinematic subject construction: "She hated the house. She wanted to go out, to enjoy herself. She liked to go to synagogue to listen to the prayers. She didn't want the home, which was just work and work and work, endless work," Seri says, now sitting down, as the lens zooms in and out to trace her changing facial expressions. What this work comprised, Seri's closed-up lips continue to list, were not only "grinding, laundering, cooking, and baking" but also to be "always pregnant, always birthing, always bleeding." Finally, Seri recounts her own failure to become a woman according to these regulations: "What is a woman? At the age of three, they say, she is already 'mareh,' [Arabic for a woman], she already knows how to work." This is the overall recollection of her early years within which, against the backdrop of a photo of her from childhood, and although the speech act is replete with talkativeness, an imperative silence inundates the words too: "People always said, 'Bracha, shut up,' even when I didn't open my mouth," Seri states, thus breaking the tabooed silence. By contrast to the instructions she received, Seri never shut up. At the same time, these activities that she talks about already ring a bell to the audience who has watched the beginning of the scene. Indeed, some sense of silencing begets from the striking compatibility between Seri's spoken voice and Seri's narrating voiceover. When Seri discusses the homemaking that she has formerly physically demonstrated—themselves reenactments of her mother's deadening work in the home—Seri also articulates the pains of procreative reproduction that her mother went through, thus metaphorically and metonymically referring to her own birth too. Linking her body and bodily practices to her mother's aching and mortal corporeality in and by her spoken voice, Seri seems to revitalize her mother's physical presence as attached to her own; in this way, she also fantasizes the vocal reconnection with, revival of, and continuity to, that concretely lost yet haunting voice of the mother. To that end, Seri's speech performance and vocal presentation resonate with her narrating voiceover's earlier establishment of the maternal grave of the home as the real source of Seri's voice. In other words, Seri's spoken voice not only talks about but also instantiates an emergence that her narrating voiceover has previously envisioned, longed for, and made possible. For, sitting in and speaking from the home that is immersed in her mother's traces and voices, Seri's spoken voice imagines its direct emergence from the vocal presence of her mother in and as the home. That, in turn, seems to indicate Seri's incarcerated state: for, she manages to speak merely from and about her mother and her mother's voice as her home and, ultimately, her grave. Seeking and shaping the real source of the voice while escorting Seri's walks in her home on the screen, the narrating voiceover encounters, amalgamates with, as well as finally appears to enable, if not enthrall, the spoken human voice of Seri's performing figure. How can we best correlate the vocal voyages toward each other with the cinematic subjectivation of *Queen Khantarisha*'s prominent narrator and protagonist in the scene? How do the voiceover and human voice affect and assemble the subjectivation of Seri, who seems to be the person that provides them? It is, after all, Seri's own voice/over sounding here: or is it?

Watching Seri seated as she speaks to the camera, we may easily imagine that the voice comes out straight from her moving mouth: the voice seems as her own, and conceived as the source of Seri's voiceover. Yet, another look at Silverman's theorizations of the cinematic voice complicates matters once again. With regard with her abovementioned claims, Silverman denounces the ways in which "Western metaphysics has fostered the illusion that speech is able to express the speaker's inner essence, that it is 'part' of him or her."[57] Reproofing specific branches of film theory and its ancestors, Silverman confronts the Westernized theorization of the subject's presumable essence and presence by insisting, "It is through the voice that the subject normally accedes to language."[58] The scene opens with the narrator's voiceover and later reincarnates as the protagonist's voice, and in this way provides us with a glimpse into the cinematic subject formation of Seri in *Queen Khantarisha*.[59] It is against the backdrop of the subjectivizing union between the previously heard voiceover of the narrator and the subsequent emergence of the voice of the protagonist that the speech act may be thought of as directly emerging from the home. In other words, it is by virtue of the sense of Seri's voiceover's homely realness, that we can imagine her culminating linguistic and vocal speech act as emerging from her real human interiority. As the voiceover corroborates and substantiates maternal meanings and material emergences, it also animates and actuates the birthing of the voice of the speech performance—thus ultimately generating Seri's overall seen and heard cinematic subjectivation. Arriving from the elsewhere of invisible narrating Seri to finally retrieving its source and, in this way, reinforcing her visualized speech act, the cinematic sound of the voiceover pieces the frames and collects the details to imbue protagonist Seri's speech act with the inner content of realness. Seri thus lets her cinematized narrator's third person cast, assemble, and signify the origins of her appeared protagonist's first person, or her outward inner voice, or her own self. If to (literally) drive this point home, Seri's speech performance may also be thought of as an elegy in and of itself: since it emerges directly from the deadening yet birthing, maternal and vocal source of the elegizing voice, Seri's spoken voice may be thus said to not only discuss, but also surface as, a dedicated elegy—an elegy to her mother, the original and spectral instructor of elegizing, homemaking, and birthing to her. Seri's voice thus not only narrates, reiterates, and reenacts her mother's place in the home but also elegizes from the place that both emblems as well as embalms the layers of her mother's histories. Situating her speech performances about elegizing as emanating from the home, the grave, and the womb, is the scene's way of instantiating the origination of Seri's voice from its maternal and vocal source. Seri's mother used to "cry over everything": using the present tense to describe the prevalent situation that overshadowed her growing-up years, Seri highlights how the brunt of the echoes of this cry are embedded in her everyday life and performance. This is the cry that Seri craves to touch through her speech performance. This is also the cry that may be facilitated by writing poetry.

Later, Seri further reflects on and complicates our understanding of crying, her practice of poetizing, and the meaning of the production and publication of poetry for her. We see Seri walking around the house, arranging her poetry books on the shelf, and explaining: "These are my books, they grow, take over, multiply … there's nothing, it's simply … a writer who doesn't read, only writes. I feel safer around my books … if my personality is not sufficient, the personality of the books is stronger." Then she sits in her kitchen and intimately relays: "I didn't cry. I don't cry, I write instead. So, I wrote … after I published my first book, I didn't want to die anymore." Finally, threading these two segments together, the camera shows Seri as she is writing a poem, with a pen, on a piece of paper, in the dimmed lights of her home. Seri not only writes instead of crying, she also publishes her poetry instead of dying: her work consists of inscribing the ink on paper to release words as tears onto it, and also of printing, publishing, and distributing of the words to share with the public and endow with life. Her published books, embracing her all around when talking, attest to Seri's industriousness as foundational to her very living, that is, her un-dying, is sustained. We may initially believe that reading is equally absent from both the elegizing women's as well as from Seri's lives. And yet, *Queen Khantarisha* introduced us to Seri as a reader—that is, a poet reading her poems to the public. If she had not shared them publicly, she would die. Whereas *Queen Khantarisha*'s portrayal of poetizing in the home scene seems to frame it as an activity of elegizing, the poetry performance scene outdoors demonstrates how poetizing must trespass the private space, walk across the threshold, and leave the home too, to encounter the public ear of the hearer, and enable Seri's vocalizations of her enlivening poetry—which is in itself a product and reenactment of poetizing.

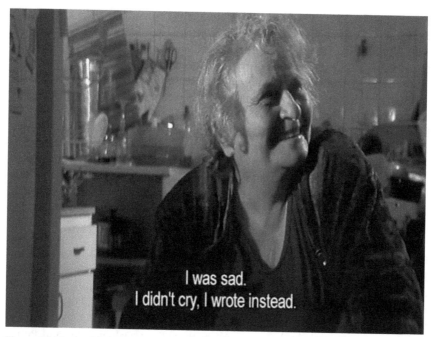

I was sad.
I didn't cry, I wrote instead.

Figure 27 *Queen Khantarisha*, Bracha Seri, "I was sad. I didn't cry. I wrote instead."

Battered and tormented under the force of the fists imprisoning her in destruction, the first-person female in "I Came to You Beaten, and Wretched, and Mute" that Seri reads had arrived at this violent setting of the poem after she has been beaten. Seri's writing hand and reading voice poetize the ongoing experience of violence as an arrival from violence, or as a constant return to, and a reiteration of, violence. Along the lines of the theme of return in her poetry, *Queen Khantarisha* syncopates Seri's performances with circular departures from the house and returns to the home to emphasize the meaning of poetizing as survival. Seri's reading of this poem in one of the first scenes of *Queen Khantarisha* is framed between two corresponsive shots, one of her departure from her home to go to the reading, and one of an arrival back at the house. Poetizing requires and becomes a repetitive ritual of trespassings out from the house and back to the home. The place from which Seri arrives and to which she is headed, the home is the site of violence from which she departs, only to return to the home and write about this violence. Concomitantly to Seri's walks out of the house and into the home, someone else leaves it without coming back in too. Part of the opening scene of *Queen Khantarisha* as well, this one-way flight is important to mention and ponder over. There, prior to the elegizing, and in fact in order for the woman's elegizing to begin, the man has to leave: she may only practice elegizing after her husband has left home. With her departing husband at the door, his wife reveals that he just cannot bear to hear the elegizing, for "he takes it too much to heart";

something about the act of elegizing threatens the runaway man, it seems. As a result, the split second in which the man appears is also when he dis/appears, for, once he enters the screen, he immediately evaporates—in this way also enacting the overall dis/appearance of men from the screen in this film.

A careful look at the threshold of the home, a threshold indicating violence and also allowing the circular promenade of trespassing and rewriting of violence, is in place here. This moment and literal point of departure in the film may be better grasped against the backdrop of the initially discussed context of Jewish Yemenite women's practices of elegizing. As we recall, while women are allowed to elegize in the home, during the first few stages of the prolonged mourning rituals, they must not leave the home and are prohibited from accessing other funeral spaces outdoors.[60] According to Madar, this sexist habit of dictating segregating spatial regulations on elegizing occurs in Jewish Yemenite communities. Yet this habit equally indicates the operative existence of various forms of patriarchy that are universally spatializing the public and private spheres to facilitate the imprisonment of women in the thralls of the home. In this spirit, Henriette Dahan-Kalev affirmed: "In the Arab and Jewish rhetoric, there are no declarative promises for equality—neither in the ultraorthodox and orthodox traditions of Judaism nor in the patriarchal Arab tradition. Mizrahi women ... were disillusioned: they found out that, here [in Israel], they exchanged Oriental patriarchal relations with Western patriarchal relations."[61] Along these lines, Dahan-Kalev and Pnina Mutzafi-Heller have stressed the need to see Mizrahi identifications of women as shaped by national, colonial, and patriarchal histories and discourses and placed in a system of intersecting power dynamics.[62] As Mutzafi-Heller noted, "If Mizrahim [men] were described as 'traditional' and 'backwards,' the common perception of the wives of these Mizrahi men was the litmus paper demonstrating the presumable lack of progressiveness of the Mizrahi community as a whole."[63]

It is impossible not to correlate the Israeli fostering of the public and private arenas as dangerous venues for Yemeni Jewish women. Seen in this light, the man that leaves the home in *Queen Khantarisha* is one in whose name patriarchy liberates men's mobility across private and public spaces while confining women's elegizing to their home, and house—a patriarchal construction made by and for men. Here, it is useful to examine the patriarchal construction of the home alongside the gendered dynamics of filmmaking that *Queen Khantarisha* manifests. To execute this endeavor, it is useful to again consult Silverman, especially her feminist exploration of the gendered dimensions of the voice in classic Hollywood cinema. Silverman depicts the construction of vocal representation as bifurcated along ubiquitously established hierarchical sex roles. Deploying its desire to produce cinematic realness, Silverman confirmed, classic cinema typically relegates the female voice to the fictional plane of the film. Thus, "the sonic vraisemblable is sexually differentiated, working to identify even the *embodied* male voice with the attributes of the cinematic apparatus, but always situating the female voice within a hyperbolically diegetic context" (emphasis in the original).[64] It is this same cinematic apparatus that "locate[s] the male voice at the point of apparent textual origin, while establishing the diegetic containment of the female voice."[65] Under the regulatory operation of cinematic synchronization that systematizes "compatibility of voice to body," female figures become but a "bewildered array of female voices marshaled at both the diegetic and extradiegetic levels for the purpose of creating direct sound."[66]

How can we understand the interrelated performances of leaving, staying, and returning that are taking place at the threshold of the homes of vocalized and/as written elegies? How can we utilize a feminist viewpoint on the gendered, patriarchal, and anti-patriarchal dynamics in *Queen Khantarisha*—a documentary by a feminist filmmaker exclusively working with and focusing on women while mostly vacating its audiovisual surface of the presence of men? Silverman's critique of Hollywood's gendering of voices is useful here as well as, complementarily, the important study of creative, subversive uses of the voice in feminist Third World and transnational documentary cinema. Writing about documentary filmmaker Kim Longinotto, Patricia White shows how a filmmaker's avoidance of obtrusiveness as an interpretive voiceover narrator and insistence on observational filmmaking "help the film's female subjects achieve their goals through witnessing."[67] In the films that White analyzed, as in *Queen Khantarisha*, "it is the subjects … who provide the film with its voice."[68] This method of centering the subjects' various enunciations in the film, coupled with an attention to questions of women's and feminism's place and role in the patriarchal public sphere, strengthens "the viewer's potential to see beyond the frame to ask questions of historical and political context."[69] Let us thus think of the threshold of the house from where the man departs, and through which patriarchy constructs, and routes its rules into, the home, as a cinematically metaphorized spatial spot that Silverman called the "apparent textual origin"—the text of patriarchy, and the rewritten and reclaimed text that Seri poetizes. Traveling through the threshold sideways, Seri's cinematized performances in *Queen Khantarisha* disavow, and also redefine, the patriarchal segregating spatialization of the private and the public sphere. This spatialization has been setting the suffocating circumstances that her voice has embodied: these are the circumstances from which elegizing emerges and in which it operates. The sound of Seri's poetizing supersedes spatial boundaries, however: her traveling voice, obtaining various roles as narrator, speaker, and poet-performer-reader, breaks away from the house, yet also returns to, and reiterates, the very making of the home. For, on the one hand, Seri violates the restrictions inflicted on women and follows the footsteps of the man, leaving the house, and releases her poetry publicly. Yet on the other hand, Seri's reading of her poetry publicly crucially invites more poetizing—elegizing, inscribing—upon returning home too, a return in turn accompanied by Seri's narration, and reiteration, of the construction of the home.

Queen Khantarisha thus foregrounds patriarchy's construction of the home as women's site of burial by escorting Seri as she returns to, and thus reiterates, the entrance of the patriarchal rules at home. Walking into it and dwelling in it, Seri here becomes the poet and performer repeating the infliction of patriarchy on and as the home: yet she is also, crucially, the one subjected to its constant injuries. Poetry is born precisely from this process of coming back home to reiterate the patriarch and rewrite the woman, mother, and mother-like body in the home: returning and/as reiterating is a self-reflexive process of registering, restaging, and reliving of the writing of the patriarchal text that dominant discourses wrote on your skin, concretizing the pain that dominant discourses engrave on our physical and affective state of being. Writing is actually always and inevitably also a rewriting; this is well known. Every poem ever written cites and reiterates those political and patriarchal regulative languages and discourses that not only signify and segregate spaces but also surround and surrender the surfacing of the poem. Yet this scene specifically foregrounds Seri's trips in and out of the house and home as formative steps on the way to, and as, inscribing poetry, to instantiate that, by virtue of the reenactment of the patriarchal writing of segregated spatialization, Seri rewrites the home with herself written in it. Such a return to, and reiteration of the entrance, home, frames her practice of poetizing—elegizing, inscribing—as an inevitable rewriting of the home on the aching, absorbing, embodying written self. *Queen Khantarisha* portrays Seri's inscriptions of her poems at home, which rely on her returning home after encountering the public sphere, as reflexively re-bringing the laws of the public sphere—the laws of patriarchy—to the home. Foregrounding Seri's trips outside and back into the home, *Queen Khantarisha* echoes the journeys of a poet that both goes to and arrives from, depicting, as well as resolutely and repeatedly suffering, violence.

In appreciating the anti-patriarchal aspect of Seri's performances in, out, and around the home, we must acknowledge filmmaker Shaer-Meoded's efforts to carve out the cinematic feminist space for Seri, and the other protagonists of *Queen Khantarisha*, to publicly demonstrate ownership of the representation of their bodies and voices—that is, ownership of layers and pieces of the film itself as cocreators. To that end, *Queen Khantarisha* conspicuously constructs its diegesis through documentary means and, in these processes, explicates Seri's multidimensional roles as the narrator in, as well as protagonist of, the documentary. Constructing Seri's speech acts as elegies, the representational mechanisms of *Queen Khantarisha* complementarily utilize the authorial agency of Seri's narrating voiceover. These vocalizations together make up her poetizing or her revised ways of elegizing. If Seri's speech performance in the home may be thought of as an elegy, and/or a penned poem, for her mother, Seri's narrations vocally simulate, and in this way remind us, that for her to fantasize the reconnection with her mother's primal voice, the cry, through the act of writing, she needs to reiterate and reclaim the language and discourse that enabled her spatial, gendered, and sexualized burial. These are, in turn, the language and discourse with which she inscribes the ink, rewrites the poem, and narrates the cinematized home. In the same way that she conducts homemaking in a house spatially constructed under patriarchy, she also re-poetizes (with/in) the master's structural tools.

Another Man, Another Grave: Naomi Amrani's Songwriting

Centering Seri as the poet protagonist of the film, *Queen Khantarisha* also spends some time with more than one poet. Naomi Amrani is a veteran songwriter who has been writing songs in Arabic for the famous Yemenite Mizrahi singer Tzion

Golan for many years, while working in house cleaning to make a living. Like Seri, Amrani speaks about her life, labor, and creative work in relation to the tradition of elegizing and to the system of patriarchy. While placing her mother as a guiding voice, Amrani politicizes her own marriage and motherhood as living conditions, limitations, and metaphors for her poetization. Upon entering her house, the lens first encounters her husband at the door, and he leads the camera in until it faces Amrani. Standing in front of the camera now, her husband still monitors Amrani from behind her, adding his commentary. This is how Amrani is situated as she shares her earliest experience of songwriting, which she has been doing "ever since I got to know myself, even without pen or paper … after my giving birth, I started writing." After she recalls, Amrani elaborates on her method of writing: "I used to write, and write, everything, I'd fill a notebook, tear it up, and throw it away. I didn't know what the meaning of this was, but the words would come out for me like that, like some sort of rain." Standing behind her, her husband reiterates, ranting: "You know how many songs she has lost? For no reason. As soon as she finished a song, she'd tear it up," he complains. Providing these accounts, Amrani reenacts the tearing with her hands. The husband then repeats her action, mimicking the tearing and the throwing. Yet there was a reason for these acts: Amrani here demonstrates to the camera how she used to write and how she used to feel while writing, and in this way conveys an approach to songwriting that remained with her and is now shared with us. Amrani states her deep regret for tearing of her poems but eloquently explains herself by correlating her practice to the tradition of live singing, which she still practices. "When people sing the lyrics, and they don't know … back then there was no recording … they just sang like that. So I didn't need it. I went, as they say, on any empty stomach, and took it out on the spot … the words … and sang," Amrani praises her practice, with her hands simulating holding a hollowed ball right outside her stomach again. Alongside this performance, we watch Amrani going around the house, taking out notebooks and cassettes that archive her work: while the written texts show her handwriting in Hebrew, the cassettes that she plays for us have the voice singing in Arabic. Amrani's fingers start dancing to the music on the counter.

"On the elegies of the women from Yemen, a genre of poetry transmitted orally, hovers over a danger of loss, which is inherent to the way of transmission," Madar confirms. On the one hand, the tradition of the oral transmission of elegies inherently harbingers the lurking loss due to its ephemerality. Yet on the other hand, writing elegies, a practice that started only after the Yemenite immigration to Israel, threatens to perish precisely this distinct ephemerality of elegizing: "Writing, by contrast to oral transmission, fixes the text in one version and impedes any changing, developing, and adapting of the texts."[70] Expanding on the element of loss embedded in elegizing, Madar highlights that "elegizing subverts the rules by virtue of the women's singing around men, but even more so, by virtue of its call to preserve contact with the dead." Gamliel contends and extends: "The wailer performs an amazing act of existential mediation: speaking with the dead and representing their point of view."[71] There is thus a conscious recognition of loss inherent to elegizing. The elegizing women elegize after the dead, while Seri and Amrani, in turn, elegize the elegy itself, affirming that some steps and routes have vanished upon the posited and positivized embracement and possession of poems through textual means. The contrast between Seri and Amrani's version on elegizing and/as poetizing and songwriting and the other elegizing women assists us in comprehending that inscribing elegies on paper not only marks a new, different way of elegizing, but also signifies the downfall of the old tradition of elegizing as it used to be conducted. Today, Amrani verbally explains, her songwriting can result in inscribing ink on paper in Hebrew, as the many lines written in Hebrew validate, or, in her recording of the songs directly to the tape, in Arabic. As the tearing apart of Hebraized paper lurks like an aching past burdening her presentation, Amrani's reenactments of the un/doing of the written songs with her hands nevertheless indicate her remembering of an embodied loss that reverberates in her recording of her songs straight onto the tape. This performance of ephemeral gestures of reproducing, fragmenting, losing, and finding elegies in the songs responds to the climactic crying that the elegizing women attain in the opening scene of *Queen Khantarisha*. While Amrani mourns the loss of many of her songs, her performance itself also mourns the ephemeral character of elegizing itself—that is, the loss of the active, formative phase of losing as an inherent part of the making of songs.

The following scene centering on Amrani extends her temporal correlation between writing songs and giving birth. With her husband no longer in the frame, she openly discusses her experience of marriage and motherhood. Amrani recounts the occurrences following her immigration to Israel as a young girl who, forced to marry when she was only nine years old, followed her husband's, her father's, and mother's commands at the time. "When I came here, my father knew he married me off young and that the law is different here, so he said, 'If you don't want your husband you can leave, it's your right, until you're 18.' Yet mother, may she rest in peace, said to him, 'What do you want, another man? Not only that you have buried her once, you want to bury her again? Let her stay with the same person.' So we stayed." Upon her mother's resolution, Amrani remained in the marriage rather than replacing it with a later, yet equally potentially deadening, bondage to another man. Reconsidering her mother's voice while rendering the father's proposition irrelevant, Amrani elucidates that the laws of the state of Israel did not apply to her, and surely did not liberate her from the marital and patriarchal pact. While the postponement of womanhood and motherhood could have hypothetically been an option for Amrani at some point, it was eventually its precipitation that dictated her life path. Shortly after her marriage and immigration to Israel, Amrani stopped going to school for good, following a visit to a doctor arranged by her husband, who took her in for hormonal injections to catalyze her period so that she can get pregnant in her early age. Later, it was the same doctor who informed Amrani: "Now you will have a baby in your belly," while she, in response, "laughed." Like Sarah the matriarch, the biblical figure and wife of Abraham, who laughed upon receiving the news of her pregnancy from the angels in her elderly years, fourteen-year-old Amrani too laughed when she received the news of a pregnancy caused by both her husband's, and her godlike Israeli doctor's, highly nonconsensual deeds.[72] It is important to discern here how the mother's reenacted advice perfectly corresponds to Amrani's subsequent articulation of her helplessness in the face of the Israeli medical institution. "Still that fear, you have it in your heart … you still haven't ingested that … it's different," Amrani describes her experience of pregnancy that was donned on her right after school's summer break. As she intimates this feeling, the camera zooms in on her frightened face first, and then rolls down to capture her arms as they embrace her chest and then her hands as they lay on her stomach. In correspondence with the way she laid them in the earlier scene when she discussed her songwriting, Amrani here holds her stomach as if it was a ball—only now, the ball seems to be one with her very stomach. "Really, I couldn't go back to school anymore … I felt that there was something else already … and that's it." Amrani's heartfelt testimony reminds us that sometimes a mother's advice is of much more value than any state legislation. A state that allows such actions as the doctor's biopolitical intervention in young girls' health and reproductive choice is a state that cannot be trusted to defend a girl or woman from her marriage or husband; this is the message that Amrani's mother put forward. Amrani's memory of her mother and her own remembered experience attest to the collaborative workings of the state and the family agents in reproducing patriarchy, depriving women's education, making marriage and economic dependence on a husband unavoidable, and as a result, burying them in the confines of a private sphere that houses endless tasks of homemaking and childcare.

One part is missing from the testimony, as Amrani says nothing about sexual relations. If we forward the film by few minutes, however, we meet the elegizing women who opened *Queen Khantarisha* and they illuminate Amrani's testimony just as they did Seri's earlier. "The girl cannot say anything" about or during sex, even if she dislikes her newly un/elected husband or resents his old age, says one of the elegizing women. If it hurts too much in the process of intercourse, "you can just put a cloth in your mouth," and it shall quickly pass, says the other elegizing woman. You are indeed supposed to force yourself into silence when having sex with your husband. The command that sex and self-silencing go together sheds an important light on Amrani's correlation between songwriting and birth giving, helping us differentiate the two procreations of life and Amrani's brave insistence on holding on to the former while having to do the latter. Whereas Amrani writes songs "on an empty stomach" through which the songs come to her and leave her like a spiritual, creative medium, she becomes a means of the state and the family patriarchal values as her stomach fills with and then releases a baby. Yet whereas that process of making and having a baby instilled fear in her, occupied her stomach from observing its useful spiritual emptiness, and was supposed to teach her how to silence herself, it has instead yielded her songwriting that keeps pouring down like rain.

The home is a grave, as Seri's mother taught us, and the father and husband are buriers, Amrani's mother corroborated. Yet as Amrani's notes and cassettes and Seri's numerous books demonstrate, the home births and houses poetry and songs too. Amrani's continued practice of singing and/as songwriting in Arabic into and/or with a tape recorder preserves and revises the tradition of elegizing.

Figure 28 *Queen Khantarisha*, "Worst case, just put a handkerchief in your mouth."

Loss is here lost and found: it is deposited in Amrani's stomach—a stomach that stands empty as if to corporeally commemorate the objectification of the body and embodiment of muteness that have occurred. While the void in her pit confirms that a rupture has occurred, leaving the inside empty, the gesture of emptiness also points to an unwillingness to learn, host, and accommodate any new imposed practice of poetizing. Poems and words pour like rain, pass through the throat and tongue, and leave through the mouth instead, motivating the hands to inscribe poems and then tear them apart, and the fingers to accompany the singing and recording onto and playing of the tape cassette. Words and poems thus definitely come straight into Amrani's heart but they cannot enter the stomach.

Arabic, Accented: The Daughters' Voices

About midway into *Queen Khantarisha*, the scene centering on the woman who collects and carries dry branches from the trees appears again for the third time. Back in the darkness of the woods with the woman at first, the scene then leads us out of the woods, as the woman hauls the pack of branches on her back and walks out with the camera following her and briefly catching her tormented facial expression. Alongside her pacing steps, we hear Seri's voice in the background, reading from her first story, *Torn*: "Blood is the soul. Where is her soul?" Seri recites from the part of the story when the rabbi invasively examines the young girl's vagina, before her parents sell her in marriage to an old man. Seri then elaborates on the writing and reception of *Torn*, which was adapted into a play in 1983. At the end of that scene, we see the woman carrying the branches for one last time, here walking by a highway jam-packed with cars, in the rain.

In this last section, I attend to how Seri describes the role and ring of Arabic in *Torn* and her relationship to it in this scene as well as in the scene that introduced her in *Queen Khantarisha* and in this chapter. I also revisit and further politicize the sounds and accent of Arabic in Amrani's account about her husband that I analyzed above alongside Seri's words. As mentioned earlier, *Torn* directly criticized the Jewish Yemenite and Zionist Israeli regulations of patriarchy that subjugate girls and women. Yet Seri's reading of it out loud, and sharing the process of its writing, brings forth additional critical messages that may evade the reader's initial impression of *Torn*. "I wrote it in two weeks, in a trance, I had earaches, I couldn't hear anything," Seri recalls. Depicting the Master's tools of fingers and knives engraving their acts on the girl-to-become woman's physical and mental faculties, Seri's sensual capacity to hear is compatibly an ecstatic and aching assault conducted by writing itself. Some sounds Seri was nevertheless able to hear: reading the play out loud, she notes that "it sounds to me like all these curses ... like ... 'impurity' ... it really rings like Yemenite, what can I say ... for me, I thought I wrote this story in Yemenite." Here, Seri's performance revives the process of writing, reconstructing it as Hebrew's verbal assault on her physical senses, an assault in turn producing the audial and ached Yemenite ringing of the text. In particular, Seri recuperates the audial echoes of Yemenite Arabic within the Hebrew word "impure," demonstrating how the sounds survive modern hegemonic Hebrew's rape and silencing of Arabic mothers' tongues. On that note, it is useful to harness our rigorous listening to notice the ways in which Arabic similarly and significantly reappeared earlier in the film, when Seri and Amrani talked about their mothers and what they used to say. "Another man? Not only that you have buried her once, you want to bury her again?" Amrani repeats her mother's response to her father's proposition that nine-year-old Amrani leave her husband and wait till she is eighteen to remarry, and required by the laws of the state of Israel. Beyond the indication of a doubled patriarchal system, the very sound of Amrani's Hebrew speech act evokes important, if implicit, messages too: it is arresting to reckon how her reiteration of the mother's employment of the word "gever," a man in Hebrew, resonates with her reiterated employment of "liqbor," to bury in Hebrew, which, in her mouth, sounds more like 'ligbor.' Amrani's speech performance thus collides the words "man" and burial" and collapses them to the same root of "g.b.r." This collision and collapse strike as fairly familiar to us audience: indeed, initially reiterating her mother's name for the home, Seri employed the actual word that the mother was using, "gabr," a grave in Arabic, and only then translated it into Hebrew as "qever," sounding more like, indeed, "gever."

Seri's and Amrani's performances remind us that, not only the female speakers, but also their spoken Arabic, were silenced and buried in the home, under the command of the gever—the Hebrew male New Jew. "From the point of view of Euro-Israeli establishment, our Baghdadi culture was perceived as the embodiment of Arab inferiority, backwardness, and savagery. To redeem us of our primal sins, we were subjected to an apparatus of erasure,"[73] Ella Shohat recounted the Zionist oppression that her family endured upon their immigration from Iraq

I had a terrible earache.
I couldn't hear a thing.

Figure 29 *Queen Khantarisha*, Bracha Seri, "a terrible earache."

in the 1950s.[74] Reviewing the linguistic and discursive decrees that she and her family had to accede, Shohat detailed the institutional and internalized efforts to strip Arab Jews of their Arabic and Arabness. Shohat vividly reconstructed her lived experience as a bilingual Arab Jewish child in Israel of the 1960s—an Israel determined to render Arabic as the tabooed and prohibited language of the enemy of the Jewish state.[75] At the heart of her autobiographical piece, Shohat's childhood home in the Jewish Israeli town Petach-Tiqua—formerly the Arab Palestinian village Mlabes—is the site where the erasure of Arabic most notably took shape, instigating intergenerational conflict. If the 1900s Jewish-Yemenite-Arab migrants were supposed to carry the Arabic language as a cultural and corporeal trait, the 1950s Arab-Jewish-Iraqi migrants that Shohat introduces to us speak about and through the linguistic entanglements that they were henceforth caught in. "Soon I learnt to master Hebrew in the socially correct form, that is, minus the Iraqi accent,"[76] Shohat recalled her first days in kindergarten. Her grandmother and parents, however, still spoke Arabic at home. The line invisibly lying between the home and the backyard she played in thus delimitated the Arabic and the Hebrew areas. Alas, while terribly affected by this segregation, the child that Shohat was demanded that her elders abandon Arabic completely. "I was becoming free from the traces of the Iraqi shackles on my tongue. I was well on my way to assimilating," Shohat recalled, noting that she was actually "relegating the Iraqi accent in Hebrew as well as my Baghdadi Iraqi dialect and culture to the private

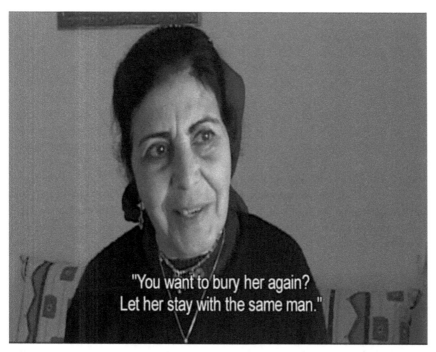

Figure 30 *Queen Khantarisha*, Naomi Amrani: "Another Man? Do You Want to Bury Her Again?"

space of home and family" in this way too. Finally, in that same home Shohat tried to suffocate the Arabic language into an inner, confined, corporeal, yet perhaps also safe, refuge: "Standing in front of the mirror, I tried to put some order in the Babel of consonants and vowels. I learnt to push all these sounds to the front of the mouth as though there was a clear border dividing the deep throat where the guttural sounds of 'qa, 'ta, 'ha, 'aa were made. I was very good, an excellent self-colonized student."[77]

To elucidate the demand of the Israeli state that immigrants like her parents and grandparents forget and eliminate their native Arabic, Shohat refers to a statement by pre-state Zionist thinker and leader Ze'ev Zabotinsky who believed that the revival of Hebrew necessitates its Westernization and thus its dissociation from any affiliation with an "Arabic accent."[78] Complementarily, Shohat elucidated the circumstances in which the Arabic accent became an object of difficult intergenerational negotiations: forbidden from the home and swallowed into the silent interiority of the body, the Arabic language compatibly emerged as an accent in speeches of migrant parents and in their children's nascent awareness. Shohat's desire to Hebraize her speech thus precipitated constant reappearances of Arabic as an accent: the encrypting of the Arabic language within the dubious auspices of the home and the throat thus birthed the Arabic accent as such. As an audial remnant evident of the forceful Hebraization occurring in its expanse, Arabic now obtained new anxious as well as subversive significances. To conceive the accent as authentically expressing an oriental cultural and corporeal character is to reproduce and reinforce the Zionist legacies of the objectification and orientalization of Arab Jews as authentic mute entities. In fact, the accent's reappearances testify on the reluctant decay of a plethora of political communications, connections, and complexities: the silencing discourse of authenticity wished to foster this decay precisely. An end-product of one's forced usage of a language that, even if is her mother tongue, is certainly not her mother's tongue, the reappearances of Arabic as an accent in and under Hebrew result from, and also resist, the prohibition on freely uttering Arabic as a public, political, and discursive language in the conquered Palestine. On that note, Arabic's imprisonment in the home and body of the young girl that Shohat relives in her text insinuates that we may seek its traces precisely in testimonies of Mizrahi women in their homes. Indeed, Amrani's and Seri's accented speech performances in Arabized Hebrew pronounce and protest the intertwined processes of gendering, racialization, and orientalization inflicted on their bodies—on women, mothers, and their mother tongues and voices.

The abovementioned ongoing delegitimization of Arabic as a native tongue of Arab Jews and its rendering as the language of the enemy—the Arab Palestinians—and also, the ridiculing of the Arabic accents especially in Israeli comedy goes hand in hand with the silencing of the Arabic-accented Mizrahi music in Israeli state-controlled television and radio and in popular culture generally.[79] Consequently, some Mizrahi singers who managed to break into the Ashkenazi-dominated realm of Israeli music gave up the Arabic accents in their singing. One relevant example here is Yizrah Cohen's broken and enraged performance of the song *Dry Twigs*. Written as a poem in the early 1980s, and later composed as a song in 1990,[80] *Dry Twigs* poetized the grim details of Makov's abuse of the women who collected dry twigs as mentioned above and, in my interpretation, cinematized into repeated excerpts throughout *Queen Khantarisha*. As the song recounts, Makov whipped the women, rode the donkey across the settlement in front of the beholding eyes and ears of residents, and/or bystanders, calling "this is the sentence of a thief!"[81] As expected, the songwriter who wrote *Dry Twigs*, Dan Almagor, received much criticism for his song, especially from the old Ashkenazi residents of Rehovot, among them Yonatan Makov's grandson.[82] Israel's state-controlled media, moreover, has conducted deliberate efforts to push the song into oblivion: while Yemenite Jewish composer and singer Yizhar Cohen had recorded and performed the song for a special television show that was to be telecast at primetime on Independence Day,[83] Israeli national television moved the planned program to 1:00 am on finding out about the incorporation of this song.[84]

The tight correlation between the silencing of the Mizrahi voice on the Israeli cultural stage and the battering of Yemenite Mizrahi women in the fields is perfectly epitomized by the exclusion of *Dry Twigs* from mainstream primetime broadcasting. It is sufficient to be somewhat familiar with the hegemonic Hebrew accent and the style of Hebrew national and popular music to notice that Cohen strictly adhered to both, in composing and performing the song for the making of *Dry Twigs*. To infiltrate the silencing mechanisms of Zionist-Israeli media, Cohen refrained from any possible musical style that might be associated with the "oriental" genre, acceding to the codes of the domineering Ashkenazi-Zionist Hebrew culture.[85] Nevertheless, his performance was banned from television representation. Almagor's lyrics and Cohen's composition of *Dry Twigs* along Hebrew linguistic and stylistic regulations comprise a conventional and still institutionally marginalized testimony on the horrendous violation of Yemeni women in Zionist Palestine. While confined within Israeli mainstream's musical norms, the jarring pain embedded in Cohen's voice and performance struggles to unearth the hardship of carrying the weight of the Hebrew language between the throat and the tongue. Did the battered women scream under the lashing of Makov's whip? We cannot know. But Cohen's broken voice burdened by Hebrew well delivers the women's experience of abuse, smuggling it through the structural walls of deafness of the Zionist Ashkenazi ear.[86]

In Conclusion: Arabic's Walkways into Hebrew

As mentioned in the opening of this chapter, the scene with the woman collector of the branches is recurrently weaved throughout the stories of Seri and Amrani and their creative work. To come full circle and follow *Queen Khantarisha's* circular fashion, let me add a final facet to my allegorical reading of these scenes. Just as the woman collector walks into the frame of the Israeli public sphere of a highway carrying the branches on her back, Cohen walks into Ashkenazi Zionist Hebrew mainstream media with a burdening, formative piece of history to deliver. Just as the scene with the bustling hyper-industrial site of the highway conflates with the woman's dreary, physical, manual labor, Seri's and Amrani's knowledge of Arabic brings about an exchangeability between the man, the burial, and the grave. Further, intended or unintended, Seri insinuates, and Amrani articulates, an intricate pun, where, in a joke, the words "man" and "grave" collide in an encounter of Hebrew and Arabic in the intimate space of the mouth hosting the accent. The pun, Avital Ronell has postulated, allows "for some degree of retention or at least a necessity of restoring an original meaning, like the great rituals of religious ceremonials, which recall, by means of reconstructive energies and incantation, a prior sense."[87] For Rebecca Schneider, the punned conflation may be regarded as an underscoring of the "certain terror(ism) at the heart of hierarchical distinctions of difference, such as civilized/primitive or male/female."[88] Exploring works of feminist performance artists, Schneider shows how "by collapsing the homophones ... the artists render the symbolic literal. Their pun confuses the space between symbolic and literal reading, and in so doing it both plays with and questions dominant habits of comprehension." Seri's and Amrani's Yemenite Arabic accent renders two words in Hebrew as audially exchangeable, in this way depriving Hebrew of conducting coherent and affirmative significations and subjectivations of the "man" of the house and digger of the grave. This is how Arabic clandestinely plots an explosive literal signification within the symbolic sovereignty of its betraying patron—Modern Hebrew. Employing the Arabic accent as pun, Seri and Amrani defy the debilitating rape that the New Jew's Hebrew inflicts on Arabic-speaking Jews.

From their first performances in the film, greeting us at the threshold of the house and walking into the home, Seri and Amrani perform a homecoming that is also an uprising against their silencing. Seri and Amrani not only quote their mothers, but also reclaim their mother tongues within their Hebrew speech performances, their accents vocally expressing the pain of the submission to Hebrew.[89] To that end, *Queen Khantarisha* pivots the diverse ways in which Seri and Amrani, and their Mizrahi women peers, elders, and ancestors, have been carrying and infusing Arabic into the hegemonic spheres of Hebrew. Seri and Amrani's creative work, and Arabic's intervention in their speech performances, recovers and repairs both the silencing of the voice of Yemenites and particularly Yemenite women in Israel, and reclaims the Arabic language as their own. The poetizing of and singing in Arabic that Seri and Amrani practice nurture the radical vision of the "outsider-within" Israeli cultural production.[90] Concomitantly, their documentary performances of Yemenite women's lived experiences in the home in *Queen Khantarisha* instantiate how their voices live on despite Zionist Hebrew's oppression of their Arabic mother tongues.

In Conclusion of Part II: "The Home"

In their introduction to *Documentary Testimonies: Global Archives of Social Suffering*, Bhaskar Sarkar and Janet Walker define "situated testimonies" as "reflective interviews delivered in situ from the very place where catastrophic events occurred and, in some cases, while the situation continues to unfold." Coined by Walker, the term proves useful to study documentaries made in various places and contexts around the world: in one of the essays of the book, Walker uses it when exploring the documentaries that came out of New Orleans post–Hurricane Katarina; in another essay, Bishnupriya Ghosh analyzed documentary testimonies delivered "in situ" in documentaries made in solidarity with the Narmada Bachao Andolan (NBA, Save the Narmada Struggle), a movement launched against the Indian federal government, the regional governments of Gujarat, Madhya Pradesh, Maharashtra, and Rajasthan, and various corporations in protest of the construction of large dam projects across contributing to climate disaster;[91] some other essays about other places also pay close attention to the documentary testimony in situ, even when the events recounted in and about those places occurred many years ago. It is precisely when we spectators immerse ourselves in the respective situated testimony and performance of each person who retells the events occurring at the place where they are at, the place we are looking at, that we are able to draw connections between the respective events in those localities and start seeking a transnational political language to articulate the similarities in the people's experiences of oppression and pain. For example, when we think of the levees breaking in New Orleans and the dams constructed in western India as manifestations of global environmental racism that bring about climate disasters. Similarly, starting to think about the colonization of Salame in 1948 and subsequent ongoing gentrification of Kfar-Shalem culminating in 2012, we may be able to cultivate language about housing injustice that rejects both forms of oppression. That shared sense of injustice around the right to stable housing begins, however, with those experiencing the deprivation of homes, displacement, and disorientation, naming their homes as such, calling those homes what they are called, regardless of whether they have physical access to those homes currently or not.

As the documentary performances of the Abu al-Hayja family in *500 Dunam on the Moon*, the shepherd in *Route 181*, and Suaad Genem in *Paradise Lost* teach us, spoken words and voiced languages come out in public despite the silencing around the Palestine of 1948 that is enduring under the state of Israel, reconnecting to and drawing strength from the other fragments of Palestine in the West Bank, Gaza, and in exile, where Palestinians hold together the whole of Palestine for the present and future. Documentary performances of Mizrahim and their past and current, unsettled and unsettling, homes are in turn an inherent part of the multidimensional real and representational flow comprising the picture of Palestine today. The designation of Mizrahi immigrants to the Judaization of places where Palestinians once lived is part of an ongoing process of the un/making of the place of Palestine into Israel since 1948, which I elaborated on in Chapter 3. My focus on Mizrahi women in Chapter 4 stresses the importance of the feminist perspective on any political discussion, and continues the thread I started in Chapter 3, discussing filmmaker Ibtisaam Mara'ana's and her protagonist Suaad Genem's conversations in *Paradise Lost* (2003). Like the Palestinian residences discussed in Chapter 3, Jaffa's neighborhood of Salame too was colonized, remapped, and renamed, part of it becoming Kfar-Shalem in Tel Aviv, where *Longing* takes place. Like the land confiscations that Abu al-Hayja refers to with regard to Ayn-Hawd in *500 Dunam on the Moon*, and which the Bedouin shepherd alludes to in *Route 181*, the evictions of Engel and her neighbors from today's Kfar-Shalem are based on the same legal foundation laid out by the 1965 Law of Planning and Construction. Since then, the Jews of Jaffa, who were destined to stay where most of Arab Palestinians were forced out of by ethnic cleansing in 1948, have been subsequently and gradually pushed out by the class-based gentrification. As we see in *Paradise Lost* and *Longing*, respectively, Suaad's and Margalit's families' long-time hometowns changed completely after 1948, with their communities suffering the loss of past habits, ways of making meaning in language, and economic precarity. However, and even though both are native Arabic speakers, Suaad and Margalit speak about the silencing of their manners of speaking from their unequal positions across the segregating Jewish/Arab hierarchical binary. Participating in the struggle to liberate Palestine, Suaad was jailed and tortured by Israel's security forces, which, among other goals, was trying to further silence her relatives and neighbors in Fureidis. Margalit joined these security forces as they were forming an army amid the establishment of the state of Israel—the Palestinians' Nakba—in 1948. Margalit thus became part of that system which later mercilessly perpetrated Suaad and many other Palestinians. Thus, the long year of 1948 not only outlined separate futures for Jews who became Israelis, and Palestinians who remained stateless—based on their identity—but it was also a formative moment in the entrenchment of those identities as enemies. When Palestine became Israel, the women starring in *Paradise Lost* and *Longing* (and/or their families) were relabeled along the ethnonational binary of Arab versus Jew, as an Israeli Arab—a citizen yet refugee in her own homeland and at times a suspected terrorist, and an Oriental Jew[92]—a resident in an appropriated neighborhood that became an arena of precarious housing and, at times, a useful spy. Moreover, Israel's renaming of places of Palestine in Zionist Modern Hebrew and the prohibition on Mizrahim from speaking Arabic in the civil public sphere—among themselves and with Arab Palestinians—further pitted Palestinians and Mizrahim against one another. The politicized pain that sparked the struggle for housing that Engel and many other Mizrahim launched led her to an acknowledgment of how intertwined the oppressions of Palestinians and Mizrahim are, as well as how intertwined their lives were within the context of the Arab geographic, cultural, and linguistic world before 1948 and, most importantly how necessary it was for Israel to segregate their lives and prevent any provision for a joint struggle against the state. In other words, as I am arguing throughout the book, the experiences of pain of Suaad and Mara'ana, Engel, Seri, and Amrani set them apart in an attempt to make them forget that their pain is stemming from the same ongoing efforts to spatially and discursively remap Palestine as Israel and turn Arabs and Jews into enemies.

Yet even if they forgot, their performed testimonies in the films help us remember that both Palestinian and Mizrahi women in Israel live on while struggling with the loss of former linguistic habits and affiliations andthe sense of emptiness that remained in them. Suaad and Mara'ana, Engel, Seri, and Amrani remind us of all the possible intricate ways of spelling out the workings, and speaking out against, this silencing. Analyzed side by side, I wish to highlight how both Palestinians and Mizrahim are similarly hindered from accessing familiar usages of language and discourse, intelligibility and credibility, and similarly speak up and retell their histories in their own voices. All the films discussed in this book focus on the impactful repercussions of the 1948 foundation of the state of Israel on their bodies and the places they called home and, by extension, on their capacities to speak about what has happened to them and to their homes. The historicization, contextualization, politicization, and de-psychologization of the pain of living is the point of departure of their reclaiming of their own identifications and their homecoming to their own languages and discourses.

CONCLUDING NOTES: LOOKING TOWARD MIZRAHI SOLIDARITY WITH THE PALESTINIAN STRUGGLE

In the introduction to this book, I described the emotional draw of the documentaries I analyzed: how easy it was to feel touched by them, to relate to the people on the screen sharing their stories of pain, and to feel empathy toward them. I also pointed out the importance of rewinding and slowing down the process of spectatorship, to pay attention to the cinematic and performative means, the historical context, and the politics of representation surrounding these documentary performances of pain. Yet it is rare that you actually see your own image reflecting back at you while watching a film at home, on your computer, when you had no idea that you appeared in one. That is what happened to me one day in the spring of 2014, as I was preparing to launch the Mizrahi Film Series at New York University with a screening of George Itzhak's *Reading Tehran in Tel-Aviv* (2014), a film about two Jewish Iranian women residing in the United States in Israel, and their cultural and political work. "I actually myself very much see it as a political act: for me it was part of my political activism," this is how Orly Noy, an Iranian-Israeli writer, translator, and activist based in Jerusalem and the star of the film, explained her Mizrahi identification and work in one of the scenes. And there I was: not remotely aware of or ready for the camera, my face wore an expression of shock—oddly reflecting my shock as a spectator watching herself.

I close the book with this moment of estranged self-recognition since it metaphorically captures the gist of this project. While *Reading Tehran in Tel-Aviv* is the first and only film in which I saw my own image, the documentaries I analyzed in this book nourish the spectator's radical identification with someone else's pain as their own. I argued that the different experiences of pain of Palestinians and Mizrahim relayed, documented, cinematized, and performed in the films commonly and powerfully demonstrate relational pain as a key representational and political tenor, cultivating human documentary performances as relational sites in the films, and conspicuously thematizing the body and the home. As Part I, "The Body," conveys, Palestinians and Mizrahim testify on and reclaim their experiences of heightened physical vulnerability and ongoing resilience in the face of state violence. Chapter 1 followed the experience of Palestinians in Jenin who witnessed destruction of bodies, houses, and their collective fabric of life while surviving the constant threat of destruction themselves due to being outlawed as

Figure 31 *Reading Tehran in Tel Aviv*, Orly Noy (center) and author (to her left) at a demonstration in Sheikh Jarrah, Jerusalem.

a "security problem." The experiences of pain as conveyed by David Deri in *The Ringworm Children* and Reuben Abergil in *Kaddim Wind: A Moroccan Chronicle*, depicted in Chapter 2, deliver their state of physical vulnerability due to the pathologization and criminalization of Mizrahim as a "social problem." In turn, that pathologization and racialization of Mizrahim mirrors the Zionist exoticization and objectification of Palestine—the colonial, orientalist, and nationalist desire to feel and touch the land of Palestine directly and un-mediatedly. Along these lines, place, displacement, disorientation, and belonging were the focus of Part II, "The Home." Chapter 3 attended to the depictions of the gradual change of the place of Palestine as experienced, narrated, and performed by '48 Palestinians. As Chapter 4 showed, in *Longing*, Margalit Engel remembered becoming a spy in order to help fight Palestinians out of their lands—although she was a Palestinian Jew herself before. In *Queen Khantarisha*, Bracha Seri and Naomi Amrani found and recovered creative practices, and their connection to their Arabic mother tongues, despite the systematic silencing, resisting their making as "mute natural workers" in the fields appropriated from Palestinians. The newly assigned spies and manual workers were supposed to materialize the Hebraization of the space of Palestine, including the eviction of Palestinians from there, with their so-called attentive ears and intuitive hands.

"The myth of 'share it and change the world' is kept alive with success stories," Jane Gaines demonstrated, way before, and more thoroughly after, the global spread of digital and cyber technologies.[1] As I claimed in Chapter 1 and explicated in what followed, reactionary maneuvers on the inabilities of documentary filmmaking only distract us from their transformative power. The documentaries I analyzed invite spectators to relate to, encounter relationality, and reflect on the positionality that have placed others and themselves in the sociopolitical and emotional economy of Israel-Palestine, wherever they are. Intuiting the emotional draw to explore one's pain and simultaneously and multidimensionally relate to the different pains of other people, I contended that the documentaries inspire us to undertake the hard task of practicing our emotional relatability to one another's different experiences of pain and expressions of pain. That is, we may rationally understand that the experiences and expressions of pain of Palestinians and Mizrahim are structurally interrelated; yet since the historical and spatial segregation and instigation do take a formative toll, we are now obliged to invest in the laborious practice of emotional relatability in order to not only know theoretically, but deeply feel, our interrelatedness. I fathomed how the effects of the ongoing Zionist and Israeli un/re/making of Palestine are represented by those living through, living on, and reliving, this history from below, gathering and threading the analyzed scenes to access a comprehensive, affective understanding of the human fabric in the place of Israel-Palestine.

Like some other Mizrahi organizers, Noy explicated in *Reading Tehran in Tel Aviv* that her path to Mizrahi organizing came out of her work in solidarity with Palestinians in Israel-Palestine—a path ultimately leading her to work in both organizing realms simultaneously. As she explains, her involvement in Palestinian anti-occupation organizing inspired her curiosity to explore the history and struggles of her own Mizrahi family and community in Israel. Writing this book, my journey walked through a similar path as Noy's narration of her politicization: I started studying visual culture in Israel-Palestine with a deep political commitment to Palestine and Palestinian freedom, and, along the way, realized I cannot offer knowledge about Palestinian lives and representation without reflecting on my own position as a Turkish-Israeli Mizrahi scholar. Further, I have learned how much formative impact the history of Palestine and Palestinians have had and continue to have on Mizrahi histories, lives, and identifications. Thus, this book is a specifically Mizrahi intervention in the field of documentary cinema in Israel-Palestine—an intervention revisiting the core matter of Palestine as it hovers over the history of Israel-Palestine, consistently shaping not only Palestinians but also Mizrahim, their everyday lived experience, their identification as such, their one-way migrations from various places in the Middle East to Israel, their economic precarity, and more. I weaved each part of this book accordingly: both Part I and Part II begin with a study of Palestinian lives and representation, and then bring in the facet of the different, racially segregated, yet interrelated, Mizrahi lives and representation. Overall, by adding the Mizrahi voice to the story of Palestine, I have endeavored to paint a fuller picture of the history of Zionism and Israel's attempted process of un/re/making, Hebraizing, and de-Arabizing Palestine, fixing the Arab/Jewish identity binary and spatial segregation, and the continuous ramified and interconnected tides of resistance to it.

Relatedly and uncoincidentally, the journey of writing this book also took place against the backdrop of the growing intersectional and transnational interconnectedness of networks of movements—movements that attempt to better understand the connections between their struggles against oppressions and state violence. In the stretch of time between 2014, the time that I started to write this book, and now, I have been carried by these hopeful pulls tightening the theoretical understandings and the human bonds between those who are leading struggles for civility and liberation around the world. One such major pull emanated from the uprising in Ferguson in 2014, following the killing of Michael Brown by police gunfire, and the acquittal of Darren Wilson, the cop who shot him (as noted in Chapter 2), and the founding of the Black Lives Matter movement. The messages of support and encouragement pouring from Palestine to the protesters in Ferguson brought about a reinvigorated examination of the historical ties between US-based and global Black movements and Palestinian movements , and a recommitment to understanding Black and Palestinian struggles as interrelated.[2] We are seeing these connections further fertilized today, in 2020, as the uprisings to protest the killing of George Floyd and so many other Black Americans in the United States throughout history are sweeping across the world—a world hit by a global pandemic disproportionately harming those already most vulnerable, racialized populations—including in Israel-Palestine. Understanding the interconnectedness of the struggles of Palestinian and Black movements, reaffirms them as an utmost core inspiration for many historical anticolonial and antiracist movements around the world, including the Mizrahi struggles in Israel-Palestine, especially those that emerged from the 1970s Black Panthers movement in Jerusalem Yet further, as Mizrahim, we have to reckon with our position of privilege and proactively acknowledge it. In the Introduction, I positioned myself in the field as a Turkish Israeli Mizrahi scholar with Jewish privilege in the Jewish state of Israel—where I am from—and with the privilege of visiting Turkey, also where I am from, unlike many of my fellow Arab Jewish Mizrahim. This attempt to transparently explicate my identification and viewpoint from the outset fuels my intersectional intervention of considering interrelated oppressions and relational pain. In acknowledging our indebtedness to interconnected anticolonial and antiracist movements, especially Black and Palestinian, and in endorsing our solidarity with them, I am encouraging more Mizrahi filmmakers, scholars, and organizers to do so too.

To that end, the current political moment of the accelerated interconnectedness of movements across the globe is different from, yet also built on, the moment of the turn of the twenty-first century, when the new trends of technology, media, and politicized self-representation discussed above, emerged in full force. The time frame I considered in *Documentary Cinema in Israel/Palestine*, the first decade of the 2000s, was a time of extreme accelerated segregation, both spatially and in terms of organizing around identity, and in filmmaking. Yet is was also a time when shared cinematic, performative, and political elements started appearing across different communities, much due to the global state of heightened digital and cyber connectivity. The pivotal challenge that this book took on is to explore and elevate the shared cinematic, performative, and political mission of representing pain relationally despite and beyond the very filmmakers' inclination to remain within the terms of segregation delimiting Palestinians from Mizrahim. That meant that, I looked at the turn of the century and identified the latent, liminal commonalities implicitly—perhaps somewhat unconsciously—manifested in separate filmic self-representations of different communities. The seeded commonalities perhaps erupted despite themselves—that is, despite the films submitting to the general fixturing of segregation rather than plunging into the interconnecting of Palestinians and Mizrahim through filmmaking. They differ from, yet precede and inform, intentional digital and cyber politicized representational collaborations across geographic borders transnationally and beyond definitions of mainstream, documentary, or experimental genres and styles, such that Patricia Zimmerman named "Public Domains."[3] Yet from where we stand now, we can retroactively view those commonalities as the seeds from which current political trends of interconnecting movement work transnationally and later branch out.

As I mentioned in the introduction, some documentaries created in the first decade of the 2000s do bring Palestinian and Mizrahi perspectives together. However, they do not intentionally deploy analyses of the prolonged structural interrelatedness of the pain of Palestinians and Mizrahim, thus running the risk of confining the conversation to the Israeli-Palestinian symmetry framework. Further, as elaborated in Chapter 4, Noy's stance as a Mizrahi organizer and thinker fostering solidarity with Palestinians as presented in *Reading Tehran in Tel Aviv*—a film made in the United States by a Mizrahi American filmmaker—is far from representative of a major trend in Israel currently. More often than not, the prominent wave of Israeli Mizrahi cultural production—sometimes called the Mizrahi cultural renaissance—such as poetry, literature, music, and cinema abundantly flourishing since 2009, and more thoroughly after 2011,[4] expanded the dedicated attention to Arab cultures that, as Chapter 4 shows, has been eminent in Mizrahi documentaries since 2000. However, similar to the following examples of documentaries that I list, the new Mizrahi wave delivered a limited spectrum of Mizrahi attention to Palestine and Palestinians, from none to some. Ron Cahlili's documentary series, *Arsim and Frechot: The New Elites* (2014), for example, gathered intimate scenes of Mizrahim, some of them organizers, thinkers, and artists, testifying on everyday racism as they encounter and understand it. Notably, the interview with Khen Elmaleh, an outspoken writer and DJ and advocate of Palestinian freedom, foregrounds the stigma that she deals with within Mizrahi communities because of her views. Similarly, spotlighting organizers, Elad Ben-Elul's and Yossi Brauman's documentary web series *The Prophets* (2015) portrays a generation of Mizrahi activists who radically criticize the state of Israel for its racist treatment of their parents, grandparents, and themselves. While a handful of these activists—Barack Cohen, for example—question the exclusively and exclusionary Jewish definition of the state and its racism toward Palestinians, most of them do not attend to that question, with one of them even endorsing the expansion of Jewish settlements over Palestinian land while framing their ideological worldview as distinctively Mizrahi. Importantly, these two series developed a veneered, hyper-edited, and hyper-commodifying aesthetic not unsimilar to the neoliberal celebration of "the subject of true feeling" appearing in films such as *The Gatekeepers*, as mentioned in the Introduction—albeit, true feeling here is Mizrahi hurt rather than Zionist-Israeli guilt. As far as *The Prophets* go, this aesthetic is at times coupled with a reactionary ideology that, especially if watched outside of Israel (the series is available with subtitles), runs the risk of "brownwashing" Israeli crimes as acts of Mizrahi nativist entitlement.[5]

Employing a different style and theme, Eyal Sagui-Bizawe's and Sara Tisfroni's *Arabic Movie* (2015) tracked down the rise of Egyptian movies to abundant popularity in Israel in the 1970s and 1980s, explicating the context of the 1967 occupation of the West Bank and Jerusalem as the backdrop. The film emphasizes Israel's goal of distributing entertainment and spreading propaganda in the newly occupied territories as the reason why the Egyptian films were made available in Israel-Palestine in the first place, including a testimony from an anonymous Palestinian person from Jerusalem about their role in that industry. Taking yet another different angle, in 2017, David Deri's film *Salah, This Is Eretz-Israel/The Ancestral Sin*, centered the filmmaker's hometown of Yerucham in the Negev/ Naqab (this is a person different from the organizer we met in Chapter 2). The film made significant waves as it explored previously undisclosed archival documents that attest to the blatant racism of the state officials who orchestrated the "population dispersal" plan in the periphery in the 1950s. The residents of Yerucham, including Deri's parents, testify about the police violence and other forms of state vengeance that they encountered upon trying to escape to seek decent work and living outside the underdeveloped town. Early in the film, a scholar of geography notes briefly when interviewed, that the main goal of the "population dispersal" plan was to repopulate the ethnically cleansed Palestinian lands of the Naqab, now called the Negev, with Jewish immigrants. Both Sagui-Bizawe and Deri directly address the backdrop of Palestinian oppression and the depopulation of Palestine constitutive to Mizrahi oppression, yet remain cautious in the screen time allocated to testimonies from and about Palestinian oppression. Relatedly, even more recently, the documentary series *Transit Camps* (Shalem Baharad, Eric Bronstein, Hila Shalem Baharad, Shay Lahav, Dina Zvi Riklis, 2019) brought together previously unheard personal testimonies from Mizrahim (and Ashkenazim) who survived the transit camps in the 1950s and 1960s, including living through harsh conditions of strict policing and punishment.

It thus seems that recent years are a time when some Mizrahi filmmakers construe the intersectional connections between the Palestinian and Mizrahi oppressions and struggles as unavoidably requiring attention: yet the direction of the narration of these intersections significantly vary, from supporting collective liberation for all, to justifying and promoting Jewish supremacy. Indeed, a key factor to assessing the politics of a Mizrahi film is how much screen time the filmmaker dedicates to Palestinian politicized self-representation in their own voice in film. In closing this book, let me briefly and symbolically concoct a thread between a film from 2000 and a recent 2016 film, both dwelling in "the Mizrahi/ Palestinian nexus," in Ella Shohat's words, to paint a broad stroke of the change in the place and representation of Palestinians in Mizrahi-centered films: the first is Nizar Hassan's and Danae Elon's *Cut* (2000), mentioned in Chapter 4, and the second is Moran Ifergan's *Palestinians: Us First* (2016). *Cut*, as Shohat wrote, "reflexively narrates a triangular encounter between a Euro-Israeli filmmaker (Elon) and a Palestinian filmmaker (Hassan), on the one hand, and Arab-Jews, on the other. It calls attention to the process—from the suspicion with which the filmmakers are greeted to their bonding with some of the interviewees."[6] Capturing an encounter between a Palestinian filmmaker, Hassan, and Mizrahi families who arrived in Agur in Israel after the village had been depopulated from Palestinians, *Cut* importantly pivoted the painful ruptures, silences, and silencing embedded in conversations between Palestinians and Mizrahim after 1948. Yet in creating an intersectional examination of a Palestinian filmmaker and Mizrahi subjects, and in foregrounding the inabilities to speak to one another, *Cut* also planted the seeds for understanding how important it is to nevertheless try to have those conversations—or at least start, as the films I analyzed did, with long-form testimonies that return to the structural historical questions related to the year 1948. Shohat wrote:

> The film itself relays an edifying story of building trust—of hopeful possibilities and anxious impossibilities ... *Cut* ends with an appreciation of the limits of trust in the war zone. The concluding acknowledgement— "This film would not have been possible without the love and the trust of 'Agur's residents'"—is cut short by the aggressive acoustic and visual presence of the military helicopters.[7]

In turn, the marking of the intimidation and silencing instigating an impasse of trust between Palestinians and Mizrahim, via all of the films I analyzed in this book, enabled the cinematic and performative bridging of this impasse in Ifergan's *Palestinians: Us First*, which captures an insightful, explicitly Mizrahi view of a '48 Palestinian as they views us Mizrahim—and specifically their thoughts on the concurrent Mizrahi cultural renaissance in Israel. A rare example of a documentary by and about Mizrahim centering not on us but, rather, on '48 Palestinians, who proudly identify as Palestinian in every way, *Palestinians: Us First* is the third episode out of the three that comprise the series *We Are the People* (Ron Cahlili, 2016) with each episode made by a Mizrahi filmmaker, exploring the approaches of Ashkenazim, Mizrahim, and Palestinians toward the "new Mizrahi discourse," respectively. In one of the most memorable scenes, Palestinian actor, writer, and thinker Firas Khory compares the hardship of his community in Israel with Ifergan's disconnect from her parents' Moroccan Arabic, while emphatically and deeply reckoning with her pain: "We're [Palestinians] unfortunate, but your people are totally miserable, totally miserable ... you see here an entire society [Palestinian], continuing to speak its language, which it has for thousands of years, and which keeps more or less the same way of life it always has, where people's lives are interlaced, while your family was brought here from Morocco, dumped in some ... housing project, cut off from everyone they knew, living in poverty, leading you to search for your identity ... and you have no connection to the land, to this place." Among my other hopes, I wish this book inspires more quests for such intimate, tough, and tender, precious moments of reciprocal recognition.

NOTES

Introduction

1 Adrienne Rich, "The Blue Ghazals," in *Collected Early Poems 1950–1970* (New York: W. W. Norton, 1993), p. 372.

2 Claudia Rankine, *Citizen: An American Lyric* (Minneapolis: Graywolf Press, 2014), p. 28.

3 Sami Shalom Chetrit, "A Mural with No Wall: A Qasida for Mahmud Darwish," in *Jews* (Somerville: Cervena Barva Press, 2014). Also appeared in *Warscapes*: http://www.warscapes.com/poetry/mural-no-wall (accessed November 23, 2019).

4 By "Israel" I am referring to the state of Israel marked by the Green Line in 1949, after the 1948 war. By "Israel-Palestine" I am referring to the entire region between the river Jordan and the Mediterranean sea that is mostly dominated by the state of Israel today. I say more about the Green Line in the following sections.

5 Inspired by Shohat's landmark, *Israeli Cinema: East/West and the Politics of Representation*, some research on Israeli cinema has moved in the direction of studying identity politics, ethnicity, and the representation of minorities in Israel. For few examples of work that elaborate on Shohat's arguments on identity politics in Israel in Israeli cinema, see Yosefa Loshitzky, *Identity Politics on the Israeli Screen* (Austin: University of Texas, 2001), Raz Yosef, *The Politics of Loss and Trauma in Contemporary Israeli Cinema* (New York: Routledge, 2011), and Miri Talmon and Yaron Peleg (eds.), *Israeli Cinema: Identities in Motion* (Austin: University of Texas Press, 2011). Joining these works, Yaron Shemer's thorough and comprehensive examination of Mizrahi film and representation in contemporary Israeli cinema has recently been published. See Yaron Shemer, *Identity, Subversion, and Place in Contemporary Israeli Cinema* (Ann Arbor: University of Michigan Press, 2013). Much research on Palestinian cinema from the West Bank and Gaza, within and outside of Israel's 1948 borders, and by exiled Palestinians around the world, has emerged since 2000 too. Reviewing the latest wave of Palestinian cinema, Nurith Gertz and George Khleifi trace the construction of "personal memory based on testimonies, individual histories, and interviews," especially after the two intifadas. See Nurith Gertz and George Khleifi, *Palestinian Cinema: Landscape, Trauma, and Memory* (Edinburgh: Edinburgh University Press, 2008), p. 191. As for Palestinian documentaries particularly, Hamid Dabashi speaks of the "traumatic anxiety" of Palestinian interviewees, pointing to their henceforth performances of "formality" as well as "authority and authenticity." See Hamid Dabashi, "Introduction," in Hamid Dabashi (ed.), *Dream of a Nation: On Palestinian Cinema* (New York: Verso, 2006), pp. 7–22. This common bifurcation stresses the significance of the framework of national cinema informing Palestinian and Israeli cinemas, fiction and documentaries alike, and yet needs to be challenged.

6 As Ella Shohat has suggested, contemporary representations of " 'Palestine' and 'Israel' are co-implicated and must be discussed relationally ... in some ways, it

is virtually impossible to speak of Israeli cinema without 'Palestine,' just as it is virtually impossible to speak of Palestinian cinema without 'Israel.'" See Ella Shohat, "Postscript," in *Israeli Cinema: East/West and the Politics of Representation*, 2nd ed. (London: I.B. Tauris, 2010), p. 273.

7 I use the term "documentary performance" to refer to an audio-visualized, mediated, documented, and cinematized appearance of a person in front of a camera and on a screen as part of a cinematic scene. In *Conceptualizing the Documentary Performance*, Elizabeth Marquis builds on both sociology and documentary film studies to offer "a framework for understanding and discussing the documentary actor's work ... which takes into account everyday performative activity (tier #1), the impact of the camera (tier #2) and the influence of specific documentary film frame-works (tier #3)." See Elizabeth Marquis, "Conceptualizing the Documentary Performance," *Studies in Documentary Film*, vol. 7, no. 1 (2013), pp. 45–60. This book engages an approach mostly drawing on visual culture and performance studies, as I elaborate in note 9, thinking through a person's performance as a human medium in constant conversation with the filmmaker, filmmaking apparatus, and mechanisms, and teases out some of the most quintessential questions informing film and documentary studies as a whole—questions about authenticity, mediation, and the construction of reality in representation. This book thus engages in conversation with the recent revisited attention given to the term "performance" by documentary scholars studying reenactments, such as Jonathan Kahana and Bill Nichols. Kahana reminds us that the questions about the ambiguous ontological status of the filmed enactment—"an enmeshment of ... *to do; to perform*" date back to the very emergence of cinema. "Because the moving image comes to us with an effect of immediacy built in ... the medium already seems to have the effect of public history, decreeing to audiences of any filmed event that *it was this way, this happened* ... it can be very difficult to distinguish 'actual' actions from performances." See Jonathan Kahana, "Introduction: What Now? Presenting Reenactment," *Framework: The Journal of Cinema and Media*, vol. 50, no. 1, article 3 (Spring and Fall 2009), p. 53. Bill Nichols stressed that "the reenacted event introduces a fantasmatic element that an initial representation of the same event lacks. Put simply, history does not repeat itself, except in mediated transformations such as memory representation, reenactment, fantasy." Bill Nichols, "Documentary Reenactment and the Fantasmatic Subject," *Critical Inquiry*, vol. 35, no. 1, (Autumn 2008), p. 73.

8 In the introduction to the special issue of *Cinema Journal* from 2006 titled "In Focus: Documentary," editor and longtime scholar of queer cinema B. Ruby Rich asserts that the growing abundant distribution and access of international documentaries alongside the more intentional emphasis on internationalism in documentaries requires that documentary scholarship be "specifically trained in international documentary practice, its local specificities, and its place in the transnational system of distribution and exhibition." Relatedly to this tenor, Rich insists on "the necessity of widening the scope of theoretical documentary analysis to look beyond the cinematic discourse." This book ventures both these missions. See B. Ruby Rich, "Documentary Disciplines: An Introduction," *Cinema Journal*, vol. 26, no. 1 (Fall 2006), p. 46. In turn, the analytic framework of "visual culture" that I employ throughout the book accommodates the needs for both interdisciplinary and local/transnational outlooks in studying documentaries as stated above, as well as addresses the accelerated fluidity in genre and media in the age of digital and cyber global distribution. As Nicholas Mirzeoff conceptualized around the turn of

the century precisely: "Visual culture has gone from being a useful phrase for people working in art history, film and media studies, sociology … to a new means of doing interdisciplinary work … the reason … for this heightened visibility is that human experience is now more visual and visualized than ever before." See Nicholas Mirzeoff, *An Introduction to Visual Culture* (London: Routledge, 1999), p. 3.

9 This book wishes to imbue the abovementioned theorizations of documentary with the overlapping understandings of "performance" and "performativity" that have been emerging at the intersection of gender and sexuality studies and trauma studies since the 1990s. In this book, to borrow from Diana Taylor, performance "function[s] as vital acts of transfer, transmitting social knowledge, memory, and a sense of identity." Performance is "an epistemology" and an "embodied practice" that operates alongside "other cultural practices" as part of the overall "aesthetics of everyday life." The theorizations of "performance" and "performativity" within gender and sexuality studies, especially Judith Butler's landmark thought, heavily drew on J. L. Austin's *How to Do Things with Words*. Eve Kosofsky Sedgewick and Andrew Parker differentiated between the theatrical "performance," which emphasizes "the extroversion of the actor" and the deconstructive "performative," linked to "the introversion of the signifier." Yet crucially, Sayidia Hartman asserts the need to consider performance and performativity together (alongside her theorization of pain as relational): "the interchangeable usage of performance and performativity is intended to be inclusive of displays of power, the punitive and theatrical embodiment of racial norms … the entanglements of dominant and subordinate enunciations … and the difficulty of distinguishing between [them]." This interdisciplinary push is required where documentaries are concerned, and especially in the digital age of accelerated visual popular culture defining our contemporary everyday. See Judith Butler, *Bodies That Matter: On the Discursive Limits of Sex* (London: Routledge, 1993); Andrew Parker and Eve Kosofsky Sedgwick (eds.), "Introduction," in *Performance and Performativity* (New York: Routledge, 1995), p. 2; Saidiya Hartman, *Scenes of Subjection: Terror, Slavery, and Self-Making in Nineteenth-Century America* (New York: Oxford University Press, 1997), p. 5; Diana Taylor, *The Archive and the Repertoire* (Durham: Duke University Press, 2003), pp. 2–3. J. L. Austin, *How to Do Things with Words* (Oxford: Claredon Press, 1962).

10 Daniel Dor, *Intifada Hits the Headlines: How the Israeli Press Misreported the Outbreak of the Second Palestinian Uprising* (Bloomington: Indiana University Press, 2004). US mainstream media painted a similar picture, especially with regard to the emphasized negative attention to Palestinians as involved in terrorism. See Amani Ismail, "Mission Statehood: Portraits of the Second Palestinian Intifada in US News Media," *Media, War & Conflict*, vol. 1, no. 2 (2008), pp. 189–92.

11 Patricia R. Zimmerman, "Public Domains: Engaging Iraq through Experimental Digitalities," *Framework: Journal of Cinema and Media*, vol. 48, no. 2 (Fall 2007), pp. 67–9.

12 Among the major Israeli film funds that supported primarily documentary cinema are the following: The New Israel Fund for Cinema and Television (1993), the Makor Foundation (1999), and the Gesher Foundation for Multicultural Cinema (2001).

13 Jonathan Kahana, "Introduction to Section VII: Documentary Transformed: Transnational and Transmedial Crossings," and Wu Wenguang, "DV: Individual Filmmaking," in Jonathan Kahana (ed.), *The Documentary Film Reader: History, Theory, Criticism* (Oxford: Oxford University Press, 2016), pp. 913–15, and pp. 956–61, respectively.

14 Shmulik Duvdevani, *First Person Camera: Personal Documentary Cinema in Israel* (Jerusalem: Keter, 2010). Raya Morag, *Waltzing with Bashir: Perpetrator Trauma and Cinema* (London: I.B. Tauris, 2013). Pablo Utin, *Requiem for Peace: Representations of the Conflict in Israeli Cinema Following the Al-Aqsa Intifada* (in Hebrew) (Tel Aviv: Safra, 2018).

15 Among the documentaries the following are noteworthy: *Checkpoints* (Yoav Shamir, 2003), *Dear Father, Quiet, We're Shooting …* (David Benchetrit, 2005), Yariv Mozer's *My First War* (2007), Tamar Yarom's *To See If I'm Smiling* (2007), Avi Mograbi's *Avenge One of My Eyes* (2005) and *Z-32* (2009), *Wasted* (Nurit Kedar, 2007), *The Law in These Parts* (Ra'anan Alexandrowitz, 2011). Despite the commonalities they share as mentioned above, the films present no unified mode—neither stylistically nor politically. Films such as those by Ra'anan Alexandrowitz and Avi Mograbi may be said to deploy a more critical line against Israel's systematic use of state violence against Palestinians, thus turning the genre's centering of the Israeli veteran on its head.

16 Among these films are *Mur (Wall)* (Simone Bitton, 2004), *Bil'in Habibti* (Shai Carmeli Pollak, 2006), *Fence, Wall, Border* (Eli Cohen, 2006), *Budrus* (Julia Bacha, 2009). With regard to *5 Broken Cameras*, Yael Friedman argues that it was shaped by problematic colonial power relations. Guy Davidi, the Jewish-Israeli filmmaker's paternalistic takeover on the script that was originally proposed by Emad Burnat, the Palestinian filmmaker and journalist and resident of Bil'in, coupled with the interventions of the authoritative auspices of Greenhouse, the Israeli-European Union production initiative that coordinated the making of the film, created conditions that were ultimately not primarily focused on Burnat and his community's struggle against the separation wall and Israel's violence, but on painting a nice picture of Israeli filmmakers as desiring of peace and partnership with Palestinians. See Yael Friedman, "Guises of Transnationalism in Israel/Palestine: A Few Notes on *5 Broken Cameras*," *Transnational Cinemas*, vol. 6, no. 1 (2015), pp. 17–32.

17 Nirit Anderman, "After Dissing Oscar Nominees, Israel's Culture Minister Urges Filmmakers to 'Self-Censor,'" *Haaretz* (February /28, 2013): https://www.haaretz.com/.premium-culture-min-to-filmmakers-censor-thyselves-1.5231790 (accessed November 23, 2019).

18 Edward Said, *After the Last Sky: Palestinian Lives* (New York: Pantheon Books, 1986), p. 61.

19 Edward Said, *The Question of Palestine* (New York: Random House, 1979); Nur Masalha, "Present Absentees and Indigenous Resistance," in Nur Masalha (ed.), *Catastrophe Remembered: Palestine, Israel, and the Internal Refugees* (London: Zed Books, 2005); Shira Robinson, *Citizen Strangers: Palestinians and the Birth of Israel's Liberal Settler State* (Stanford: Stanford University Press, 2013).

20 Robinson, *Citizen Strangers*, p. 1.

21 This is according to Israel's Central Bureau of Statistics: https://www.cbs.gov.il/en/mediarelease/Pages/2019/Israel-in-Figures-Selected-Annual-Data-2019.aspx (accessed November 23, 2019).

22 For extended discussions on the many imposed namings and self-identifications of '48 Palestinians in Israel, see Azmi Bishara, "On the Question of the Palestinian Minority in Israel" (in Hebrew), *Theory and Criticism*, vol. 3 (Winter 1993), pp. 7–20; Danny Rabinovich, "Oriental Nostalgia: How the Palestinians Became 'Israeli Arabs'" (in Hebrew), *Theory and Criticism*, vol. 4 (Fall 1993), pp. 141–51; David Grossman, *Present Absentees* (in Hebrew) (Tel Aviv: Hakibutz Hameuchad, 1992), pp. 31–46.

23 Gil Hochberg, *Visual Occupations: Violence and Visibility in a Conflict Zone* (Durham: Duke University Press, 2015), pp. 7–21.

24 Ibid., p. 7.

25 Ibid., p. 17.

26 Amit M. Schejter, "'The Stranger That Dwelleth with You Shall Be unto You as One Born among You'—Israeli Media Law and the Cultural Rights of the 'Palestinian-Israeli' Minority," *Middle East Journal of Culture and Communication* vol. 1, no. 2 (2008), pp. 160–76. Amal Jamal, "Manufacturing 'Quiet Arabs' in Israel: Ethnicity, Media Frames, and Soft Power" *Government and Opposition*, vol. 48, no. 2 (2013), pp. 245–65; Amal Jamal and Noa Lavie, "Constructing Ethnonational Differentiation on the Set of the TV Series, *Fauda*," *Ethnicities* vol. 19, no. 6 (2019), pp. 5–6.

27 Helga Tawil Souri, "Cinema as the Space to Transgress Palestine's Territorial Trap," *Middle East Journal of Culture and Communication*, no. 7 (2014), pp. 170–2; Gertz and Khleifi, *Palestinian Cinema*, pp. 134–70.

28 Helga Tawil Souri and Miriyam Aouragh, "Intifada 3.0? Cyber Colonialism and Palestinian Resistance," *Arab Studies Journal*, vol. 22, no. 1, Special Issue: Cultures of Resistance (Spring 2014), pp. 107–19; Helga Tawil-Souri, "Media, Globalization, and the (Un)Making of the Palestinian Cause," *Popular Communication: The International Journal of Media and Culture*, vol. 13, no. 2 (2015), pp. 150–1.

29 Dabashi, "Introduction," in Dabashi (ed.), *Dream of a Nation*.

30 Nadia Awad, "Nostalgia for the Future," *The New Inquiry*, March 22, 2015: https://thenewinquiry.com/nostalgia-for-the-future/ (accessed November 23, 2019).

31 Tawil-Souri, "Cinema as the Space to Transgress Palestine's Territorial Trap," p. 172.

32 Ibid., pp. 172–4.

33 Ibid., pp. 178–80.

34 Ella Shohat, "The Invention of the Mizrahim," *Journal of Palestine Studies*, vol. 29, no. 1 (Autumn 1999), pp. 13–17; Sami Shalom Chetrit, "Mizrahi Politics in Israel: Between Integration and Alienation," *Journal of Palestine Studies*, vol. XXIX, no. 4 (Summer 2000), p. 51; Smadar Lavie, *Wrapped in the Flag of Israel: Single Mothers and Bureaucratic Torture* (Lincoln: University of Nebraska Press, 2014), p. 2.

35 Albert Memmi, *Jews and Arabs*, translated from the French (1974) by Eleanor Levieux (Chicago: J. P. O'Hara, 1975).

36 Ella Habiba Shohat, "Reflections by an Arab Jew," in *Bint Jbeil: Frontier of Our Soul*: https://www.marxists.org/history/etol/newspape/atc/626.html (accessed December 12, 2020).

37 Shlomo Svirsky and Dvora Bernstein, "Who Worked in What, for Whom, and for How Much? The Economic Development of Israel and the Consolidation of Labor Division" (in Hebrew), *Notebooks for Research and Criticism*, no. 4 (1980), pp. 5–66; Ishak Saporta and Yossi Yonah, "Pre-Vocational Education: The Making of Israel's Ethno-Working Class," *Race, Ethnicity, and Education*, vol. 7, no. 3 (2004), pp. 251–75; Lavie, *Wrapped in the Flag of Israel*, p. 4.

38 Noa Hazan, "The Racialization of Jews in Israeli Documentary Photography," *Journal of Intercultural Studies*, vol. 31, no. 2 (2010), pp. 161–182; and "Learning to See Race in Hebrew, of Photo-Off Photo-Photo Opp," in Ktzia Alon (ed.), *The Other Side Of Israeli Photography* (Gama Israel, 2017).

39 Ktzia Alon, "On Photography and Ethnicity in Israel: A Telegraphic Doodle of Three Steps," in Noa Hazan and Sivan Rajuan Shtang (eds.), *Visual Culture in Israel: An Anthology* (in Hebrew) (Tel Aviv: Hakibutz Hameuchad, 2017), p. 655. Alon quotes from the following 2009 report: Shula Keshet, Ortal Ben Dayan, and Shira Ohayon

(eds.), *Bureaucracy of Inequality—Cultural Resources in Israel 2008–2011: A Report by the Coalition "East at Heart"* (in Hebrew) (Tel Aviv: Achoti Publications for Women in Israel, 2011).

40 Sami Shalom Chetrit, *The Mizrahi Struggle in Israel, 1948–2003* (in Hebrew) (Tel Aviv: Am Oved, 2004), pp. 281–95; Moshe Karif, *The Mizrahit: The Story of the Mizrahi Democratic Rainbow Movement* (in Hebrew) (Tel Aviv: Globes, 2005).

41 In 2001, Ron Cahlili created the cable channel *Breeza*, slating content targeting Mizrahi audiences. In 2003, organizers, scholars, and artists such as Osnat Trabelsi and Moshe Behar initiated the film series *Encounters from a Dark Angle* in Tel Aviv's Cinematheque. Shohat, "Postscript," in *Israeli Cinema*, 2nd ed., p. 317. Even before, Channel 2 broadcasted Ron Cahlili and Shoshana Gabai's documentary series, *Sea of Tears* in 1998, about the history of Mizrahi music in Israel, in New York. Additionally, the First Sephardi Film Festival was launched in 1999.

42 Yigal Nizri (ed.), *Mizrahi Appearance/Mother Tongue* (Tel Aviv: Babel, 2002).

43 This is not to say that people who are Palestinian and Mizrahi in Israel do not work or appear together in the film or media industry. My point here addresses the limited intentional effort to highlight the systemic interrelatedness of their histories, oppressions, and identifications, which increases the risk of falling into the Israeli-Palestinian symmetry framework. Still, it is important to note several moments where the parallel lines of Palestinian and Mizrahi documentary representation did meet and explored what Ella Shohat has called the "Mizrahi/Palestinian nexus." Shohat employed this term in analyzing Nizar Hassan and Danae Elon's documentary *Cut* (2000), which follows several mixed Mizrahi families consisting of Iraqi and Turkish Jews who immigrated to Azur in Israel after its foundation. *Cut* is a unique example for a documentary centering on Mizrahim and made by a Palestinian filmmaker and citizen of Israel, Hassan (in partnership with Elon), and provides a profound account of the difficulty of Mizrahim to verbally explain, not to mention relate to, Palestinians and the question of Palestine and Zionism as a whole. For more on *Cut*, see the concluding notes. In *The Bombing* (1998), Simone Bitton interviews Palestinian and Jewish families who lost their children in a suicide attack in Jerusalem—both as bombers and as victims—in 1998. Sharon Hemo and Avi Hershkowitz's *Fantasia: A Different Land* (1998) follows two drag queens: Sami Jaber, a Palestinian from Jaffa, and Michael Shimon, a Mizrahi from the religious town Bnei-Darom. In 1998, Duki Dror and Rashid Masharawi created *Stress*, a compilation of two films, each by one of the filmmakers, about the stressful days of the decline of the Oslo Accords and spread of violence in Israel and in Gaza, respectively. Dror was also very involved in the production of Ibtisaam Mara'ana's *Paradise Lost*, discussed in Chapter 3. *Men on the Edge: A Fishermen's Diary* (Avner Geingelrent and Maccabit Abramson, 2005) follows the lives of fishermen in Gaza and in the towns adjacent to it on the Israeli side and their experiences of violence on both ends of the fence. Finally, it is important to mention Avi Mograbi's *I Once Went into the Garden* (2012), which critically focuses on the story of Ali al-Zahari, a '48 Palestinian, and his family and community's experiences of the Nakba, while reminiscing about the days when Mograbi's family used to travel between Syria and Palestine prior to 1948, but without including much mention of the Mizrahi oppression that took place in Israel after its foundation.

44 The films about Palestinians analyzed below did not receive funding from Israeli funds, including *500 Dunam on the Moon* made by Rachel Leah Jones, who is an

Ashkenazi Israeli woman. The exception is Ibtisaam Mara'ana's *Paradise Lost*, which did receive some funding, albeit on condition that she omits a factual mention of the massacre conducted by Jewish soldiers in Tantura during the 1948 war. See Ibtisaam Mara'ana, "The Sovereign Has Decided for Me" (in Hebrew), in *Haaretz*, May 13, 2018: https://www.haaretz.co.il/literature/.premium-1.6070425?utm_source=App_ Share&utm_medium=Email&utm_campaign=Share (accessed November 23, 2019).

45 Yael Friedman, "The Camera and the National Ethos: The 'Battle of Jenin' in Recent Palestinian Cinema" (in Hebrew), in Eyal Sivan and Yael Munk (eds.), *South Cinema Notebooks: Cinema, Destruction & Trauma* (Sapir Academic College and Pardes Publishers, vol. 2, 2007), pp. 5–7.

46 Alon, "On Photography and Ethnicity in Israel," pp. 658–60; Sami Shalom Chetrit, "On Mizrahi-Palestinian Collaboration in Israel," in Adi Ophir (ed.), *Real Time: The Al Aqsa Intifada and the Israeli Left* (in Hebrew) (Jerusalem: Keter, 2001), pp. 290–1.

47 For the most comprehensive studies about Zionist immigration and settlement since 1882 from a post/anti/colonial perspective, see Nur Masalha, *The Bible and Zionism: Invented Traditions, Archeology, and Post Colonialism in Israel-Palestine* (London: Zed Books, 2007); Baruch Kimmerling, *Zionism and Territory: The Socio-Territorial Dimensions of Zionist Politics* (Berkeley Institute of International Studies: University of California, 1983); Gershon Shafir, *Land, Labor and the Origins of the Israeli-Palestinian Conflict 1882–1914* (Berkeley: University of California Press, 1996).

48 Shohat, "Postscript," p. 321.

49 Jasbir Puar, *Terrorist Assemblages: Homonationalism in Queer Times* (Durham: Duke University Press, 2007), pp. 37–40, 51–61, 119.

50 Nirit Anderman, "Not Only 'Our Boys': What Ben-Gurion Did Not Want You to See on the Screen" (in Hebrew), *Haaretz*, September 1, 2019. More about the television show *Our Boys* in note 54.

51 Chetrit, "On Mizrahi-Palestinian Collaboration in Israel," p. 295.

52 Bryan Ruby, *The Mizrahi Era of Rebellion: Israel's Forgotten Civil Rights Struggle 1948–1966* (Syracuse: Syracuse University Press, 2015), pp. 29–31.

53 Chetrit, *The Mizrahi Struggle in Israel, 1948–2003*, pp. 310–12.

54 In "Mizrahi Hangers," Omri Ben-Yehuda explains how currently popular television shows such as *Fauda* and the reality show *District of Jerusalem* essentialize and depoliticize the criminalization of Palestinians and the predominant Mizrahi percentage in the Israeli police and Border Patrol, overall de-historicizing the ethnonational conflict for propaganda purposes. See Omri Ben-Yehuda, "Mizrahi Hangers," *Haaretz*, August 5, 2019. For popular representation that embarks on more critical reflection of the sociopolitical conditions informing the positions of Palestinians and Mizrahim against each other, see the recent television show, *Our Boys* (Tawfik Abu-Wael, Yosef Cedar, Hagai Levy, 2019), produced by the Israeli Keshet International and HBO. The show portrays the complex sociopolitical backdrop around the killing of the Palestinian boy from East Jerusalem, Muhammad Abu Khdeir, by a Mizrahi ultraorthodox boy, Yosef Haim Ben-David, right before the break of the attacks on Gaza in the summer of 2014. For a fascinating photographic reflection on the systematic tracking of Mizrahim and Jews of Color to low-ranked security roles, see Matti Milstein's project from the years 2004 to 2015, *Black Labor*: https://matimilstein.com/post/129007864677/blacklabor (accessed November 23, 2019).

55 Oren Yiftahel, "Israeli Society and Jewish-Palestinian Reconciliation: 'Ethnocracy' and Its Territorial Contradictions," *Middle East Journal*, vol. 51, no. 4 (Autumn 1997), pp. 505–8; Daniel De Malah, "Where Is the Occupation, Discrimination, and Imperialism? Notes on the Discussion on the Implications of Globalization in Israel" (in Hebrew), *Theory and Criticism*, no. 35 (Fall 2009), pp. 116–22; Lavie, *Wrapped in the Flag of Israel*, pp. 8–12.

56 Edward Said, *Peace and Its Discontents: Essays on Palestine in the Middle East Peace Process* (New York: Vintage, 1996), and "Introduction: The Right of Return At Last," in Naseer Aruri (ed.), *Palestinian Refugees: The Right of Return* (New York: Pluto Press, 2001), pp. 1–6; Talal Asad, *On Suicide Bombing* (New York: Columbia University Press, 2007), p. 46; Eyal Weizman, *Hollow Land: Israel's Architecture of Occupation* (London: Verso, 2007), pp. 7, 139–44.

57 Yehouda Shenhav, *In the Trap of the Green Line: A Jewish Political Essay* (in Hebrew) (Tel Aviv: Am Oved, 2010), pp. 13–14; Ariella Azoulay and Adi Ophir, *The One-State Condition: Occupation and Democracy in Israel/Palestine* (Redwood City: Stanford University Press, 2012), pp. 12–15.

58 Weizman, *Hollow Land*, pp. 161–85.

59 Yiftahel, "Israeli Society and Jewish-Palestinian Reconciliation," p. 506.

60 I use the term "racialization" along the lines of Jasbir Puar's working definition in *Terrorist Assemblages*. Puar describes a process of racialization as such that "informs the very distinctions between life and death, wealth and poverty, health and illness, fertility and morbidity, security and insecurity, living and dying" (p. xi). Puar also explains: "I deploy 'racialization' as a figure for specific social formations and processes that are not necessarily or only tied to what has been historically theorized as 'race'"(p. xii). See Puar, *Terrorist Assemblages*, pp. xi and xii.

61 Nur Masalha, "Present Absentees and Indigenous Resistance," pp. 23–55; Hillel Cohen, *The Present Absentees: The Palestinian Refugees in Israel since 1948* (Jerusalem: Van-Leer Institute, 2000), pp. 66–71.

62 Cohen, *The Present Absentees*, pp. 35–42.

63 Robinson, *Citizen Strangers*, p. 1.

64 Shohat, "The Invention of the Mizrahim," pp. 8–13.

65 Moshe Behar, "Interpreting the Pre-Israeli and Intra-Israeli Sociopolitical History of Arabized Jews" (in Hebrew), *Politika: The Israeli Journal of Political Science & International Relations*, no. 14 (2005), pp. 109–24; Yehouda Shenhav, "Arab Jews, Population Exchange, and the Palestinian Right of Return," in Ann M. Lesch and Ian S. Lustick (eds.), *Exile and Return: Predicaments of Palestinians and Jews* (Philadelphia: University of Pennsylvania, 2008), pp. 225–40. Also see Zvi Ben-Dor Benite's talk, "The Mizrahim and the Nakba" in Zochrot's *Conference of Return*, March 21, 2016: https://www.youtube.com/watch?v=puXe8T94vBc (accessed January 19, 2020). It is also worth noting, as these scholars do, that before 1948, in contrast to the accelerated waves of Jewish immigration to Palestine from Europe since the late 1880s, Jews from the Arab world and Middle East were neither too interested in settling in Palestine as part of the Zionist organized efforts, nor were they encouraged to join these efforts by the Zionist movement, except when recruited as cheap labor as in the case of the Jews of Yemen. These conditions changed in the early 1940s, when the Zionist establishment started realizing the horrific proportions of the Holocaust and sought alternative ways to increase Jewish presence in Palestine, resolutely conducting more outreach in Jewish communities

that had otherwise experienced almost no systematic oppression against them in the Arab and Muslim world for centuries.

66 Avi Picard, "The Beginning of Selective Migration to Israel in the 1950s," *Reviews of the Resurrection of Israel*, vol. 9 (1999), pp. 338–94.

67 This is well detailed in Avraham Abbas's comprehensive report from 1958. See Avraham Abbas, "From Ingathering to Integration: The Communal Problem in Israel," in Moshe Behar and Zvi Ben-Dor Benite (eds.), *Modern Middle Eastern Jewish Thought* (Waltham: Brandeis University Press, 2013), pp. 225–48.

68 Ella Shohat, "Sephardim in Israel: Zionism from the Perspective of Its Jewish Victims," *Social Text*, no. 19/20 (Autumn 1988), pp. 18–19.

69 See Adrianna Kemp, "The Border as a Janus Face: Space and National Consciousness in Israel" (in Hebrew), *Theory and Criticism*, vol. 16 (Spring 2000), and "The Migration of Peoples or the Great Explosion: State Control and Resistance in the Israeli Periphery," in Hannan Hever, Pnina Mutzafi Haler, and Yehoudah Shenhav (eds.), *Mizrahim in Israel: A Critical Observation into Israel's Ethnicity* (in Hebrew) (Jerusalem: Van Leer Institute, 2002), pp. 36–67. Benny Nurieli and Hayim Yaakobi discuss the placement of immigrants from Iraq in the formerly Palestinian and newly evacuated neighborhoods of Lod/Lyddia, far remote from job opportunities and the city center. See Benny Nurieli, "Foreigners in a National Space: The Arab Jews in the Ghetto of Lod 1950–1959," *Theory and Criticism*, vol. 26 (Spring 2005); Hayim Yaakobi, "The Third Space, Architecture, Nationalism, and the Postcolonial Gaze," *Theory and Criticism*, vol. 30 (Summer 2007). Also see Yiftahel, "Israeli Society and Jewish-Palestinian Reconciliation," pp. 506–13; and "Ethnocracy: The Politics of Judaizing Israel/Palestine," *Constellations*, vol. 6, no. 3, pp. 364–90.

70 Shalom Chetrit, *The Mizrahi Struggle in Israel, 1948–2003*, pp. 61–2; Shohat, "The Invention of Mizrahim," pp. 8–13; Ella Shohat, "Rupture and Return: Zionist Discourse and the Study of Arab Jews," *Social Text* 75, vol. 21, no. 2 (Summer 2003), pp. 51–5, and more. Also see Yehudah Shenhav, "Jews from the Arab World in Israel: The Divided Identity of Mizrahim in the Districts of National Memory," in Hever, Mutzafi Haler, and Shenhav (eds.), *Mizrahim in Israel*, p. 139.

71 As Kemp, Yiftahel, Shalom Chetrit, and Shohat demonstrate, examples of this abound. In their precarious homes in public housing projects, Mizrahim were the first to encounter and be harmed by Palestinian returnees who were trying to return to their homes. Mizrahim and '48 Palestinians were also competing for working-class jobs: after 1967, Palestinians from the West Bank and Gaza were competing for these jobs too. Thus, Mizrahim were placed in positions and situations of utter vulnerability in front of the even more vulnerable Palestinian refugees and discriminated indigenous minority who were surviving and resisting the state of Israel's displacement and oppression of them. Suspicion and animosity, naturally, kept growing between Palestinians and Mizrahim. The racialization of Mizrahim as Oriental Jews and the attempted erasure of their Arab and/or Middle Eastern affiliations should be understood alongside the racialization of Palestinians as always already potential terrorists and/or assisting traitors. In other words, the differential orientalizing, discursive, and materialized racializations and segregating oppressions of Palestinians and Mizrahim pitted two oppressed Arab/Middle Eastern populations that could have otherwise organized together against the Ashkenazi-Zionist Jewish ethnocracy of the state of Israel.

72 Manar Makhoul, "The Palestinian Citizens of Israel: The Progression of a Name," in Areej Sabbagh-Khoury and Nadim N. Rouhana (eds.), *The Palestinians in*

Israel: Readings in History, Politics and Society, Volume 2 (Haifa: The Mada Al-Carmel Arab Center for Applied Social Research, 2015), pp. 11–15.

73 In the 1990s, '48 Palestinians founded several not-for-profits dedicated to cultivate legal and representational struggles for civil justice. For example, *Adalah: The Legal Center for Arab Minority Rights in Israel*: https://www.adalah.org/, and *Mada Al Carmel: Arab Center for Applied Social Research* was founded in 2000: https://www.mada-research.org/en/home-eng/ (accessed November 23, 2019).

74 See Amal Jamal, *Arab Minority Nationalism in Israel: The Politics of Indigeneity* (London: Routledge, 2011), p. 270.

75 Ibid., p. 279.

76 Jamal, *Arab Minority Nationalism in Israel*, pp. 268–79; Hillel Cohen, *Good Arabs: The Israeli Security Agencies and the Israeli Arabs, 1948–1967*, trans. Haim Watzman (Berkeley: University of California Press, 2011), p. 10; Thabet Abu Ras, "The Uprising of October 2000," in *The Palestinians in Israel*, pp. 20–1.

77 Gil Eyal, *The Disenchantment of the Orient: Expertise in Arab Affairs and the Israeli State* (in Hebrew) (Jerusalem and Tel-Aviv: Van-Leer Institute and Hakibutz Hameuchad, 2005), p. 147.

78 Shalom Chetrit, *The Mizrahi Struggle in Israel*, pp. 53–60.

79 Kemp, "The Migration of Peoples or the Great Explosion," pp. 364–90.

80 Ruby, *The Mizrahi Era of Rebellion*.

81 Shalom Chetrit, *The Mizrahi Struggle in Israel*, pp. 160–9.

82 Notable are the foundation of the Sephardi-Mizrahi religious party Shas in 1983, the foundation of the landmark not-for-profit organization, the *Mizrahi Democratic Rainbow* in 1996 and its promotion of an anti-capitalist agenda for the redistribution of land and resources.

83 Ibid., pp. 228–304.

84 Ella Shohat, "A Voyage to Toledo Twenty-Five Years after the 'Jews of the Orient and Palestinians' Meeting," *Jadaliyya*, September 30, 2014: https://www.jadaliyya.com/ Details/31283/A-Voyage-to-Toledo-Twenty-Five-Years-After-the-%60Jews-of-the-Orient-and-Palestinians%60-Meeting (accessed November 23, 2019).

85 The 1986 bill constituted against meetings between Palestinians and Israelis (and primarily with Mizrahim) was called the "Law For Fighting Terrorism." See Shalom Chetrit, *The Mizrahi Struggle in Israel*, pp. 272–5.

86 Ibid., pp. 232–42.

87 Shoshana Gabai, "We the Sentimentalists: The Mizrahi Struggle as the Loyal Servant of Neoliberal Media" (in Hebrew), *Haoketz*: https://bit.ly/33ilRHy (accessed November 23, 2019).

88 Said, *The Question of Palestine*, pp. 56–114.

89 Shohat, "Sephardim in Israel."

90 Said, *The Question of Palestine*, p. 57.

91 Ibid., p. 68.

92 Shohat, "Sephardim in Israel," p. 1.

93 Ella Shohat, "The Narrative of the Nation and the Discourse of Modernization: The Case of the Mizrahim," *Critique: Critical Middle Eastern Studies*, vol. 6, no.10 (1997), pp. 9–10; "The Shaping of Mizrahi Studies: A Relational Approach," *Israel Studies Forum*, vol. 17, no. 2 (2002), pp. 86–93, and elsewhere.

94 Shohat, "The Narrative of the Nation," p. 10.

95 Differing in approaches, these scholars are taking part in the larger trend of studying the Israel/Palestine geography as a whole to disrupt the canonical symmetry in

studies about the Israel-Palestine or Israeli/Arab conflict, and the delimitation between studies on the Arab-Palestinian or the Jewish-Israeli culture, media, and representation. Zachary Lockman's approach to studying the "relational history" of Palestinians and Jews in Palestine, e.g., emphasized the histories of interaction, exchange, and conflict of people due to, as well as across and against, the Zionist/Palestinian national division. See Zachary Lockman, *Comrades and Enemies: Arab and Jewish Workers in Palestine, 1906–1948* (Berkeley: University of California Press, 1996). Additionally to the work of Ella Shohat, this book builds on scholarship in anthropology and cultural studies typically engaging in critical and comparative anti-/postcolonial and race studies, and sometimes gender and queer studies too, such as Ariella Azoulay, "The Ghost of Yigal Amir" (in Hebrew), *Theory and Criticism*, vol. 17 (Fall 2000), pp. 9–26; Noa Hazan, "Order Please! The National Museum and Political Initiation," in Hazan and Shtang (eds.), *Visual Culture in Israel*, pp. 52–74; Gil Hochberg, *In Spite of Partition: Jews, Arabs, and the Limits of Separatist Imagination* (Princeton: University of Princeton, 2007); Smadar Lavie, "Blowups in the Borderzones: Third World Israeli Authors' Gropings for Home," in Smadar Lavie and Ted Swedenburg (eds.), *Displacement, Diaspora, and Geographies of Identity* (Durham: Duke University Press, 1996); Rebecca L. Stein and Ted Swedenburg (eds.), *Palestine, Israel, and the Politics of Popular Culture* (Durham: Duke University Press, 2005).

96 As Ella Shohat notes: "War … is the friend of binarisms, leaving little place for complex identities. The Gulf War, for example, intensified a pressure already familiar to the Arab Jewish diaspora in the wake of the Israeli-Arab conflict: a pressure to choose between being a Jew and being an Arab." See Ella Habiba Shohat, "Reflections by an Arab Jew."

97 Gil Hochberg, "Forget Pinkwashing, it's Brownwashing Time: Self-Orientalizing on the US Campus," in *Contending Modernities: Exploring How Religious and Secular Forces Interact in the Modern World*, November 24, 2017: https://contendingmodernities.nd.edu/theorizing-modernities/forget-pinkwashing-brownwashing-time-self-orientalizing-us-campus/ (accessed November 23, 2019).

98 Zvi Ben-Dor Benite criticized the cynical co-optation of the Mizrahi struggle by Likkud's minister of culture and sports (2015–19), Miri Regev. See Zvi Ben-Dor Benite, "Unleash: Miri Regev and the Black Panthers," *Haoketz*, March 18, 2016: https://bit.ly/2OFoJsO (accessed November 23, 2019).

99 Hochberg, *In Spite of Partition*, pp. 4–5.

100 Sara Ahmed, "The Contingency of Pain," in *The Cultural Politics of Emotion* (Edinburgh: Edinburgh University Press, 2014), p. 31.

101 Rebecca L. Stein and Ted Swedenburg, "Introduction: Popular Culture, Transnationality, and Radical History," in Stein and Swedenburg (eds.), *Palestine, Israel, and the Politics of Popular Culture*, p. 10.

102 Shohat, *Israeli Cinema*, pp. 234–46.

103 This is a point Ilana Szobel and I discuss elaborately in our article. See Shirly Bahar and Ilana Szobel, "Confessions of IDF Soldiers in Autobiographical Documentaries from Israel" (in Hebrew), *Mikan*, vol. 17 (March 2017).

104 Close-up shots serve to invoke the failed fantasy of both the camera lens and the speaker to touch and capture things as they really are. Lamenting an inherent inability to see things in the world without shaping them through the seeing or, in other words, to mediate things unmediatedly, the close-ups simultaneously speak to the tireless wish and will to do so. Mary Ann Doane's discussion of the effect of

close-ups in cinema is relevant here and useful to understanding this. Ann Doane
theorized the close-up as one of various cinematic tactics employed as part of a
cinematic fantasized attempt to reliably represent real time. Attempts at real-time
representation accommodate the promise of distilled, optimal documentation,
aspiring instantaneity, simultaneity, and immediacy, and presumably offering an
experience of pure—indeed, unmediated— connectivity and interactivity to the
spectator. "Ideally, there would be no gap between the phenomenon and its analysis,"
the real-time fantasy goes (p. 24). Yet while processes of representation are an
inherent part of it, Doane claims that, at least potentially, "the concept of real time
is itself, of course, a denial of mediation, of the very presence of the technology"
(p. 24). In cinematic representation, upon its "irreversible temporal flow of film
… the reified terms 'life-like,' true-to-life,' and the appeal to 'life itself' constitute
the ultimate rebuttal … appealing to a universal, undifferentiated, and undeniable
experience shared by all" (p. 31). To resist this potential perception, Doane embarks
on a journey to trace and depict the mechanisms of what she here usefully calls
"unreal time," standing for "a technologically produced and mediated time" (p. 24).
See Mary Ann Doane, "Real Time: Instantaneity and the Photographic Imaginary,"
in David Green and Joanna Lowry (eds.), *Stillness and Time: Photography and the
Moving Image* (Brighton: Photoworks, 2006), pp. 24–31.

105 Lauren Berlant, "The Subject of True Feeling: Pain, Privacy, and Politics,"
in Sarah Ahmed, Jane Kilby, Maureen McNeil, and Beverley Skeggs (eds.),
Transformations: Thinking through Feminism (London: Routledge, 2000), p. 34.

106 Ibid., p. 35.

107 Shohat, "Postscript," p. 300.

108 Some notable examples for documentaries centering (sometimes remorseful) on
executors or perpetrators of violence from the 2000s are *Bowling for Columbine*
(Michael Moore, USA, 2002), *Capturing the Freedmans* (Andrew Jarecki, USA, 2003),
S-21: the Khmer Rouge Killing Machine (Rithy Panh, Cambodia and France, 2003),
Standard Operations Procedure (Errol Morris, USA, 2008), *The Act of Killing* (Joshua
Oppenheimer, USA, 2013). Some notable examples for documentaries focusing on
individuals experiencing and resisting political pain are *Mighty Times: the Children's
March* (Hudson and Houston, US, 2004), *When the Levees Broke: A Requiem in Four
Acts* (Spike Lee, USA, 2005), *The Road to Guantanamo* (Michael Winterbottom, UK,
2006). The most famous, albeit very different, earlier examples for documentaries
that focused on testimonies of survivors of oppression and violence are *Shoah*
(Claude Lantzman, France, 1986) and *Tongues Untied* (Marlon Riggs, USA, 1989).

109 Phyllis R. Klotman and Janet K. Cutler (eds.), *Struggles for Representation: African
American Documentary Film and Video* (Bloomington: Indiana University Press,
1999), pp. xvii–xviii. Similar to black American documentaries, the filmmakers
I discuss "have adopted the documentary mode to assert their view of reality."
Introduction, *Struggles for Representation*, p. xvii.

110 Bhaskar Sarkar and Janet Walker, "Introduction: Moving Testimonies," in Bhaskar
Sarkar and Janet Walker (eds.), *Documentary Testimonies: Global Archives of Social
Suffering* (New York: Routledge, 2010). The essays in this important collection
analyze documentaries from Cambodia, Darfur, India, Indonesia, Korea, Norway,
Rwanda, South Africa, and the United States. They do not cover any documentaries
from Israel-Palestine, however.

111 Sarkar and Walker, "Introduction," pp. 2 and 7.

112 Ibid., p. 12.

113 Ibid., p. 17.

114 The two most notable examples of scholars of Israeli documentary cinema who employ Freudian psychoanalytic perspectives to analyze the Israeli traumatized subject are Shmulik Duvdevani and Raya Morag . Duvdevani theorized the new Israeli documentary cinema of testimonial and autobiographical monologues since the 1990s, mostly from psychoanalytic perspectives. See Duvdevani, *First Person Camera*. Raya Morag wrote about Israeli documentary cinema, also focusing on psychoanalytic examinations of what she calls "the perpetrator's trauma." See Raya Morag, *Waltzing with Bashir*. Morag also edited and prefaced the special issue *Radical Contextuality* on Israeli documentary cinema. See Raya Morag, "Radical Contextuality: Major Trends in Israeli Documentary Second Intifada Cinema," *Studies in Documentary Film*, vol. 6, no. 3 (September 2012), pp. 253–72. Both Duvdevani and Morag mark the second intifada in September 2000 as a historical hurtful moment motivating abundant production of documentaries. Yet Duvdevani and Morag's research largely focus on the liabilities, legacies, and, mainly, on the traumas of Zionist military and hegemonic culture(s) as addressed in documentaries. The framework of trauma is used by the following scholars writing about Palestinian cinema too—Hamid Dabashi, Nurith Gertz and George Khleifi, and Yael Friedman—albeit with a sufficiently elaborated political criticism of the sociopolitical context in Israel/Palestine that births trauma.

115 Cathy Caruth defined trauma as "an overwhelming experience of sudden or catastrophic events." As in Caruth's interpretation, "the traumatic experience, as Freud indicated suggestively, is an experience that is not fully assimilated as it occurs," and the inassimilable traumatic experience is deeply embedded in any writing or telling of history. Trauma was first conceptualized by Sigmund Freud, and later developed by many, among them psychoanalysis theorists Jacques Lacan and Salvoj Zizek. For the latter two, trauma involves a significant loss—a loss inherently pertinent in language and constitutive to subjectivity. Loss is primordial, and whether it actually happened or not matters less, because it is in any case mostly unknown to us, always irrepresentable, a lack in our perception of reality constitutive of subjectivity and language. Lacan and Zizek sometimes relate the trauma of loss embedded in language to their psychoanalytically defined dimension of "The Real." See Slavoj Zizek, *The Sublime Object of Ideology* (London: Verso, 1989), pp. 171–227; *An Unclaimed Experience: Trauma, Narrative, and History* (Baltimore: Johns Hopkins University, 1996), p. 11.

116 For a notable example of political theorizations of cultural trauma, refer Angela Onwuachi-Willig: building on Kai Erikson's scholarship on collective trauma and Jeffrey Alexander's definition of cultural trauma as occurring "when members of a collective feel they have been subjected to a horrendous event," Angela Onwuachi-Willig employs a lens of structural racism to contend that cultural trauma occurs "not only when the routine is disrupted," as commonly held, "but also when regularly expected occurrences—the matters that communities have come to know and take for granted—occur and in fact get reaffirmed in a public or official manner." Angela Onwuachi-Willig, "The Trauma of the Routine: Lessons on Cultural Trauma from the Emmett Till Verdict," *Sociological Theory*, vol. 34, no. 4 (2016), p. 336. Complementarily, Lauren Berlant resists the predominance that Caruth's theorization of trauma has obtained, encouraging cultural theorists to "think of trauma through the affective conventions of genre ... as a style of responding to a happening, a style of mediating it into event." Berlant defies viewing

trauma as "self-evident" or as "detach[ing] the subject from the historical present."
Instead, she proposes to consider the traumatic event as "an affective concept" that
"bridges" various relationships to time and place, a "mess of temporalization"; for,
"trauma, after all, does not make experiencing the historical present impossible,
but possible ... it transforms the work of survival without much of a normative plot
or guarantees." Lauren Berlant, *Cruel Optimism* (Durham: Duke University Press,
2011), pp. 80–1.

117 Elaine Scarry famously theorized the difficulty of expressing physical pain in
language, correlating this difficulty to the inability to articulate physical pain.
"Whatever pain achieves, it achieves in part through its unsharability, and it
ensures this unsharability through its resistance to language," *The Body in Pain*,
p. 4. Endorsing Scarry's observations that "the threat of violence is a threat to
language, its world-making and sense-making possibility," Butler asked: if "pain
shatters language," that is, "if certain kinds of violence disable language," then "how
do we account for the specific kind of injury that language itself performs?" Judith
Butler, *Excitable Speech: A Politics of the Performative* (New York: Routledge, 1997),
p. 6. To account for the specific kind of injurious language that causes continuous
pain, it is useful to think along Sayidia Hartman's determination that "pain must
be recognized in its historicity and as the articulation of a social condition of
brutal constraint, extreme need, and constant violence: in other words, it is the
perpetual condition of ravishment." Insinuatingly referring to Scarry's work,
Hartman contends that "if this pain has been largely unrecognized and unspoken,
it is due to the sheer denial of the black sentience rather than the inexpressibility
of pain." See Saidiya Hartman, *Scenes of Subjection*, p. 51. To name a prominent
exception, Susan Sontag's *Regarding the Pain of Others* from 2003. It is an account
by the famous thinker of photography about the power and perils of photographs
of war and atrocities, especially, when utilized by an overtly commercialized media,
and the limitations embedded in photography's capacity to politicize spectators.
In addressing mostly historical events that have been widely accepted as horrific,
and their victims/survivors acknowledged for their pain, and in undermining
photography's ability to represent otherwise underrepresented instances of
oppression, Sontag chooses a very different approach from what the thinkers about
pain noted above—and different from this book. Susan Sontag, *Regarding the Pain
of Others* (New York: Picador, 2003).

118 Ahmed, "The Contingency of Pain," pp. 22–3. It is probably not a coincidence that,
for this article, she looks not at Freud's definition of trauma but rather of pain, as
"an external and internal perception, which behaves like an integral perception even
when its source is in the external world." Quoted on page 24.

119 Ibid., p. 56

120 Affect is a key term in this book, and one of the hardest to define—since it is so
intimately embedded in the world of experience. If performance de-essentializes the
body, then affect de-essentializes emotion. Let me share briefly some theorizations
of "the affective turn" that I found most inspiring. "Affect arises in the midst
of in-betweenness, in the capacities to act and be acted upon ... affect is an
impingement or extrusion of a momentary or sometimes more sustained state of
relation as well as passage (or duration of passage) of forces or intensities," write
Melissa Gregg and Gregory Seigworth in the introduction to *The Affect Theory
Reader* (p. 1). A space where "forces of encounter" coalesce, affect is "at once intimate

and impersonal, affect accumulates across both relatedness and interruptions of relatedness, becoming a palimpsest of forces-encounters … between bodies …. affect marks a body's belonging to a world of encounters … also, in non-belonging … through all these far sadder de-compositions" (p. 2). This definition is useful for this book, where affect marks a dynamic array of political experiential encounters and interrelations between people and a dominant and violent discourse. Indeed, affect, Sarah Ahmed reminds us, most significantly carries within it the concept of being affected by something (p. 29). Building on Ahmed's framing of affect as a placement of bodies along racial lines, Claire Hemming emphasizes that "only for certain subjects can affect be thought of as attaching in an open way; others are so over-associated with affect that they themselves are the object of affective transfer." Thus, "some bodies are captured and held by affect's structured precision." See Claire Hemmings, "Invoking Affect: Cultural Theory and the Ontological Turn," *Cultural Studies*, vol. 19, no. 5 (September 2005), p. 562. I use "affect" to discuss and politicize feelings, while trying to communicate feelings as material and physical substance and political structures, or in other words, communicate the substance and structure of feelings, feelings that can be discerned and shared. This is my attempt to move beyond narrow, psychological, and often depoliticized concepts of emotions and consciousness (p. 7). See Melissa Gregg and Gregory Seigworth (eds.), *The Affect Theory Reader* (Durham: Duke University Press, 2009). In her landmark writing about affect, Eve Kosofsky Sedgwick correlated between affect and texture, famously contending that "texture and affect, touching and feeling, seem to belong together … what they have in common is that at whatever scale they are attended to, both are irreducibly phenomenological." That is, they are experiential, evasive of thick description, and resistant to any subject-versus-object dualistic definitions. See Eve Kosofsky Sedgwick, *Touching Feeling: Affect, Pedagogy, Performativity* (Durham: Duke University Press, 2003), p. 21.

121 Very much like Sarkar and Walker, this book strives to "[recognize] testimony's relational essence" while wishing to "engage with testimony as, all at once: the most intimate manifestation of the survivor-witness relationship and the product of intercalated institutions and practices; profoundly human and incontrovertibly cyborgian; a performative act continually in the making; and, at the level of methodology, both a circumscribed object of documentary studies and the gold standard for global human rights initiatives," Sarkar and Walker, "Introduction," pp. 4–5.

122 *My Favorite Scene*, an excerpt from a students' project for the Sam Spiegel film school. See http://e.walla.co.il/item/1775530 (accessed November 23, 2019).

123 In 2011, right before his passing from cancer, Ronny Koven and Naama Lansky created the documentary *Cult Movie* for the television investigative show, *Fact*. In the film, Shiloah's daughter presented footage that she took of her father, where he tells about his immigration to Israel, the hardship involving the labor market, and more. See http://www.mako.co.il/tv-ilana_dayan/2012-6368621b91af3310/Article-001b6c5a079f331006.htm (accessed November 23, 2019).

124 Among much other activity, Shiloah also attended the abovementioned Toledo conference in Spain in 1989.

125 Ahmed, *The Contingency of Pain*, p. 30.

126 Tourmaline, "Preface," in Larry Mitchell, *The Faggots and Their Friends between Revolutions* (New York: Nightboat Books, [1977] 2019), p. viii.

Chapter 1

1 Gadi Sukenik interviewing Mohammad Bakri and David Tzanegen, Channel Two, December 2009. To watch the interview see https://www.youtube.com/watch?v=ZQaLuwnZKOw (accessed November 16, 2019).

2 "The bill will put an end to the neglect of the blood and the good name of our warriors, so that an appropriate toll will be charged from the creators of false propaganda such as *Jenin Jenin*," declared Knesset member Yariv Levin in support of the bill adequately named "the Jenin Jenin law." See https://law.acri.org.il/he/26968. Intending to modify the already existent law forbidding libel against private individuals, this new bill from May 2013 aims to consider speech acts that critique the Israeli Defense Force (IDF) as defamation that may potentially lead to the prosecution of the critic; it thus rejects the definition of the IDF as a public institution liable for critique. See http://www.hahem.co.il/friendsofgeorge/?p=3382. The law aims to center on "the honor and status of the IDF *soldiers*" rendered as individuals rather than merely presumably materializing the local risk of "sabotaging the security interest of Israel." See http://news.walla.co.il/?w=/2689/2639876.

3 Jewish-Israeli film critic Meir Schnitzer notes about this wave: "The insistence of both sides of the conflict in the Middle-East to specifically capture the Jeninian case, that presumable 'true' story, reflects a collective psychological compulsion, which is of no lesser importance than the historical narrative that these movies aspire to endow." Meir Schnitzer, "Jenin Is Hollywood," in the daily *Maariv*, April 18, 2003.

4 Nurith Gertz and George Khleifi, *Palestinian Cinema: Landscape, Trauma, and Memory* (Edinburgh: Edinburgh University Press, 2008), p. 173. The untimely death of Mer-Khamis in 2011 further amplified the interest in his cultural and political activism in Jenin that *Arna's Children* exemplified. See Adam Shatz, "The Life and Death of Juliano Mer-Khamis," *London Review of Books*, http://www.lrb.co.uk/v35/n22/adam-shatz/the-life-and-death-of-juliano-mer-khamis. Mark Levine, "A Year after Juliano Mer-Khamis' Murder, It's Time to Board the Freedom Bus," *Aljazeera*, http://www.aljazeera.com/indepth/opinion/2012/04/20124483146411159.html.

5 Ramzy Baroud, "Introduction," in Ramzy Baroud and Mahfouz Abu Turk (eds.), *Searching Jenin: Eyewitness Accounts of the Israeli Invasion, 2002* (Seattle: Cune Press, 2003), p. 23.

6 Talal Asad, *On Suicide Bombing* (New York: Columbia University Press, 2007), p. 48.

7 Judith Butler has famously critiqued the framework of "the lack," wondering "whether the notion of a lack taken from psychoanalysis as that which secures the contingency of *any* and *all* social formations is itself a presocial principle universalized at the cost of every consideration of power, sociality, culture, politics, which regulates the relative closure and openness of social practices." To that end, one patriarchal, dangerous line of thought connects the opinion that a harmful event is typically fantasized, always already lost, and/or irrepresentable, and doubting the validity of the testifier that somebody inflicted a very real harm on her. Judith Butler, *Bodies That Matter: On the Discursive Limits of Sex* (London: Routledge, 1993), p. 202. Emphases in the original.

8 Hillel Cohen, *Good Arabs: The Israeli Security Agencies and the Israeli Arabs, 1948–1967*, trans. Haim Watzman (Berkeley: University of California Press, 2011), p. 10.

9 Chapter 2 elaborately reads Habibi's novel "The Pessoptimist."

10 Ofer Matan, "Under Censorship: An Interview with Mohammad Bakri" (in Hebrew), *Tel Aviv's Ha'ir Weekly*, January 29, 2010.

11 Ginger Assadi, "Upholding the Palestinian Image in Israeli Cinema: An Interview with Mohammad Bakri," *Cineaste USA*, vol. 29, no. 4 (2004), p. 41.

12 Ibid., p. 42.

13 Edward Said, *After the Last Sky: Palestinian Lives* (New York: Pantheon Books, 1986), p. 51.

14 David Grossman explores the processes by which Jewish Israelis—the authorities as well as the people—got accustomed to commonly referring to the Palestinians who found themselves receiving citizenship in Israel after 1948 as "Arab-Israelis," and details the intricate repercussions that this affiliation has evoked. See David Grossman, *Present Absentees* (in Hebrew) (Tel Aviv: Hakibutz Hameuchad, 1992).

15 Edward Said, "The Essential Terrorist," *Arab Studies Quarterly*, vol. 9, no. 2 (Spring 1987), p. 149.

16 Ibid., p. 150.

17 Ibid., p. 152.

18 Ibid., p. 153.

19 Ibid., p. 154.

20 Arjun Appadurai, *Fear of Small Numbers: An Essay on the Geography of Anger* (Durham: Duke University Press, 2006).

21 Ibid., p. 90.

22 Ibid., p. 91.

23 Ibid., p. 89.

24 Ibid., p. 90.

25 Ibid., p. 92.

26 The exception is Yael Friedman's analyses of *Jenin Jenin* and *Arna's Children*, albeit being quite brief. See Yael Friedman, "The Camera and the National Ethos: The 'Battle of Jenin' in Recent Palestinian Cinema" (in Hebrew), in Eyal Sivan and Yael Munk (eds.), *South Cinema Notebooks: Cinema, Destruction & Trauma* (Sapir Academic College, vol. 2, 2007), pp. 5–7.

27 Quoting Israeli journalist Boaz Evron, Noam Chomsky interpreted the IDF invasion of Jenin in 2002 as one more attempt to remind the Palestinians that "the whip is held over their heads" constantly. Chomsky also linked the invasion to Israel's infamous common belief that as long as it does not come across as conducting "a purposeful massacre of hundreds of civilians in the Jenin refugee camp" in global media, it can get away with anything. See Noam Chomsky, "Preface," in Baroud and Abu Turk (eds.), *Searching Jenin*, pp. 17–18.

28 From Mohammad Bakri's appeal to the Israeli Supreme Court, p. 74.

29 Ibid., p. 78.

30 Ibid., p. 79.

31 Ibid.

32 Ibid.

33 Alongside the consensus about documentary media's ontological disability, some have stressed that documentaries nevertheless always possess, and possibly risk, the aspiration to transmit *a reality* of some sort, often seeking some degree of reliability. Today, the unattainable desire for reality is even more extensively acted on and investigated by digital contemporary documentary films. Whether one ascribes the coining of the term "documentary" to Jeremy Bentham for his early nineteenth-century dictionary entry (Paula Rabinowitz, p. 2), or to John Grierson for his review of Robert Flaherty's 1926 film *Moana* (Brian Winston,

p. 2), grappling with the documentary seems to continuously require addressing questions about truth, evidentiality, and authenticity ever since its inception. See Paula Rabinowitz, *They Must Be Represented: The Politics of Documentary* (New York: Verso, 1994); Bryan Winston, *Claiming the Real: The Griersonian Documentary and Its Legitimations* (London: British Film Institute, 1995). Jane Gaines endorsed and underscored foundational documentary thinker Andre Bazin, who was "simultaneously able to give the impression that realism is both achieved through artifice and unproblematically expressed, and able to create the sense that 'reality' is found as well as constructed." Jane Gaines, "Introduction: The Real Returns," in Jane Gaines and Michael Renov (eds.), *Collecting Visible Evidence* (Minneapolis: University of Minnesota Press, 1999), pp. 1–19. The documentary medium, Michael Renov claimed, "shares the status of all discursive forms with regards to its tropic or figurative character ... it employs many of the methods and devices of its fictional counterpart." Renov engaged Jacque Derrida to claim that truth "in which reality is subjected to the heat and pressures of the creative imagination ... demands the detour through fictive constructs." Michael Renov, "Introduction: The Truth about Non-Fiction," in Michael Renov (ed.), *Theorizing Documentary* (New York: Routledge, 1993), pp. 3 and 6. Studying "the spectacle of actuality" from the lens of the Lacanian Real, Elizabeth Cowie describes the documentary filmmaker and apparatus' aspirations and mechanisms of recording reality as driven by "a desire for reality held and reviewable for analysis as a world of materiality available to scientific and rational thought, a world of evidence confirmed through observation and logical interpretation. It is a desire for a symbolic or social reality ordered and produced as signification." See Elizabeth Cowie, "The Spectacle of Actuality," in Gaines and Renov (eds.), *Collecting Visible Evidence*, p. 19. Finally, as filming devices grow smaller by the day and live broadcasting more widespread, digital filmmaking may be said to fantasize the minimization of the time, means, and labor necessary for the display and distribution of an event as an end product, which may precipitate aspirations to access and deliver reality accurately. At the same time, digital filmmaking also carries more potential to intricately reflect on the multilayered and contingent means, materiality, and processes of filmmaking. Indeed, the instantaneous, constantive, and ubiquitous character of digital moving images tend to reveal more of the traces of their making. Computer-based production of imagery both celebrates hyperrealism as well as harbingers questions about the credibility and authenticity of the images. With the advent of digital media, new technologies, techniques, and methods are harnessed in filmmaking. Lev Manovich contends that, today, "digital media redefines the very identity of cinema." The core character of filmmaking, which has "emerged out of the same impulse which engendered naturalism," has changed drastically, since "it is now possible to generate photorealistic scenes entirely in a computer using 3-D computer animation" and "cut, bend, stretch and stitch digitized film images into something which has perfect photographic credibility," Manovich explains. Lev Manovich, "What Is Digital Cinema?" in Timothy Corrigan and Patricia White (eds.), *Critical Visions in Film Theory* (New York: Bedford, 2011), pp. 1058–70.

34 Ryan Watson, "Art under Occupation: Documentary, Archive, and the Radically Banal," *Afterimage*, vol. 36, no. 5 (March/April 2009), p. 7.

35 Jane M. Gaines, "The Production of Outrage: The Iraq War and the Radical Documentary Tradition," *Framework*, vol. 48, no. 2 (Fall 2007), p. 40.

36 David Tzanegen, "Seven Lies about Jenin": https://www.news1.co.il/MemberLogin. aspx?ContentType=1&docid=1858&subjectid=3. For a television debate between Tzanegen and Bakri, see http://www.youtube.com/watch?v=ZQaLuwnZKOw.

37 Ibid.

38 Moshe Reinfeld, "The State to the Supreme Court: *Jenin Jenin* is Full of Falsifications," *Haaretz*, March 8, 2003: http://www.haaretz.co.il/misc/1.866850.

39 Giorgio Agamben, *Remnants of Auschwitz: The Witness and the Archive* (New York: Zone Books, 2002), p. 17.

40 Ibid.

41 Ibid.

42 Ibid., p. 33.

43 Ibid., p. 34.

44 Ibid.

45 Faisal Devji, *Landscapes of the Jihad: Militancy, Morality, Modernity* (London: Hurst, 2005), p. 94.

46 Ibid., pp. 94–5.

47 Rebecca Schneider, *Performing Remains: Art and War in Times of Theatrical Reenactment* (London: Routledge, 2011). p. 10.

48 Ibid., p. 36.

49 Ibid., p. 38.

50 Devji, *Landscapes of the Jihad*, p. 94.

51 Ibid.

52 Ibid., pp. 95–9.

53 Ibid., pp. 97–8.

54 Yael Friedman discusses the representation of trauma in *Jenin Jenin*, *Invasion*, and *Arna's Children*. See Friedman, "The Camera and the National Ethos," first published in Hebrew in Makhbarot Kolnoa Darom (South Cinema Notebooks).

55 Ibid., p. 100.

56 Devji, *Landscapes of the Jihad*, p. 94.

57 Avital Ronell, *The Test Drive* (Urbana: University of Illinois Press, 2005), p. 103.

58 Ibid., p. 107.

59 Ibid., p. 111.

60 Devji, *Landscapes of the Jihad*, p. 101.

61 Ibid.

62 Juliano was the son of the film's star, Arna Mer, who is a Jewish woman originally from Rosh-Pina, and Saliba Khamis, a Palestinian from Nazareth. See Shatz, "The Life and Death of Juliano Mer-Khamis."

63 Gertz and Khleifi, *Palestinian Cinema*, pp. 171–2.

64 Ariella Azoulay and Adi Ophir, *This Regime Which Is Not One: Occupation and Democracy between the Sea and the River (1967–)* (in Hebrew) (Tel Aviv: Resling, 2008), pp. 225–7.

65 Ibid., p. 227.

66 Ibid.

67 Emine Fisek, "I Want To Be a Palestinian Romeo! *Arna's Children* and the Romance with Theater," *Theater Research International*, vol. 37, no. 2 (July 2012), pp. 104–17.

68 Ibid., p. 108.

69 Ibid.

70 Ibid., p. 112.

71 Ever since the foundation of the Palmach, its young soldiers and advocators—named the "Palmach generation"—were obsessed with imitation and adoption of oriental and Arab cultural symbols. They wore Arab costumes and kaffiahs, reiterated Bedouin rituals, acquired sayings in Arabic and more. This cultural appropriation signifies the Zionist orientalistic fascination with the native Palestinian and the Zionists' attempts to resemble, if not become, natives themselves. See Oz Almog, *The Sabra: A Portrait* (in Hebrew) (Tel Aviv: Am Oved, 1997), pp. 305–8.

72 Fisek, *A Palestinian Romeo*, p. 111.

73 Ibid., p. 112.

74 Ibid.

75 Ibid.

76 Ariella Azoulay, "When a Demolished House Becomes a Public Square," in Ann Laura Stoler (ed.), *Imperial Debris: On Ruins and Ruination* (Durham: Duke University Press, 2013), pp. 194–226.

77 Ibid., p. 201.

78 Ibid.

79 Ibid., p. 201.

80 Ibid., p. 203.

81 Shatz, "The Life and Death of Juliano Mer-Khamis."

82 Laura Mulvey, *Death 24x a Second: Stillness and Moving Image* (London: Reaktion Books, 2006), p. 173.

83 Ibid., pp. 173–5.

84 Ibid., p. 174.

85 Schneider, *Performing Remains*, p. 88.

86 Ibid., p. 89.

87 Ibid., pp. 89–90.

88 Ibid., p. 89.

89 Ibid., p. 90.

90 Ibid., pp. 90–6.

91 Ibid., p. 48.

92 Ibid., p. 90.

93 Ibid., p. 92.

94 Asad, *On Suicide Bombing*, pp. 48–9.

95 Ibid., p. 49.

96 Ibid., p. 42.

97 Ibid., p. 45.

98 Ibid., p. 49.

99 Shatz, "The Life and Death of Juliano Mer-Khamis."

100 Ibid.

101 Fisek, *A Palestinian Romeo*, p. 109.

102 Schneider, *Performing Remains*, p. 100.

103 Ibid., p. 102.

104 Ibid., p. 36.

Chapter 2

1 Gideon Maron, "The Horror Film of Filmmaker Benchetrit: An Interview with David Benchetrit" (in Hebrew), *Yediot Ahronot*, April 30, 2004.

2 For Senyora (Sini) Bar David's eulogy/Facebook post (in Hebrew), see https://www.facebook.com/sini.bardavid.1/posts/103103577124001

3 For some of the praising reviews of the documentary, see Clyde Haberman, "Behind the Arab Veil, a Human Face," *New York Times*, October 31, 1992: https://www.nytimes.com/1992/10/31/movies/behind-the-arab-veil-a-human-face.html (accessed November 16, 2019); and Ethan Bronner, "Israeli Filmmaker Looks through the Veil," *Sunday Boston Globe*, November 8, 1992.

4 Ilan Shaul, "The Dark Side of the Light Torch: An Interview with David Benchetrit," *Ynet*, September 18, 2002: https://www.ynet.co.il/articles/0,7340,L-2124533,00.html (accessed November 16, 2019).

5 Carl Frankenstein, "The Problem of Ethnic Differences in the Absorption of Immigrants," *Judaism: A Quarterly Life of Jewish Life and Thought*, vol. 2, no. 3 (July 1953), p. 217. Like most of his writings, the essay also appears here: http://www.carl-frankenstein.com/HTMLs/page_736.aspx?c0=464&bsp=419 (accessed December 20, 2012).

6 Ibid., p. 219.

7 Ruth Bondy, *Sheba: A Doctor of All People* (in Hebrew) (Tel Aviv: Zmora-Beitan, 1981), p. 307.

8 Ibid., p. 308.

9 Ibid., p. 300.

10 Ella Shohat, "Sephardim in Israel: Zionism from the Perspective of Its Jewish Victims," *Social Text*, no. 19/20 (Autumn 1988), pp. 3–7.

11 Nissim Rejwan, *Outsider in the Promised Land: An Iraqi Jew in Israel* (Austin: University of Texas Press, 2006), p. 16.

12 These include Shohat, "Sephardim in Israel," p. 5; Nissim Mizrahi, "From Badness to Sickness: The Role of Ethnopsychology in Shaping Ethnic Hierarchies in Israel," *Social Identities*, vol. 10, no. 2 (2004), pp. 222–30; Henriette Dahan-Kalev, "You Are So Beautiful, You Don't Look Moroccan," *Israel Studies*, vol. 6, no. 1 (2001), pp. 1–14.

13 Ella Shohat, "The Invention of the Mizrahim," *Journal of Palestine Studies*, vol. 29, no. 1 (Autumn 1999), pp. 6–8.

14 Bryan Ruby, *The Mizrahi Era of Rebellion: Israel's Forgotten Civil Rights Struggle 1948–1966* (Syracuse: Syracuse University Press, 2015), p. 29.

15 Ibid., p. 31.

16 Photo credit: Teddy Bruner, @copyright Israel's Government Press Office ("la'am"). Photo taken from Ella Shohat, "Mizrahim in Israel: Zionism from the Perspective of Its Jewish Victims," in *Forbidden Memories: An Introduction to Multicultural Thought* (in Hebrew) (Tel Aviv: Keshet Hamizrah, Bimat Kedem Lesifrut, 2001), p. 170. This type of Zionist and later Israeli government sponsored photos of medical examinations of immigrants from the Middle East and/or of Palestinians were very common. For more on that and for more pictures of this kind, see: Dafna Hirsch, *We Are Here to Bring the West: Hygiene Education and Culture Building in the Jewish Society of Mandate Palestine* (in Hebrew) (Sede Boker: Ben Gurion University in the Negev, 2014); Noa Hazan, "When the Hadassah Nurses Educated the Mothers of the Orient," in *Haoketz*, June 20, 2018; https://bit.ly/3qOwheq (accessed December 20, 2020).

17 Frankenstein, "The Problem of Ethnic Differences in the Absorption of Immigrants,"
    p. 218.
18 Ibid., p. 219.
19 Ibid., p. 218.
20 Sami Shalom Chetrit, *Intra-Jewish Conflict in Israel: White Jews, Black
    Jews* (New York: Routledge, 2010), p.17, quoting Edward Said, *Orientalism*
    (New York: Random House, 1978), p. 104.
21 Frankenstein, "The Problem of Ethnic Differences in the Absorption of Immigrants,"
    p. 218.
22 Ibid., p. 219.
23 Ibid., pp. 220–2.
24 Ibid., p. 219.
25 Ibid., p. 218.
26 Ibid., p. 222.
27 Ibid.
28 Ibid., p. 219.
29 Mizrahi, "From Badness to Sickness," p. 220.
30 Frankenstein, "The Problem of Ethnic Differences in the Absorption of Immigrants,"
    p. 223.
31 Ibid.
32 Ibid.
33 Interestingly enough, the caption accompanying the figure may assist in such a
    reading, as it mentions that Salah was a "real-estate agent" in Iraq using the Hebrew
    word "metavech" that literally and connotatively speaking may also mean "mediator."
    See Figure 13.
34 Frantz Fanon, *Black Skin White Masks*, trans. Richard Philcox (New York: Grove
    Press, 2008), p. 89.
35 Ibid.
36 Ibid., p. 91.
37 Ibid.
38 Ibid.
39 Ibid., p. 90.
40 Ibid., p. 92.
41 Stuart Hall, "The After-life of Frantz Fanon: Why Fanon, Why Now? Why Black
    Skin White Masks?," in Alan Read (ed.), *The Fact of Blackness: Frantz Fanon and
    Visual Representation* (London: Institute of Contemporary Arts; Seattle: Bay Press,
    1996), p. 16.
42 Ibid., p. 21.
43 Avi Picard, "Immigration, Health, and Social Control: Medical Aspects of the Policy
    Governing *Aliyah* from Morocco and Tunisia," *Journal of Israeli History: Politics,
    Society, Culture*, vol. 22, no. 2 (November 2003), p. 42.
44 Rhona Seidelman, Ilan Troen, and Shifra Shvarts, " 'Healing' the Bodies and Souls of
    Immigrant Children: The Ringworm and Trachoma Institute, Sha'ar ha-Aliyah, 1952–
    1960," *Journal of Israeli History: Politics, Society, Culture*, vol. 29, no. 2 (September
    2010), p. 196.
45 Ibid.
46 Bondy, *Sheba*, pp. 152–4.
47 "The Secrets of Ringworm," a documentary report created for the investigative
    television show *The True Face* with Amnon Levy, on Israel's Channel 13, was

broadcast on November 4, 2018: https://13news.co.il/10news/panim/175427 (accessed November 16, 2019).

48 "The Secrets of Ringworm."

49 Meirav Aloush-Lavron, "The Mizrahi Memory and the Zionist Dominance: Voices from the Margins in Contemporary Documentary Cinema" (in Hebrew), *Israel: A Journal, for the Study of Zionism and the State of Israel: History, Culture, Society*, vol. 14 (2008), pp. 127–50.

50 Picard, "Immigration, Health, and Social Control," p. 35.

51 Seidelman, Troen, and Shvarts, " 'Healing' the Bodies and Souls of Immigrant Children," p. 192.

52 Ibid., p. 197.

53 Ibid., p. 198.

54 Bondy, *Sheba*, p. 153.

55 Ibid., p. 134.

56 Ibid., p. 300.

57 Ibid. For more similar opinions, see Rafael Falk, *Zionism and the Biology of the Jews* (in Hebrew) (Tel Aviv: Resling, 2006), pp. 178–9.

58 Ibid.

59 Ibid.

60 Ibid., pp. 198–202.

61 Ibid., pp. 136–7.

62 Akira Mizuta Lippit, *Atomic Light (Shadow Optics)* (Minneapolis: University of Minnesota Press, 2005), p. 52.

63 Ibid., p. 57.

64 Allen W. Grove, "Rontgen's Ghosts: Photography, X-Rays, and the Victorian Imagination," *Literature and Medicine*, vol. 16, no. 2 (1997), pp. 141–73 (quote from p. 144).

65 Ibid.

66 Lippit, *Atomic Light*, p. 50.

67 Frankenstein, "The Problem of Ethnic Differences in the Absorption of Immigrants," p. 219.

68 Ibid., p. 223.

69 Ibid.

70 Ibid., p. 224.

71 Dahan-Kalev, Henriette, "You Are So Beautiful, You Don't Look Moroccan," *Israel Studies*, vol. 6, no.1 (2001), pp. 8–9.

72 Shalom Chetrit, *Intra-Jewish Conflict in Israel*, pp. 48–9. Yossi Yonah and Yitzhak Sporta, "Pre-Vocational Education and the Making of the Working Class in Israel" (in Hebrew), in Hannan Hever, Yehudah Shenhav, Pnina Mutzafi-Haler (eds.), *Mizrahim in Israel: A New Critical Study* (Tel Aviv: Hakibutz Hameuchad, 2002), pp. 79–84.

73 Conceptualized in the late 1950s, prevocational programs of education were designed with pupils arriving from Arab and Muslim countries in mind; while some ministers and educators worriedly saw the "social selection" process coming, others wished for it, deliberately designating the immigrants to these programs. By contrast to initial plans, the vocational programs were mostly practiced in towns and neighborhoods populated by immigrants of Arab and Muslim countries; several educational figures explained this by conveying the special importance of such programs for children who would otherwise find themselves lazily hanging out doing nothing. The programs were to provide professional foundations and direct the children toward

productivization, dimensions assumed to be missing from their disposition. In this way, they would serve as part of the system that destined itself to educate, promote, and redeem the traditional immigrants from their dark and unsophisticated ways. Presuming beyond doubt the degradedness of immigrant/s' children here assisted in conditioning and confirming the maintenance of these children in institutions especially designed for their transitional state of in-between. Outlining the immigrant students' professional path to low-income occupations, these processes contributed to the positioning and fixing of the immigrants of Arab and Muslim countries in the underprivileged classes. See ibid., pp. 79–101.

74 Zelshik describes how the psychiatric institution prepared and/or, rather, found itself unprepared, to treat the immigrants in need: since their first arrivals in the early 1950s, psychiatrists tended to ignore the immigrants of Arab and Muslim countries. Gradually, during the 1950s, psychiatrists shifted from denying the few treated immigrants' social and cultural backgrounds to meticulously studying and, to a large degree and in ways not dissimilar to Frankenstein's, shaping and stereotyping it. Accordingly, the psychiatric institution regarded, positioned, and treated the immigrants as newly arrived individuals in a state of transition. Largely ascribing their illness to difficulties in socialization and absorption, the doctors anticipated and hoped for their hastened acculturation, after which they will be treated just like any other (Ashkenazi) person. They thus became psychiatric objects designated for improvement. See Rakefet Zelshik, *Ad Nefesh: Immigrants, Ascendents, Refugees, and the Psychiatric Institution in Israel* (in Hebrew) (Tel Aviv: Hakibutz Hameuchad, 2008), pp. 193–226.

75 Carl Frankenstein, *Externalization—Its Social Aspects* (in Hebrew) (Tel Aviv: Am Oved, 1983), p. 164. Also appears in: http://www.carl-frankenstein.com/HTMLs/page_792.aspx?c0=516&bsp=419 (accessed December 15, 2019).

76 Ibid.

77 Ibid., p. 181.

78 Ibid.

79 Ibid., p. 182.

80 Mizrahi, "From Badness to Sickness," p. 228.

81 Ibid., p. 227.

82 Shalom Chetrit, *Intra-Jewish Conflict in Israel*, pp. 81–140.

83 Raz Yosef, "Ethnicity and Sexual Politics: The Invention of Mizrahi Masculinity in Israeli Cinema" (in Hebrew), *Theory and Criticism*, vol. 25 (Fall 2004), p. 36.

84 Noa Hazan, "Display of Institutional Power between Race and Gender" (in Hebrew), *Israeli Sociology* vol. 14, no.2 (2012), pp. 358–66.

85 Ibid., p. 344.

86 Ibid., p. 359.

87 Paula Rabinowitz, "Street/Crime: From Rodney King's Beating to Michael Brown's Shooting," *Cultural Critique*, vol. 90 (2015), p. 144.

88 Ibid.

89 Ibid., p. 146.

90 Paula Rabinowitz, *They Must Be Represented: The Politics of Documentary* (New York: Verso, 1994), p. 211.

91 Ibid.

92 Rabinowitz, "Street/Crime," p. 144.

93 Avital Ronell, "Trauma TV: Twelve Steps beyond the Pleasure Principle," in *Finitude's Score: Essays for the End of the Millennium* (Lincoln: University of Nebraska Press), p. 70.
94 Ibid., p. 76.
95 Ibid., p. 71.
96 Ibid., p. 82.
97 Frankenstein, *Externalization—Its Social Aspects*, p. 164.
98 Ibid., p. 181.
99 Theresa De Lauretis, "Difference Embodied: Reflections on Black Skin White Masks," *Parallax*, vol. 8, no. 2 (2002), p. 56.
100 Ibid.
101 Ibid., p. 55.
102 Fanon, *Black Skin White Masks*, p. 91.
103 Hall, "The After-life of Frantz Fanon," p. 16.
104 De Lauretis, "Difference Embodied," p. 55.
105 Ibid., p. 57.
106 Ibid.
107 After Andre Bazin, Margulies reminds us that filmed representations "have actual effects on reality and in particular the reality of the profilmic bodies," i.e., one must consider that the experience that the performing person is communicating has been formative to the way their body looks like, to how their voice sounds like, to how they perform their self-identifications in everyday life and not just in front of cameras. Ivone Margulies, "Bodies Too Much," in Ivone Margulies (ed.), *Rites of Realism: Essays on Corporeal Cinema* (Durham: Duke University Press, 2003), p. 1.
108 As Taylor notes, "The *is/as* underlines the understanding of performance as simultaneously 'real' and 'constructed,' as practices that bring together what have historically been kept separate as discrete, supposedly free-standing, ontological and epistemological discourses." See Diana Taylor, *The Archive and the Repertoire* (Durham: Duke University Press, 2003), p. 5.

Chapter 3

1 From the DVD cover.
2 Ilan Pappe, "The Tantura Case in Israel: The Katz Research and Trial," *Journal of Palestine Studies*, vol. 30, no. 3 (Spring 2001), p. 24.
3 Ibid.
4 Nurith Gertz and George Khleifi, *Palestinian Cinema: Landscape, Trauma, and Memory* (Edinburgh: Edinburgh University Press, 2008), p. 132.
5 Helga Tawil-Souri, "Cinema as the Space to Transgress Palestine's Territorial Trap," *Middle East Journal of Culture and Communication*, vol. 7, no. 2 (2014), p. 172.
6 From the DVD cover. The new village of Ayn-Hawd was officially recognized in 2005, thus was not recognized at the time the film came out (2002).
7 Hillel Cohen, *The Present Absentees: The Palestinian Refugees in Israel since 1948* (Jerusalem: Van-Leer Institute, 2000), pp. 35–42.
8 Ibid., pp. 66–71.

9   Naama Meishar, "Fragile Guardians: Nature Reserves and Forests Facing the Arab Village," in Haim Yacobi (ed.), *Constructing a Sense of Place: Architecture and the Zionist Discourse* (Burlington: Ashgate, 2004), p. 304.

10 Ibid., p. 306.

11 Irus Braverman, *Planted Flags: Trees, Land, and Law in Israel/Palestine* (New York: Cambridge University Press, 2009), pp. 1–2.

12 Ibid., p. 4.

13 Ibid., p. 11.

14 Ibid., p. 79.

15 Ibid., p. 43.

16 Meishar, "Fragile Guardians," p. 306.

17 Braverman, *Planted Flags*, pp. 9–14.

18 Meishar, "Fragile Guardians," pp. 308–10.

19 Braverman, *Planted Flags*, pp. 40–7.

20 Meishar, "Fragile Guardians," p. 306.

21 Ubiquitously incorporated into Zionist propaganda, the olive tree is commonly constructed as linked to, and thus symbolic of, the ancient Hebrew culture of Palestine or, for Zionists, Eretz-Israel. Decorating Israeli nature preservation websites within descriptions of various landscapes, quotes from the Bible attempt to ascertain that biblical Hebrew denoted and connoted plants native to the promised land such as the olive trees. Below are websites indicating touristic and hiking attractions in Israel that construct the olive tree as a remnant from the Hebrew biblical culture of Eretz-Israel and, as the quotes demonstrate, allegedly accordingly mentioned in the Bible. See https://greenwin.kkl.org.il/features/forest/trees/israel_trees/olive/about_olive_trees/; https://bit.ly/3qv88bU; https://bit.ly/3c9pIgC

22 Benvenisti affirms that "all of the new names it [the Negev Names Committee] … chose were determined in direct reference to the old [Arabic] names, and no fewer than 333 of the 533 new names were either transliterations of Arabic or Hebrew names that had been decided upon on the basis of their similarity in sound to Arabic names," Meron Benvenisti, *Sacred Landscape: The Buried History of the Holy Land since 1948* (Berkeley: University of California Press, 2000), p. 17.

23 Daniel Bertrand Monk, *An Aesthetic Occupation: The Immediacy of Architecture and the Palestine Conflict* (Durham: Duke University Press, 2002), p. 19.

24 Susan Slyomovics, *The Object of Memory* (Philadelphia: University of Pennsylvania Press, 1998), p. 50.

25 Ibid.

26 Ibid., p. 51.

27 Ibid., p. 52.

28 Ibid., p. 53.

29 Ibid., pp. 34–5.

30 Monk, *An Aesthetic Occupation*, p. 23.

31 Ann Laura Stoler (ed.), *Imperial Debris: On Ruins and Ruination* (Durham: Duke University Press, 2013), p. 21.

32 Ibid., "Introduction," p. 2.

33 Ibid., p. 9.

34 Far from unfamiliar, the man's words, including the gaps and postponements that dwell between them, sound so familiar. "There was a war," proclaimed David Grossman too in his *Absent Present* (translated to English as *Sleeping on a Wire*), using the exact same words that the man used, when he wrote about Ayn-Hawd and

Ein-Hod about a decade prior to the making of *500 Dunam on the Moon*. Grossman reiterates the statements of his neighbor, the resident Giora Ben-Dov, whom Grossman interviewed earlier. "There was a war. It's over, and now there's a situation," said Ben-Dov confidently in their conversation. David Grossman, *Absent Present* (in Hebrew) (Tel Aviv: Hakibutz Hameuchad, 1992), p. 76.

35 Braverman, *Planted Flags*, p. 41.
36 See the JNF website: http://www.wildflowers.co.il/kkl/plant.asp?ID=236.
37 Nicholas Mirzeoff, *The Right to Look: A Counterhistory of Visuality* (Durham: Duke University Press, 2011), p. 3.
38 Ibid., p. 6.
39 Ibid., p. 239.
40 Ibid., p. 232.
41 Ibid., p. 241.
42 Nabil I. Matar, "Renaissance Cartography and the Question of Palestine," in Ibrahim Abu-Lughod, Roger Heacock, and Khalen Nashef (eds.), *The Landscape of Palestine: Equivocal Poetry* (Ramallah: Birzeit University, 1999), pp. 139–40.
43 Ibid., p. 151.
44 Ibid., p. 139.
45 Gil Hochberg, *In Spite of Partition: Jews, Arabs, and the Limits of Separatist Imagination* (Princeton: Princeton University Press, 2007), p. 74.
46 Ibid., pp. 74–5.
47 Ibid., p. 76.
48 Ibid.
49 Hochberg notes that Eastern Europe was Orientalized by eighteenth- and nineteenth-century Western Jewry who desired to differentiate themselves from those they perceived as primitive, "backward and traditional," ibid., p. 11.
50 Ahmad Amara, "The Negev Land Question: Between Denial and Recognition," *Journal of Palestine Studies*, vol. 42, no. 4 (Summer 2013), pp. 29–41; Oren Yiftahel and Sandi (Alexander) Kedar, "On Power and Land: The Israeli Regime of Land" (in Hebrew), *Theory and Criticism*, vol. 16 (Spring 2000), pp. 85–95.
51 Emile Habiby, *The Secret Life of Saeed, the Ill-Fated Pessoptimist: A Palestinian Who Became a Citizen of Israel*, trans. Salma Khadra Jayyusi and Trevor Le Gassick (London: Readers International, 1985), p. 41.
52 Ibid., p. 43.
53 Ibid., p. 117.
54 Ibid., p. 119.
55 Ibid., p. 158.
56 Ibid., p. 4. As Jayyusi points out, Saeed "recounts the secrets of his life to an unnamed friend … after he is safely ensconced somewhere in outer space," ibid, p. xi.
57 As Jayyusi contends, Saeed "is an informer for the Zionist State, but his stupidity, uncanny candour, and cowardice make him more the victim than the villain," ibid., p. xii.
58 Edward Said, *After the Last Sky: Palestinian Lives* (New York: Pantheon Books, 1986), p. 61.
59 Ibid.
60 Ibid., p. 52.
61 Ibid., p. 56.
62 Ibid., p. 63.
63 Pappe, "The Tantura Case in Israel," p. 24.
64 Sara Ahmed, *Living a Feminist Life* (Durham: Duke University Press, 2007), p. 260.

Chapter 4

1   Gil Eyal, *The Disenchantment of the Orient: Expertise in Arab Affairs and the Israeli State* (in Hebrew) (Tel Aviv: Hakibbutz Hameuchad, 2005), pp. 63–9.

2   Ella Habiba Shohat, "A Reluctant Eulogy: Fragments from the Memories of an Arab Jew," in Nahla Abdo and Ronit Lentin (eds.), *Women and the Politics of Military Confrontation* (Oxford: Berghahn, 2002), pp. 264–7.

3   Vered Madar, "Elegies of Women from Yemen: Chains of Intergenerational Transmission in Its Cultural Context," in Shlomit Lir (ed.), *To My Sister: Mizrahi Feminist Politics* (in Hebrew) (Tel Aviv: Babel, 2007), pp. 235–7.

4   Eitan Bronstein Aparicio, "The Mizrahi Communities Destroyed by Israel," in *+972*, December 28, 2017: https://972mag.com/the-mizrahi-communities-destroyed-by-the-israeli-establishment/131968/ (accessed October 16, 2019). This article is based on a report prepared for the organization Decolonizer/Zochrot. See https://www.de-colonizer.org/ (accessed October 16, 2019).

5   "Natalie Baruch Interviewing Aharon Madouel" (in Hebrew), *Sedek: A Journal about the Nakba That Is Here*, vol. 2 (January 2008), pp. 85–7. Avi Blarchman, "The Residents of Kfar Shalem Renew Their Struggle" (in Hebrew), *Local Call*, April 28, 2014: https://mekomit.co.il/ (accessed October 16, 2019); Omer Cohen, "From Pioneers to Invaders: Three Generations, One Struggle" (in Hebrew), in *Davar*, June 28, 2016: https://www.davar1.co.il/22013/ (accessed October 16, 2019).

6   For more about the struggles of the Mizrahi residents of Giv'at Amal (formerly Jamusin Al-Ghrarbi) and the Argazim neighborhood in Tel Aviv, see: Smadar Lavie, "Gaza 2014 and Mizrahi Feminism," *PoLAR: Political and Legal Anthropology Review*, vol. 42, no. 1 (2019), pp. 85–109. Orly Noy, "Corruption Lies in the Thread Connecting Givat Amal and Al-Arakiv" (in Hebrew), *Local Call* (2017): https://bit.ly/3iGUhxd (accessed December 25, 2017) Adi Cohen, "An Apartment for 75K Shekels: Who Actually Profits from the Eviction Plan for the Argazim Neighborhood?" (in Hebrew), *The Marker* (April 17 2019): https://www.themarker.com/realestate/.premium-1.7133475 (accessed December 11, 2020).

7   Gil Eshed, "An Interview with Bracha Seri," in Henriette Dahan-Kalev (ed.), *In Blessing Secret: The Poetry of Bracha Seri* (in Hebrew) (Jerusalem: Carmel, 2013), p. 136.

8   Shani Littman, "Who Said Erotica Is for the Secular? An Interview with Israela Shaer-Meoded," *Haaretz*, May 27, 2019: https://www.haaretz.co.il/gallery/cinema/docaviv/.premium-1.7288124 (accessed December 11, 2020).

9   Elon Gilad, "The Strange Word That Made It to Court," *Haaretz*, September 12, 2018. See https://www.haaretz.co.il/magazine/the-edge/mehasafa/.premium-1.6468480 (accessed October 8, 2020).

10 For more on the humor in the poem "Queen Khantarisha," see Leah Bertz, "An Examination of the Collection, 'Daughter of Wine,' by Bracha Seri" (in Hebrew), *Browsed Humor*, vol. 1 (October 2011), pp. 68–9.

11 See Adrianna Kemp, "The Border as a Janus Face: Space and National Consciousness in Israel" (in Hebrew), *Theory and Criticism*, vol. 16 (Spring 2000), pp. 13–44. With regard to other places in Israel, see Benny Nurieli, "Foreigners in a National Space: The Arab Jews in the Ghetto of Lod 1950–1959," *Theory and Criticism*, vol. 26 (Spring 2005), pp. 13–42; Haim Yaakobi, "The Third Space, Architecture, Nationalism, and the Postcolonial Gaze," in *Theory and Criticism*, vol. 30 (Summer 2007), pp. 63–88. Also see Ella Shohat, "Sephardim in Israel: Zionism from the Perspective

of Its Jewish Victims," *Social Text*, no. 19/20 (Autumn 1988), p. 170; and Moshe
Karif, *The Mizrahit: The Story of the Mizrahi Democratic Rainbow Movement* (in
Hebrew) (Tel Aviv: Globes, 2005). Additionally, Eli Hamo and Sami Shalom Chetrit's
documentary *Black Panthers (in Israel) Speak* (2003) provides information about the
Zionist unequal distribution of space among its Jewish residents with statements
such as: "Mizrahim carried out the drying of the Hula swampland, but the land was
distributed to Kibbutzim only."

12 This chapter focuses on the labor exploitation of Yemenite Mizrahim in particular,
though the general process of designating Mizrahim to manual labor was inflicted
on all Mizrahim. For a comprehensive historical account on this, see Shlomo Svirsky
and Dvora Bernstein, "Who Worked in What, for Whom, and for How Much? The
Economic Development of Israel and the Consolidation of Labor Division" (in
Hebrew), *Notebooks for Research and Criticism*, vol. 4 (1980), pp. 5–66.

13 Dahan-Kalev, "Mizrahi Women: Identity and History," in Galit Hazan-Rokem,
Ruth Kark, Margalit Shilo (eds.), *The New Hebrewesses: Women in the Yishuv and in
Zionism in Light of Gender* (Jerusalem: Yitzhak Ben-Zvi Foundation, 2001), p. 50, and
Pnina Mutzafi-Heller, "Knowledge, Identity and Power: Mizrahi Women in Israel," in
Shlomit Lir (ed.), *To My Sister*, pp. 89–90.

14 Manar Hasan, "The Politics of Honor: Patriarchy, the State and the Murder of Women
in the Name of Family Honor," *Journal of Israeli History: Politics, Society, Culture*, vol.
21, no. 1–2 (June 2002), p. 1.

15 The entire quote from Hasan is worth detailing here: "First, he injects and implements
government policy within the society under investigation, shaping it along the lines
of the state's agenda, then he studies that same society, only to contend in the end
that his 'research finding' spring from fixed and unchanging cultural or religious
elements," in ibid., p. 2.

16 Eshed, "An Interview with Bracha Seri," p. 134.

17 Ibid.

18 Ella Shohat, "Postscript," in *Israeli Cinema: East/West and the Politics of
Representation*, 2nd ed. (London: I.B. Tauris, 2010), p. 299.

19 Cofounded by Vicky Shiran, Sami Shalom Chetrit, Doly Benhabib, Yehuda Shenhave,
Moshe Karif, and other Mizrahi activists, the *Mizrahi Democratic Rainbow* is a not-
for-profit organization founded in 1996 to launchhuman rights and representation
struggles in the name of Mizrahim in Israel. One of their most famous and partly
successful struggles was an appeal to the Supreme Court in 2001 demanding the
reallocation of land resources formed as the state-owned Kibbutzim and Moshavim
and predominantly populated by Ashkenazim. For more, see Karif, *The Mizrahit*.
As does *Black Panthers (in Israel) Speak*, *Breaking the Walls* also elaborates on how
Israel placed Mizrahi immigrants in the Palestinian urban neighborhoods evicted in
1948 and comprising the edges and fortifications of the borders of the newly founded
state—one of which being Musrara.

20 Heart at East: The Coalition for Equal Distribution of Cultural Funds in Israel, *A
Bureaucracy of Inequality: Discrimination in the Allocation of Cultural Resources in
Israel—the Case of Mizrahi Culture in 2009*.

21 In the early 1990s, Mizrahi and feminist women activists called for recognition
not only of women's oppression in Israel in general but also of the oppression,
discrimination, and exclusion of Mizrahi women in particular, and of the
racism of the predominantly Ashkenazi Feminist Movement in Israel itself. The
formative event marking the emergence of Mizrahi feminist activism in the

Ashkenazi-dominated public sphere in Israel was a panel discussion delivered by Ella Shohat, Tikva Levi, and Mira Eliezer at the plenary session of the 10th feminist conference in Givat Haviva, in July 1994. These Mizrahi feminist speakers called out the racism of the feminist movement itself, bringing to the forefront the specific needs and demands of Mizrahi women in Israel, which were formerly only addressed by the organization HILA, the Association for Education in the Poor Neighborhoods and Development Towns. Theses speakers were the first Mizrahi feminists to call attention to both the intersections between different forms of oppression in Israel. The speakers were later joined by other Mizrahi feminist activists such as Vicky Shiran, Neta Amar, and Henriette Dahan-Kalev. For the talks, see Ella Shohat, "Breaking the Silence," publication of Ella Shohat, Tikva Levy, and Mira Eliezer's speeches, delivered at the plenary session of the 10th Feminist Conference, Givat Haviva, Israel, July 17–19, 1994; published in Hebrew, "Lishvor et Ha-shtika," *Hila News*, vol. 50, August 1994; and in English in *News from Within*, vol. 10, no. 8 (August 1994). For more on this, see Ktzia Alon, "The Voice of the Mizrahi Women Deviating from the Stereotype Is Not Heard" (in Hebrew), in the website of the organization *The Mizrahi Democratic Rainbow*, first published in *New Horizons*: http://www.ha-keshet.org.il/articles/feminisim/kolan_alon.htm. Two years later, in a special piece for *News from Within* Ella Shohat situated Mizrahi feminism as part of a larger global wave of Third World feminism around the world, stressing that "it is within the broad context of Third World gender, race, and class struggles that I want to situate an inclusive Mizrahi feminist agenda ... to contextualize Mizrahi feminism within racial and national Third World struggles." See Ella Shohat, "Mizrahi Feminism: The Politics of Gender, Race, and Multiculturalism," published simultaneously in three languages: English (*News From Within*), Arabic (*Rou'iya Oukhra*), and Hebrew (*Mitzad Sheni*), vol. 12, no. 4 (April 1996), pp. 17–26. Following the rebellion in Givat Haviva, the Mizrahi feminist organization The Achoti (My Sister) Movement was established in 2000. For more on this, see Henriette Dahan-Kalev, "Achoti Movement: Foundational Pangs" (in Hebrew), in Shlomit Lir (ed.), *To My Sister*.

22   Shoshana Gabai, "We the Sentimentalists: The Mizrahi Struggle as the Loyal Servant of Neoliberal Media" (in Hebrew), *Haoketz*: https://bit.ly/33ilRHy (accessed November 23, 2019).

23   Arieh Bruce Saposnik, *Becoming Hebrew: The Creation of a Jewish National Culture in Ottoman Palestine* (New York: Oxford University Press, 2008), pp. 69–70.

24   Nissim Yaakov Malul, "The Question of Hebrew Teaching of Arabic," and the Editors' Note, in Moshe Behar and Ben-Dor Benite (eds.), *Modern Middle Eastern Jewish Thought* (Waltham: Brandeis University Press, 2013), pp. 64–6.

25   Liora R. Halperin, "Orienting Language: Reflections on the Study of Arabic in the Yishuv," *Jewish Quarterly Review*, vol. 96, no. 4 (Fall 2006), p. 485.

26   Matti Shmuellof, "To Heal the Rupture" (in Hebrew), *Haoketz*, November 18, 2010. See http://www.haokets.org/2010/11/18/ (accessed October 16, 2019).

27   Madar, "Elegies of Women from Yemen," in Shlomit Lir (ed.), *To My Sister*, pp. 235–7.

28   Ibid., 231.

29   Tova Gamliel, *Aesthetics of Sorrow: The Wailing Culture of Yemenite Jewish Women* (Detroit: Wayne State University Press, 2014), p. 9.

30   Madar, "Elegies of Women from Yemen," in Shlomit Lir (ed.), *To My Sister*, p. 236.

31   Ibid., p. 235.

32 Shoshana Madmoni-Gerber, *Israeli Media and the Framing of Internal Conflict: The Yemenite Babies Affair* (New York: Palgrave-Macmillan, 2009), pp. 22–30.

33 Ibid., pp. 25–7.

34 Ibid.

35 Ibid., pp. 28–9.

36 Sara Hinsky, "The Lace Female Sewers from Betzalel" (in Hebrew), *Theory and Criticism*, vol. 11 (Winter 1997), pp. 177–205.

37 Ibid., pp. 179–86.

38 Ibid., p. 186.

39 Ibid., p. 187.

40 Ibid.

41 Ibid., p. 186.

42 Ibid., pp. 191–3.

43 Ibid., p. 192. On this matter, however, the Palestinian Jewish women at the center of Hinsky's argument differ from the Yemenite Jews that she mentioned in passing: for, unlike the former who spoke mainly Ladino and Yiddish, the latter group spoke Arabic. This utterly significant detail requires much attention: for, the Zionists had, and still have, a very particular, impactful, and destructive view of, and approach toward, Arabic—which I elaborate on shortly.

44 Zvi Ben-Dor, "Ib, Hshuma, Infjarat Kunbula: Towards a History of Mizrahim and the Arabic" (in Hebrew), in Yigal Nizri (ed.), *Eastern Appearance/Mother Tongue* (Tel Aviv: Babel, 2002), p. 35.

45 Matti Shmueloff, "A Social and Cultural Struggle and the Reception of Bracha Seri's Earlier Work," in Dahan-Kalev (ed.), *In Blessing Secret*, pp. 196–7 and 207.

46 For this pseudonym, Seri incorporated her youth surname "Meridor," which literally comprises the word "rebel" and "generation" and, for the first name, she uses the noun "storm" in the female, which may also be read as the verb "steamed" in the female pronoun. See ibid., p. 206.

47 Ibid.

48 Ibid., p. 205. For more about the Tents protest and movement, which was a landmark in Mizrahi struggles in Israel, see Zvi Ben-Dor Benite, "The Wondrous History of the Mizrahim" (in Hebrew), in Inbal Perlson (ed.), *The Mizrahi Revolution: 3 Essays on Zionism and the Mizrahim* (Jerusalem: Center for Alternative Information, 1999), pp. 87–106; Sami Shalom Chetrit, *The Mizrahi Struggle in Israel 1948–2003* (in Hebrew) (Tel Aviv: Am Oved, 2004), pp. 186–7.

49 Yael Levy Hazan , "Reality Is Larger Than Poems: War and Protest in the Poems of Bracha Seri," Ashkelon Academic College, 2013, pp. 230–62.

50 Yaron Shemer, *Identity, Subversion, and Place in Contemporary Israeli Cinema* (Ann Arbor: University of Michigan Press, 2013), p. 190.

51 Ronit Hacham, "Living in the Word: Reading Some of the Poems of Wanderings," in Dahan-Kalev (ed.), *In Blessing Secret*, p. 33.

52 Ibid., p. 34.

53 Ibid.

54 Below, I address the subject of motherhood and daughter-mother relationships in relation to poetry and to poetizing, by focusing on film and feminist scholar Kaja Silverman's employment of this subject, in her writings about the voice, its associations with motherhood, and its manifestation in cinema. It is important to mention other eminent scholars that have paved the path for Silverman's work. Julia Kristeva's multifaceted notion of the maternal as deriving and comprising

the preoedipal stages and factors in language development is notable. See Julia Kristeva, *Revolution in Poetic Language*, trans. from French by Margaret Waller (New York: Columbia University Press, 1984 [1974]). Adrienne Rich traced women's fundamental relationship to motherhood that exists by virtue of them being born to mothers, and regardless of whether they themselves choose to mother. Poetry, to Rich, is the ultimate way to reflect on both the institution—ideas and constructs—and the lived experience of women's relation to motherhood. See Adrienne Rich, *Of Woman Born: Motherhood as Experience and Institution* (Norton: New York, 1976). Employing Silverman's writings on voice in cinema and its association with motherhood, my analysis below distances itself from rigid psychoanalytic frameworks and shows how documentary cinema constructs, reconstructs, reiterates, and complicates such frameworks, emphasizing their ideological preconceptions and manifestations.

55 Kaja Silverman, *The Acoustic Mirror: The Female Voice in Psychoanalysis and Cinema* (Bloomington: Indiana University Press, 1988), pp. 74–5. Silverman's theorizations build on and problematize Kristeva's work on the maternal voice, which the latter conceives "as a 'mobile receptacles' which absorbs the infant's 'anaclytic facilitations'" (p. 72), quoted from Julia Kristeva, "Place Names," in *Desire in Language: A Semiotic Approach to Literature and Art*, trans. Thomas Gora, Alice Jardine, and Lon S. Roudiez (New York: Columbia University Press, 1980), p. 282. Generally, Silverman's theorizations of cinematic images of the maternal, the voice, the receptacle, as precisely that—images—emphasize that they dwell in a socially constructed and politically shaped representational economy.

56 Ibid., p. 43.

57 Ibid., p. 43.

58 Ibid., p. 44.

59 While we are well trained and tamed to consciously identify the voiceover as Seri's own voice, it is necessary to think against this normative perception and consider the specific cinematic composition that the scene manifests here. It is useful to recall Judith Butler's conceptualization of subjectivation alongside subjection on this note. Butler emphasized that the subject as a critical theme is primarily designated as a "linguistic category [and] occasion." For Butler, the subject may only become one after seeking, finding, and forming intelligibility through language; paradoxically, such subjectivation is "circular," thus not only utilizing, but also stemming from and relying on, one's subjection to language. In this process, the speaker "refer[s] to its own genesis … by taking a third-person perspective on itself" to deploy "the narration of how the subject is constituted." She thus "must refer to what does not yet exist." See Judith Butler, *The Psychic Life of Power: Theories in Subjection* (Stanford: Stanford University Press, 1997), p. 11.

60 Madar, "Elegies of Women from Yemen," in Shlomit Lir (ed.), *To My Sister*, p. 237.

61 See Dahan-Kalev, "Mizrahi Women," in Hazan-Rokem, Kark, and Shilo (eds.), *The New Hebrewesses*, p. 51. Compatibly, Rachel Eli'or has also depicted this patriarchal practice as prevalent in all Jewish traditions. See Rachel Eli'or, "Like Sophia, Marcel, and Lizzie" (in Hebrew): http://mikrarevivim.blogspot.com/2014/08/blog-post.html (accessed December 11, 2014).

62 Dahan-Kalev, "Mizrahi Women," in Hazan-Rokem, Kark, and Shilo (eds.), *The New Hebrewesses*, p. 50. Pnina Mutzafi-Heller, "Knowledge, Identity, and Power: Mizrahi Women in Israel" (in Hebrew), in Dahan-Kalev (ed.), *To My Sister*, pp. 89–90.

63 Mutzafi-Heller, "Knowledge, Identity, and Power," p. 93.

64 Silverman, *The Acoustic Mirror*, p. 45.

65 Ibid.
66 Ibid., p. 46.
67 Patricia White, "Cinema Solidarity: The Documentary Practice of Kim Longinotto," *Cinema Journal*, vol. 46, no. 1 (Autumn 2006), p. 124.
68 Ibid.
69 Ibid., p. 126.
70 Silverman, *The Acoustic Mirror*, p. 46.
71 Gamliel, *Aesthetics of Sorrow*, p. 35.
72 The renowned doctor, hospital manager, and policy maker Chaim Sheba, whose ideology I discussed in Chapter 2, has also advocated for the need to encourage birth within Jewish Yemenite communities, and was opposed to abortion. See Ruth Bondy, *Sheba: Physician for All People* (Tel Aviv: Zmora-Betan and Modan, 1981), p. 287.
73 Shohat, "A Reluctant Eulogy," in Abdo and Lentin (eds.), *Women and the Politics of Military Confrontation.*
74 Ibid., p. 264.
75 Ibid., pp. 264–7.
76 Ibid., p. 265.
77 Ibid., p. 266.
78 Ibid., p. 264.
79 It is important to note that, since its emergence, Ashkenazi, Zionist, Eretz-Israeli music was itself very preoccupied by what it saw as "eastern" sounds—that is, tunes from the Middle East, Asia, and Africa, especially Yemenite Jewish and Non-Jewish melodies. This interest was based on their orientalist preconception that Yemenite Jews are the "true" offspring of the old Israelites. Their music faced no cultural exclusion—to the contrary, it was celebrated as the "authentic" sound of the historically and geographically fixed and inevitably Israelite Land of Israel. See Edwin Seroussi and Motti Regev, *Popular Music and National Culture in Israel* (in Hebrew) (Tel-Aviv: Open University, 2013), pp. 249–62; and Amy Horowitz, *Mediterranean Israeli Music and the Politics of the Aesthetic* (Detroit: Wayne State University Press, 2010), pp. 261–6. Many scholars, activists, and Mizrahi musicians have shown how Israeli national cultural institutions operated systematically to silence and invisibilize Mizrahi music. That is, since the foundation of the state in 1948, Mizrahi music was never taken on by the major all-Ashkenazi music producers in Israel; it was banned from the national radio stations and from national television, since its foundation in 1968; those very few channels of media access were then the only ones available in Israel. The very few alleged attempts to promote restorative discrimination had a purely orientalist outlook toward them. For example, Yosef Ben-Israel, one of the only Mizrahim working on national TV, advocated the creation of one or two limited frameworks such as the "Mizrahi Music Festival." Yet Ben-Israel believed that the Mizrahi clubs and cassettes' music was shallow, primitive, and altogether inferior, and that was why, he thought, it should progress to become "high-quality," as would happen under the proper auspices of the state. See Seroussi and Regev, *Popular Music and National Culture in Israel*, pp. 250–2; Horowitz, *Mediterranean Israeli Music and the Politics of the Aesthetic*, pp. 261–6. Notably, Ron Kahlili's TV documentary series *A Sea of Tears* from 1998 brought testimonies of many Mizrahi musicians, activists, as well as people from the Zionist entertainment institution, who have exposed experiences and stories about the ongoing systematic racial discrimination and labeling of Mizrahi musicians in Israel. The series can be viewed on http://www.youtube.com/watch?v=1lzRQAzMJWg (accessed October 16, 2019). Rightly claimed

by many, this source is certainly worth mentioning more elaborately. On the silencing of the Sephardi and Mizrahi piut, see Haviva Pedaya, "Prelude," in Haviva Pedaya (ed.), *The Piut as a Cultural Window: New Directions in the Study of the Piut and Its Cultural Construction* (in Hebrew) (Tel Aviv: Hakibutz Hameuchad, 2012), p. 14.

80 Shimon Cohen, "A Historic Closure for *Dry Twigs*," in Channel 7, June 17, 2018: http://www.inn.co.il/News/News.aspx/176328 (accessed October 16, 2019).

81 For Dan Almagor's lyrics of *Dry Twigs* in Hebrew: http://shironet.mako.co.il/ artist?type=lyrics&lang=1&prfid=518&wrkid=21512 (accessed October 16, 2019).

82 Cohen, "A Historic Closure for *Dry Twigs*."

83 To watch Yizhar Cohen performing the song *Dry Twigs*: http://www.youtube.com/ watch?v=OSdlNAYte4I (accessed October 16, 2019).

84 Cohen, "A Historic Closure for *Dry Twigs*."

85 On that note, an interesting scene from *A Sea of Tears* centers on a criticism against Jewish Yemenite musicians Margalit Tzanani and Hayim Moshe who, in the early 1990s—around the time Cohen's song was broadcast—had started singing music in the style of popular Hebrew culture, composed by Ashkenazi writers. "Margalit neglected Eastern Music. I'm telling her that on TV. Like Hayim Moshe. She betrayed Eastern music. She went along with the Ashkenazim," say people from her Mizrahi audience, promising that her sales will decrease among them. Tzanani herself communicates that she became a huge star when she incorporated other "Westernized" musical styles in her music, claiming that she loves a variety of musical tenets and would like to "obey no law." See http://www.youtube.com/ watch?v=1lzRQAzMJWg (accessed October 16, 2019).

86 Pnina Mutzafi-Haller, "An Ashkenazi Woman Taken Captive" (in Hebrew), in Tova Cohen and Shaul Regev (eds.), *A Woman in the East—A Woman from the East: The Story of the Jewish Women from the East* (Ramat-Gan: Bar-Ilan University, 2005), pp. 273–4.

87 Avital Ronell, "The Sujet Suppositaire: Freud, and/or the Obsessional Neurotic Style (Maybe)," in *Finitude's Score: Essays for the End of the Millennium* (Lincoln: University of Nebraska Press, 1994), pp. 110–11.

88 Rebecca Schneider, *The Explicit Body in Performance* (New York: Routledge, 1997), p. 2.

89 Many Arab Jewish poets chose, or were compelled to, write their poetry in Hebrew once they had immigrated to Israel, for reasons that I elaborated on. For more about other Arab Jewish poets writing in Hebrew since the 1980s, see Almog Behar, "Identity and Gender in the Poetry of Amira Hess" (in Hebrew), *Peamim*, vols. 125–7 (Ben-Tzvi Institute for Research of the Communities of Israel in the East, 2011), pp. 319–22.

90 Inspired by Patricia Hill-Collins, Mutzafi-Heller stressed that Mizrahi women need to keep working "within" Israel's institutions (in her example, academic) while utilizing a radical perspective of the excluded "outsider." See Mutzafi-Haller, "Knowledge, Identity and Power," pp. 89–90. Originally, Hill-Collins had coined the term to elucidate the position of Black feminist thought in the White American academy. See Patricia Hill-Collins, *Black Feminist Thought: Knowledge, Consciousness, and the Politics of Empowerment* (New York: Routledge, 1999), pp. 1–12, 251–3.

91 Bishnupriya Ghosh, "We Shall Drawn, Not Move," in Bhaskar Sarkar and Janet Walker (eds.), *Documentary Testimonies: Global Archives of Social Suffering* (New York: Routledge, 2010), p. 59.

92 While both mean "Oriental" in Hebrew, my differentiation here between "Oriental" and "Mizrahi" follows the differentiation between the state-imposed term and the self-defining, resistant, reclaiming term, respectively.

Concluding Notes: Looking toward Mizrahi Solidarity with the Palestinian Struggle

1 Jane Gaines, "The Production of Outrage: The Iraq War and the Radical Documentary Tradition," *Framework*, vol. 48, no. 2 (Fall 2007), p. 40.
2 For more on this, see Noura Erakat and Marc Lamont Hill, "Black-Palestinian Transnational Solidarity: Renewals, Returns, and Practice," *Journal of Palestine Studies*, vol. 48, no. 4 (Summer 2019), pp. 7–14.
3 Patricia R. Zimmerman, "Public Domains: Engaging Iraq through Experimental Digitalities," *Framework: The Journal of Cinema and Media*, vol. 48, no. 2 (Fall 2007), pp. 1–28.
4 For more about the Mizrahi cultural renaissance and in particular the revolutionary poetry movement Arspoetica, see Ayelet Tsabari, "Mizrahi Artists Are Here to Incite Cultural War," in: http://forward.com/opinion/335653/mizrahi-artists-incite-culture-war-against-israeli-elite/.
5 For more on this, in addition to Hochberg's piece about "brownwashing" mentioned in the introduction, it is also worth mentioning Lihi Yona's related recent piece on Mizrahi-washing. See Lihi Yona, "Mizrahi-Washing: The New Face of Israeli Propaganda," *+972 Magazine*, June 25, 2020: https://www.972mag.com/mizrahi-washing-hasbara-israel-propaganda/ (accessed August 1, 2020).
6 Ella Shohat, "Postscript," in *Israeli Cinema: East/West and the Politics of Representation*, 2nd ed. (London: I.B. Tauris, 2010), p. 299.
7 Ibid., p. 301.

BIBLIOGRAPHY

Abdo, Nahla and Lentin, Ronit (eds.), *Women and the Politics of Military Confrontation: Palestinian and Israeli Gendered Narratives of Dislocation*. New York: Berghahn Books, 2002.

Abu-Baker, Haula and Rabinowitz, Danny, *The Erect Generation* (in Hebrew). Jerusalem: Keter, 2002.

Abu-Lughod, Ibrahim, Heacock, Roger, and Nashef, Khalen (eds.), *The Landscape of Palestine: Equivocal Poetry*. Ramallah: Birzeit University, 1999.

Agamben, Giorgio, *Remnants of Auschwitz: The Witness and the Archive*. New York: Zone Books, 2002.

Ahmed, Sara, "The Contingency of Pain," in *The Cultural Politics of Emotion*. Edinburgh: Edinburgh University Press, 2014.

Alcalay, Ammiel (ed.), *Keys to the Garden City: New Israeli Writing*. San Francisco: Lights Books, 1996.

Almog, Oz, *The Sabra: A Portrait* (in Hebrew). Tel Aviv: Am Oved, 1997.

Aloush-Lavron, Meirav, "The Mizrahi Memory and the Zionist Dominance: Voices from the Margins in Contemporary Documentary Cinema," (in Hebrew), *Israel: a Journal for the Study of Zionism and the State of Israel: History, Culture, Society* no. 14 (2008), pp. 127–50.

Al-Raheb, Hani, *The Zionist Character in the English Novel*. New York: Zed Press, 1985.

Anidjar, Gil, *Semites: Race, Religion, Literature*. Stanford: Stanford University Press, 2007.

Appadurai, Arjun, *Modernity at Large: Cultural Dimensions of Globalization*. Minneapolis: University of Minnesota Press, 1996.

Appadurai, Arjun, *Fear of Small Numbers: An Essay on the Geography of Anger*. Durham: Duke University Press, 2006.

Asad, Talal, *On Suicide Bombing*. New York: Columbia University Press, 2007.

Assadi, Ginger, "Upholding the Palestinian Image in Israeli Cinema: An Interview with Mohammad Bakri," *Cineaste USA*, vol. 29, no. 4 (2004), pp. 41–3.

Austin, J. L., *How to Do Things with Words*. Oxford: Claredon Press, 1962.

Awad, Nadia, "Nostalgia for the Future," *The New Inquiry*, March 22, 2015.

Azoulay, Ariella, *How Does It Look Like to You? 25 Conversations, 44 Photographs* (in Hebrew). Tel Aviv: Bavel, 2000.

Azoulay, Ariella, *The Civil Contract of Photography*. New York: Zone Books, 2008.

Azoulay, Ariella and Ophir, Adi, *This Regime Which Is Not One: Occupation and Democracy between the Sea and the River (1967-)* (in Hebrew). Tel Aviv: Resling, 2008.

B'shara, Azmi, "On the Question of the Palestinian Minority in Israel" (in Hebrew), *Theory and Criticism*, vol. 3 (Winter 1993), pp. 7–20.

B'shara, Azmi, "A Hundred Years of Zionism" (in Hebrew), *Theory and Criticism*, no. 12–13 (1998), pp. 507–22.

Bahar, Shirly and Szobel, Ilana, "Confessions of IDF Soldiers in Autobiographical Documentaries from Israel" (in Hebrew), *Mikan*, vol. 17 (March 2017): 251–77.

Baudrillard, Jean, *Simulacra and Simulation*, trans. Sheila Faria Glaser. Ann
    Arbor: University of Michigan Press, 1994.
Behar, Moshe, "Interpreting the Pre-Israeli and Intra-Israeli Sociopolitical History
    of Arabized Jews" (in Hebrew), *Politika: The Israeli Journal of Political Science &
    International Relations*, no. 14 (2005), pp. 109–29.
Behar, Moshe and Ben-Dor Benite, Zvi (eds.), *Modern Middle Eastern Jewish Thought*.
    Waltham: Brandeis University Press, 2013.
Benjamin, Andrew, *Art, Mimesis, and the Avant Garde: Aspects of a Philosophy of
    Difference*. New York: Routledge, 1991.
Ben-Tzvi, Tal, *Self Portrait: The Art of Palestinian Women* (in Hebrew). Tel-Aviv:
    Andelus, 2001.
Benvenisti, Meron, *Sacred Landscape: The Buried History of the Holy Land since 1948*.
    Berkeley: University of California Press, 2000.
Berkowitz, Michael, *Zionist Culture and West European Jewry before the First World War*.
    Cambridge: Cambridge University Press, 1993.
Berlant, Lauren, "The Subject of True Feeling: Pain, Privacy, and Politics," in Sara Ahmed,
    Jane Kilby, Maureen McNeil, and Beverley Skeggs (eds.), *Transformations: Thinking
    through Feminism*. London: Routledge, 2000, pp. 33–47.
Berlant, Lauren, *Cruel Optimism*. Durham: Duke University Press, 2011.
Bhabha, Homi K., "The Other Question … Homi K. Bhabha Reconsiders the Stereotype
    and Colonial Discourse," *Screen*, vol. 24, no. 6 (1983), pp. 18–36.
Bhabha, Homi K., "Of Mimicry and Man: The Ambivalence of Colonial Discourse,"
    October, vol. 28, *Discipleship: A Special Issue on Psychoanalysis* (Spring 1984),
    pp. 125–33.
Bhabha, Homi K., *The Location of Culture*. London: Routledge, 2008 [1994].
Boyarin, Daniel, *Unheroic Conduct: The Rise of Heterosexuality and the Invention of the
    Jewish Man*. Berkeley: University of California Press, 1997.
Braverman, Irus, *Planted Flags: Trees, Land, and Law in Israel/Palestine*. New York:
    Cambridge University Press, 2009.
Bresheeth, Haim and Hammami, Haifa (eds.), "The Conflict and Contemporary Visual
    Culture in Palestine & Israel," *Third Text*, vol. 20, nos. 3/4 (May/July 2006), pp. 287–91.
Bruss, Elizabeth W., "Eye for I: Making and Unmaking Autobiography in Film," in James
    Olney (ed.), *Autobiography: Essays Theoretical and Critical*. Princeton: Princeton
    University Press, 1980.
Butler, Judith, *Bodies That Matter: On the Discursive Limits of Sex*. London: Routledge,
    1993.
Butler, Judith, *The Psychic Life of Power: Theories in Subjection*. Stanford: Stanford
    University Press, 1997.
Caruth, Cathy, *An Unclaimed Experience: Trauma, Narrative, and History*.
    Baltimore: Johns Hopkins University, 1996.
Césaire, Aimé, *Discourse on Colonialism*, trans. from French by Joan Pinkham, in *Monthly
    Review Press*, New York 2000 [1972].
Chakrabarty, Dipesh, *Provincializing Europe: Postcolonial Thought and Historical
    Difference*. Princeton: Princeton University Press, 2000.
Chatterjee, Partha, *Nationalist Thought and the Colonial World: A Derivative Discourse*.
    Minneapolis: University of Minnesota Press, 1993 [1986].
Chatterjee, Partha, *The Nation and Its Fragments*. Princeton: Princeton University
    Press, 1993.

Chatuka, Tali, *Moments of Redress* (in Hebrew). Tel Aviv: Resling, 2005.

Chetrit, Sami Shalom, "Mizrahi Politics in Israel: Between Integration and Alienation," *Journal of Palestine Studies*, vol. 29, no. 4 (Summer 2000), pp. 51–65.

Chetrit, Sami Shalom, *The Mizrahi Struggle in Israel, 1948–2003* (in Hebrew). Tel Aviv: Am Oved, 2004.

Chetrit, Sami Shalom, *Intra-Jewish Conflict in Israel: White Jews, Black Jews*. New York: Routledge, 2010.

Cheyette, Bryan, *Constructions of "the Jew" in English Literature and Society: Racial Representations, 1875–1945*. Cambridge: Cambridge University Press, 1993.

Clifford, James, *Routes: Travel and Translation in the Late Twentieth Century*. Cambridge: Harvard University Press, 1997.

Cohen, Hillel, *Present Absentees: The Palestinian Refugees in Israel since 1948* (in Hebrew). Jerusalem: Van Leer Institute, 2000.

Cohen Hillel, *Good Arabs: Israeli Intelligence and the Arabs in Israel* (in Hebrew). Jerusalem: Keter, 2006.

Cohen, Hillel, *Good Arabs: The Israeli Security Agencies and the Israeli Arabs, 1948–1967*, trans. Haim Watzman. Berkeley: University of California Press, 2011.

Cowie, Elizabeth, *Recording Reality, Desiring the Real*. Minneapolis: University of Minnesota Press, 2011.

Dabashi, Hamid (ed.), *Dream of a Nation: On Palestinian Cinema*. New York: Verso, 2006.

Dahan-Kalev, Henriette, "You Are So Beautiful, You Don't Look Moroccan," *Israel Studies*, vol. 6, no.1 (2001), pp. 1–14.

Dahan-Kalev Henriette (ed.), *In Blessing Secret: The Poetry of Bracha Seri* (in Hebrew). Jerusalem: Carmel, 2013.

De Lauretis, Theresa, "Difference Embodied: Reflections on Black Skin White Masks," *Parallax*, vol. 8, no. 2 (2002), pp. 54–68.

De Malah, Daniel, "Where Is the Occupation, Discrimination, and Imperialism? Notes on the Discussion on the Implications of Globalization in Israel" (in Hebrew), *Theory and Criticism*, vol. 35 (Fall 2009), pp. 111–40.

Deleuze, Gilles, *Cinema*. Minneapolis: University of Minnesota, 1986.

Deleuze, Gilles, *Cinema 2: The Time-Image*. London: Continuum, 2005 [1989].

DeRosa, Robin (ed.), *Simulation in Media and Culture: Believing the Hype*. Lanham: Lexington Books, 2011.

Devji, Faisal, *Landscapes of the Jihad: Militancy, Morality, Modernity*. London: Hurst & Company, 2005.

Doane, Mary Ann, "Real Time: Instantaneity and the Photographic Imaginary," in David Green and Joanna Lowry (eds.), *Stillness and Time: Photography and the Moving Image*. Brighton: Photoworks, 2006, pp. 23–38.

Dor, Daniel, *Intifada Hits the Headlines: How the Israeli Press Misreported the Outbreak of the Second Palestinian Uprising*. Bloomington: Indiana University Press, 2004.

Duvdevani, Shmulik, *First Person Camera: Personal Documentary Cinema in Israel* (in Hebrew). Jerusalem: Keter, 2010.

Eliad, Yoaz, *Land/Text: The Christian Roots of Zionism* (in Hebrew). Tel Aviv: Resling, 2008.

Lúcia Nagib and Cecília Mello (eds.), *Realism and the Audiovisual Media*. New York: Palgrave Macmillan, 2009.

Etgar, Rafi (ed.), *Worth and Worth-Less*. Jerusalem: Museum of the Seam, 2006.

Eversley, Shelly, *The Real Negro: The Question of Authenticity in Twentieth-Century African American Literature*. New York: Routledge, 2004.

Eyal, Gil, *The Disenchantment of the Orient: Expertise in Arab Affairs and the Israeli State* (in Hebrew). Jerusalem: Van-Leer Institute, 2005.

Falk, Rafael, *Zionism and the Biology of the Jews* (in Hebrew). Tel Aviv: Resling, 2006.

Fanon, Frantz, *Black Skin White Masks*, trans. Richard Philcox. New York: Grove Press, 2008 [1952].

Feldstein, Ariel L., *Pioneer, Work, Camera: Eretz-Israeli Cinema and the Zionist Idea 1917–1939*. Tel Aviv: Am Oved, 2009.

Feldt, Jakob, *The Israeli Memory Struggle: History and Identity in the Age of Globalization*. Odense: University Press of Southern Denmark, 2007.

Fisek, Emine, "I Want to Be a Palestinian Romeo! *Arna's Children* and the Romance with Theater," *Theater Research International*, vol. 37, no. 2 (July 2012), pp. 104–17.

Foster, Hal, *The Return of the Real: The Avant-Garde at the End of the Century*. Cambridge: MIT Press, 1996.

Foucault, Michel, *Security, Territory, Population: Lectures at the Collège de France, 1977–78*, trans. Graham Burchell. New York: Picador, 2007 [2004].

Friedman, Yael, "The Camera and the National Ethos: The 'Battle of Jenin' in Recent Palestinian Cinema" (in Hebrew), in Eyal Sivan and Yael Munk (eds.), *Makhbarot Kolnoa Darom (South Cinema Notebooks)—Cinema, Destruction & Trauma*. Sapir Academic College and Pardes Publishers, vol. 2, 2007, pp. 125–36.

Fuss, Diana, "Interior Colonies: Frantz Fanon and the Politics of Identification," *Diacritics*, vol. 24, nos. 2/3, *Critical Crossings* (Summer/Autumn 1994), pp. 19–42.

Fuss, Diana, *Identification Papers*. New York: Routledge, 1995.

Gabai, Shoshana, "We the Sentimentalists: The Mizrahi Struggle as the Loyal Servant of Neoliberal Media" (in Hebrew), *Haoketz*, January 16, 2015.

Gaines, Jane and Renov, Michael (eds.), *Collecting Visible Evidence*. Minneapolis: University of Minnesota Press, 1999.

Gaines, Jane M., "The Production of Outrage: The Iraq War and the Radical Documentary Tradition," *Framework*, vol. 48, no. 2 (Fall 2007), pp. 36–55.

Gertz, Nurith and Khleifi, George, *Palestinian Cinema: Landscape, Trauma, and Memory*. Edinburgh: Edinburgh University Press, 2008.

Gluzman, Michael, *The Zionist Body: Nationalism, Gender, and Sexuality in the New Israeli Literature* (in Hebrew). Tel Aviv: Hakibutz Hameuchad, 2007.

Gordon, Adi (ed.), *Brith Shalom and Binational Zionism: The Jewish Question as an Arab Question* (in Hebrew). Jerusalem: Karmel, 2008.

Gregg, Melissa and Seigworth, Gregory (eds.), *The Affect Theory Reader*. Durham: Duke University Press, 2009.

Grossman, David, *The Yellow Wind* (in Hebrew). Tel Aviv: Hakibutz Hameuchad, 1987.

Grossman, David, *Present Absentees* (in Hebrew). Tel Aviv: Hakibutz Hameuchad, 1992.

Haberman, Clyde, "Behind the Arab Veil, a Human Face," *New York Times*, October 31, 1992.

Habiby, Emile, *The Secret Life of Saeed: The Pessoptimist*, trans. Salma Khadra Jayyusi and Trevor LeGassick. New York: Vantage Press, 1992 [1974].

Hall, Stuart, "Cultural Identity and Cinematic Representation," *Framework: Journal of Cinema and Media*, no. 36 (1989), pp. 68–82.

Hartman, Saidiya, *Scenes of Subjection: Terror, Slavery, and Self-Making in Nineteenth-Century America*. New York: Oxford University Press, 1997.

Hasan, Manar, "The Politics of Honor: Patriarchy, the State and the Murder of Women in the Name of Family Honor," *Journal of Israeli History: Politics, Society, Culture*, vol. 21, nos. 1–2 (June 2002), pp. 1–37.

Hazan, Noa, "The Racialization of Jews in Israeli Documentary Photography," *Journal of Intercultural Studies*, vol. 31, no. 2 (2010), pp. 161–82.

Hazan, Noa and Rajuan Shtang, Sivan (eds.), *Visual Culture in Israel: An Anthology* (in Hebrew). Tel Aviv: Hakibutz Hameuchad, 2017.

Hemmings, Claire, "Invoking Affect: Cultural Theory and the Ontological Turn," *Cultural Studies*, vol. 19, no. 5 (September 2005), pp. 548–67.

Hever, Hannan, Shenhav, Yehuda, and Mutzafi-Haler, Pnina (eds.), *Mizrahim in Israel: A New Critical Study* (in Hebrew). Tel Aviv: Hakibutz Hameuchad, 2002.

Hinsky, Sara, "Eyes Wide Shut: On the Acquired Albinism Syndrome in the Israeli Art Field," in Yehuda Shenhav (ed.), *Colonialism and the Postcolonial State*. Jerusalem: Van Leer Institute, 2004.

Hochberg, Gil Z., *In Spite of Partition: Jews, Arabs, and the Limits of Separatist Imagination*. Princeton: Princeton University Press, 2007.

Hochberg, Gil, *Visual Occupations: Violence and Visibility in a Conflict Zone*. Durham: Duke University Press, 2015.

Jamal, Amal, *Arab Minority Nationalism in Israel: The Politics of Indigeneity*. New York: Routledge, 2011.

Jamal, Amal, "Manufacturing 'Quiet Arabs' in Israel: Ethnicity, Media Frames, and Soft Power," *Government and Opposition*, vol. 48, no. 2 (2013), pp. 245–64.

Jameson, Fredric, *The Geopolitical Aesthetic: Cinema and Space in the World System*. Bloomington: Indiana University Press, 1992.

Johnson, E., *Appropriating Blackness: Performance and the Politics of Authenticity*. Durham: Duke University Press, 2003.

Kahana, Jonathan, "Introduction: What Now? Presenting Reenactment," *Framework: The Journal of Cinema and Media*, vol. 50, no. 1, article 3 (Spring and Fall 2009).

Kahana, Jonathan (ed.), *The Documentary Film Reader: History, Theory, Criticism*. Oxford: Oxford University Press, 2016.

Kaplan, Caren, *Questions of Travel*. Durham: Duke University Press, 1996.

Karif, Moshe, *The Mizrahit: The Story of the Mizrahi Democratic Rainbow Movement* (in Hebrew). Tel Aviv: Globes, 2005.

Kemp, Adriana, "The Border as a Janus Face: Space and National Consciousness in Israel" (in Hebrew), *Theory and Criticism*, vol. 16 (2008), pp. 13–44.

Khalidi, Rashid, *Palestinian Identity: The Construction of Modern National Consciousness*. New York: Columbia University Press, 1997.

Kimmerling, Baruch, *Zionism and Territory: The Socio-Territorial Dimensions of Zionist Politics*. Berkeley Institute of International Studies: University of California, 1983, pp. 257–77.

Kimmerling, Baruch, *Immigrants, Settlers, Natives: State and Society in Israel: Between Multiple Cultures and Culture Wars* (in Hebrew). Tel Aviv: Am Oved, 2004.

Klotman, Phyllis R. and Cutler, Janet K. (eds.), *Struggles for Representation: African American Documentary Film and Video*. Bloomington: Indiana University Press, 1999.

Krauss, Rosalind E., *Perpetual Inventory*. Cambridge: MIT Press, 2010.

Lacan, Jacque, "The Mirror Stage as Formative of the 'I' Function as Revealed in Psychoanalytic Experience," in *Ecrits: The First Compete Edition in English*, trans. Bruce Fink. New York: Norton, 2006, pp. 73–81.

Lavie, Smadar, *Wrapped in the Flag of Israel: Single Mothers and Bureaucratic Torture*. Lincoln: University of Nebraska Press, 2014.

Lavie, Smadar and Swedenburg, Ted (eds.), *Displacement, Diaspora, and Geographies of Identity*. Durham: Duke University Press, 1996.

Lesch, Ann M. and Lustick, Ian S. (eds.), *Exile and Return: Predicaments of Palestinians and Jews*. Philadelphia: University of Pennsylvania, 2008.

Levy, Yagil, "Militarist Policy, Interracial Relationships, and the Internal Expansion of the State: Israel 1948–1956" (in Hebrew), *Theory and Criticism*, vol. 8 (1996), pp. 203–23.

Lewis, Reina, *Gendering Orientalism*. New York: Routledge, 1996.

Lir, Shlomit (ed.), *To My Sister: Mizrahi Feminist Politics* (in Hebrew). Tel Aviv: Babel, 2007.

Lockman, Zachary, *Comrades and Enemies: Arab and Jewish Workers in Palestine, 1906–1948*. Berkeley: University of California Press, 1996.

Long, Burke O., *Imagining the Holy Land: Maps, Models, and Fantasy Travel*. Bloomington: Indiana University Press, 2003.

Loshitzky, Yosefa, *Identity Politics on the Israeli Screen*. Austin: University of Texas, 2001.

Lubin, Orly, *Woman Reading Woman* (in Hebrew). Haifa: Haifa University Press, 2003.

MacCarthy, Anna, "Reality Television: A Neoliberal Theatre of Suffering," *Social Text* 93, vol. 25, no. 4 (Winter 2007), pp. 17–42.

Madmoni-Garber, Shoshana, *Israeli Media and the Framing of Internal Conflict*. New York: Palgrave, 2009.

Madsen, Deborah L. (ed.), *Native Authenticity: Transnational Perspectives on Native American*. Albany: Literary Studies State University of New York Press, 2010.

Mamdani, Mahmood, *Citizen and Subject*. Princeton: Princeton University Press, 1996.

Margulies, Ivone (ed.), *Rites of Realism: Essays on Corporeal Cinema*. Durham: Duke University Press, 2003.

Marquis, Elizabeth, "Conceptualizing the Documentary Performance," *Studies in Documentary Film*, vol. 7, no. 1 (2013): 45–60.

Masalha, Nur, *Expulsion of the Palestinians: The Concept of "Transfer" in Zionist Political Thought 1882–1948*. Washington, DC: Institute for Palestine Studies, 1992.Masalha, Nur, *A Land without a People: Israel, Transfer and the Palestinians 1949–96*. London: Faber and Faber, 1997.

Masalha, Nur, "Present Absentees and Indigenous Resistance," in Nur Masalha (ed.), *Catastrophe Remembered: Palestine, Israel, and the Internal Refugees*. New York: Zed Books, 2005.

Mbembe, Achille and Roitman Janet, "Figures of the Subject in Time of Crisis," *Public Culture*, vol. 7, no. 2 (1995), pp. 323–52.

Mbembe, Achille and Roitman Janet, *On the Postcolony*. Berkeley: University of California Press, 2001.

Memmi, Albert, *Jews and Arabs*. Chicago: J. P. O'Hara, 1975.

Mirzeoff, Nicholas, An Introduction to Visual Culture. New York: Routledge, 1999.

Mirzeoff, Nicholas, *The Right to Look: A Counterhistory of Visuality*. Durham: Duke University Press, 2011.

Mishori, Elik, *Straighten, Lo and Behold* (in Hebrew). Tel Aviv: Am Oved, 2000.

Mitchell, Larry, *The Faggots and Their Friends between Revolutions*, 2nd edition. New York: Nightboat Books, 2019 [1977].

Mitchell, Timothy, Prakash, Gyan, and Shohat, Ella (eds.), "Palestine in a Transnational Context," *Social Text*, vol. 75 (Summer 2003), pp. 1–162.

Mizrahi, Nissim, "From Badness to Sickness: The Role of Ethnopsychology in Shaping Ethnic Hierarchies in Israel," *Social Identities*, vol. 10, no. 2 (2004), pp. 219–43.

Monk, Daniel Bertrand, *An Aesthetic Occupation: The Immediacy of Architecture and the Palestine Conflict*. Durham: Duke University Press, 2002.

Morag, Raya, "The Living Body and the Corpse-Israeli Documentary Cinema and the Intifada," *Journal of Film and Video*, vol. 60, nos. 3–4 (Fall/Winter 2008), pp. 3–24.

Morag, Raya (ed.), "Radical Contextuality: Major Trends in Israeli Documentary Second Intifada Cinema," *Studies in Documentary Film*, vol. 6, no. 3 (September 2012), pp. 253–72.

Morag, Raya, *Waltzing with Bashir: Perpetrator Trauma and Cinema*. London: I.B. Tauris, 2013.

Morris, Benny, *The Birth of the Palestinian Refugee Problem 1947–1949*. Cambridge: Cambridge University Press, 1987.

N. Hayles, Katherine, *How We Became Posthuman: Virtual Bodies in Cybernetics, Literature, and Informatics*. Chicago: University of Chicago Press, 1999.

Neumann, Boaz, *Land and Desire in Early Zionism* (in Hebrew). Tel Aviv: Am Oved, 2009.

Nichols, Bill, "Documentary Reenactment and the Fantasmatic Subject," *Critical Inquiry*, vol. 35, no. 1 (Autumn 2008), pp. 72–89.

Nizri, Yigal (ed.), *Mizrahi Appearance/Mother Tongue: Present Moving in the Knot of Its Arabic Past* (in Hebrew). Tel Aviv: Bavel, 2004.

Obenzinger, Hilton, *American Palestine: Melville, Twain, and the Holy Land Mania*. Princeton: Princeton University Press, 1999.

Onwuachi-Willig, Angela, "The Trauma of the Routine: Lessons on Cultural Trauma from the Emmett till Verdict," *Sociological Theory*, vol. 34, no. 4 (2016), pp. 335–57.

Ophir, Adi (ed.), *Real Time: The Al Aqsa Intifada and the Israeli Left* (in Hebrew). Jerusalem: Keter, 2001.

Ouellette, Laurie and Murray, Susan, *Reality TV: Remaking Television Culture*. New York: New York University Press, 2004.

Pappe, Ilan, "The Tantura Case in Israel: The Katz Research and Trial," *Journal of Palestine Studies*, vol. 30, no. 3 (Spring 2001), pp. 19–39.

Parker, Andrew and Sedgwick, Eve Kosofsky (eds.), *Performance and Performativity*. New York: Routledge, 1995.

Penslar, Derek J., *Zionism and Technocracy: The Engineering of Jewish Settlement in Palestine, 1870–1918*. Bloomington: Indiana University Press, 1991.

Porath, Yehoshua, *The Emergence of the Palestinian-Arab National Movement, 1918–1929*. London: Cass, 1974.

Puar, Jasbir, *Terrorist Assemblages: Homonationalism in Queer Times*. Durham: Duke University Press, 2007.

Rabinowitz, Paula, *They Must Be Represented: The Politics of Documentary*. New York: Verso, 1994.

Rabinowitz, Paula, "Street/Crime: From Rodney King's Beating to Michael Brown's Shooting," *Cultural Critique*, vol. 90 (2015), pp. 143–7.

Ram, Uri, *The Time of the Post: Nationalism and the Politics of Knowledge in Israel* (in Hebrew). Tel Aviv: Resling, 2006.

Raz-Karkotzkin, Amnon, "Exile within Sovereignty: Criticism of the Negation of Exile, Part 1 and 2" (in Hebrew), *Theory and Criticism*, vols. 4 and 5 (1993–4), pp. 23–55 and 113–32.

Renov, Michael, "The Subject in History: The New Autobiography in Film and Video," *Afterimage*, vol. 17, no. 1 (1989), pp. 4–7.

Renov, Michael (ed.), *Theorizing Documentary*. New York: Routledge, 1993.

Renov, Michael, "Video Confessions," in Michael Renov and Erika Suderburg (eds.), *Resolutions: Contemporary Video Practices*. Minneapolis: University of Minnesota Press, 1996, pp. 78–101.

Renov, Michael, *The Subject of Documentary*. Minneapolis: University of Minnesota Press, 2004.

Robinson, Shira, *Citizen Strangers: Palestinians and the Birth of Israel's Liberal Settler State*. Stanford: Stanford University Press, 2013.

Ronell, Avital, "Trauma TV: Twelve Steps beyond the Pleasure Principle," in *Finitude's Score: Essays for the End of the Millennium*. Lincoln: University of Nebraska Press, 1994.

Ross, David, "Truth or Consequences: American Television and Video Art," in John G. Hanhardt (ed.), *Video Culture: A Critical Investigation*. Rochestor: Visual Studies Workshop Press, 1986, pp. 167–78.

Rotberd, Sharon, *White City Black City* (in Hebrew). Tel Aviv: Bavel, 2006.

Ruby Rich, B., "Documentary Disciplines: An Introduction," *Cinema Journal*, vol. 26, no. 1(Fall 2006), pp. 108–15.

Ruby, Bryan, *The Mizrahi Era of Rebellion: Israel's Forgotten Civil Rights Struggle 1948–1966*. Syracuse: Syracuse University Press, 2015.

Sabbagh-Khoury, Areej and Rouhana, Nadim N. (eds.), *The Palestinians in Israel: Readings in History, Politics and Society, Volume 2*. Haifa: The Mada Al-Carmel Arab Center for Applied Social Research, 2015.

Said, Edward, *Orientalism*. New York: Random House, 1978.

Said, Edward, *The Question of Palestine*. New York: Random House, 1979.

Said, Edward, *After the Last Sky: Palestinian Lives*. New York: Pantheon Books, 1986.

Said, Edward, *The Politics of Dispossession*. New York: Pantheon, 1994.

Samooha, Sami, "The Israeli State Regime: Non-Democracy, Citizenry Democracy, or Ethnic Democracy?" (in Hebrew), *Israeli Sociology: Israeli Society Research Journal*, vol. 2, no. 2 (2000), pp. 568–617.

Saposnik, Arieh Bruce, *Becoming Hebrew: The Creation of a Jewish National Culture in Ottoman Palestine*. New York: Oxford University Press, 2008.

Sarkar, Bhaskar and Walker, Janet (eds.), *Documentary Testimonies: Global Archives of Social Suffering*. New York: Routledge, 2010.

Scarry, Elaine, *The Body in Pain: The Making and Unmaking of the World*. New York: Oxford University Press, 1985.

Schneider, Rebecca, *Performing Remains: Art and War in Times of Theatrical Reenactment*. New York: Routledge, 2011.

Sedgwick, Eve Kosofsky, *Touching Feeling: Affect, Pedagogy, Performativity*. Durham: Duke University Press, 2003.

Segev, Tom, *1967: Israel, the War, and the Year That Transformed the Middle East*. New York: Metropolitan Books, 2007.

Sela, Rona, *Photography in Palestine/Eretz Israel in the 1930s and 1940s* (in Hebrew). Tel Aviv: Hakibutz Hameuchad, 2000.

Shafir, Gershon, *Land, Labor and the Origins of the Israeli-Palestinian Conflict, 1882–1914*. Berkeley: University of California Press, 1996.

Shapira, Anita, *Land and Power: The Zionist Resort to Force, 1881–1948*. New York: Oxford University Press, 1992.

Shemer, Yaron, *Identity, Subversion, and Place in Contemporary Israeli Cinema*. Ann Arbor: University of Michigan Press, 2013.

Shenhav, Yehuda, *In the Thralls of the Green Line: A Jewish Political Essay*. Tel Aviv: Am Oved, 2010.

Shmuellof, Matti, "To Heal the Rupture" (in Hebrew), *Haoketz*, November 18, 2010.

Shohat, Ella, "Sephardim in Israel: Zionism from the Perspective of Its Jewish Victims," *Social Text*, no. 19/20 (Autumn 1988), pp. 1–35.

Shohat, Ella, "The Narrative of the Nation and the Discourse of Modernization: The Case of the Mizrahim," *Critique: Critical Middle Eastern Studies*, vol. 6, no. 10 (1997), pp. 3–18.

Shohat, Ella, "The Invention of the Mizrahim," *Journal of Palestine Studies*, vol.29, no. 1 (Autumn 1999), pp. 5–20.

Shohat, Ella, *Forbidden Memories: An Introduction to Multicultural Thought* (in Hebrew). Tel Aviv: Keshet Hamizrah, Bimat Kedem Lesifrut, 2001.

Shohat, Ella, "Rupture and Return: Zionist Discourse and the Study of Arab Jews," *Social Text* 75 (vol. 21, no. 2) (Summer 2003), pp. 49–74.

Shohat, Ella, *Taboo Memories, Diasporic Voices*. Durham: Duke University Press, 2006.

Shohat, Ella, *Israeli Cinema: East/West and the Politics of Representation*, 2nd ed. London: I.B. Tauris, 2010.

Silverstein, Lawrence J., "New Historians and Critical Sociologists between Post-Zionism and Postmodernism" (in Hebrew), *Theory and Criticism*, vol. 8 (1996), pp. 105–22.

Slyomovics, Susan, *The Object of Memory*. Philadelphia: University of Pennsylvania Press, 1998.

Stein, Rebecca Swedenberg, Ted (eds.), *Palestine, Israel, and the Politics of Popular Culture*. Durham: Duke University Press, 2005.

Sternhell, Zeev, *Building a Nation or Redressing a Society? Socialism and Nationalism in the Israeli Labor Movement 1904–1940* (in Hebrew). Tel Aviv: Am Oved, 1995.

Stoler, Ann Laura (ed.), *Imperial Debris: On Ruins and Ruination*. Durham: Duke University Press, 2013.

Svirsky, Shlomo and Bernstein, Dvora, "Who Worked in What, for Whom, and for How Much? The Economic Development of Israel and the Consolidation of Labor Division" (in Hebrew), *Notebooks for Research and Criticism*, vol. 4 (1980) pp. 5–66.

Talmon, Miri and Peleg, Yaron (eds.), *Israeli Cinema: Identities in Motion*. Austin: University of Texas Press, 2011.

Taussig, Michael, *Mimesis and Alterity: A Particular History of the Senses*. New York: Routledge, 1993.

Tawil-Souri, Helga, "Cinema as the Space to Transgress Palestine's Territorial Trap," *Middle East Journal of Culture and Communication*, vol. 7, no. 2 (2014), pp. 169–89.

Tawil Souri, Helga and Aouragh, Miriyam, "Intifada 3.0? Cyber Colonialism and Palestinian Resistance," *The Arab Studies Journal*, vol. 22, no. 1, *Special Issue: Cultures of Resistance* (Spring 2014), pp. 102–33.

Tawil Souri, Helga, "Media, Globalization, and the (Un)Making of the Palestinian Cause," *Popular Communication: The International Journal of Media and Culture*, vol. 13, no. 2 (2015), pp 145–57.

Taylor, Diana, *The Archive and the Repertoire*. Durham: Duke University Press, 2003.

Troen, Ilan S., *Imagining Zion: Dreams, Designs, and Realities in a Century of Jewish Settlement*. New Haven: Yale University Press, 2003.

Tsoffar, Ruth, "Baghdad-Tel Aviv: Roundtrip to the Promised Land," *Anthropological Quarterly*, vol. 79, no. 1 (Winter 2006), pp. 133–44.

Virilio, Paul, *The Vision Machine*, trans. Julie Rose. Bloomington: Indiana University Press, 1994.

Weizman, Eyal, *Hollow Land: Israel's Architecture of Occupation*. London: Verso, 2007.

Wenzel, Jennifer, "Remembering the Past's Future: Anti-Imperialist Nostalgia and Some Versions of the Third World," *Cultural Critique*, vol. 61 no. 1 (Winter 2006), pp. 1–32.

Winston, Bryan, *Claiming the Real: The Griersonian Documentary and Its Legitimations*. London: British Film Institute, 1995.

Yacobi, Haim (ed.), *Constructing a Sense of Place: Architecture and the Zionist Discourse*. Burlington: Ashgate, 2004.

Yacobi, Haim, "The Third Place: Architecture, Nationalism, and the Post-Colonial Gaze" (in Hebrew), *Theory and Criticism*, vol. 30 (Summer 2007), pp. 63–88.

Yiftachel, Oren, "The Ethnic Democracy Model and Arab-Jewish Relations in Israel: Geographic, Historical, and Political Perspectives" (in Hebrew), *Horizons in Geography*, no. 37/38 (1993), pp. 51–9.

Yiftahel, Oren, "Israeli Society and Jewish-Palestinian Reconciliation: 'Ethnocracy' and Its Territorial Contradictions," *Middle East Journal*, vol. 51, no. 4 (Autumn, 1997), pp. 505–19.

Yosef, Raz, *Beyond Flesh: Queer Masculinities and Nationalism in Israeli Cinema*. New Brunswick: Rutgers University Press, 2004.

Yosef, Raz, *The Politics of Loss and Trauma in Contemporary Israeli Cinema*. New York: Routledge, 2011.

Young, Robert, *Postcolonialism: An Historical Introduction*. Malden: Blackwell, 2009 [2001].

Zalmona, Yigal (ed.), *Kadima: The East in the Art of Israel* (in Hebrew). Jerusalem: Israel Museum, 1998.

Zelshik, Rakefet, *Ad Nefesh: Immigrants, Ascendants, Refugees, and the Psychiatric Institution in Israel* (in Hebrew). Tel Aviv: Hakibutz Hameuchad, 2008.

Zerubavel, Yael, *Recovered Roots: Collective Memory and the Making of Israeli National Tradition*. Chicago: University of Chicago Press, 1995.

Zimmerman, Patricia R., "Public Domains: Engaging Iraq through Experimental Digitalities," *Framework: The Journal of Cinema and Media*, vol. 48, no. 2 (Fall 2007), pp. 66–83.

Ziv, Amalia, "Between Sexual Commodities and Sexual Subjects: The Feminist Controversy on Pornography" (in Hebrew), *Theory and Criticism*, vol. 25 (Fall 2004), pp. 163–94.

Zizek, Slavoj, *Welcome to the Desert of the Real!: Five Essays on September 11th and Other Dates*. New York: Verso, 2002.

INDEX

Lightning Source UK Ltd.
Milton Keynes UK
UKHW020614300123
416164UK00008B/1401